D1130365

SPACE IS OPEN FOR BUSINESS

THE INDUSTRY THAT CAN TRANSFORM HUMANITY

BY ROBERT C. JACOBSON

PRAISE

"Robert Jacobson makes a compelling case in *Space Is Open for Business* for how both continued private and public investment into the space sector helps people and our planet. Jacobson wrote a must-read for anyone interested in the business and commerce of space. This book will open your eyes, heart, and mind to the possibilities and potential solutions derived from space."

Lori Garver | Chief Executive Officer, Earthrise Alliance; Former Deputy Administrator, NASA

"Like the universe in which it operates, space commerce is expanding, challenging, and full of opportunity. *Space Is Open for Business* is an exceptional guide that defines how investors, entrepreneurs, and business leaders can make the most of the space frontier."

Shelli Brunswick | Chief Operating Officer, Space Foundation

"Robert Jacobson has been promoting and investing in the NewSpace revolution since before it was cool. Now that NewSpace has become not just cool—but in some instances, profitable—*Space Is Open for Business* provides a valuable introduction to the industry and will assist investors in imagining the multiple avenues for investment that could be opened up by humankind's ventures beyond Low Earth Orbit."

Rich Smith | Space Lawyer; Contributing Writer, *The Motley Fool*

"*Space Is Open for Business* is the best overall view of the rapidly changing space industry that I've read. I lived through one of the fastest growing Silicon Valley space startups while building and launching over 300 satellites at the Earth imaging company Planet; few books really capture the nuances of how an agile Silicon Valley approach to space is completely changing the art of the possible in space. Robert captures the interplay between fast-moving, disruptive startups, public space programs, and billionaire interest in space. I came away from the book with a greater overall picture of the space industry and a new inspiration for what is coming next. The space industry is rapidly changing and growing—and it is about to get much more exciting."

Ben Haldeman | Founder & Chief Executive Officer, LifeShip

"Space is no longer for just billionaires. Any investor who is looking for the next hot sector needs to pick up Robert Jacobson's book, as it gives a fair and thorough overview of why space could be the ultimate investment market."

Brian Deagon | Technology Journalist, *Investor's Business Daily*

"Robert Jacobson's new book shares how entrepreneurs are mining the sky, and it's not what you might first think. Jacobson's vision for the intersection of space and business looks both practical and promising for investors. Visionaries like Musk, Bezos, and Branson, aren't interested in space for no reason!"

Harry S. Dent, Jr. | Author of *Zero Hour* and *The Great Depression Ahead*

"Robert Jacobson has written an insider's account of the emerging NewSpace industry. Anyone wanting to understand why some of our planet's smartest people and savviest investors are embracing NewSpace should read this book."

Bob Werb | Cofounder, Space Frontier Foundation

"Jacobson's book is a terrific survey of the visionaries and dreamers who have been inspired by space to create a better world. A must-read for anyone curious to know the magnitude to which space has influenced humanity—and why space is a crucial part of our future."

Nik Halik | Astronaut & Thrillionaire Entrepreneurial Alchemist

"*Space Is Open for Business* paints a clear picture of the space sector and the new territory created by commercial entrants, highlighting both the vast opportunities as well as the complex challenges. Jacobson's book is a well-presented introduction to this nuanced industry. It provides crucial insights around immediate actions we need to take nationally and globally for a safe and prosperous future. A must-read for those interested in the new frontiers of the business of space."

J. Patrick Michaels | Founder, Chief Executive Officer, & Chair, Communications Equity Associates

"Robert Jacobson does a great job with *Space Is Open for Business*, which is an insightful work detailing the synergies required and adapted from the world's desire and necessity to explore and commercialize space. This is a marvelous wonder through the present day 'state-of-the-art' space systems, industry players, and economics, as well as a brilliant and valuable discussion of the 'art-of-the-possible' for all those areas. His business-minded approach to space exploration is refreshing and multifaceted, making this a must-read for those considering investing in space-related industries."

Commander Joseph Dituri, Ph.D., US Navy, Ret. |
Director, International Board of Undersea Medicine

"Robert has a clear understanding of the all-encompassing nature of the space industry for the future of humanity in this book. We thank Robert for his contribution as the private commercial space industry continues to grow. Let's reach for the stars."

Tarek Waked | General Partner, Type One Ventures

"A sweeping guide that will inspire you to think big about space, the space economy, and your role within it."

"There's so much to learn about the space sector, and a whole world to explore for space investing. If you want to get involved in what is becoming a trillion-dollar economy, read *Space Is Open for Business*, which gives an intensive and elucidative introduction to this extraordinary and surprisingly accessible industry. Space is Internet 2.0, and it's happening now—emerging startups and space opportunities are seeking mentorship, partnerships, investments, and more. Don't miss out."

"Robert has distilled a decade's worth of knowledge and experience into an intelligent, engaging, and fun read. This book should be required reading for anyone interested in the emerging space economy."

"Buzz Aldrin said that exploration is wired into our brains. If we can see the horizon, we want to know what's beyond it. But one does not discover new lands without consenting to lose sight of the shore for a very long time. Science fiction enables us to dream of those bold futures, and books such as *Space Is Open for Business* enable us to build them."

"*Space Is Open for Business* is an insightful read for any investor and entrepreneur interested in in the space sector. It's captivating and makes a compelling case for why investing in space is important."

"Space is about to be globally transformative on a scale we have never seen before, and now is the time to start tapping into that potential. Read *Space Is Open for Business*, which paints the big picture of the industry within its covers and shows how our connection with space can create a better world."

"Robert has been one of the innovative thinkers on how to help drive entrepreneurial development of space for the benefit of all. Hopefully, his book will help inspire more investment and innovation."

"Space: the next, not final, frontier for venture capital investment. Robert Jacobson's book, *Space Is Open for Business*, takes us through how some of the leading-edge luminaries think about investing in space. Get on board! It will be quite a ride."

Timothy Draper | Founder, Draper Fisher Jurvetson

"Human innovation is reaching a tipping point that is ushering in an era of space travel, extraterrestrial inhabitance, and Moon mining. *Space Is Open for Business* gives a glimpse into what's to come."

Scott Amyx | Chair & Managing Partner, Amyx Ventures

"Robert eloquently explains why smart, forward-looking investors need to start tracking the space sector for investment and commerce. New doors are opening—fast—and those who act now will build the future. The rest will be left behind in the stardust."

Adil Jafry | Chief Executive Officer, Chandah Space Technologies

"The creation of commercial business models that operate in the vacuum of space is a necessity to accelerate human exploration of the final frontier. *Space Is Open for Business* paints the history of the commercial space industry well and outlines with depth the potential it holds for entrepreneurs and humanity alike. Robert Jacobson has created a primer that should inspire entrepreneurs and investors to turn their efforts to creating sustainable businesses in space while unlocking investment returns and huge potential for the human race."

Colin Ake | Principal, VentureLab at Georgia Tech

"Jacobson's captivating read is a testament to the fact that even the most far-out passions truly *can* become success stories. NewSpace proves over and over that there has never been a better time to take a bold chance on your dreams. This book is a must-read for 'dream big, go big' entrepreneurs—or anyone looking for inspiration."

Allen Clary | Cofounder, Tampa Bay WaVe; Managing Director, Signal Point Ventures

"In this comprehensive book, space-investment veteran Robert Jacobson shows how to grow a third of a trillion-dollar industry to a trillion-dollar business in ten years."

Howard Bloom | Author of *The God Problem*; Founder, Space Development Steering Committee

"As the founder of a space startup, I appreciated the unique perspectives on the current state of the NewSpace market and its challenges and opportunities moving forward—in particular, the insights into some of the past failures and how to learn from them as we move toward the commercialization of space."

Kartik Kumar | Cofounder, satsearch

"In *Space Is Open for Business,* Jacobson not only helps us understand how we got to where we are now but clues us into the amazing business potential that space represents today and in the years ahead. I foresee a space gold rush starting in 2020, and the publication of this book will be seen as a starter's gun to that end. Jacobson demonstrates quite clearly why space is both the new frontier and the next hot business for the private sector. This new space race is on!"

Alon Rozen, Ph.D. | Dean & Professor of Innovation and Management, École des Ponts Business School

"This is awesome. Robert's unique access and point of view offer insights that blow my mind."

Shaun Arora | Managing Director, MiLA Capital

"Space truly is open for business! At this moment in time, entrepreneurial energy, renewed governmental commitment, and investor interest are all making space the place to be. Jacobson's must-read book explores the confluence of innovation, inspiration, and investment required to conquer this lucrative new domain."

Greg Autry | Director, Southern California Commercial Spaceflight Initiative, Marshall School of Business, University of Southern California

"Space is no longer just a place to visit or explore; it is increasingly the place where new commercial services will be created that will improve our lives on Earth and allow for continued exploration of the heavens. Robert Jacobson makes an effective and convincing argument in this book, *Space Is Open for Business,* that public and private sector investment must continue to ensure continued benefits and leadership roles for our nation.

Robert's book injects a fantastic new energy into this discourse. I especially like the fact that he has included so many industry views in this volume. *Space Is Open for Business* is an informative and important guide for leaders, investors, and entrepreneurs who care about the key role of space activities in our future."

Kevin M. O'Connell | Director, Office of Space Commerce, US Department of Commerce

"NewSpace has grown by leaps and bounds thanks to demands for new data sets, communications, and deeper analytics and insights. Thanks to radically cheaper satellites and more launch options, the sector is rapidly growing to fill this need. Robert shares clearly why NewSpace could be one of the most important industries of the twenty-first century, successfully illustrating the subtly nuanced and multi-disciplinary aspects to this sector that drew me in as an entrepreneur. The keen insights shared by Robert and his collaborators in *Space Is Open for Business* summarize what has taken me nearly eight years to learn on my own in the space industry."

Marshall Culpepper | Cofounder & Chief Executive Officer, Kubos

"From my perspective of having founded a space company in an artist's studio in Pasadena, this book lays bare the opportunities ahead for anyone who wants to participate in the next giant leap. You no longer have to be a government, a global corporation, or a billionaire to do something important in this ecosystem."

Simon R. Halpern | Founder, Aether Industries; Vice President of Strategy, Kubos; Founder & Former Chief Executive Officer, Phase Four

"Will the Martian economy have a stock market or a dedicated currency? In his new book, Robert makes an extremely compelling argument that Space will fundamentally change both our understanding of and the earth-bound rules around trade and commerce. This will have profound effects on Earth's future."

Brett King | Bestselling Author; Founder, Radio Host

"Science fiction has long inspired the dreams of doers and, by extension, has shaped the reality we recognize today. The science fiction-inspired technology that we take for granted today is already well beyond the ultra-visionary fiction showcased in Roddenberry's *Star Trek*, Asimov's *Foundation,* and on and on. Today, sci-fi such as *The Expanse* embraces the ideas that will be realities tomorrow. I appreciate Robert's entertaining, educational, and truly insightful writings on what got us here, as well as his blueprint for space exploration and the 'astropreneurs' of today.

I'm fortunate to be one of Virgin Galactic's first 603 to briefly see our blue gem from above; STEAM educational programs will ensure that this generation, and those ahead, grow up with the skills to thrive, drive, and literally soar to new heights. They will lead the out-of-this-world discoveries on our Moon, Mars, and throughout our solar system—above and beyond. Robert illustrates just how far we've come, how fast we're moving, and the great opportunity for humanity."

Larry O'Connor | Founder, Other World Computing; Avid Science Fiction Fan

"Robert Jacobson has written a fantastic, comprehensive history of the space industry that is both fascinating and accessible to readers."

Josie Enenstein | Aspiring Astrophysicist

SPACE IS OPEN FOR BUSINESS

THE INDUSTRY THAT CAN TRANSFORM HUMANITY

BY ROBERT C. JACOBSON

LOS ANGELES, CALIFORNIA

2020

First Printing.
ISBN 978-1-7342051-0-7 (Paperback)
ISBN 978-1-7342051-1-4 (Hardcover)
978-1-7342051-2-1 (eBook)

Designed by Julie Karen Hodgins
Cover design by Richard Ljoens Design LLC
Interior illustrations by Fates.com

Publisher's Cataloging-In-Publication Data
(Prepared by The Donohue Group, Inc.)

Names: Jacobson, Robert C., 1975- author.
Title: Space is open for business : the industry that can transform humanity / by Robert C. Jacobson.
Description: Los Angeles, California : [Robert C. Jacobson], 2020. | Includes bibliographical references and index.
Identifiers: ISBN 9781734205107 (paperback) | ISBN 9781734205114 (hardcover) | ISBN 9781734205121 (ebook)
Subjects: LCSH: Space industrialization--Technological innovations. | Space industrialization--Social aspects. |
   Aerospace industries--History. | Aerospace industries--Finance.
Classification: LCC HD9711.75 .J33 2020 (print) | LCC HD9711.75 (ebook) | DDC 338.0999--dc23

Printed in the United States of America.

www.robertjacobson.com

Dedicated to my mother, Cynthia Jacobson.

*She was a ray of sunshine
who shared her gifts of serenity, creativity, joy,
and love for family, friends, and animals.*

*Thank you for always telling me to follow my passions,
no matter how far into space they may take me.*

CONTENTS

FOREWORD

Thirty years ago, I was working on my first tech startup, developing software and packaging for the WristMac, a digital watch that could upload and download data from a Mac computer—a quarter-century before the introduction of the Apple Watch. It was a fun product that garnered a fair amount of press, but I was sure it would be of interest only to a small group of geeky enthusiasts. Imagine my surprise when I received a call from NASA suggesting that the watch might be useful on the next Shuttle mission to help the astronauts with their scheduling and asking if we could work with them to enhance and adapt it. I immediately agreed, and the watches flew on Space Shuttle Atlantis, mission STS-43, on August 2, 1991. For the first time, I realized "space" was not just a mythical place in science fiction or the province of governments and rocket scientists, but a down-to-earth market that was just as real as more traditional ones.

As it turned out, a key part of NASA's mission statement even then was "investing in America's future … contributing to economic growth and security and developing and transferring cutting-edge technologies." In the decades since STS-43, I have helped to fund several new space-related ventures as an angel investor, including Zero-G (providing microgravity simulation flights for NASA, tourists, and filmmakers) and Rocket Racing League (a spectator sport based on rocket-powered aircraft). I also became a founding member of Space Angels, an early-stage investment consortium that specifically seeks to invest in space-related startups.

That there even *are* space-related startups is a consequence of a major policy shift at NASA, beginning in 2010 and accelerating in 2017. For the first half-century following its founding in 1958, NASA's space program (and that of every other country) was the epitome of a Big Government project. Whether putting humans on the Moon or building a research station in low Earth orbit, the assumption was that only a government could design, build, and operate things in space; NASA would, therefore, hire contractors to create things to its specifications. But the dramatic shift in 2010—variously known as "Commercial

Space," "NewSpace," and "Space 2.0"—turned that paradigm on its head. Private sector organizations became partners rather than contractors, and NASA began to purchase services and outcomes instead of hardware. A new path opened up for innovative private-sector opportunities through competitive challenges, research partnerships, and expanded fast-track processes for "low-budget" projects under $150 million.

Around 2010, I was invited by Guillermo Söhnlein to become one of the founding members of the first space-focused angel group in the world, Space Angels Network. As I worked with the other founders to build the technical infrastructure and investment side of the business, Robert Jacobson was working in the management sphere. With his prior experience investing in space companies and working in private equity, Robert helped to build the personnel infrastructure through his existing network in the space community. The passion and dedication that I saw in him and the other early members of Space Angels was more than inspiring; they provided a glimpse into the expanding community of investors and entrepreneurs who were determined to evolve this emerging space ecosystem.

Today, there are space-related enterprises across the country—and the globe. At a recent meetup where I spoke on a panel with fellow space investors Esther Dyson and Howard Morgan, in attendance were over two dozen space-related companies, all based in New York City. This book by Robert Jacobson is the first general introduction to NewSpace, and it does an exceptional job of putting this movement into historical and business contexts while providing a practical guide to getting started, whether you are an entrepreneur, an investor, or just an interested citizen. Robert himself has occupied all three of those roles and thus has a unique perspective that has allowed him to illuminate the intricacies of this sector.

As you continue reading, there is one fundamental concept that will be crucial to keep in mind—an idea so critical that, unless you have first truly internalized it, you will find yourself at a serious disadvantage in understanding the full importance of NewSpace... and this book. That concept is the *exponentially accelerating pace of technological change.*[†] In a nutshell, with *linear* growth, every step forward in time moves technological power one step up; but with *exponential* growth, every step forward *doubles* the power of the existing technology. As a result, after twenty steps of linear growth, technology would have advanced by a factor of twenty. After the same period with exponential growth, technology will have advanced by a factor of over one million. We have all been raised to expect evolutionary systems (e.g., technology) to grow in linear terms; what is actually happening in our world, however, is exponential growth.

Once you let that sink in, you will realize that the iPhone in your pocket has one hundred thousand times the power—and seven million times the memory—of the Apollo Guidance Computer that put Neil Armstrong and Buzz Aldrin on the Moon. Think of that power *doubling* every twelve to eighteen months, and it becomes apparent that the vastness of space and the complexity of moonshots are no longer mythically unreachable. They are, instead, the next logical step in the progress of human knowledge, achievement, and commerce. Space is, indeed, open for business.

David S. Rose

Founder, New York Angels
Associate Founder, Singularity University

February, 2020
New York, NY

[†]This concept was first brought to public attention in Ray Kurzweil's seminal book *The Singularity is Near,* and then disseminated and given structure through the work of Singularity University, founded by Kurzweil and Peter Diamandis (who had previously cofounded International Space University).

PREFACE

The original *Star Wars* was one of the first films I recall seeing. I was about two years old. Something about the scenes of spacecraft, exotic deserts, and alien lifeforms attracted me. Clearly, I was not the only one; this single franchise touched millions around the world and is still regarded as one of the most highly influential pieces of popular culture in history. A few years later, I found *Star Trek*; its focus on humanity's evolution, both technologically and socially, had an even deeper impact. Becoming a space-faring human immediately felt like an obvious and natural path to me, and I found myself wondering why we weren't further along in our efforts to explore and understand what lies above Earth. Why did we spend so much time and energy on getting to the Moon in the 1960s and 1970s if we haven't tried to go back since? I was determined to become heavily involved in the industry. When I was in junior high school, I attended two programs at Space Camp in Huntsville, Alabama. While there, I realized that becoming a NASA astronaut would be a limited route; the agency no longer held the energetic visions that had guided my interest up to that point. Nevertheless, I retained my interest in space—if, for some time, only as a spectator.

Fast-forward to today, and the landscape has changed dramatically—to the point where many of the ideas articulated in sci-fi are coming to fruition. The fictional technology described in the first *Star Trek* series, set in the twenty-third century, exists in many forms today: cell phones, tablets, Bluetooth earpieces, smart watches, virtual assistants, and video calls. Advancements in 3D printing are catching up with *replicators* (twenty-fourth-century machines that can create and print anything), and groups are developing what is essentially a medical *tricorder* (a scanning, analysis, and diagnostic device), as directly inspired by *Star Trek* and initiated through an XPRIZE competition. Translation in almost real-time is here—Google Translate instantly converts text from one language into another, and groups like Skype are experimenting with real-time voice translation. Martin Cooper, who helped develop the world's first mobile phone for Motorola, said that *Star Trek's* communicator device directly inspired him.

Then, "[H]e and his team took only 90 days in 1973 to create the first portable cellular."[1] That, to me, is breathtaking. We live in a time when nonfiction is, in many ways, becoming more fascinating than science fiction.

A s of 2020, less than six hundred people have visited space, which is too small of a sample of humanity if we intend to share the potentiality of space and the beauty of our planet Earth with wider communities around the world. Simultaneously, the pace of technology's developments is challenging to keep up with—even for professional analysts and writers. As a result, my initial role in space evolved from fan-enthusiast to advocate. Today, I continue to advance my position in the NewSpace industry as an advisor, thought leader, investor, and entrepreneur.

Back in 2007, my business partner and I established 62MileClub, a company that was dedicated to connecting the public with the evolving commercial spaceflight industry. At the time, the space industry was an exclusive niche; we described as being closed off by a velvet rope. We therefore aimed to advocate for and promote greater access to space for the mainstream and beyond. The effort ultimately happened too early, and I ended up pivoting to other areas in NewSpace. I went on to serve as a principal for Space Angels Network, cofound the Aerospace & Defense Forum, attend the International Space University, and join the Arch Mission Foundation. All the while, I continued developing relationships in and around the space community.

Over the years, in getting to know some of my colleagues in the space sector, I learned that for most, the industry is a conduit for them to merge their extraordinary intellects with their hearts for the greater good. Their passion for space intertwines with a desire to make humanity better, stronger, and more resilient. They are the early investors, the creators, the trailblazers, the innovators. We might call them rocket scientists, geeks, or space enthusiasts, but these labels tell only a fraction of who these mighty individuals really are. One of my intentions for this book is to highlight some of the stories and knowledge from these pioneers, deep thinkers, and astropreneurs—humans who have the skills *and* determination to help us elevate our civilization.

The aim of this book is not, however, to select industry winners. Instead, I hope to develop a framework for those outside of the industry to understand its relevance and potential, to become a guide and inspirational tool for future astropreneurs, to encourage more people to contribute to or become an active part of this ecosystem, and to offer steps and directions for policymakers, investors, and bold leaders to accelerate the industry's growth.

T his endeavor started as a challenge from a friend who wanted me to write a book. Over the summer of 2016, during an extended visit to Israel as part of a professional development program at the Technion University in Haifa, I started interviewing a few of my peers in the program and began writing daily journal entries late at night as my long day was winding down. Some of these entries would provide the kernels that evolved into the book's guiding thoughts.

The original purpose of this project was to give the person who perhaps has not invested in this sector yet a framework to incorporate into their own investment strategy—whether in time, funds, energy, or ideas. Whether you're a seasoned institutional investor or sharp, early-stage investor, the space sector is more nuanced than many might first imagine. Yes, there's rocket science, but it's also heavily regulated and interdisciplinary. It's still relatively nascent, with many unproven models. These risks might deter the typical investor, but for certain visionaries, it is an incredible sector that is ripe for investment.

When I began working on this book in 2016, I intended to balance my own ideas with insights and opinions from other experts. The original scope expanded significantly over the years—largely as a result of the fascinating conversations I had with those who shared their own inspiring outlook on this evolving industry. In total, over one hundred individuals contributed their knowledge, the majority of which you will find in the coming pages. You may also be surprised that the list includes not only engineering and finance mavens but experts in policy, law, and the arts.

The text that follows is intended to provide critical context that led to the commercial space sector, and to help the reader understand its emerging opportunities, new paradigms, investment potential, and the influence of arts and culture on the sector. While the different pieces of this book may seem disparate at first glance, they each provide a crucial layer of understanding what might be possible. To say that this area of focus is large is an understatement;

I contend that it could one day become the greatest area for humanity to focus on, especially if you take into account the size, scale, and availability of resources available in our solar system—and beyond.

The following pages pack in wisdom gained from over a decade of exploring this area of deep interest; my intention is to save you time and broaden your horizons for how incredibly valuable space truly is. As it stands today, the finished work is meant for anyone who desires to better understand the space sector—and my hope is that many will. While it covers economics, investment activity, and policy, it is fundamentally non-technical in an effort to provide inspiration and insights to all.

This book is a snapshot in time to help you understand where we are in 2020, though there are ideas which hopefully will remain timeless. It's difficult to predict exactly which way things will go; that trajectory is truly up to the individuals who are involved today and those who decide to become involved in the future. I hope that providing personal observations and experiences from my own life and from the many accomplished professionals included in this book will illuminate the nuances and granular elements that make the space sector so spectacular—both in its challenges and its potential.

I'd like to make a final note in light of the unexpected circumstances that arose just before the publication of this book's first edition. Like every other industry, the space sector has been affected by the COVID-19 pandemic. At this time, the extent of the pandemic's impact on the industry as a whole as well as its many individual companies is impossible to know with any real certainty. For this reason, I have decided to present the contents of this book as things stood in the first quarter of 2020, prior to the mass disruption the virus has had on all of our lives. Of course, this means that some of the companies mentioned—perhaps even the most promising—might not exist within the next year, and industry projections are likely to shift while the global economy experiences this abnormal pause in activity. That said, I ask for the reader's flexibility and understanding as things continue to unfold. I'd also like to request that the reader consider, as you read on, how we will respond to a global catastrophe in the future—and how a vibrant space economy might allow us to do things differently. [†]

[†] Updates and information on the space sector, including developments related to the pandemic, will be available online at tools.spaceisopenforbusiness.com

I wholeheartedly believe that space is a global, interconnected, and complex sector that deserves more attention, investment, and accelerated initiatives. By the end, I hope you will feel the same way.

Robert C. Jacobson

April, 2020
Earth, Solar System, Gould Belt, Orion Arm, Milky Way,
Virgo Supercluster, Laniakea Supercluster, Universe

ACKNOWLEDGMENTS

My endless gratitude to the following people
for helping make this book possible.

My advisors
Thank you for your patience, encouragement, and time—
and for taking on all of my (sometimes unconventional) requests.

My editor, Vanessa de Horsey
You took on a colossal responsibility and are my hero.
I'm grateful for all of the energy you contributed to this project.

My copy editor, Catherine Palmer
Thank you for brainstorming and helping identify
a feasible path to completion.

My fellow experts and interviewees
Thank you for being open to sharing your
wisdom and insights for this project.

My wife, Michelle
Thank you for your unwavering support and love. ♥
Your curiosity, zeal for exploration, and love for life are inspiring.

My father, Mel
Your generosity and kindness are exemplary.

Nova Spivack
Thank you for your encouragement to publish
this book here on Earth and beyond.

International Space University

Thank you for your generous gift, which allowed me to participate in the Space Studies Program. The experience completely changed my life.

Friends, family, and colleagues who knew about this project

Thank you for being you and for being a part of my life.

To the reader

Thank you for your time and for being open
to reading about this exciting sector.

And to the astropreneurs of today and tomorrow

Our civilization needs you. Onwards!

Special thanks to all those who contributed their time, talent, and wisdom.
There are too many of you to list, but I have attempted to do so.

Adam Bellow, *Book Advisor*
Christopher Stott, *Project Advisor*
Dr. Armin Ellis, *Technical Advisor*
Dennis Wingo, *Technical Advisor*
Jeff Garzik and SpaceChain, *Book Sponsor*
Ben Lamm and Hypergiant, *Book Sponsor*

Aaron Oesterle	Avi Blasberger	Cesar Sciammarella, Ph.D.
Adam Bellow	Berin Szoka	Charles Hildebrant
Adisakdi Tantimedh	Blaze Sanders	Charles Lurio, Ph.D.
Ali Binazir	Bob Werb	Chris Biddy
Allison Dollar	Brandon Farwell	Christopher Stott
Amaresh Kollipara	Bruce Ha	Christopher Tucker, Ph.D.
Amir Blachman	Bruce Pittman	Clifford W. Beek
Andrew Barton, Ph.D.	Brian Cogswell	Colleen Howard
Andrew Campbell	Bryan Landers	Dana Huffman
Andrew Dempster, Ph.D.	Camillo Andres Reyes	Daniel Abraham
Andrew Mayne	Carey Fosse	Daniel Campbell
Anthony Freeman, Ph.D.	Carissa Bryce Christensen	Daniel Faber
Arnin Ellis, Ph.D.	Cenan Al-Ekabi	Daniel Katz

Danny Salinas	Hoyt Davidson	Kirsten Kramer
Dario Nardi	Hsuan-Kuang Hsieh	Kyle Acierno
David A. Barnhart	Ian Fichtenbaum	Kyu Hwang
David Cowan	Ian Hattwick	Larry Niven
David Goldsmith	Ian Thiel	Drs. Larry and Emily Lai
David Jacobson	Ivan Rosenberg, Ph.D.	Lars Krogh Alminde
David Livingston, Ph.D.	James E. Dunstan	Lisa Rich
David Lizerbram	James Mellman, Ph.D.	Loryn Napala
Dawn McGinty	Jane Kinney	Luca del Monte
Debra Eckerling	Jay Gibson	Lynette Kucsma
Dennis Wingo	Jason Aspiotis	Mandy Sweeney
Dezsö Molnár	Jason Dunn	Marc Serres, Ph.D.
Don Brancato	Jeff Balis	Margeaux Sullivan
Doug Hegebarth	Jeffery Ferguson	Mark Boggett
Douglas Campbell	Jeff Garzik	Mark Siegfried
Douglas Messier	Jeff Greason	Matthew Dean
Eddie Van Pelt	Jeffrey Manber	Matthew Hoerl
Eduardo Sciammarella	Jeffrey Mathews	Meagan Crawford
Edward Story	Jenny Kaptein	Melissa Cecchine
Eliza & Moshe Shloush	Jeremy Conrad	Michael A. Smith
Elizabeth Kennick	Jesse Norton	Michael Carey
Ellen Chang	Jim Cantrell	Michael Clive
Emma Vardimon	James A. M. Muncy	Michael Mealling
Eric W. Golden	Joerg Kreisel	Michael Potter, Ph.D.
Fábio Teixeira	John Jaquish	Mickael Torrado
Federico Sciammarella, Ph.D.	John Paffett, Ph.D.	Monica Jan
Flavia Tata Nardini	John Spencer	Nahum Romero
Frank Lago	Joseph Naus	Nancy Davis
Frank Salzgeber	Josh Jones Dilworth	Neil Baliga
Gareth Keane, Ph.D.	Joyce Lu, Ph.D.	Nick Marks
Gary Marx	Judah Ben Jehoshua	Nick Slavin
George T. Whitesides	Karina Drees	Nova Spivack
Guillermo Söhnlein	Kartik Kumar	Oliver Eberle
Gwynne Shotwell	Keegan Kirkpatrick	Opher Brayer
Haley Jackson	Ken Davidian., Ph.D.	Patrick Gray
Hannah Petersson	Kent Verderico	Penn Arthur
Harold Davidson, Ph.D.	Keri Kukral	Peter Platzer
Heyward Bracey	Khaki Rodway	Piedra Stone

Rafal Modrzewski · Scott Thompson · Thomas Olson
Ray Podder · Sean Mahoney · Maj Gen. Thomas Taverney
Rex Ridenoure · Shahin Farshchi, Ph.D. · Timothy Draper
Richard Godwin · Shaun Arora · Troy McCann
Richard Kaplan · Sheri Anstedt · Uma Subramanian
Richard Leamon · Simon "Pete" Worden, Ph.D. · Van Espahbodi
Richard Pournelle · Stefan Bucher · Wen Hsieh, Ph.D.
Rick Tumlinson · Stephany Oosting · Will Porteous
Rob Coneybeer · Steve Goldberg, Ph.D. · William "Bill" Miller
Robert M. Davis · Stevie Rhim · Yasemin Denari
Roger Gilbertson · Stewart Bain · Yevgeny Tsodikovich
Sam Coniglio, IV · Takeshi Hakamada · Yonatan Winetraub
Sam Reiber · Tony and Marie Thomas · Yossi Yamin
Scott Farkas · Tonya "Tbird" Ridgely · Zeev Kirsh
Scott Farr · Theresa Saso

Thank you to the following organizations for their respective guidance
and assistance on this project, and for their roles in nurturing
this wonderful and endlessly complex sector.

Arch Mission Foundation · NASA
Blue Ribbon Studios · National Space Society
Bryce Space and Technology · NOAA
European Space Agency · Planet
Exploration Institute · Seraphim Capital
Fates · Space Frontier Foundation
International Institute of Space Commerce · The Space Show
Luxembourg Space Agency · Tikun Olam Media

INTRODUCTION

A DREAM WITHIN REACH

During a winter road trip to Mount Shasta, California, my wife and I took an evening walk through a snowy neighborhood. The trees, iced in white and set below the scale of the dramatic night sky, resembled decorations on a beautifully frosted cake. Without streetlights, the sky above seemed to expand forever, showcasing the twinkling stars like an endless display of cosmic jewels. As we walked through the snowdrifts and dark, forested lanes, surrounded by the magnificence of nature's creations, it gave me pause to realize that the cosmos are both our origin and our destination—perhaps even our future home.

The feeling most humans describe after seeing Earth from space is known as the "Overview Effect," a transcendent experience of empathy and connectedness. When viewed from an extreme distance, the planet resembles a beautiful blue marble; all our Earth-bound complexities become simplified in that moment, bringing the viewer the universal awareness that we each belong to this great life together. The understanding that we are each one small, tiny part of a much bigger world, sitting among this expansive universe, seems to unlock a sense of elevated compassion. The importance of our Earth—caring for it, maintaining it, and extending that care to all its inhabitants—eclipses the minutiae of our daily problems and distractions.

We often forget that we are not the center of the universe—that we are each just grains of sand among infinity. Space is not outside of our world or separate from us; we are part of it. Space influences us, and always has, even when we were not aware of it. The Moon and our ocean tides; meteors that have destroyed different eras; the Sun's evolution; the beginning of human life, starting from atoms of hydrogen and helium that evolved over billions of years to become intelligence and consciousness.

The space sector can open the universe for humanity; it is also a catalyst for transformation and a tool for wealth creation. The more we learn about space and understand it, the more we benefit. As we have explored and studied the realms beyond our own atmosphere, we have created solutions, technologies, and applications that have changed the way we live. There was a time before humans knew what lay inside the oceans; tenacious individuals resolved to explore these great waters, figure out how to use them for travel, understand their part in our planet. Space is similar. As we dare to explore outward, incredible results unfold in front of us.

For hundreds of thousands of years, humanity focused on space as a location. It was a place that inspired our dreams; we hid our secrets there in the stars, intertwined with myths of human imagination. Its impact is nothing if not universal. The profound energy that comes from interacting with space, even in intimate moments of introspection, can transform the way we think and feel about the world and ourselves. Space is not just a destination; it is a domain, an ecosystem, and an enabler. When we dream of improving our lives on Earth, we find answers within the great mysteries that the universe above us contains. At night, we look up into the stars and are filled with a sense of wonder, possibility, curiosity, and vitality. It's no surprise that we find endless ways to incorporate space into our daily lives, from the films we watch to the GPS we use during our commute—or why interactions with space tend to leave such lasting impressions. We want to explore; we want to understand. We want to believe.

PART I

BEYOND OBSERVATION

CHAPTER ONE
SPACE BECOMES AN INDUSTRY

The express object of an observatory is the increase and diffusion of knowledge by new discovery. ... The influence of the Moon, of the planets, our next door neighbors of the solar system, of the fixed stars, scattered over the blue expanse in multitudes exceeding the power of human computation, and at distances of which imagination herself can form no distinct conception; the influence of all these upon the globe which we inhabit, and upon the condition of man, its dying and deathless inhabitant, is great and mysterious. ... But to the vigilance of a sleepless eye, to the toil of a tireless hand, and to the meditations of a thinking, combining, and analyzing mind, secrets are successively revealed ... which seem to lift him from the Earth to the threshold of his eternal abode.[1]

John Quincy Adams, "Report of the Select Committee of the House of Representatives of the United States (J.Q. Adams, Chair), on the Smithsonian Bequest," March 5, 1840.

The United States' official interest in space goes back to John Quincy Adams. In the 1800s, he championed the beginning of the space exploration effort with a fervid passion for building astronomical observatories across the country, stemming from his belief that the vast unknown above would inspire us here on Earth and promote interest in the sciences. Within this persistent crusade, Adams made various requests to Congress for observatories, during both his presidency and later career in the House of Representatives. As a champion for science and knowledge, Adams was the leading force in establishing the US Naval Observatory in 1844—and in persuading Congress to establish the Smithsonian Institution as a scientific research and learning facility in 1846. One century later, plans to leverage space began in earnest.

Since the Space Age of the mid-twentieth century began, government programs and a handful of contractors have traditionally comprised the modern space sector. World War II and the decades that followed catalyzed a surge of interest in space, led by the Soviet Union (USSR) and the United States. From launching the first satellite in 1957 and putting the first person in space in 1961, the USSR pushed the boundaries in space, prompting other countries to follow suit. In this original "space race," the two global powers challenged and motivated each other to accomplish the seemingly impossible: establishing surveillance satellites, launching rockets into space and safely returning them to Earth, putting humans in space, and eventually planting a flag on the Moon. The twentieth century is thus understood as a period of "flags and footprints," with strategic and national security interests serving as paramount catalysts for early space programs and missions. In this era, goals to visit a destination in space, leave both literal and metaphorical marks, and return to Earth superseded any further concrete action related to leveraging space or its resources.

After accomplishing key capabilities and milestone missions, the United States, the USSR, and other ambitious countries began to explore new uses for space. For the latter part of the twentieth century, space extended beyond symbolic achievements with several subsectors emerging: rockets, satellites, crewed exploration, and uncrewed exploration.

NASA'S ROOTS

The conception and evolution of the National Aeronautics and Space Administration (NASA) are much more profound than most realize. Created as a defense infrastructure during the Cold War, it provided the United States with accurate missile-targeting capabilities. As space industry pioneer Jeff Greason explained, whereas the USSR knew precisely where to send their missiles, "The only way the United States knew what to target in the Soviet Union was to secretly fly spy planes over them. Eisenhower knew that we wouldn't be able to keep doing that forever; his advisers told him that eventually, we would do that reconnaissance from space."[2] NASA, therefore, was imperative in preserving the safety and strength of the United States during an incredibly fragile period of global history.

Another crucial aspect of NASA's origins was that Eisenhower formed it as a defense tool—but he deliberately kept it separate from the military. Even though the defense department could have developed the needed rockets, missiles, and satellites more quickly, "The precedent of peaceful overflight was much more important than who was first and who was second," Greason stated.

It was strategically vital to the United States that space be a domain that was free for the innocent passage of all. So, when [the successful launch of] Sputnik forced Eisenhower to take some kind of action, instead of nationalizing and making the military go to space, he created NASA. That way, when we went to space, it would be as a civilian agency.

Jeff Greason*

NASA's creation is a testament to forward-thinking, and an understanding of how today's actions will affect generations to come. Many of the Agency's programs promote continuous improvement in technology and partnership opportunities for the private sector, from the Innovative Advanced Concepts program and the Technology Transfer Program to the Commercial Resupply Services, Commercial Crew Development, and Commercial Lunar Payload Services programs. These offerings provide far more than internal benefits; they spur progress in industries that affect civilian life, and NASA investments in early-stage research and development (R&D) can be powerful enablers for

★ **Jeff Greason** is a trailblazer in commercial space. He has been a key player in regulatory improvements for the commercial space industry, having worked with the Federal Aviation Administration Office of Commercial Space Transportation (FAA/AST) since 1998, and as a member of the Commercial Space Transportation Advisory Committee (COMSTAC) focused on reusable launch vehicles. He led the development of the Commercial Space Launch Agreement of 2004 and has been a member of the Review of United States Human Space Flight Plans Committee since 2009. Additionally, Greason has founded numerous private space companies and organizations, including the Commercial Spaceflight Federation, XCOR Aerospace, and Agile Aero. He is currently the cofounder and chief technologist of Electric Sky, a startup developing wireless energy sources for launch vehicles, and the chair of Tau Zero Foundation.

various markets, especially in cases where private sector ideas are too expensive to pursue or too early for investment.

In NASA's peak years, large numbers of people signed up to become test pilots, astronauts, and volunteers for other high-risk career opportunities, despite the danger and challenges. American citizens, driven by authentic passion and excitement, joined the efforts of the space program. Consider how many people today, including entrepreneurs, scientists, cultural influencers, and more, were deeply affected by the NASA Moon landing in 1969—over half a century ago.

n the past, United States policies via NASA and the White House Office of Science and Technology Policy (OSTP) alluded to extending Earth's economic ecosystem to include space. We have decades of thought leadership and ideas around the possibilities of what space holds for humanity, and NASA has a luminous track record of inspiring achievements.

However, NASA has slowed substantially in recent decades. The issues of stagnation and aversion to risk are surprisingly common in a sector so reliant on innovation and experimentation. Factors like changes of administration, public interest, and budgets all play a part, though most notably, this shift has resulted from governments allocating budgets to "higher priority" items.

CHAPTER TWO
POST-APOLLO

After the Apollo program ended in 1972, the Nixon administration attempted to compensate for the loss with the NASA Space Shuttle program. The Space Shuttle was the first reusable rocket in history, intended to fly fifty times per year and serve interests including the Department of Defense (DoD), intelligence and security, satellite operations, exploration, and in-space research; it was also meant to help reduce launch costs.[1]

In a statement issued in March 1970, President Nixon explained his ambitions with NASA and the Shuttle program. "We must think of [space activities] as part of a continuing process ... and not as a series of separate leaps, each requiring a massive concentration of energy. Space expenditures must take their proper place within a rigorous system of national priorities." He continued: "What we do in space from here on in must become a normal and regular part of our national life and must therefore be planned in conjunction with all of the other undertakings which are important to us."[2]

Such enthusiastic promises quickly fell flat. Nixon repeatedly gouged the NASA budget throughout his presidency, rejecting space proposals across the board, with the Shuttle as his only real focus. And still, the Space Shuttle never achieved its original goal; in fact, it never came close to those initial targets. The lofty objective of fifty flights per year shattered with the reality of the Challenger explosion in 1986. From that point on, the risks and challenges of launches overshadowed the potential benefits. Simultaneously, military satellites increased in capabilities and began launching more often on lower-cost, single-use rockets.[3]

NASA's conception informs its current paradox. Formed to solve a near-impossible problem, it succeeded with flying colors. However, once the Cold War ended, so did its purpose. When the Space Shuttle program concluded with neither strong replacement nor direction, the crewed space program headed into the doldrums—though many experts will contend that the United States was in the space doldrums back when it decided to end the Apollo program. This was part of the reason why I (and many others) became disillusioned with NASA in the 1980s and 1990s. The Shuttle was too slow, too expensive, and it looked highly unlikely that it would ever include the rest of us. In 2004, President George W. Bush announced that NASA would retire the program; after the Atlantis landed back at the Kennedy Space Center (KSC) in 2011, the program was officially over.[4]

As Professor John Logsdon noted in his book, *After Apollo? Richard Nixon and the American Space Program,* President Nixon's assistant Tom Whitehead commented that "no compelling reason to push space was ever presented to the White House by NASA or anyone else." This resulted in what Logsdon describes as "the least desirable outcome," citing that for the forty-plus years following the space boom of the 1960s, "there has been a mismatch between space ambitions and the resources provided to achieve them."[5]

While NASA's beginnings stemmed from noble intentions, it has suffered from its isolation from the high-powered government agencies. Because there was never a national discussion or agreement about *why* we go to space, NASA exists with an unclear purpose, regardless of its track record. Even after the Soviet Union's collapse, Russia continued to move forward in space with the Roscosmos State Corporation for Space Activities (Roscosmos). And after NASA retired its Space Shuttle program, the United States began paying Russia to send crews to the International Space Station (ISS).

oday, NASA's funding is minuscule compared to other government programs. Since its high point in 1966 of $5.6 billion (4.4 percent of the federal
budget), it continues to drop year by year.[6] In fiscal year (FY) 2017, NASA's
budget was a mere 0.489 percent of the entire $4 trillion budget and only 0.4
percent of the FY2019 budget.[7] While NASA's budget increased to a projected
$23 billion for FY2020 (mainly due to a proposal for an additional $1.5 billion
for a new Moon mission), it still clocks in at 0.4 percent of the federal budget;
the Department of Defense, in comparison, will receive $750 billion: 16 percent
of the federal budget.

It is certainly worth noting that despite the small sliver of the pie NASA
receives, it generates much more than exciting expeditions and technologies. NASA's 2005 budget was $16.1 billion, and a report from the Space
Foundation estimated that space-related activities in that year resulted in $180
billion added to the United States economy. [8] This means that every dollar
spent within NASA yielded a ten-fold return; other studies agree that NASA
returns between $8 and $10 in economic growth per dollar it receives—quite a
significant margin from an investment standpoint.[9]

While it seems logical to allocate a higher percentage of the budget to
NASA, the common issue with government funding is that space tends to be
low on the totem pole. General Michael Carey, who retired from the United
States Air Force (USAF) after over three decades of technical and political
experience in satellite and space operations, explained that the wrestling match

for budget always leans in the direction of security.* "What *does* win the battle is the requirement to sustain our communications capabilities and sustain our warning capabilities," Carey relayed, noting that new efforts, exploration, and research are not considered as crucial.[10] As such, NASA must prioritize the areas assessed as the most significant needs for its mission directives.

Furthermore, policymakers have proved time and again that other interests take priority, developing a culture of distrust and establishing a precedent that finishing projects results in punishment: if the goal is accomplished, the programs get shut down and budgets get cut. As such, NASA operates mostly in survival mode, keeping a tight grip on its projects rather than taking more significant risks and self-protecting to retain the funding it has left.

Of course, NASA continues its inspiring work, leading to technological advancements and applications that most of us today couldn't imagine living without—still, most of these achievements fly under the radar. Without a greater understanding of why NASA and its success matters, it's impossible to solve the Agency's more granular issues. Given NASA's ongoing challenges, the current status of the civil space sector in the United States is now seriously in question. The United States used to take risks, but its current approach to space focuses on avoiding as much risk as possible. If the leading champion in space is losing steam, what does that mean for the rest of us?

★ **Michael Carey** is the cofounder and chief strategy officer of ATLAS Space Operations, a satellite communications company based in Michigan and focused on bringing affordable access to space via its cloud-based software platform. Carey also serves as an advisor for Syndicate 708, a deep space technology accelerator based in Los Angeles, and as the president of his own defense and leadership consultancy. He is a retired US Air Force General with thirty-four years of military service and expertise in satellite and space operations.

PART II

TADPOLES, UNICORNS, AND ZEBRAS

CHAPTER THREE
NEW ENERGY, NEW SPACE

Space tends to be slow. Although the United States space program went from zero to the Moon in less than ten years, it required billions of dollars and hundreds of thousands of people to focus on it. Even now, the traditional methods of developing space technology are much too expensive for most governments.

While space programs around the world suffered from a lack of interest and lack of funding in the decades following the end of the Apollo program, confident individuals and companies remained determined not to lose faith in the potential space holds. The result of their passions and efforts opened a new era for space and its myriad applications.

Now, twenty years into the twenty-first century, the space sector is finally gaining newfound traction. Though much of this activity happens behind the scenes, there is now more involvement in space globally than ever before in history. This new era, led by private space efforts, is known as "NewSpace"—a movement that views space not as a location or metaphor, but as a well of resources, opportunities, and mysteries yet to be unlocked.

Though certain leaders historically dominated the industry, over fifty nations have national space programs today. More than a dozen new companies are now significant players in the manufacturing and launch of complete vehicles, while thousands of companies supply parts, engineering, logistics, and other space-focused products and services.

Commercial companies in the United States now develop spacecraft in places like Austin, Texas; Kent, Washington; and Hawthorne, California. They leverage existing facilities in sites such as KSC (NASA's primary launch center) and the ISS.[1] SpaceX is building an assembly line for its orbital launch vehicles in Los Angeles, and Planet makes satellites in downtown San Francisco that are small enough to hold in two hands.

With decentralized computing, crowdsourcing, additive manufacturing, advances in computing and robotics, lean methodology (technology convergence), and everything in-between, the industry landscape has transformed dramatically. Simultaneously, some governments have gradually relaxed their hold on the space sector—with new contract models that favor fixed-price bids, reductions in burdensome paperwork, and modified security restrictions—making it easier for startups and smaller organizations to work with or for governments.

Perhaps most inspiring in the expansion of the NewSpace sector is the involvement of students around the world; these young minds all believe in the future of space exploration. Equally amazing are the select entrepreneurs who commit to seeing these risky endeavors to completion. And, of course, the industry has attracted some of the world's ambitious, public-facing billionaires, who have helped bring "space" back into the vernacular—whether it's Elon Musk suggesting we need a backup for humanity, Jeff Bezos envisioning trillions of humans inhabiting the solar system, or Sir Richard Branson intending to take millions of regular people to space, there is no shortage of earnest efforts behind these moonshots. Simply put, a plethora of talented people are working tirelessly to push the limits of technology and discovery. Roadmaps are being drawn and plans are being made, whether from the bright youth still in school, highly funded startups, or established governments.

CHAPTER FOUR
FROM EVOLUTION TO REVOLUTION

The XPRIZE was one of those magical moments where history was made—and you were a part of it. And it was all done with the best of intentions: for a positive view of the future, entrepreneurism, American spirit, taking risks, and being willing to put it all on the line. It worked, and it was a wonderful experience to be an observer of that whole thing.[1]

John Spencer*

The idea of a private space sector is not new. It's been a movement for decades, advocated for by individuals and groups—such as Space Frontier Foundation, which may have been the first to actively use and promote the term "New Space"—who took an active leadership role in the commercial space industry's early days. But key moments have defined NewSpace's transformation so far; these milestones helped break through established power structures and industry standards, allowing private efforts to surge forward with serious momentum.

It's important to understand that while space as a place and concept is widely admired, it is rarely understood in its totality. It is still difficult for most people

★ **John Spencer** is the founder and president of the Space Tourism Society, an organization focused on establishing and expanding a space tourism industry. He is also an outer space architect, internationally renowned for his design and creation of in-space structures and facilities and for space-themed structures on Earth. For his innovative architectural design work on the International Space Station, NASA awarded Spencer with the Space Act Award and the Certificate of Recognition.

to get past the notion that the space sector could be something more than just rockets, scientific exploration, or satellites used for weather and communications. Space remains one of the most contested areas; it's a highly competitive sector, and there are government-mandated regulations and security controls around the industry that add friction to the collaborative elements. Technologies for space exploration tend to have extreme requirements, given that repairs, modifications, and other changes once in space are notoriously difficult, if not considered virtually impossible.

In the 1990s, there were no public plans on private space projects. Jeff Greason explained that "The idea was so laughable that for years we had a secret business plan. We had a cover story to explain why we were building a rocket." The breakthrough was when Dennis Tito flew as a private citizen to space, paid for by himself, in 2001.[2] A domino effect followed, with ideas and dreams becoming plausible realities.

Historically, some of the first of the commercial space flight efforts began with Robert Truax (1970s), Kistler Aerospace (1993), the XPRIZE Foundation (1996), Beal Aerospace (1997), MirCorp (1999), and Blastoff! Corporation (1999). Many private efforts followed in their footsteps, first intermittently, and in recent years a fully-fledged ecosystem has developed.

> *Suborbital is not a word you heard very often in 1999, so we looked at the suborbital market. People paid money to climb Mount Everest. People paid to go to the South Pole. It seemed obvious that people would spend money to go to space.*[3]
> **Jeff Greason | Cofounder & Chief Technology Officer, Electric Sky; Chair, Tau Zero Foundation; Cofounder, XCOR Aerospace & Commercial Spaceflight Federation**

EARLY STEPS

The United States-based XPRIZE Foundation emerged in 1996 as one of the first organizations that sought to advance private spaceflight. Unlike government-sponsored projects, the XPRIZE served as a competition for commercial efforts to create and launch a reusable, uncrewed aircraft.

XPRIZE founder Dr. Peter Diamandis spent years promoting the competition around the world in the search for financial sponsors who might be willing to fund the $10 million prize for a successful uncrewed flight to space. For a long time, there was interest—but no takers. However, the effort inspired several groups to at least announce their intention of entering the prize competition. Diamandis finally ended up securing a prize sponsorship by the Texas-based Ansari family, who put up the money for what is known as a hole-in-one insurance prize.

The competition required a vehicle to fly 100 kilometers (62.5 miles—the distance to space from sea level) twice within two weeks while carrying a weight equal to three passengers.[4] Ultimately, there was only one credible effort: Burt Rutan's SpaceShipOne. Many other groups had the technical acumen but didn't have the financial backing or passionate interest in pursuing the prize.

Investing in the XPRIZE ended up being a smart move for the Ansari family. Burt Rutan is a legendary airplane designer; he created the Voyager aircraft, which was the first to circumnavigate the globe without refueling. And the late Paul Allen, cofounder of Microsoft, financially backed SpaceShipOne's development. Given Burt's excellent track record of designing experimental vehicles, coupled with a strong financial backer, the effort and eventual prize-winning flights generated significant global coverage.

It was a seriously wild-ass idea at that time—
people building spaceships for suborbital,
people risking their lives on vehicles, and all kinds of stuff.[5]

**John Spencer | Space Architect; Founder & President, Space
Tourism Society; Chief Designer, Mars World Enterprises**

Witnessing this first flight of SpaceShipOne on June 21, 2006 ended up being the most pivotal space experience in my adult life. Among a crowd of ten thousand others, I watched the spacecraft soar into history, reaching a height of 100.124 kilometers and becoming the first privately developed and funded vehicle to reach space. This event affected me at my core—as if it had changed my DNA—and repositioned my life for a role of astropreneurship and exploration. SpaceShipOne provided obvious clues that there could be roles for private individuals and groups in space. While I didn't yet know what my role would be, from that day forward I decided to orient my life to consciously face space. Space was, indeed, closer than I or anyone else thought.

The XPRIZE helped prove that smart, strategic sponsorship can be a powerful way to generate steady deal flow for future business and socially related opportunities. The entire endeavor helped give this space renaissance steam, inspiring the next wave of people to immerse themselves in NewSpace. One significant impact worth noting was on Sir Richard Branson, who announced Virgin Galactic in between the first and second flights of SpaceShipOne by making a deal with Rutan's Scaled Composites and Paul Allen to license and leverage SpaceShipOne's technology. Branson and Rutan then partnered to develop SpaceShipTwo, the Virgin Galactic spacecraft created specifically for space tourism.

Once an idea is proven, and evidence exists that there is an opportunity, more activities begin to take shape. Efforts like the XPRIZE competition are crucial milestones for NewSpace: they shed light on a formerly obscure industry and inspired those who thought it *might* be possible to have private, crewed missions to space and motivated them to pursue concrete actions. Activities like these set up the possibility that space can experience exponential growth, and it's precisely this potential that has ambitious individuals taking a chance on their boldest visions for the future.

CHAPTER FIVE
SUCCESSFUL ENDEAVORS

There's a fundamental generational shift going on as well—not just a shift in the cost and time of access to space, but people realizing, like a big slap in the face, what they can do now. What's holding you back? Nothing is holding your back.[1]
Christopher Stott*

N ewSpace draws on lessons learned in the business world to establish new—and previously thought impossible—offerings. In recent years, new companies have worked on solutions to make in-space work, manufacturing, and repairs a sustainable possibility. There is also a rise in quality business plans, spearheaded by entrepreneurs who understand that it takes more than engineering to successfully execute a space-enabled or space-focused initiative. Let's look at a few of the top venture-backed space startups and how they got here.

SPACEX

When something is important enough, you do it even if the odds are not in your favor.[2]
Elon Musk | Founder, SpaceX

S pace Exploration Technologies (SpaceX) is arguably the most famous of the NewSpace companies—and for good reason. Founded in 2002 by engineer and technology magnate Elon Musk, SpaceX has been successful in financing, creating, and operating new orbital vehicles.

Before his entry into the space sector, Elon Musk made several fortunes in internet startups, most notably as a cofounder of PayPal. A longtime space enthusiast, he invested approximately $100 million (a significant portion of personal capital) into SpaceX.[3] Musk's tenacity and level of seriousness caught the attention of the Defense Advanced Research Projects Agency (DARPA)—the

DoD agency that develops technology for the military—which became one of the company's first customers and provided behind-the-scenes political support after SpaceX's first rocket exploded in 2006.

It's worth a reminder that Musk was not always a billionaire. After putting his entire PayPal payout into SpaceX, Tesla, and SolarCity, he spent a decade pouring all of his income back into his various companies—to the point where, in 2010, he reported that he was "out of cash" and had been taking loans from friends. Like any other entrepreneur, he would rely on third-party investors to keep his ambitious space company alive. Luke Nosek, a fellow PayPal cofounder and later a cofounder of Founders Fund, was SpaceX's first investor, providing $20 million in 2008 via Founders Fund.[4] Other early funding came from Draper Fisher Jurvetson (DFJ), a venture capital (VC) firm that had previously backed Tesla and SolarCity.[5] Musk effectively parlayed those prior relationships into putting DFJ on the radar for the NewSpace community, which had few VC players at the time. Other investors included members of the Pritzker family, Fidelity, and Google—all of which helped bolster SpaceX financially.

Still, success does not tend to happen overnight. Govenment contracts, traditional space organizations, and launch incumbents all dismissed SpaceX's efforts many times over the years. Despite this, the disruptive startup continued to develop and launch, even leveraging the judicial process to level the playing field by convincing the United States Air Force to allow SpaceX to fly defense payloads—which had been the sole domain of United Launch Alliance since 2006.[6]

★**Christopher Stott** is the cofounder, chief executive officer, and chair of ManSat, the world's largest commercial provider of satellite spectrum, which he founded with his father in 1998. ManSat is a pioneering success story of the private space sector and established the Isle of Man, where it is based, as a hub for commercial space efforts. A space entrepreneur with experience in government policy and regulation, Stott previously served as the director of international commercialization and sales for Lockheed Martin Space Operations' contract with NASA. He worked on the Delta Launch Vehicle Program at McDonnell Douglas and for Boeing Space & Communications. Stott is a fellow of the Royal Astronomical Society and the International Institute of Space Law, an alumnus and faculty member of the International Space University, and a founder of the International Institute of Space Commerce. He continues to support NewSpace through his involvement in space and STEM education, by serving on several boards, and by contributing to multiple space-related publications.

A lthough some of SpaceX's first flights weren't 100 percent successful, the SpaceX team consistently learned from its mistakes, allowing it to forge a steady path of progress. Even after an explosion on a launchpad in Florida in September 2016, SpaceX quickly licked its wounds and successfully launched seventeen Falcon 9 rockets in 2017—including its first launch of a United States national security mission. In 2019, the Falcon Heavy rocket launched its first commercial communications satellite into geostationary orbit, both completing its task and safely landing the three rocket boosters back on Earth—where SpaceX can use them again.[7]

SpaceX's newest endeavor is the reusable Starship vehicle, which is now in rapid development. The company is using an internal competition to increase speed, testing, and improvements, with two separate teams working on pro-totypes. After visiting both Starship sites in early August 2019 (one in Texas and one in Cape Canaveral), Musk tweeted that while both teams are racing to orbit, "a success by both in close proximity would be amazing [and] each would count as a win."[8] This form of "collaborative competition," a successful method often used in software development, is yet another indicator of SpaceX's ability to push the boundaries in an effective, efficient way.[9]

From its beginnings in 2002 to winning a grant of $3 million from NASA in October 2019, SpaceX boasts twenty-seven investors and approximately $3.3 billion in total funding over twenty-five rounds.[10] In the summer of 2017, Luke Nosek formed a new investment group, Gigafund, to focus specifically on raising capital for SpaceX. Since then, the firm has invested "[hundreds] of millions into SpaceX after partnering with Stephen Oskoui [a former venture partner from Founders Fund]," as noted on the Gigafund website.[11] A Series K financing round in May 2019 brought in $535.74 million from Gigafund, Quantum Global Partners, and FoundersX Ventures, followed by another round in June from the Ontario Teachers' Pension Plan for an estimated $314.2 million.[12] SpaceX thus completed three successful financing rounds by the end of Q2 in 2019, amounting to $1.32 billion, and its valuation continues to grow. While CNBC designated a $33.3 billion valuation after the Starlink test launch in May 2019, Morgan Stanley published a report in September 2019 stating that the Starlink constellation increases the company's value far more significantly—from a base of $52 billion up to an astonishing $120 billion "Bull Case."[13] As the leader of the private space launch sector, coupled with its new Starlink satellite constellation and reusable Starship, SpaceX stands as a lucrative and promising venture.[14]

SUPERIOR SATELLITES

While rockets and their missions into space tend to receive the most attention from the public and the media, some of the greatest NewSpace successes come from the massive satellite market. Planet and Spire Global are leaders in the field, each creating their own satellites for various purposes that improve our world.

In 2010, former NASA Ames scientists Will Marshall, Robbie Schingler, and Chris Boshuizen created a startup out of garage space at the co-living house in Cupertino known as Rainbow Mansion. The stucco home has attracted bright, space-friendly professionals over the near-decade that it has operated as a shared living space. The garage area, used for ongoing hardware projects, served as the first office for Cosmogia—known today as Planet.

While many Earth observation efforts exist today, Planet started as a rare creature. Its founders saw the possibility of leveraging small satellites (also known as "smallsats") for Earth observation. As Boshuizen recounted in NASA's 2016 *Spinoff* publication, NASA Ames Research Center's director of engineering, Pete Klupar, "had this shtick ... where he'd pull out a Government-issued BlackBerry from his pocket and tout how a smartphone has more capabilities than many satellites, as it has a bigger computer and better sensors." Klupar would proceed to ask the room why satellites cost so much more than a phone—before putting the phone away and continuing with his regular programming. One day, Boshuizen and Marshall interjected: "We said, 'Pete, don't put that back in your pocket. We're going to make that into a satellite.'" The pair soon began leading the NASA PhoneSat project: CubeSats that leveraged cheap smartphone components to take photographs once in orbit. PhoneSats cost under $7,000 to build; the least expensive satellite that NASA had been able to develop up to that point cost $10 million.[15]

Following the success of the PhoneSat tests, Marshall, Boshuizen, and fellow Ames colleague Robbie Schingler left NASA in 2010 and formed their own CubeSat company with an ambitious goal: "to image the whole world every day, making change visible, accessible, and actionable," Schingler said.[16] Planet's imaging and data benefit sectors ranging from human rights to agriculture, environment to shipping investments.

Planet is one of the first private, venture-backed, Earth observation startups using smallsat platforms. While most startups tend to start with a friends and family round, proceed to an angel round, and then to the venture capital round (a well-known path to establishing credibility), Planet went through several quick rounds of early-stage funding with venture capital groups. These investments resulted from Planet's savvy decision to use the tech industry approach of presenting a minimum viable prototype to investors *before* spending time and money on analysis and systems development—a strategy the founders refer to as "agile aerospace." Once Planet proved that its product would work, funding began to flow in, and the startup hired engineers before promptly moving toward its goal of rapidly imaging Earth. Planet successfully deployed Flock-1, its first commercial constellation of twenty-eight Earth-sensing CubeSats (called Doves), from the ISS in 2014. As of Q1 2020, the company has deployed over 200 Doves into orbit.[17]

Planet's early and continued success resulted from a strong combination of factors. First, the startup's founders leveraged new technology—smartphone components and off-the-shelf parts—to develop an inexpensive but innovative product with robust processing capabilities. They had a tenacious business model of "release early, release often," which attracted substantial capital investments and support; and because the technology they used continued to improve while becoming more affordable, so did their products—allowing them to compete with the established satellite magnates and cater to both existing and emerging markets. In addition, the affordability of Planet's CubeSats reduces risk for the company and stakeholders in the event of damage or destruction; in 2014, for example, thirty-four Doves were destroyed in two separate rocket failures. Such losses would typically be catastrophic to a company, but Planet barely batted an eyelash.[18]

In its first ten years, the company received over $300 million in private investments from DFJ, Felicis Ventures, Capricorn Investment Group, Data Collective, and AME Cloud Ventures.[19] Planet acquired satellite operating companies Black Bridge in 2015 and Terra Bella in 2017 (from Google, making Google an equity shareholder), as well as geospatial software company Boundless Spatial in 2018. After a 2018 funding round, Planet's valuation was estimated to be over $1.4 billion.[20] The startup now has hundreds of employees and partners in over forty countries, working in markets that include agriculture, government, defense and intelligence, emergency management, energy, and finance.

> *We started Planet because of its potential to aid*
> *humanitarian causes, and then we realized that*
> *the best way to have that impact and be sustainable*
> *was to develop a highly profitable business model.*[21]
> **Will Marshall, Ph.D. | Cofounder & Chief Executive Officer, Planet**

S pire Global (Spire), another small satellite constellation play, emerged in 2012 and has since been successful in fundraising as well as generating a mini ecosystem for different uses of its satellites. When founder Peter Platzer first conceived of Spire, it looked more like a space-education opportunity. Platzer pitched an earlier iteration of the company, known as NanoSatisfi, at the Space Frontier Foundation's New Space Business Plan Competition in 2012. When the startup did not win the competition, Platzer ended up reorienting; he quickly pivoted the opportunity as Spire Global and raised several tens of millions of dollars. To date, Spire has raised over $160 million over ten funding rounds, the last of which occurred in September 2019. Investors include the Luxembourg government, Luxembourg Future Fund, Itochu Corporation and Mitsui & Co. (two of Japan's largest trading companies), and London-based Seraphim Capital.[22]

In September 2015, Spire launched four satellites aboard an Indian rocket as part of its emerging commercial weather satellite network.[23] Spire has also partnered with the National Oceanic and Atmospheric Administration (NOAA) and the European Space Agency (ESA) to gather weather data that improves global forecasting. In 2018, Platzer told CNBC that he estimates this data to be worth close to $3 billion for his company over the next twenty-five years.[24]

S atellites are, of course, far more valuable when paired with revolutionary software. Such software is responsible for nearly every function and application we use on our smartphones and our computers. As we understand more and more how to use the data available via satellites, some companies are making considerable strides in applying them to successful business models.

Orbital Insight, established in 2013 and based in Silicon Valley, is a geospatial Big Data company that uses satellites and Earth observation technologies to create custom data sets for its customers. By leveraging various forms of data, the company analyzes human activity and then trains its artificial intelligence (AI)-enabled software to construct trends that help others determine business solutions. From figuring out where a grocery store chain should open a new location (based on foot and auto traffic in a given area), to providing insight on the housing market (based on existing buildings, where there is free space, and what kind of buildings are in development), to monitoring agricultural activity, Orbital Insight is proving the worth of Smart Data analysis.

The company's data sets are customized based on specific timespans and geographical locations, all dependent on the client's goals and target markets. Partners include satellite data providers like Planet and Netherlands-based Airbus; the latter announced a collaboration with Orbital Insight in 2018 to form Airbus' OneAtlas Digital Platform, which uses the Airbus satellite imagery and Orbital Insight's analytics services to provide premium data services to the world.[25] Orbital Insight also partnered with Energy Aspects in 2018 to provide tracking and analysis of global oil storage levels. As Energy Aspects CEO Fredrik Fosse explained, "This partnership with Orbital Insight will drive innovation in the energy industry, equipping clients with the latest technology to make the best possible investment, trading, and strategic decisions."[26]

Orbital Insight has raised close to $80 million in funding from investors, most notably $50 million from Sequoia Capital in 2017.[27] Other investors include Lux Capital, Intellectus Partners, and Bloomberg Beta.[28] *Fast Company* named Orbital Insight as one of its "Most Innovative Companies," citing that its data analysis application can detect social and economic trends around the world, which results in intelligent information that can be leveraged effectively by a range of businesses, from nonprofits to large corporations to governments.[29]

RIDESHARE

Because rockets often have extra room for additional payloads, "rideshare" companies provide that extra space as a useful and lower-cost launch alternative. Groups like Nanoracks, Rocket Lab, and Spaceflight have been effective intermediaries for groups looking for quick access to space. These companies also provide services that allow smaller satellite developers and operators to spend less time on paperwork, integration issues, and communications—which are not core parts of their respective businesses. These services increase efficiencies, spread risk, and help astropreneurs focus their energies on their expertise and market propositions.

Nanoracks, based in Houston and founded in 2009, is the first brokerage company to help a wide variety of private and public customers access the International Space Station. Nanoracks doesn't have exclusive access to the ISS, but it has strong capabilities in navigating complex NASA bureaucracy, thus enabling the company to deliver payloads for a wide variety of customers, from schools to nation-states. [30]

Nanoracks' capabilities are strong enablers for NewSpace as a whole. After successfully identifying an existing demand for research on the space station, the company has been able to provide unprecedented access to the ISS. In a 2017 press release celebrating Nanoracks' seventh anniversary, CEO Jeffrey Manber* noted how the company had been consistently accomplishing its goal of aiding the growth of other commercial space startups; among those companies, Manber named Spire, Planet, NanoAvionics, and GomSpace.[31] Dan Katz, CEO of hyperspectral satellite startup Orbital Sidekick, relayed how Nanoracks played an instrumental role in providing access to the ISS National Lab.* Katz shared

★**Jeffrey Manber** is the chief executive officer of Nanoracks, a company focused on products and services related to the commercial use of space. He began his career in space as a writer on microgravity business opportunities for the likes of *The New York Times* and McGraw-Hill before the Reagan Administration asked him to help develop the Office of Space Commerce (Department of Commerce). Manber went on to help the Soviet Union in privatizing its space efforts, later joining MirCorp, where he headed the Mir space station business (and signed Dennis Tito's private visit to Mir). In 2009, Manber cofounded Nanoracks, one of the most successful NewSpace companies in the world, which leverages the ISS for commercial and government services and has sent over 900 payloads to the space station.

that after receiving funding from the Center for the Advancement of Science in Space (CASIS, the organization that manages the ISS National Lab), the wait time to reach the ISS was close to two years. Orbital Sidekick decided to work with Nanoracks, which provided a grant as well as a rideshare slot twelve months away. CASIS then ended up matching the grant, approving the new timeline, and helping get the payload delivered to the ISS. "We were able to leverage a very aggressive schedule, with the reality of us of actually executing a contract with Nanoracks, to push CASIS to get on board with what we were doing," Katz explained of the success.[32] With nearly one thousand payloads launched to date, Nanoracks is proving to be one of the stronger space-enabled businesses.

NANORACKS ACCOMPLISHMENTS INCLUDE:

- Nearly 1,000 payloads launched between 2009 and 2019, most of which have been ISS missions. Blue Origin and India's Polar Satellite Launch Vehicle (PSLV) account for some of the few non-ISS missions.

- Over 250 CubeSats launched as of 2020, which includes Nanoracks' External Cygnus Deployer and India's PSLV.

- 100 percent success rate: only two launches with Nanoracks payloads failed, and Nanoracks was able to refly all customer payloads from those launches.

- Starting in 2020, Nanoracks will begin numerous off-ISS missions, including a demonstration mission for its in-space Outpost (Habitat) program. Contracted by NASA, these "wet lab" habitats, which are converted upper-stage rockets, evolved out of the 2016 NASA NextSTEP effort and will act as commercial space stations in Low Earth Orbit (LEO).

Rocket Lab, founded in New Zealand in 2006 by Peter Beck (and now headquartered in Long Beach California), is another rideshare startup with a focus on reducing launch costs and increasing launch frequency. As of Q1 2020, the company successfully deployed forty-eight satellites between its commercial and government customers, which include Spire Global and GeoOptics, into LEO.[33] The company is booked with monthly launches, and as Rocket Lab focuses on increasing its manufacturing capability to build one reusable Electron rocket per week, CEO Peter Beck expects that they'll soon be able to launch every week.[34]

To date, Rocket Lab has raised $215 million in total funding, notably $140 million in Series E from Future Fund.[35] In 2018, Beck received the Royal Aeronautical Society's Gold Medal "in recognition of his exceptional work in creating a novel, affordable launch capability for small satellites," and for his "crucial role in establishing international treaties and legislation to enable orbital launch capability from New Zealand."[36]

Spaceflight Industries, based in Seattle, has been successful in raising funds, acting as a steadfast broker of services in the satellite market, branching out with ownership, and managing its own satellites. In 2016, Spaceflight Industries received $18 million in Series B funding from Mithril and $150 million in Series C from Mitsui & Co. Other investors include RRE Venture Capital, Vulcan Capital, and Razor's Edge Ventures, bringing Spaceflight's total to $203.5 million in investments.[37]

Electron spacecraft from Rocket Lab

★ **Daniel Katz** is the cofounder and chief executive officer of Orbital Sidekick, a hyperspectral monitoring company focused on both the commercial and civil sectors, serving markets ranging from agriculture to defense/intelligence. Orbital Sidekick currently has a payload operating on the ISS and plans to build a constellation of five nanosatellites by 2021. Katz previously worked at SSL (formerly known as Space Systems Loral) as a senior propulsion engineer and at PGH Wong Engineering as a civil inspector and technical analyst.

The company has two subsidiaries. Spaceflight Inc. innovates on rideshare services by offering simplified pricing plans with its global network; BlackSky offers geospatial intelligence, satellite imaging, and global monitoring services via its smallsat constellation. For rideshares, Spaceflight identifies appropriate launches, manages the process, and helps with integrating the payload; the company has launched hundreds of satellites for customers since 2013. In February 2016, Spaceflight was awarded the first US General Services Administration Professional Services contract for satellite launch services. Effectively, the US Government and Spaceflight agreed with pre-negotiated terms for prices; this collaboration "reduces administrative costs and overhead and potentially increases how frequently the agencies access space."[38]

We should expect to see rideshare providers and service options increase while the price to access space continues to decrease. Rocket Lab is beginning to tackle the onerous challenge of making its Electron booster reusable as part of the effort to drive down flight costs (which recently increased from $5 million to $7.5 million per flight). Perhaps more interesting is Elon Musk entering the rideshare arena; in August 2019, SpaceX announced its new Smallsat Rideshare Program, which would charge between $2.25 million and $6 million depending on satellite size—significantly more affordable than Rocket Lab's costs. Then, SpaceX announced a revised price: a mere $1 million per 200 kilogram (440 lb) satellite, and in February 2020, the company released an online booking tool to schedule rideshares.[39] This new program will open many more doors for startups leveraging smallsat capabilities—and will likely push others in the rideshare market to create more cost-saving solutions.

Along with these NewSpace companies' individual successes, their work and accomplishments have driven the industry forward and paved the way for others. These NewSpace pioneers are establishing new paradigms for cost, frequency, on-Earth benefits, and exploration alike. The impacts of private NewSpace efforts also mean that barriers for entry into the space sector are lowering by the day.

CHAPTER SIX
NEW PARADIGMS

The single greatest contribution that SpaceX has made to the launch market is that launch now has a price. Before, if you wanted to launch something into space, you couldn't even write your business plan, because you couldn't get a price until after you had your money—and you couldn't get your money until after you had a price.

It's just all been kind of congested to date, and the way to break that free is to establish a price: let the market work and find out whether there is actually economic value in human beings doing things, and that will start the cascade. There will be a demand for more people doing more things. The price will then come down because the volume will go up, and that will expand the range of things that people can do in space.[1]

**Jeff Greason | Cofounder & Chief Technology Officer,
Electric Sky; Chair, Tau Zero Foundation; Cofounder,
XCOR Aerospace & Commercial Spaceflight Federation**

NewSpace now functions as a fast-paced, innovation-centric powerhouse. Commercial and private interests continue poking holes in the belief that space is the exclusive domain of governments—in fact, it's more accurate to say that the private sector has shattered that myth.

NASA and established aerospace organizations such as Lockheed Martin, Boeing, and United Launch Alliance (ULA) have traditionally dominated the space sector. These incumbents came out of the post-World War II effort to further industrialize and work in partnership with the US government to advance space technologies, as mandated by President Eisenhower with Congressional support.

Until now, the prime NASA contractors had no incentive to do things differently. The budgets were mighty, and "business as usual" typically meant that Congressional interests catered to the concerns of their district's space industry incumbents rather than NASA's long-term visions. However, these traditional space organizations can no longer rely upon open checkbooks from governments to pay for new technology development.

Today, NewSpace efforts surpass government programs and incumbents alike with their various technological and exploratory advancements. Some of the better-known NewSpace companies started out serving the US government with the value proposition that they can offer products and services in a better, more efficient way than the government can. In some cases, these fresh players built upon what already existed, such as private groups like Nanoracks, SpaceX, and Blue Origin, which leverage the ISS as a platform for research and business endeavors.

Space startups and companies such as SpaceX, which have graduated from startup status to growth companies, pushed the ceiling and created their own timelines. They put pressure on incumbents to consider reusability, to lower costs, and even to seriously recognize the commercial market. They use commercial trade groups and lobbyists, work with other nimble space startups (like Nanoracks), leverage the latest technologies (such as rapid manufacturing), and are open to the philosophy of failing fast—while expecting results in a much quicker way.

In October 2018, the USAF awarded $2.3 billion in Launch Services Agreement (LSA) contracts to ULA, Northrop Grumman, and Blue Origin; the companies will receive $967 million, $791 million, and $500 million, respectively, to develop new launch systems.[2] Exciting as these contracts are for the launch providers, the LSA program's other goal is to end the United States' reliance on Russian engines.[3] It's also worth noting that ULA selected Blue Origin to provide the main engine for its Vulcan rocket; even as many companies compete with each other to become industry leaders, there is a widespread understanding that setting rivalries aside to leverage the top technologies and innovations is crucial to both individual and sector-wide success.[4]

In February 2019, the USAF awarded launch contracts to SpaceX and ULA for $297 million and $441.76 million, respectively. These contracts came out of the Evolved Expendable Launch Vehicle (EELV) program, now called the National Security Space Launch (NSSF) program, which focuses on providing space access to the DoD and other government agencies.[5]

In March 2019, NASA and SpaceX partnered to send a Crew Dragon space-craft to the ISS as a test for future crewed missions. In this expedition, known as Demo-1, the Crew Dragon only carried supplies to the space station; still, it gets the United States back on track to conduct crewed missions that don't rely on outside nations for launch, vehicles, engines, or other capabilities.[6] "For the first time in history, a commercially built and operated American crew spacecraft and rocket, which launched from American soil, is on its way to the International Space Station," NASA celebrated in a press release.[7]

The coming online of the SpaceX Crew Dragon and the Boeing Starliner is one of the key events that we all need to be looking at in the history of space business. This is a key moment because once that capability exists—once you can send things on a rocket or fill rockets with paying customers—you can identify current markets of people who would pay $10 million or $50 million for that. These changes matter.[8]

Ian Fichtenbaum*

Within the NewSpace industry, it is common to hear the debate of government versus private. However, it's not an either-or situation. Governments can be great customers, as they are typically unlikely to default on financial obligations and can provide stable future activity. And while NASA focuses on advanced technology R&D and exploration, the private sector can't yet engage in those two areas wholly. On the other hand, the sole reliance on the government to advance the myriad interests of the space sector is too slow and inefficient.

★ **Ian Fichtenbaum** is the senior vice president and the space and satellite specialist of the American Industrial Acquisition Corporation (AIAC), a privately held industrial investment portfolio. Through his role with AIAC, he serves as the director of Bradford Space Group, a global space company that specializes in manufacturing, propulsion systems, altitude and orbit control systems, deep space missions, and space station facilities. He previously served as vice president and associate of Near Earth LLC, where he led startup investments as well as acquisition strategies within the space and satellite markets. Fichtenbaum is an International Space University alumnus.

In the space-for-profit sector, companies often have increased flexibility for addressing new markets and creating new products; private companies can be mostly agnostic regarding their customers and markets.

While we cannot expect the government to develop all technology to a commercially ready level, it can leverage large, existing infrastructures and funding programs that place potentially viable technology in the private sector's line of vision. General Michael Carey, who is also the founder and chief strategy officer of ATLAS Space Operations, noted that "the commercial world could absolutely compensate or make up for that shortfall in capability," particularly in areas like culture, programmatics, acquisition systems, and procedures. "If a space startup company has a bad day, the world doesn't shudder," he stated.[9] This creates a substantial window for NewSpace startups and other organizations to step in and get involved.

One of NASA's greatest private-public collaborative successes was its Commercial Orbital Transportation Services program (COTS). The goal of this competitive program was to spur the commercial industry to develop new vehicles to help carry out NASA's mission of getting cargo to and from the ISS. NASA initially awarded contracts to RocketPlane-Kistler (RpK) and SpaceX, but RpK was later replaced with Orbital ATK after failing to secure enough private funds.[10] COTS ultimately resulted in two new transportation vehicles. Research by KSC's Edgar Zapata found that SpaceX and Orbital ATK's vehicle costs amounted to $89,000 and $135,000 per kilogram of cargo, respectively—one-third to one-half the cost of NASA's space shuttle, which was costing $272,000 per kilogram of cargo.[11]

Aside from cost savings, the COTS program provided NASA with increased flexibility and diversification to ensure successful deliveries to the ISS, all while supporting private sector growth. For instance, the KSC report shows that the $140 million investment from NASA into the Falcon 9 spacecraft allowed SpaceX to then provide launch to over twenty private sector clients within the United States. Zapata concluded, "The over $1 billion (net difference) is US economic activity that would have otherwise mostly gone abroad. This is very different from the economic benefit when NASA is a sole user of a system."[12] In addition, COTS provided NASA with the ability to apply its learnings to future programs.

The NASA Commercial Crew & Cargo Program Office (C3PO), formally established in November 2005 ... represented the culmination of years, even decades, of initiatives to encourage the growth of the private spaceflight sector in the U.S. Although the Commercial Orbital Transportation Services (COTS) government-private sector partnerships established by C3PO represented a new way of doing business in the realm of human spaceflight, such symbiotic relationships have occurred throughout U.S. history. In the first half of the 20th century, the 1925 Contract Air Mail Act (more commonly referred to as the Kelly Act) incentivized commercial aviation by allowing the U.S. Post Office to contract with private companies for mail delivery. This eventually led to the use of commercial aircraft for affordable passenger travel, as air travel transitioned from a dangerous, daredevil pastime to a routine operation.[13]

**NASA, "Commercial Orbital Transportation
Services: A New Era in Spaceflight," 2014.**

Other ongoing NASA programs are geared toward various sectors within the science and space industries, all aimed at creating a foundation for innovators to develop their best work. Bruce Pittman,* a space industry veteran who helped develop the COTS program, noted in an interview that for entrepreneurs trying to enter NewSpace, "I would recommend that they go through the NIAC [NASA Innovative Advanced Concepts] and the SBIR [Small Business Innovation Research]–related databases. See what's being developed out there and if there's something that they think is exciting or a technology that could be viable or profitable."[14]

★**Bruce Pittman** has more than twenty years of experience in the commercial space industry and is currently the senior vice president and senior operating officer of the National Space Society. He has served as a member of the startup team for the SpaceHab Space Research Laboratory, participating in the initiation and development of the NASA Commercial Orbital Transportation Services concept, and co-developing the Innovative Lunar Demonstrations Data Program. He has authored numerous technical papers and received high honors for his work, such as the NASA Exceptional Public Service Medal.

The Innovative Advanced Concepts program "nurtures visionary ideas that could transform future NASA missions with the creation of breakthroughs—radically better or entirely new aerospace concepts—while engaging America's innovators and entrepreneurs as partners in the journey."[15] With the Small Business Innovation Research program, NASA selects from over one hundred proposals every year to fund small businesses with projects aligned with the Agency's needs. This program is a stellar example of productive collaboration: the businesses selected for each phase receive funding to complete that leg of their project with the intent of producing something of both innovative and commercial value.

NASA SPINOFF TECHNOLOGIES INCLUDE:

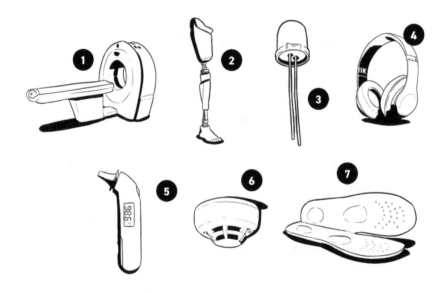

1   Digital image processing: used in MRIs and CT scans (1960s)

2   Dynamic artificial limbs (2004)

3   Light-emitting diode (LED) development for medical therapies (1990s)

4   Wireless headsets (1960s)

5   Infrared aural thermometers (1991)

6   Smoke detector with adjustable sensitivity (1970s)

7   Aerogel: temperature-controlling insulation, commonly used for shoe inserts (1993)

ASA also has a strong record of sharing its technologies and applications via its Technology Transfer Program (founded in 1964), which has yielded broad economic and social returns, from innovative technologies that spur economic growth to efficiencies that save money across multiple industries. NASA's free publication, *Spinoff* (founded in 1976), highlights the "nearly 2,000 products and services that began as, or have benefited from, NASA technology," ranging across various industries including environment and agriculture, transportation, computer technology, health and medicine, and public safety. [16]

For instance, SpaceX has a non-exclusive license to use NASA's Phenolic Impregnated Carbon Ablator (PICA) heat shield technology, which helped the company reduce risks in creating the PICA-X heat shield for its Dragon capsule. The PICA-X is ten times less expensive to manufacture than NASA's version, and because the Dragon vehicle was contracted for government missions, SpaceX's improved technology saves substantial federal budget. [17]

I think we'll always try to do what no one has done before—the search for planets around other stars and the search for life and its origin in our solar system. I think we will also see several ocean-worlds missions, exploring moons that have oceans buried under kilometers of ice, which have the ingredients—water, minerals, energy, and a lack of radiation—for life. But in about a decade, I also see us doing that quite differently from the way we do it now. I see advanced manufacturing coming into play, I see miniaturization coming into play, and I see software coming into play. We are long overdue for an injection of the kind of software capability that the commercial aerospace and automotive industries take for granted. [18]

Anthony Freeman, Ph.D.*

★**Anthony Freeman, Ph.D.** works with the Innovation Foundry at NASA's Jet Propulsion Laboratory (JPL), a federally funded research and development center that operates at the California Institute of Technology and specializes in robotic space and Earth science missions.

A s NewSpace takes advantage of advances from other industries, we all benefit from reduced research and development costs, increased innovation, and new capabilities. If we think of NASA as the parent of the space sector, NewSpace activities are the children who are quickly growing up and ready to expand in their own right. NASA reflects an era of linear thinking, with specific goals, clear timelines, and direct expectations. NewSpace reflects our current culture and economy, where innovation is king, and merging different industries and capabilities leads to unexpected results. NewSpace embraces ambiguity, with leaders who are open to experimentation, failure, and risk—all in the name of progress.

It's time that we look to the growing ranks of astropreneurs to further our development of space. Best results will come from being supportive, identifying the inefficiencies on both sides, and increasing collaboration between the civil and commercial sectors to propel the industry forward.

PART III

THE CASE FOR NEWSPACE

CHAPTER SEVEN
SPACE IS OPEN FOR BUSINESS

*We are no longer technology-limited on humans developing
the solar system economically. We are limited in organization,
management, and funding, but we are not technology-limited.[1]*
Dennis Wingo*

A t this moment in our history, we are in the early days of a space renaissance. Public and private organizations now participate in various roles and capacities as a combination of collaborators, partners, and customers. The space sector has evolved so that it's intertwined with countless other subjects, allowing anyone with interest to participate; whether you work in finance, science, medicine, the arts, construction, or another industry, there are many ways to interact with space. From using space-derived modeling techniques, licensing technologies from NASA and other research institutions, or leveraging space as a theme for marketing and promotion, there is no real limit on who could benefit from these partnerships.

The space industry is newly available for more extensive commercial utilization—and is now in desperate need of our attention and conscious awareness. This frontier has started to become economically viable, much like the internet in the 1990s. When the internet emerged, it existed only as a concept for most people. The vast possibilities were impossible to predict during its conception, or even through its many developments. In the 1990s, we might have seen immediate

---

★**Dennis Wingo,** founder and chief executive officer of Skycorp Inc., has decades of experience in the computer and aerospace industries. Prior to Skycorp, he served as an executive for Greentrail Energy and Orbital Recovery Corporation. Wingo is an advocate for lunar development and has published various papers over the years to explore the benefits of the Moon. His book, *Moonrush: Improving Life on Earth with the Moon's Resources*, dedicated to the topic.

applications such as Amazon and email—but we would have had a harder time imagining revolutionary services like rideshare (e.g., Uber), home-share (e.g., Airbnb), dating apps, or in-depth navigation tools (like real-time traffic updates from Waze or Google Maps).

Similarly, the space frontier presents us with immediately apparent uses. But rockets, satellites, and space stations should be seen as infrastructures rather than just objects with a single purpose: they provide a platform for other opportunities—facilitating transport, data, and research opportunities, respectively—much like internet infrastructure company Cisco, which established foundational capabilities that enabled companies like Google to create applications that other organizations could then build upon or leverage. This is all to say that the real growth will come from future developments once we've had the opportunity to spend more time exploring and understanding the possibilities.

While the scope of these potential markets is, for now, unknown, the economic transition is already underway. Three primary segments of orbital space are already open for business: low Earth orbit (LEO), medium Earth orbit (MEO), and geostationary orbit (GEO). Geosynchronous orbit, polar orbit, Sun-synchronous orbit, high Earth orbit, and semi-synchronous orbit are also useful for specific satellites and Earth imaging applications—albeit lesser-used at this stage.

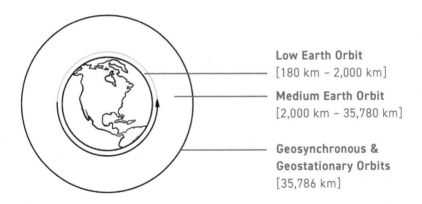

Low Earth Orbit
[180 km – 2,000 km]

Medium Earth Orbit
[2,000 km – 35,780 km]

Geosynchronous &
Geostationary Orbits
[35,786 km]

Low Earth orbit accounts for many communications, remote sensing, and Earth-imaging satellites; it has housed all space stations to date and is where the ISS resides; and all crewed flights to space have occurred in LEO (apart from the Apollo program from 1968–1972). MEO hosts communications satellite constellations as well as the Global Navigation Satellite Systems (GNSS), which provides global positioning and navigation capabilities (otherwise known as GPS).[2]

Right above MEO and just below high Earth orbit (HEO), there is a sweet spot at an altitude of 35,786 km (22,236 miles) known as geosynchronous orbit (GSO). In GSO, satellites orbit exactly in sync with Earth's rotational period. Geostationary orbit (GEO) is also known as geosynchronous equatorial orbit, the key difference being that this orbit remains fixed with Earth's equator. GEO and GSO therefore always monitor a specific area—allowing them to detect changes in that region over time, which is useful for military insights, agriculture, satellite radio, and communications. GEO's primary value lies in the fact that its orbits have zero inclination and therefore are always in the same spot relative to their receiving stations on Earth (hence appearing stationary in the sky). Because they remain in this fixed position, satellites in GEO provide consistent and broad coverage, without the on-Earth provider needing to adjust its receivers; and, its location above the equator gives GEO satellites the largest coverage of any position in space: 42 percent of Earth's surface.[3] GEO, then, is particularly valuable for communications (and therefore hosts many of Earth's telecom satellites), weather monitoring, and solar activity monitoring. Additional opportunities for GEO include private weather satellites, satellite servicing businesses, and in-space manufacturing.

The suborbital market is moving at a slower pace than the orbital market (which includes LEO, MEO, and HEO), but many anticipate its expansion. Suborbital refers to the area in space that is still within the planet's atmosphere (the Kármán Line, 100 km above sea level, indicates the atmospheric cut-off between suborbital and orbital); an object or spacecraft in suborbital flight is still impacted by enough of the planet's gravity that it will be pulled back down rather than engaging in orbit. Blue Origin president Rob Meyerson said in a *Space* interview that he considers suborbital research "an untapped market."[4] While many companies use suborbital flights for launch tests, the emerging commercial companies focused on space tourism will provide trips to space via suborbital flights.

When it comes to space, there is no shortage of opportunities within our reach. For instance, how could the insurance sector better take advantage of space-derived data for its use? How could the energy sector borrow modeling software to design better turbines, use satellite data to identify target areas for renewable energy activities, or optimize existing functionalities? As the infrastructures' pieces develop, an increasing number of smaller, more nimble organizations can look at ways to leverage these newer space offerings. Just as we see the emergence of the LEO economy, we'll see new ways to measure our social, political, and economic confidence in allowing commercial and private interests to operate in space.

SPACE IS AN ECOSYSTEM

n the late 1980s, space conglomerate Rockwell International created the first "Integrated Space Plan" to give a visual representation showing how the major space infrastructure elements fit together.[5] Today, the idea of a single, top-down plan for space development has been superseded by an organic, multi-path process involving hundreds or thousands of independent entities, all working in their own ways to succeed in their field of endeavor. Space is no longer a project—it is an industry or an ecosystem.

MANUFACTURING   ENGINEERING   TESTING   SOFTWARE   REGULATIONS   MARKETING   COMMUNI-
                & DESIGN   & LOGISTICS   & DATA   & LEGAL   & SALES   CATIONS

We now understand space as a literal and metaphorical high ground. There's much more involved than launch vehicles, satellites, and space stations. Space-enabled advancements grow every day, with new systems, products, logistics, applications, job roles, and technologies developing in parallel. According to *Space Safety Magazine*, the definition of the space value chain is "the whole range of activities, including design, production, marketing, logistics and distribution to support to the final customer, that organizations engage in to bring a product to the market, from conception to final use. Each step adds some form of value."[6]

While these activities may seem like niche interests when considered individually, they all contribute to the total space network. However, most of the economic activity and media attention on space today tends to focus on launch efforts to transport humans, cargo, and spacecraft from point A to B. There is less attention to the critical infrastructure that will connect all the dots.

Space is a culmination of many disciplines, and it works in tandem with various industries. The sector's growth depends on merging different fields with cutting-edge technologies, fantastical ideas with logical applications. From Hollywood to navigation, communications devices to streaming services, medical discoveries to robotics, agriculture to energy, all these industries affect space and are affected by space—much like bees pollinating flowers. It is also the sector with the most unlimited potential for progress and collaboration. When space advances, other industries benefit. When other industries advance, space benefits as well—and innovations and growth multiply.

CHAPTER EIGHT
LOWER COSTS,
LOWER BARRIERS

I think that all this miniaturization is going to continue to have a huge, huge impact—just tremendous capabilities—mostly in electronics and satellites. You'll be able to put CubeSats or combinations of multi-CubeSat cables into orbit for Earth observation and communications, and they'll be very capable. No matter how it works out, there will be a lot more connectivity over the next five to ten years. It's interesting because there have been ideas and projects like this before, but the timing has never been better than now. If someone started this whole kind of concept seven years ago, or even five years ago, the world wasn't quite there. And now, I think that everything is there.[1]

Michael Potter, Ph.D.*

With parallel advancements in artificial intelligence, software-enabled agreements, blockchain technology, and quantum computing, there are many possibilities for a variety of new economic markets, each with their own compelling traits for space. Much of this success depends on reliable and lower-cost access to space, which is steadily emerging. Startups around the world are creating business models, software, and new techniques to build spacecraft that continue to drive traditional costs related with space into more affordable territories—and they're working fast.

★**Michael Potter, Ph.D.** is the founder of Geeks Without Frontiers, a foundation focused on bringing internet connectivity to underserved parts of the world via satellites and space-enabled applications, with an ultimate goal of eradicating global poverty. He is also the founder and director of Paradigm Ventures, a firm dedicated to supporting and developing technology efforts. In addition, Dr. Potter was the first entrant in the Google Lunar XPRIZE through his team, Odyssey Moon.

THE SMALLSAT REVOLUTION

T he satellite industry is in transformation, in large part due to the increased flurry of activity within the smallsat segment of the nearly $280 billion global satellite sector. The miniaturization of electronics has reenergized the sector and attracted new entrants to growing areas of opportunity.

What started off as this hobbyist movement became the basis for disrupting the entire space infrastructure. Suddenly, Moore's Law came rushing into the space industry and completely changed to how people think about it. Instead of spending a billion dollars to put a satellite in GEO—instead of spending twelve years on building and designing it, and then buying a multi-hundred-million-dollar rocket to get it there, and having a mission that's going to last for thirty years—for a tiny, tiny fraction of that cost you could build these little CubeSats out of cell phone components, and you can put up ten or a hundred or a thousand of them in low Earth orbit and just replenish them.[2]

David Cowan*

The larger, traditional satellites that currently provide weather and navigation services are designed and built for high performance and high reliability (mostly because of their typical fifteen-to-twenty-year operations goal), and most commonly are made as one-offs or in low volumes. They cost hundreds of millions of dollars each and typically orbit between MEO and GSO, in an altitude range of 1,200 to 22,236 miles above Earth. Smallsats operate much closer to Earth, in LEO. Radically smaller and less expensive, smallsats are individually less

★ **David Cowan** is a renowned investor and entrepreneur. He was featured on the *Forbes* Midas List Hall of Fame for "the best dealmakers in high-tech venture capital" after appearing on the Midas List fourteen times since 2001. Cowan is currently a partner at Bessemer Venture Partners, a global leader in cloud infrastructure, cyber security, technology, and space tech investments. He invested in Rocket Lab and Spire Global through Bessemer, and is also now a board member at Rocket Lab.

powerful than their larger siblings. However, when operated in more significant numbers, the capabilities rival traditional satellites.

The disruptive idea is to lower the cost of building and launching a new spacecraft (i.e., smallsat) enough that replacing it with more modern, more capable models becomes feasible. The paradigm shift centers on moving from fewer, larger satellites with longer lifetimes, complicated development efforts, and less-advanced technology to a vastly larger amount of smaller, faster satellites that have shorter development timelines and better, newer technology. Smallsats are disrupting NewSpace the same way the smartphone disrupted mobile communications—and, like the smartphone, are likely to have profound effects on the world far beyond their initial expectations.

Much of the investment activity going into areas such as small satellites focus on commercializing the sector's technology. Though this technology first emerged in the 1950s—Sputnik 1, the world's first satellite, was a smallsat—it has mostly operated in academic or otherwise limited capacities.[3] Today, much of the current activity focuses on developing infrastructures to spur future applications from space-enabled assets. For instance, strapping tools, sensors, and other instruments onto smaller satellites is another frontier of possibility.

Research and Markets released a report titled "Prospects for the Small Satellite Market" in 2019, wherein the global market research firm projected that 7,000 smallsats will launch between 2018 and 2027. Notably, the 2019 report's forecast for the smallsat market's growth over the next ten years increased by 13 percent from the last report in 2018, signifying the rapid evolution of the subsector over the course of one year coupled with the "[untapped] potential of several applications and regions of the world." The report also anticipated a rate of 580 smallsats launched per year by 2022 and an increase to 820 per year by 2027; a main driver of these increased quantities will come from satellite constellations, which Research and Markets expects to account for 82 percent of the predicted 7,000 smallsats.[4]

A forecast from SpaceWorks in 2019 further predicted 2,000–2,800 nano or microsatellites will launch in over the next five years between the military, commercial, and civil sectors. This segment of satellites already increased in launch and production by 25 percent from 2017 to 2018; in 2018, 253 of the

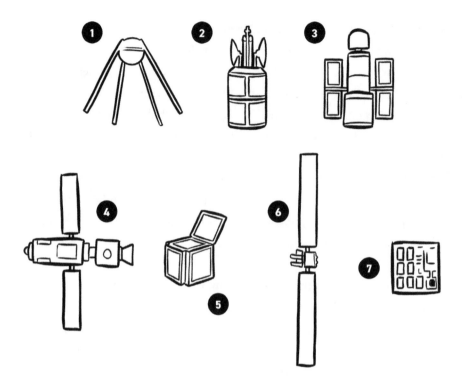

1   SPUTNIK 1 (1957, Soviet Union)
First artificial satellite
Specs: 23-in. diameter sphere;
Four antennas, 7.9 ft (two)
& 9.5 ft (two); 184 lb

2   INTELSAT IV F-3 (1971, Intelsat (US))
International communications satellite
with solar panels and transponders
(twenty). *Specs: 22 ft 11 in. (height);*
7 ft 9 in. (diameter); 3,335 lb

3   HUBBLE SPACE TELESCOPE
(1990, NASA)
World's largest space telescope
Specs: 43.3 ft × 13.8 ft; 24,490 lb

4   ZARYA (1998, US)
First International Space Station module
Designed and built by Russia/Soviet Union,
funded by the United States
Specs: 41.2 ft × 13.5 ft; 42,600 lb

5   CUTE-1
(2003, Tokyo Institute of Technology)
One of the earliest standardized,
miniature CubeSats
Specs: 10 cm (3.9 in.) cube; 1 kg (2.2 lb)

6   XM-3 (2005, XM Satellite Radio (US))
Commercial radio satellite,
built by Boeing Satellite Systems
Specs: 47.9 meters long (~157 ft);
10,346 lb

7   KICKSAT SPRITE PROTOTYPES
(2011, KickSat (US))
Miniature satellite chip attached to the
ISS via Endeavor (NASA Space Shuttle)
Specs: 10 grams; about the size of a
postage stamp

planned 262 nanosatellites actually launched, reflecting "Greater launch consistency and better execution on the part of small satellite operators."[5] Factors like the Internet of Things (IoT), demand for communications data, and increased need for Earth observation are all helping to drive this market.[6]

Forty-five percent of all launches included smallsats in 2019. Bryce Space and Technology's "Smallsats by the Numbers 2020" report highlighted trends in the subsector from 2012 to 2019.[7] Of the 1,700+ total smallsats launched in that timespan, 899 were commercial, 1,126 were CubeSats, and 81 percent were manufactured by US companies; main uses were remote sensing, communications, technology development, and scientific research. There was a significant increase in commercial smallsats from 6 percent in 2012 to 62 percent in 2019 (243 of the 389 smallsat launches in 2019 were commercial), and of the 133 commercial smallsat operators, 70 percent of commercial smallsats were owned by Planet, Spire, and SpaceX (Planet owned 55 percent of the remote sensing smallsats and SpaceX owned nearly half of the communications smallsats). Non-commercial operators between 2012 and 2019 were either government (353 smallsats launched), academic (348 smallsats launched), or

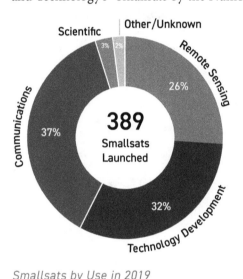

Smallsats by Use in 2019

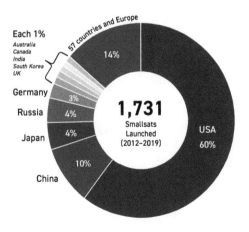

Percentage of Smallsats by Operating Country from 2012–2019

Data and tables courtesy of Bryce Space and Technology[8]

Overview of global small satellite manufacturers

What's interesting is that if you think about space infrastructure coupled with the burgeoning small satellite industry, and you look at who has been putting the small satellites together, it's not the large aerospace companies. While the government helps, the really big constellations—and small constellations, too—come completely from the commercial side. That implies that there's a huge push from the commercial side to get mass to orbit.[9]

David A. Barnhart*

This infographic only includes companies selling satellites commercially, and does not include companies that manufacture satellites as a means to sell services to end-users.

Cubesat (1-15 Kg)   ## Microsatellite (15-150 Kg)

*Data and visual courtesy of **satsearch.co**. Released on February 3, 2020.*

★ **David A. Barnhart** is a research professor in the Department of Astronautical Engineering at the University of Southern California (USC), director and cofounder of the USC Space Engineering Research Center (SERC), and director of the Space Systems and Technology Division at USC/Information Sciences Institute (ISI). He formerly worked as a senior space project manager for DARPA.

nonprofit (111 smallsats launched). The United States held the highest amount of smallsat operators (60 percent), followed by Europe (14 percent between fifty-seven countries), China (10 percent), Japan and Russia (both 4 percent), Germany (3 percent), and Australia, Canada, India, South Korea, and the United Kingdom (1 percent each). Bryce noted that this upward trend will continue based on the smallsat sector's proven business models and "ability to generate significant revenue." The analytics and engineering firm expects that smallsat constellations and the development of small launch vehicles will be important areas to watch as this niche continues to progress.[10]

To further illustrate how rapidly the smallsat market is growing, a Euroconsult research report from 2016 predicted that 3,600 smaller satellites would launch by 2026 and create a $22 billion market.[11] Research and Markets expects even more, predicting smallsat manufacturing itself to reach $22 billion by 2027 to comprise 58 percent of the projected $38 billion market (with launch services accounting for the other 42 percent of the market growth).[12] United Kingdom-based growth strategy and research firm Frost and Sullivan forecasts the smallsat launch market will generate a whopping $69 billion in revenue by 2030, with new satellites, constellations, and replacement missions accounting for nearly 12,000 launches.[13] These reports all point to the accelerating plans for new satellite constellations, emerging smallsat entrants, lower costs to manufacture and launch smallsats, and improved capabilities that are propelling the subsector forward.

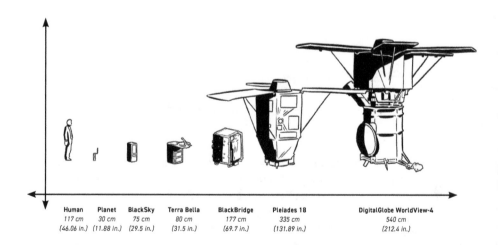

Human	Planet	BlackSky	Terra Bella	BlackBridge	Pleiades 18	DigitalGlobe WorldView-4
117 cm	30 cm	75 cm	80 cm	177 cm	335 cm	540 cm
(46.06 in.)	(11.88 in.)	(29.5 in.)	(31.5 in.)	(69.7 in.)	(131.89 in.)	(212.4 in.)

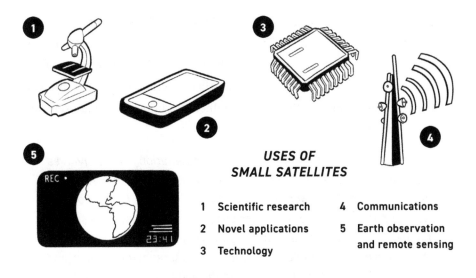

USES OF SMALL SATELLITES

1 Scientific research   4 Communications

2 Novel applications   5 Earth observation
                             and remote sensing
3 Technology

teve Jurvetson, cofounder of venture capital firms Draper Fisher Jurvetson and Future Fund, has watched the rise of the smallsat subsector. Jurvetson noted that the smallsat boom is "a really, really big opportunity with very attractive economics," and he predicts "a whole other wave of businesses that build on the data streams or are ancillary to these smallsat companies."[14] DFJ invested in nanosatellite imaging startup Planet in 2016. In 2019, Dr. Neil Jacobs of the NOAA stated, "The CubeSat industry is just now, I believe, starting to take off, and the data that they're providing, particularly with the GPS radio occultation data, is incredibly valued."[15]

One example comes from SpaceFab.US, which plans to launch its first Waypoint space telescope via a SpaceX Falcon 9 rocket in 2020 and hopes that its satellite will provide observational capabilities for civilians, corporations, and researchers alike.[16] This CubeSat telescope, called the Waypoint 1, will be one in an ultimate constellation of sixteen that focuses on ultraviolet light resulting from supernovae.[17]

Lars Krogh Alminde, cofounder and chief commercial officer of Denmark-based nanosatellite startup GomSpace, believes that in five years, "the market will be in hypergrowth—we'll be in a more mature market with more established players and more established value creations." The challenge is the availability of financing mechanisms that more mature markets benefit from, he said: "Banks need to be willing to issue guarantees in deals related to NewSpace technology.

Insurance providers who insure the big traditional satellite market should also go into the nanosatellite market. Things like that need to happen for the market to grow and to establish ways to finance the customer."[18] Though many of the startups leveraging smallsat technology are still in development mode, they will continue to work alongside the more prominent traditional satellites to unveil new applications for our future.

> *The next step is not just putting up a constellation, which involves individual satellites. It's starting to think about how to make truly space-based solar power or how to make a massive fuel depot that will support these large aerospace companies that want to do service things. Does it have to be with large aerospace? Or can you merge the construct of small satellites, low-cost manufacturing, fast and efficient rollout, and small launch with the ability to actually put things together in space and then move them to where they need to be?*[19]

> **David A. Barnhart | Research Professor, Department of**
> **Astronautical Engineering, University of Southern California**

FUTURE TECHNOLOGIES

NewSpace is preparing for the future. Just like the first space race gave us GPS and satellite communications, the NewSpace rush is providing cutting-edge technologies enabling supersonic spaceflight, rovers on Mars, and far more. In the technology sector, additive manufacturing is one area exploding with applications, promising capabilities, and ways to work with other new advances.

Additive manufacturing, also known as 3D printing, has skyrocketed over the past few years as a method to build more efficiently and cost-effectively. Because launching objects into space relies on high-strength, lower-weight materials, both startups and established companies now leverage the technology for a variety of purposes.

The US government also invests in additive manufacturing to aid a variety of its agencies, including the US Air Force, the National Science Foundation, and, of course, NASA.[20] Research and Markets' 2017 report projected that by 2027, "the yearly value of additive manufactured parts in the space industry will reach $4.7 billion, driving nearly $1 billion in yearly sales of 3D-printed equipment, software, and materials."[21]

ertain commercial companies are already pursuing additive manufacturing and proving its worth. Rocket Crafters spearheads the use of 3D-printed combustion chambers as part of its quest for safer, better-performing hybrid engines.[22] SpaceX and Rocket Lab use additive manufacturing to print nearly the entire engines for their Dragon thrusters and Electron main engines, respectively. And Relativity Space, which secured $140 million in Series C funding in October 2019, is on track to launch its entirely 3D-printed rocket by 2021—which would make it the first company to do so. Relativity's ambition will likely have even greater impacts on the commercial industry; while even the most innovative companies still need multiple years to develop and build their rockets, Relativity's 3D manufacturing process, integrated with machine learning and robotics, requires less than two months to build a launch-ready rocket.[23]

In February 2019, the United Kingdom's Orbex Space unveiled the world's largest 3D-printed engine. Later that same month, Brooklyn-based startup Launcher claimed to have 3D-printed an even *larger* engine—completed by its five-person team.[24] Launcher founder Max Haot told CNBC that the ability to achieve these cutting-edge results with such a small team stems from the innovative technology itself. "With 3D printing, we're now in a world where a startup like us can now access [advanced] liquid oxygen propulsion technologies," Haot explained.[25]

3D metal printing has allowed companies like SpaceX to develop much better rockets and to do it much faster than anyone's ever been able to develop them before. More durations and faster durations really push the performance and efficiency to levels that we haven't seen before.[26]

David Cowan | Partner, Bessemer Venture Partners

ther 3D printing applications are changing the sector as well as on-Earth applications and manufacturing. Let's explore some examples of this revolutionary capability. Boeing uses 3D printing to make parts for its Starliner space taxis.[27] These parts are cheaper to manufacture and result in structures that weigh 60 percent less than if built using traditional materials and methods.

In 2018, Boeing invested in additive manufacturing startup Morf3D through its investment entity, HorizonX Ventures, which "focuses on identifying startups developing revolutionary concepts around the world."[28]

Founded in 2015 and based on the edge of Los Angeles in El Segundo, Morf3D develops 3D-printed applications for the aerospace sector. Boeing has been a key client from the beginning, with Morf3D supplying 3D-printed parts for the aerospace giant's satellites and helicopters—using titanium and aluminum materials that offer improved performance and are more cost-effective compared to traditionally manufactured materials.[29] On the other side of the country, Florida-based Harris Corporation researches ways to use 3D printing to develop parts for future spacecraft, which could save "up to $400,000 per satellite."[30] Harris is developing this project with Israel-based Nano Dimensions to reduce satellite development time.

Meanwhile, MIT scientists designed a substance out of graphene—reported to be "one of the strongest lightweight materials" in existence. This material is "ten times stronger than steel but is only 5% as dense."[31] While the current version of this material is too expensive to implement on a large scale, a significant aspect of the graphene's strength is due to its "unusual geometrical configuration," which could theoretically be applied to other materials. If a cost-effective version existed, this kind of technological advancement could quickly change the landscape of construction and fabrication—both on Earth and in space.

Apis Cor revolutionized 3D printing to build an entire house, which it printed on-site in Russia in twenty-four hours for just over $10,000. Apis Cor won the first construction round of NASA's Phase 3 3D-Printed Habitat Competition in 2018, a competition centered on innovative 3D printed habitats for deep space exploration.[32] Founder Nikita Chen-yun-tai states on the Apis Cor website, "We want to change public views that construction can't be fast, ecofriendly, efficient and reliable at the same time."[33]

Other companies, like RedWorks Construction Technologies, are taking 3D printing to its logical conclusion. RedWorks was a finalist in the first and third phases of NASA's 3D-Printed Habitat Competition in 2015 and has been the only team to focus on finding solutions for 3D printing using exclusively in-situ materials—in other words: dirt.

RedWorks created a way to 3D-print solid rock from virtually any source of dirt or sand around the world—and beyond. The company's founder, Keegan Kirkpatrick, speaking at the launch of the Construction Robotics Forum, stated that RedWorks' goal is to make construction independent of supply chains so that eventually, homes could be built without needing to deliver any materials or people to a build site. If companies like RedWorks are successful, they will bring about the most considerable economic shift in construction since the invention of cement.

The development, engineering, and manufacturing of space-enabling materials is a massive market with many challenges. And if we can manufacture in space, the mechanical loads that the equipment needs to survive during its in-space operation will be dramatically less than any traditional launch loads. With additive manufacturing, robotics, and the use of materials from the Moon and asteroids, that becomes possible.

REUSABILITY

The space shuttle was often used as an example of why you shouldn't even attempt to make something reusable. But one failed experiment does not invalidate the greater goal. If that was the case, we'd never have had the light bulb.[34]

Elon Musk | Founder, SpaceX

Reusability is currently a central focus for NewSpace companies, and many believe it is the key to the industry's sustainable success. Blue Origin, SpaceX, Virgin Galactic, and others have been working hard to turn reusability into a functional business model. The Ultra Low-Cost Access to Space (ULCATS) Symposium, held in 2017, brought together the civil and commercial sectors to discuss future space system collaborations. ULCATS worked on increasing space vehicle reusability and lowering costs of space-related activities, specifically by reducing current launch costs by a factor of ten. In its report on ULCATS, the USAF's Air University suggested that public-private partnerships outside of traditional acquisition approaches are necessary for the US government to achieve cheaper and lower-cost access to space.

*If the launch providers can get some of the lower-cost
launches or smaller launches sorted out, and if we can
start to reduce the price of slightly higher performance
satellite platforms, then many of these new business
models and services can start to come to fruition.[35]*

John Paffett, Ph.D.*

Reusability is not only important for launch vehicles but for satellites as well. Morgan Stanley published an article in November 2018 that illuminated how both subsectors' costs have reduced dramatically because of reflying. Satellite launch costs have dropped from $200 million each to $60 million, and Morgan Stanley predicts that they could decrease to just $5 million per launch. The firm also expects satellite production costs could decrease by a factor of one thousand: from the current price of $500 million per satellite down to a mere $500,000.[36] These massive savings will make satellite data more affordable and free up budgets to spend on new technology development, which will result in more sustainable business models across many industries.

*We think of reusable rockets as an elevator to low Earth
orbit ... Just as further innovation in elevator construction was required before today's skyscrapers could dot
the skyline, so too will opportunities in space mature
because of access and falling launch costs.[37]*

Adam Jonas, "Space: Investing in the Final Frontier,"
***Ideas*, Morgan Stanley, July 2, 2019.**

★**John Paffett, Ph.D.** is a space systems engineering, project, and management expert with over thirty years of experience. He is currently the managing director of KISPE, a project engineering, system design, and implementation company that works with the space, telecommunications, and electronics industries. Before KIPSE, Dr. Paffett spent nearly twenty-nine years with Surrey Satellite Technology in various roles ranging from project manager to chief executive officer. He is based in the United Kingdom and is a member of the board of directors of the Swedish Space Corporation, the managing director of Applied Space Solutions, and the chief architect and evangelist for Open Source Satellite.

A ctual applications of reusability became a more prominent theme in 2019, with startups like Exos Aerospace reflying one of its rockets, and companies like Blue Origin and SpaceX developing reusable vehicles while pushing for industry and policy shifts to favor sustainable, long-term spacecraft activity. By helping to radically reduce the cost of launch through his efforts with Blue Origin, Jeff Bezos wants to create essential infrastructures and enable other entrepreneurs to develop the assets and applications that could fuel the NewSpace age. Bezos argued that "The number one thing that we need to do is to have truly operational, reusable launch vehicles. And they can't be reusable only in name; they need to be designed from the beginning to be reusable like commercial airliners."

Blue Origin's reusable rocket, New Shepard, completed its eleventh uncrewed test mission on May 2, 2019, launching into suborbital space with thirty-eight scientific experiments to perform in the microgravity environment and landing safely back to Earth several minutes later. Blue Origin expects that it will continue improving New Shepard's capabilities, driving down launch costs, and soon bringing humans along on its trips.[38] Bezos contends that if we make space access cheap enough, we'll see new uses that will no doubt surprise and benefit us all.

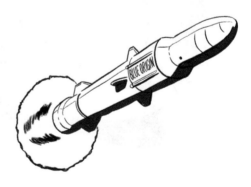

The objective to [develop] infra-structure is always expensive. Amazon was easy to start in 1994 because the transportation system was already in place, payment systems existed, and the telecom network existed, so the internet could ride on top of them. All those things would have cost billions of dollars. You cannot start an inter-esting space company today from your dorm room; the price of admission is too high, and the reason for that is the infrastructure doesn't exist. So, my mission with Blue Origin is to help build that infrastructure, that heavy-lifting infrastructure, so that future generations will be able to stand on top of it the way I was able to stand on top of the US Postal Service and so on. That's critical, and that's all about reusability.[39]

Jeff Bezos | Founder, Blue Origin

Virgin Galactic CEO George T. Whitesides* echoed Bezos's sentiment. He explained, "The reason that a 747 or 787 [airplane] ticket costs so little is that you're essentially only paying for the amortized cost of the labor and the fuel. There's functionally very little hardware cost in your ticket, and that's because they're flying that aircraft ten thousand times." The economic benefit of reusability will be lowering costs of launch, access to space, and more.

T he United States' commercial aviation industry exploded during the post-war boom when metallurgical engineering and propulsion technology finally allowed affordable mass air travel and cargo rates to catch up with

★ **George T. Whitesides** is the chief executive officer of Virgin Galactic, the commercial space company founded by Sir Richard Branson. Through his role with Virgin Galactic, Whitesides seeks to increase access to space through reusable spacecraft and space tourism offerings. Prior to Virgin Galactic, Whitesides served as the chief of staff for NASA and as the chair of the Reusable Launch Vehicle Working Group for the FAA's Commercial Space Transportation Advisory Committee. He is the vice chair of the Commercial Spaceflight Federation and a board member of various other space foundations around the world.

predicted industry demands. The government then shifted toward integrating commercial players into the aviation sector. We can expect the same trend with the space industry: as launch costs decrease and launch opportunities increase, there will be additional opportunities for edgier, riskier, and more unique avenues for experimentation.

Reusability is sort of the byword of the space launch community right now, and I absolutely think that's true—I've been pushing on that for many, many years. The interesting opportunity we have is not just to refly a vehicle two, five, ten times, but to refly a vehicle hundreds of times—or potentially thousands of times.

The opportunity for our vehicle is to integrate aircraft technology with rocket technology. If we can fly Unity one thousand, two thousand, three thousand times, the cost of that hardware will be an exceedingly small piece of the overall component of the ticket cost. That's a great leap forward when it comes to space transportation, and from an underlying economic level, that's what's exciting. It's a platform that is hopefully going to offer access to space—the very frequent access to space for human beings—at an incredibly low cost, in a relative sense.[40]

George T. Whitesides | Chief Executive Officer, Virgin Galactic

Software engineer and bitcoin developer Jeff Garzik noted that the space industry is now in a similar position as the internet was when it evolved beyond the mainframe computer.* "We have people who are exploring business plans that fuse industrial, assembly-type techniques with zero gravity and low Earth orbit; people who fuse art and space; people like us who want to fuse software and money and financial technology with space. We're going to see the proverbial

★ **Jeff Garzik** is known as a pioneer in software engineering and development. He played crucial roles in the 1990s to first integrate CNN.com with the internet, followed by creating open source projects like the Linux kernel—the operating system used by the five hundred most powerful supercomputers, all Android devices, and endless other computing devices. After discovering bitcoin in 2010, Garzik went on to become a global blockchain leader (the number three bitcoin developer and the most active for many years) before transitioning from building software to building companies. He founded Bloq in 2015, a Chicago-based blockchain technology company that provides open-source, decentralized blockchain infrastructure, applications, and solutions to the business world. He is also the cofounder and chief technology officer of SpaceChain, the first open-source blockchain-based satellite network that has created a community platform to allow its users to create its own space applications from anywhere in the world.

'long tail of the web' repeating the pattern in space," said Garzik. He also relayed that "Wiring together one hundred of the cheapest PCs you could get on eBay was far more cost-effective and ultimately led to far more powerful computing versus a similar capacity mainframe. The cost for these new cloud computers was literally about one one-thousandth of the old mainframes."

Now, the same thing is happening with space. "The cost of rocket launch is not coming down by half, it's coming down to one one-thousandth of the previous cost, and this is enabling new businesses that simply weren't possible before," Garzik emphasized. "So, with the cost of space falling through the floor, people around the world will be enabled and empowered in new ways. We're going to see a generous number of small businesses that really find their niche—and the good news is that it's going to be a lower cost, volume-type market rather than a hit-or-miss, multi-billion-dollar contract once every five years."[41] As Garzik also emphasized, "Economics drive everything in this world." The benefits of space won't continue without consistent investment and support. This sector needs the world's creativity, attention, and hard-earned dollars—which I believe could be the most impactful contribution current generations could make for humanity.

CHAPTER NINE
A DATA-DRIVEN WORLD

Observation via satellites is an incredibly powerful tool to address the challenges of Earth and space. Water shortage, food shortage, environmental damage due to fire or natural disaster, quality of drinking water, urban development, pollution, management of our forests and wildlife, energy and resource development, transportation, all those things—they are all critical. For us to survive as a species, we must get really good at addressing these challenges really quickly.[1]

Stewart Bain*

Once you have access to a valuable capability, could you imagine life without it? Think for a moment about your GPS and how much you rely on it to navigate every single day. There is little doubt about the steadily increasing volume of, variety of, and voracity for data today.

Satellites, which are typically uncrewed spacecraft orbiting Earth, have become indispensable tools for humanity—particularly as data providers. From defense and security to communication and research, the challenges we would face without satellites would be crippling to our lives on Earth.[2] Space allows us to generate insights about our planet, our solar system, and beyond. Leveraging this environment enables new perspectives and a deeper understanding of our changing world and its evolving needs.

★**Stewart Bain** has been involved globally in aerospace technology and business development since 1989. He is the cofounder and chief executive officer of NorthStar Earth & Space, an Earth observation, imaging, and tracking company that leverages its satellite constellation to monitor and protect the planet's natural environment. NorthStar is based in Montréal and serves both government and commercial customers.

Consider a day without satellites: No internet connection. No weather updates. No cell phone service. Paper maps for directions. Cash-only transactions. No airplane travel. This brief list isn't even the tip of the iceberg when you consider the amount of technology and infrastructure, both nationally and globally, that depends on satellites today. Industries, governments, businesses big and small, and civilians would feel the effects; most of the world would be at a standstill.

n response to the many challenges our population and our planet face, venture-funded satellite initiatives are shaking things up with existing and promised capabilities. Companies around the world are working toward solutions to bring connectivity to the planet, preserve Earth's environment, and improve various industries.

> I started thinking about how business in space actually improves the quality of life on Earth—about the GPS functionality or the Earth observation capability for identifying areas of pollution. So, I honestly feel in my heart of hearts that a lot of the improvement of quality of life on Earth is managed from space. And that's intriguing to me; it's something that's captured my spirit.[3]
>
> **Clifford W. Beek***

One company is already using satellites to revolutionize data security. Cloud Constellation Corporation's SpaceBelt Data Security as a Service is a constellation of ten satellites in LEO that provides unprecedented cybersecurity made possible by space capabilities.[4] "Think of it as a Dropbox in space," said Cliff Beek, Cloud Corporation's president and CEO. SpaceBelt "leverages the isolation of a space-based cloud infrastructure," operating independently of the internet and leased lines—because terrestrial networks are vulnerable to data breaches. SpaceBelt is

---

★**Clifford W. Beek,** a global cybersecurity expert, is the president and chief executive officer of Cloud Constellation Corporation, a data security company that provides space-based cloud data storage through its patented service, SpaceBelt. He is also the cofounder of Star Asia Technologies, an information and technology services company based in Singapore; a board member of CMC – Asia, a renewable energy company; and a board member of Advanced Training & Learning Technology, an interactive gaming software company focused on math and education.

therefore ideal for companies and governments who need to transfer sensitive and valuable data globally, "whether it's data about a financial transaction, an environmental issue, or something ultra-sensitive for the department of defense," Beek said. "We're able to protect that data as it moves around the world by keeping it above-ground and then delivering it directly to the target company or device or location on Earth," he continued. "We could be in Bahrain, we could be in Saudi—we can be in any city on the planet, and we can pull the data down without it having to go across any international network."[5]

On a broader level, SpaceBelt is an important step in the direction of securing critical data within space assets themselves—which are a key part of our digital infrastructure and, therefore, vulnerable to cyberattacks. Given our dependence on space, from weather to financial transactions to national security, it will be imperative to expand cybersecurity capabilities in the space domain, especially as the sector continues to grow.

The satellite sector is full of opportunities, providing immense economic and social benefits ranging from navigation to weather forecasting to disaster relief.[6] However, there is much more we can do with them, including helping farmers become more productive, better managing Earth's natural resources, and tracking migration.[7] Additional satellite applications include analyzing of shipping traffic, optimizing solar panel location placement, creating base maps for urban planners, scheduling airplanes, tracking water productivity, estimating surface water reserves, monitoring illegal logging and deforestation, and detecting underground water and mineral sources.

EARTH OBSERVATION & REMOTE SENSING

Satellites and aerial platforms can carry a variety of sensors to support their missions. These remote sensing capabilities range from spatial resolution, spectral resolution, radiometric resolution, and temporal resolution. Optical remote sensing, visible light spectrum, and multispectral imaging all extend beyond the visible light range.

Aerial platforms for Earth observation are also increasing in viability,
particularly high-altitude pseudo-satellites (HAPS). Tucson-Based World
View Enterprises, a private American
near-space exploration and technology
company, launched a high-altitude
balloon in a successful stratospheric
mission in 2017. This uncrewed,
remotely controlled balloon called the
"Stratollite" was able to carry a communications payload for the United States
Southern Command, which believes
it can use the vehicle "to help combat
human and drug trafficking and maritime piracy."[9]

Earth observation involves using
telescopes mounted on spacecraft,
aimed back towards Earth, to collect
useful information.

Other uses for the Stratollite, or balloons like it, include communications,
weather, disaster responses, defense, and others. The most compelling feature is
the high-bandwidth data transfer from high altitudes, which World View says
will be "crucial to delivering … real-time data to future commercial customers."
In 2017, World View cofounder (and former NASA astronaut) Mark Kelly
lamented in a *Space* interview that there are "trillions of dollars spent within

Optical remote sensing makes
use of visible, near infrared and
short-wave infrared sensors
to form images of the Earth's
surface by detecting the solar
radiation reflected from targets
on the ground. Different materials
reflect and absorb differently at
different wavelengths.[8]

**Center for Remote Imaging,
Processing and Sensing**

the atmosphere, hundreds of billions of dollars spent in orbit around the Earth. But in the stratosphere, basically nothing."[10] Luckily, that may be changing. Tom Olson, the director of business development for UK-based early-stage investment firm Avealto, sees HAPS as a huge opportunity, arguing that it is a "$40 billion untapped market," and that many around the world are now viewing it as such.* "Multiple companies are developing solutions, some of which received funding from the EU, the UK, and ESA," Olson said.[11]

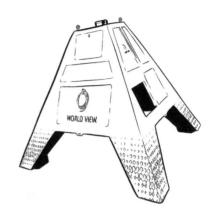

Stratollite, High-Altitude Balloon from World View

Avealto is currently developing high-altitude platforms focused on providing internet and mobile services. While this market might be untapped now, we're likely to see that change as successful initiatives continue.

CONSTELLATIONS FOR CONNECTIVITY

While in the United States and many other global areas, it is impossible to imagine a world without internet, the shocking truth is that nearly 50 percent of Earth's population lives without internet connection and cannot afford traditional satellite services at current price levels.[12] However, there is now a growing movement to change that fact via satellite applications. Many NewSpace companies intend to use satellite constellations to deliver internet to those without regular and reliable connections.

★Tom Olson is the director of business development for Avealto, an early-stage investment firm in the United Kingdom that is developing High Altitude Platforms to provide internet and mobile services. He previously founded and served as the managing partner for Exodus Consulting Group, a firm focused on connecting tech startups with investors. Olson has over thirty years of experience as a business systems engineer and analyst in the communications, aerospace, and publishing industries. He is the founder and chair of the Center for Space Commerce and Finance, a nonprofit based in Texas and the parent organization of the NewSpace Business Plan Competition.

O3b Networks' constellation has been operational in medium Earth orbit since 2013 and is now comprised of twenty satellites, the last of which went into orbit in April 2019. O3b, which stands for "Other three billion," refers to the world's population without internet access. Luxembourg-based SES, the commercial satellite leader that became Europe's first private satellite operator in 1985, purchased O3b in 2016 as a wholly owned subsidiary company and is now preparing the next generation of O3b satellites, with plans to launch in 2021. OneWeb launched the first six of its planned constellation (of 650 satellites in total) in February 2019.[13] SpaceX launched sixty of its Starlink satellites in May 2019, and after a March 2020 launch, had over 300 of the constellation's planned 1,584 satellites in orbit. But that's just the beginning: the Federal Communications Commission (FCC) has approved SpaceX to launch close to twelve thousand total satellites for this project, and the company confirmed in October 2019 that it had filed a request for permission to launch an additional 30,000 Starlink satellites—which makes sense, since CEO Elon Musk noted that SpaceX is manufacturing Starlink satellites faster than the company is able to launch them.[14] Other emerging startups participating in this effort include Fleet Space Technologies, Sky & Space Global, and Kepler, each of which has plans to develop a constellation of smallsats to help connect devices around the globe. Even Amazon, operating separately from Blue Origin in this case, announced in April 2019 that it had plans to launch a constellation of over three thousand satellites to provide internet to "unserved and underserved communities around the world."[15]

PREPARING FOR DISASTER

Every minute, the world loses an area of forest the size of 48 football fields. Better data about the location of deforestation and human encroachment on forests can help governments and local stakeholders respond more quickly and effectively. Planet is releasing thousands of image chips from the Amazon basin, labeled with information about atmospheric conditions and the presence of roads, mining, agriculture, human habitation, rivers, and more.[16]

Planet

H urricanes, earthquakes, tsunamis, forest fires, and other natural terrestrial disasters splash across headlines every year—displacing families, causing billions of dollars in damages, and destroying areas from neighborhoods to entire cities. While such events often appear impossible to prevent, or even prepare for, space-enabled technology can provide crucial insights that would improve how natural disasters affect humanity.

In August 2018, Planet became the first private-sector data provider to partner with the International Charter on Space and Major Disasters to aid global disaster relief efforts. In a press release from Planet, the company stated, "From Hurricane Maria to massive floods in India, the increasing occurrence and intensity of natural disasters around the globe has created a need for greater coordination between the private and public sectors to improve disaster preparedness and emergency management."[17]

This partnership could drastically improve the handling of disaster relief: "Timely access to daily high-resolution PlanetScope imagery will help to more efficiently and accurately respond to both natural and human-made disasters. With recent pre- and post-event PlanetScope imagery of a particular area or multiple sites, responders can verify damages with confidence, allocate resources, and provide aid more effectively."[18]

Planet also launched its Kaggle Competition in 2017 to prompt accurate satellite dataset labeling of the Amazon basin. Planet believes this initiative "will be the foundation for new advances in deep learning and forestry research at high spatial and temporal resolution." This competition aims to improve the existing satellite data at our disposal, as well as "help scientists, businesses, governments, and others monitor the entire Amazon basin."[19] Hopefully, Planet will mark the beginning of private sector initiatives to create solutions for Earth's fragile environments.

Others use satellite data and tracking to help manage outbreaks of diseases and viruses—and then help eradicate them. Dr. Martin Wikelski, managing director at the Max Planck Institute for Ornithology devised the ICARUS Initiative (International Cooperation for Animal Research Using Space) to start accurately tracking the wildlife on Earth. Using Ebola as an example, Wikelski explained, "We can take a blood sample and check if [the animals] have Ebola, put tags on them, let them go, recapture them and take another sample. ... We can then say that bats that have been through this part of the Congo have seen Ebola."[20]

The ICARUS tracking technology is robust. It includes GPS and the ability to transmit information, and it can measure things like the temperature, the amount of light in the region, and the pace of an animal's movement. The applications from this innovation are vast and have garnered the attention of researchers around the globe. It is inspiring to see how the private sector can lend itself to global issues, particularly with space-enabled technology making these efforts possible.

SATELLITE WEATHER

If you look at the economic value of weather, it's pretty enormous— you think about everything from food production to resource extraction, all of which depend on optimal weather conditions to get the optimal outcome. We believe that there will be a competitive advantage for many businesses, enterprises, and their business processes as they think about how weather can affect those over time.[21]

Gareth Keane, Ph.D.*

Weather affects each of us every single day. From television to newspapers, mobile applications to radio, weather data derived from satellites comes into the mix at some point. This subsector is another perfect place for private-public collaboration. Traditionally, governments provide weather services for free as a form of soft-diplomacy and public good. However, new commercial entrants within the NewSpace industry are entering the market to both complement and extend weather forecasting abilities.

From analysts to farmers to corporations, several weather technologies might help augment US government satellites and potentially provide higher resolution data sets, which could be critical for shipping, agriculture, environmental issues, and weather forecasts. Startups such as PlanetIQ, Spire Global, GeoOptics, and Koolock are in various levels of development and operations; time will tell if they will successfully complement existing government weather assets and do so in a sustainable way.[22]

In 2016, the National Oceanic and Atmospheric Administration awarded contracts to two weather startups, Spire and GeoOptics, as part of a pilot project to acquire weather data from commercial providers. Purchasing data through the private sector had multiple advantages, as described by the NOAA: "Efficiency, low cost, ease of use, and continuity of operationally required data." Looking to the future, NOAA stated that the agency "envisions ultimate success as a space-based observing system [composed] of a mix of US Government, international partners, and commercial data sources contributing to NOAA's products and services on which the nation depends."[23] The first two rounds of these NOAA contracts focus on what is known as GPS radio occultation. For instance, Spire uses its smallsats to collect data for global weather forecasting. Positioned on opposite sides of the planet, the satellite sensors detect different frequencies as they bend through Earth's atmosphere. "By comparing how different frequencies bend, Spire can learn about the temperature, pressure, and humidity of the atmosphere, and feed that into its weather model," NOAA attested.[24]

NOAA next plans to focus on broader data types—not just GPS radio occultation—that will help the agency with various types of weather modeling and forecasting. As the agency said, "Success of future pilots will depend on the commercial availability of additional data for NOAA to assess that can fulfill NOAA data requirements while demonstrating lower-cost ways of providing data on shorter development timelines."[25]

Spire completed a $40 million funding round in September 2019, which included investments from Global Public Offering (GPO) in New York and Japan's Itochu Corporation and Mitsui Group. Peter Platzer told CNBC that this new funding will help the company develop its data and analytics and "keep on pushing the boundary of the accuracy of extreme weather forecasting," particularly bringing its satellite capabilities to the underserved Asia Pacific region.[26] If commercially developed satellites can provide more profound insights into our weather, especially in storm-prone areas, it may be possible for emergency responses to save more lives and structures through more accurate forecasts.

★**Gareth Keane, Ph.D.** is a partner at Promus Ventures, a firm that invests in ambitious, early-stage deep tech software and hardware companies. With a background in both business and electronic engineering, Dr. Keane previously worked for Qualcomm Ventures, National Semiconductor, Texas Instruments, PMC-Sierra, and various other technology firms in both the hardware and software spheres.

AGRIBUSINESS

F eeding the world will forever exist as a global industry, and with populations increasing in more resource-constrained areas, there are compelling reasons to look across the technological landscape for ways to improve the quality of food, crop yield, land management, and water management. As emerging satellite platforms get closer and closer to real-time coverage of Earth, agribusiness is one of the primary industries benefitting from satellite applications.

Farmers now have an array of options that include satellites as well as other aerial platforms, such as uncrewed aerial vehicles. This is not a new use for the agriculture and farming industry, which has been using GPS and several types of Earth observation to aid them for decades, beginning with John Deere's GPS receiver—known as "green eggs and ham"—for tractor cabs in 1996.[27]

What *is* new is that more products and services are catering to the agriculture market and are not solely reliant on public space assets. Satellite constellations, distributed computing, machine learning, and AI provide ample room for astropreneurs and others to mix their ideas, which may result in solving challenges the food sector faces. Remote sensing capabilities can detect what type of vegetation is growing, the vegetation's health and vigor, and even what the environmental conditions are. Agricultural applications and benefits include detecting and measuring soil moisture, more accurate weather forecasts, increased crop production levels, more efficient cattle grazing via pasture maps, weather synchronization for crop life cycles, early warning for crop pests and diseases, and monitoring environmental conditions.

In 2015, international management consulting firm McKinsey & Company reported, "Food and agribusiness have a massive economic, social, and environmental footprint—the $5 trillion industry represents 10 percent of global consumer spending, 40 percent of employment, and 30 percent of greenhouse-gas emissions."[28] Grand View Research published a report that valued the 2018 global precision farming and agriculture market at $4.07 billion; with a compound annual growth rate (CAGR) of 14.2 percent over the forecast period, the firm expects the industry to reach $10.23 billion by 2025. The report further states, "The high growth can be attributed to the growing proliferation of Internet of Things (IoT) and use of advanced analytics by farmers."[29]

Work on agricultural crop stem cells in space has shown great promise as researched on the ISS by Zero Gravity Solutions in conjunction with the University of Florida. This company has also worked in highly efficient bio-stimulants that would allow us to grow food in space, or on the Moon or Mars. The product works incredibly well, proving itself to be an amazing dual use of technology.[30]

Richard Godwin*

Actions to enhance the agriculture industry are already in motion in the commercial sector, with corporations developing innovative technology and collaborating with one another to maximize these efforts. Bayer, Monsanto, Climate Corporation, and Fall Line Capital are among those in the private sector making meaningful strides to leverage space for improved farming on Earth.

In 2016, Bayer partnered with Planetary Resources, Inc. to leverage the startup's data for its Digital Farming Initiative in an effort to improve and create global, data-based benefits for farmers.[31] "Bayer intends to provide farmers all over the world with practical decision-making aids based on the precise evaluation and combination of diverse data such as weather data or topographic maps. Using these individualized recommendations, farmers can optimize their business management and lower costs," *Parabolic Arc* reported.[32] Specific applications of this initiative include saving water with timed irrigation systems, using planting date recommendations for better crop yield, and surveying the water-holding capacity in the land's soil.

Climate Corporation, a company that came out of Silicon Valley in 2006, leverages satellite imagery for its products and services from companies such as BlackBridge (which Planet acquired in 2015).[33] With a "technology platform combining hyper-local weather monitoring, agronomic data modeling, and high-resolution weather simulations to deliver a complete suite of full-season monitoring, analytics, and risk-management product," Climate Corporation is

★ **Richard Godwin** is the president of Space Technology Holdings, a strategic development group focused on commercializing and bringing to market intellectual property related to government and private space research. He is also the founder of Starbridge Venture Capital, a venture capital fund that invests in dual-use advanced technologies derived or designed for spaceflight.

able to extract in-season and historical field information for farmers to evaluate crop health and identify issues before they impact yield.[34] In the fall of 2013, Monsanto announced that it acquired Climate Corporation for $930 million; then, in 2017, Bayer and Monsanto merged—creating a "global powerhouse in agriculture" that heavily relies on Climate Corporation's data to improve the farming industry.[35]

Satellite data and imagery have proven both lucrative and helpful for Clay Mitchell, cofounder and managing director of Fall Line Capital. As Mitchell prospects land to buy for his equity fund, he uses satellite-based information to survey historical information; this information shows him the potential gains, losses, and room for growth in the farms he considers.

Precision agriculture, enabled by satellite imagery, can return degraded farmland to productive use. Well-managed farmland is like an oil well that never goes dry.[36]

Clay Mitchell | Cofounder & Managing Director, Fall Line Capital

One growing opportunity is to provide comphrensive analyses of the assembled data so that the information is both meaningful and actionable for farmers and other agriculture stakeholders. Hyperspectral imaging, which is even more precise than multispectral, is emerging for this reason.

Orbital Sidekick (OSK), a hyperspectral monitoring company based in the Bay Area, focuses on both the commercial and civil sectors, OSK serves markets ranging from agriculture to defense and intelligence, has a payload operating on the ISS, and plans to build a constellation of five nanosatellites by 2021. OSK partnered with Corning Optical Communications in 2018 to leverage hyperspectral imaging from the ISS. While its main clients hail from the oil and gas industries, Orbital Sidekick cofounder and CEO Dan Katz expects that the company's technology can apply to various other business cases. "Through our collaboration with Corning, we see significant potential for this technology in disaster monitoring and in the defense, agriculture, and infrastructure sectors," Katz said in a press release. Curt Weinstein, senior vice president of Original Equipment Manufacturers and Advanced Networks at Corning further explained that "Now more than ever, industries are driven to conserve natural resources and to reduce human impact on the environment," and that "Corning is continually innovating and investing in capabilities like hyperspectral imaging so our customers can offer next-generation services that change lives."[37]

Hypercubes, a San Francisco-based startup, uses hyperspectral imaging sensors on nanosatellites, aided by artificial intelligence, to provide hyperspectral data for industries ranging from precision agriculture to environmental monitoring. Fábio Teixeira, cofounder of Hypercubes, explained in an interview that his company focuses on addressing the global challenges that lie in the decades ahead. "By leveraging advances in satellite imaging that allow us to see what was previously unseen, Hypercubes is putting technologies into space that will unveil unprecedented details of our planet," Teixeira said. "By scanning the entire globe daily, our sensor network will deliver the fundamental component in a truly sustainable future, information."

The need for this level of precision comes from the understanding that while agriculture may be one market sector, each crop needs to be treated as its own sector "because they each have requirements that are completely different from each other," Teixeira explained. For this reason, Hypercubes' hyperspectral data picks up on daily changes, which is a giant step up from previous technology that could only provide updates every two weeks. Hypercubes then compiles all the data and can use it to detect patterns and create custom-level mappings of the agriculture and crops.

Satellites are not only useful for the farmers but for their insurers. With increasing interest in urban farming, global trade, and hyper-local initiatives, there is a multitude of opportunities to continue expanding and improving the world's agricultural markets.

By 2050, the United Nations is predicting that there will be 9.6 billion people on this planet. The challenge of ensuring that everyone on this planet has enough food, water, and energy falls to our generation. Hypercubes is here to answer that challenge.

Most farmers using satellite data are using a statistical model to quantify extremely basic phenomena. However, if you want to become effective, we need new models that respond to specific biomarkers. For example, citrus, soy, and sugar cane are all very, very different. So, we wrap our instrument with artificial intelligence because our goal here is to give this network of sensors the ability to learn what's important, what's not, how to classify, and how to find specific biomarkers.[38]

Fábio Teixeira | Cofounder, Hypercubes

SMART DATA

Any data produced for use on the ground becomes even more valuable when adding insights, analytics, and intelligence. Data providers not dependent on satellites or remote sensing include Internet of Things sensors, socio-economic metrics, customer relationship management (CRM) data, commodities data, and government and public datasets. Between these data sectors, space-enabled technologies more and more frequently improve the way we collect, transmit, and understand the vast information at our fingertips.

The Internet of Things and its predecessor, Machine to Machine (M2M), play an influential role in pushing the sector forward. These capabilities use satellites to communicate with physical devices on Earth. M2M and IoT have skyrocketed as industries in recent years, most widely known for making our lives easier with devices like the Amazon Alexa and Nest home thermostats—but they are also aiding industries like precision agriculture. ORBCOMM, a provider of industrial IoT and M2M communications solutions, has been using these functionalities since 1993 to provide "hardware devices, modems, web applications and data services delivered over multiple satellite and cellular networks."[39]

While M2M uses embedded hardware that allows two machines to interact with each other (think of pairing a Bluetooth speaker with your phone, or an ATM receiving authorization to dispense funds), IoT takes things to the next level by connecting unlimited things via internet. These "things" either collect and send data (e.g., a moisture sensor that alerts the user when it's time to water their plant), receive data and then take an appropriate action (e.g., an app-controlled device that will water your plants on command), or do both (e.g., a device that detects when a plant needs to be watered, and then waters the plant autonomously).[40]

Plugging an address into your GPS and receiving a recommended route that shows traffic levels is an everyday example of M2M. Waze is a famously successful version of GPS, which builds on the M2M capability by using IoT to provide more accurate information in near real-time. The mobile application provides routes, directions, and traffic, but it also allows app users to report accidents or potholes in specific places—which are then marked for other Waze users to see (and avoid).

These data capabilities not only have functional business models; they make our lives more convenient, increase safety, save time and energy, and contribute to incredibly lucrative and ever-growing industries. They also led to an emerging subset of the satellite industry: an extension of the Big Data movement that has been taken to its logical extreme. Smart Data applications (and other geospatial developers) now use machine learning, artificial intelligence, and other analytics to generate more profound insights from Big Data.[41] For instance, investment management company BlackRock uses computers to sift through satellite images that monitor construction in China, helping the company make decisions on whether or not to sell Chinese construction-related securities.[42]

Fleet Space Technologies (Fleet), based in South Australia, uses IoT enabled by low-cost satellites to create affordable industry solutions. For example, climate change has severely impacted farmers in South Australia in recent years. Adverse effects include droughts, increased fires, and decreased livestock output. These issues also lead to higher prices for consumers; fruits and vegetables increased in price by 43 percent and 33 percent, respectively, between 2007 and 2018.[43]

Fleet's IoT sensors are low cost and low power, making solutions accessible and affordable to the everyday farmer. These sensors use smart irrigation to maintain the correct moisture levels needed for the soil to produce each crop, and the systems avoid waste by only watering when and where the land needs it. Farmers can then plant seeds and tend to their crops properly—which solves a glaring problem because, with the recent ecological changes, it can be difficult for farmers to determine the optimal time to plant.

The low-cost satellite systems also provide the necessary internet connection for the IoT sensors and machines to work together, solving another previous challenge for large farmlands as they tend to lack internet coverage from traditional (and expensive) terrestrial providers.

The underlying message is simple and clear: climate change has already affected agriculture and irrigation on a near-disastrous scale. The many different ways that technology can help farmers with the problems they face from global warming and infrequent rainfalls only goes to show that technology can and will be a powerful way to overcome the challenges created by climate change.[44]

Fleet Space Technologies

Flavia Tata Nardini, cofounder and CEO of Fleet, spoke at length about IoT's increased adoption and future applications.* "I started diving into what this IoT revolution means for the world," she said. "It's transitioning from connecting people to connecting things, and what it does is create amazing efficiency. The Industrial Revolution happened for a reason: to increase industry efficiency. The third revolution was internet for people; this one is internet for things—and it's happening because it has to happen," Tata Nardini explained.[45] She pointed to our planet's growing population and the problem of sustaining resources, noting that IoT applications will help us improve the way industries operate—saving food, water, energy, time, and other valuable resources.

You must go to the customer, understand their value, and figure out whether geospatial data is useful to them. If it is, what do we do next is figure out whether there's a very particular set within geospatial data that's useful; if that's the case, we try to answer the question of

★**Flavia Tata Nardini** is the cofounder and chief executive officer of Fleet Space Technologies, a NewSpace startup that combines satellite imaging services with the Internet of Things and Industrial Internet of Things to solve connectivity and industry challenges in its home base of South Australia. Tata Nardini previously worked as a propulsion engineer for the European Space Agency and the Netherlands Organisation for Applied Scientific Research (TNO).

whether we can provide it. Right now, the full customer requisition process—from the moment you've met them to when they are in operation—is three years.[46]

Rafal Modrzewski*

A s the proliferation of Big Data and Smart Data spreads, satellites will play a key role in the creation and distribution of newly available data sets. In 2017, *Forbes* predicted that the Big Data business and analytics market would likely jump from $130 billion in global revenue in 2016 up to $200 billion by 2020, noting that data monetization has further untapped potential. In 2019, International Data Corporation reported that global Big Data revenues would hit $189 billion, and analysts now expect that by 2022, the Big Data market will account for $274 billion in revenue.[47]

While an increase in data streams to Earth might decrease the cost of data, its intriguing new value will stem from future applications. We already see this with some of the small satellite manufacturers, which develop wherever possible within their market. These companies rapidly innovate through iterations of new satellites: spend less, lower capital costs to invest in small satellites, and put them up in higher numbers.

T ata Nardini's earlier allusion to the "IoT Revolution" is another fascinating topic with growing momentum. Each Industrial Revolution we've had so far has drastically shaped the way our industries and economies operate. The first brought us water and steam-powered machine factory systems and manufacturing. The second, known as the Technological Revolution, saw the emergence of electrically-powered mass production, leading to telecommunications systems (like the telegraph, radio, and eventually telephone) and

★ **Rafal Modrzewski** is the cofounder and chief executive officer of ICEYE, a NewSpace Earth observation data company that provides actionable radar satellite imaging information and services to industries including maritime, disaster management, insurance, finance, security, and intelligence. ICEYE's data comes from its synthetic-aperture (SAR) small satellite constellation; ICEYE also stands as the world's first company to develop and launch SAR satellites with a mass below 100 kilograms.

transportation infrastructure (both railways and the rise of the automotive industries) that transformed our ability to travel, communicate, and share information. The third, or Digital Revolution, is still ongoing, characterized by the shift from analog to digital interfaces, the adoption of computing technologies, robotics, and further mechanization that has further impacted the way we coexist. And, of course, each of these revolutions led to unpredictable new markets, economic growth, and countless other innovations.

Now, many believe we are on the precipice of the fourth industrial revolution, which we might understand as the "Data Revolution." This period will

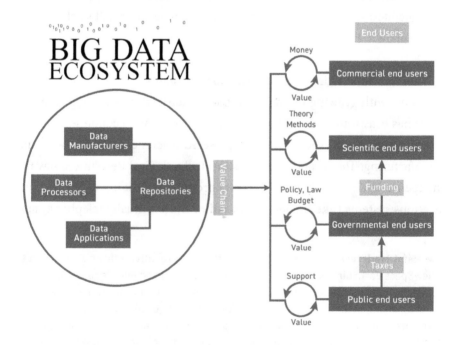

Key stakeholders and end users in the Space Big Data value chain

Data and visual courtesy of the 2016 Space Studies Program of the International Space University

be categorized by automation and optimization of data-driven solutions. With technologies like IoT, Industrial IoT (IIot), AI, machine learning, quantum computing, biotechnology, and nanotechnology, these "smart" digital applications will work together, create new solutions, improve efficiency, and develop new business models that change the way we live and work.[48]

We are fortunate to live in a time where data about our planet is not only becoming more ubiquitous, but the growing intelligence behind it will help us all make more informed, smarter decisions in our respective fields. Many predict that as more people and organizations, such as non-governmental organizations, citizen scientists, and entrepreneurs, become aware of the benefits of space data, we'll see an increasing trend in space-derived or enabled applications—and that we on Earth will ultimately become the beneficiaries of these applications.

CHAPTER TEN
OFF-WORLD OPPORTUNITIES

The global economy has been transformed from a material-based economy into a knowledge-based economy. Previously the main sources of wealth were material assets such as gold mines, wheat fields and oil wells. Today the main source of wealth is knowledge.[1]

Yuval Noah Harari, *Homo Deus: A Brief History of Tomorrow* (2017). †

Earth's resources evolved over billions of years, and humans have consistently leveraged them in varied ways to improve our lives. Within these limits, we have explored caves, chasms, ocean floors, and mountaintops in search of new lands and their resources to increase our ability to make, manufacture, and transform our environment.

From powering our cars, manufacturing medicines, industrializing agriculture, and energizing our economy, could we have imagined that coal and oil—both carbon-based fuels—would enable the immense, broad technological complexities integrated deep and wide within the modern economy? However, terrestrial resources will forever be a closed-loop, and we are now in a race against Earth's ecological clock. Yuval Noah Harari's excellent work, *Homo Deus*, shows that Earth's economic and technological growth in its current form will end up crippling both our ecosystems and our standard of living if we don't preserve our natural environment.

Becoming more efficient will only do so much. Dennis Wingo describes "renewable energy" as a term that's used carelessly, often employed as a convenient way to make people feel better about the energy sources they use. However, what we see advertised as sustainability and renewable energy is mostly a shrouded promise for developing countries.

---

†Quotes from pp. 15, 213–24 of *Homo Deus* by Yuval Noah Harari. Copyright © 2017 by Yuval Noah Harari. Used by permission of HarperCollins Publishers.

As we look twenty years into the future, we confidently expect to produce and consume more in 2036 than we do today. ... The real nemesis of the modern economy is ecological collapse. Both scientific progress and economic growth take place within a brittle biosphere, and as they gather steam, so the shock waves destabilise the ecology.[2]

Yuval Noah Harari, *Homo Deus: A Brief History of Tomorrow* (2017).

M ost people live with the assumption that we're constrained by Earth and its materials. However, space has the resources, visible and invisible, that will enable all of humanity on Earth to reach a standard of living even higher than we have today. Jeff Bezos argues that going into space is a crucial next step for humanity's continued survival, and much of that survival is reliant on resources. At the 2016 Pathfinder Awards at Seattle's Museum of Flight, Bezos noted that "If you take baseline energy usage on Earth and compound it at just 3 percent per year for less than 500 years, you have to cover the entire surface of the Earth in solar cells. That's just not going to happen."[3]

Every person on the planet uses an average of 16 kilograms of resources each day—metals, fossil energy, bio-mass, and minerals—that must be mined or extracted from Earth. Those in the Western world use up to 57 kilograms of resources daily. In 2019 alone, we mined over 55 billion tons of terrestrial resources.[4]

16 KILOS of material
extracted from Earth every day

We can only clean up our act here at home—meaning learning to live sustainably on this planet—because we discovered how planets work in our push outwards. All that space science gave us the much-needed view (and understanding) of Earth's functioning as a planet in its full totality. So, yes, it seems we were born to explore and push outwards. The combination of evolution and culture made us explorers and wanderers. Now—with so much to gain—we should recognize that explicitly and see exactly where our next frontier lies. At our feet and far overhead.[5]

Adam Frank, "Are Humans Evolved to Explore and Expand into Space?" *NPR*, 2016.

Imagine a world where energy is clean, inexpensive, and immediately accessible to all. Imagine a world where communications, whether voice, video, or text, is available to all. Imagine a world where internet access is free to all, regardless of where you live.

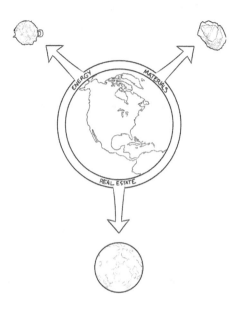

These worlds can exist, and not just in our wildest dreams. There are compelling arguments that even our standard of living in "First World" countries should be more advanced by now. We live in a time when we have tools to develop our available resources such that our quality of life surpasses anything we see today. Though unspoken by many terrestrial-focused economists and financial analysts, the only way to have continuous growth is to incorporate space as part of Earth's economic influence and activity.

> *I think there are important things in the world that need to get done. Some people don't like change, but you need to embrace change if the alternative is disaster.*[6]
>
> **Elon Musk | Founder, SpaceX**

At the 2016 *Forbes* Women's Summit, former astronaut Mae Jemison (and the first black woman to go to space), spoke about the fact that those outside the ultra-wealthy bracket, including the most impoverished populations, still have much to gain from space exploration. While working on the 100 Year Starship project, which aims to create capabilities for humans to travel beyond our solar system within the next hundred years, Jemison said: "So much of what I saw could be positively impacted by space technologies. ... The reality is the majority of us will not get off this planet. ... So, the long run is, some kind of space exploration has to benefit us here on Earth."[7]

The benefits Jemison pointed to could, in the immediate future, impact GPS, water purification systems, cell phones—results that could reach anyone and everyone on Earth. It isn't difficult to imagine some of the other potential applications, some of which already exist. For example, Dr. Alain Gachet, a geologist and the founder of Radar Technologies International, developed a method to identify drinking water using remote-sensing satellite data in the early 2000s. His WATEX system leverages NASA's Shuttle Radar Topography Mission (the first high-resolution dataset of global topography), NASA's Spaceborn Imaging Radar, and Landsat satellites (a joint program between NASA and the US Geological Survey). This technology has impacted millions of lives in places such as Darfur, Angola, Kenya, and Iraq, notably locating clean water during the 2004 Darfur crisis and later finding 66 trillion gallons of water in drought-plagued Kenya.[8]

Another example is the Space Solar Power Initiative (SSPI), a collaboration between the California Institute of Technology and Northrop Grumman, which developed an in-space solution that leverages cost-effective solar power that sends clean energy to Earth. As SSPI explains, "The beauty of this system is that there is no need for costly energy infrastructure on the Earth. Remote and impoverished regions, lacking a groundwork for energy transmission, are easily furnished with this space-based solar power. Simple antennas and receiving stations are all that's needed."[9] The program began in 2015 and continues to design and prototype its ultralight energy converter.[10] Innovations like this have profound effects, not only for the energy they create but for democratizing power around the world and making a better life for our planet as a whole.

I am a proponent of increasing efficiencies and becoming master stewards of our home planet. I also don't believe I have the right to deny access to others who also want a similar standard of living that I (and many others) currently enjoy. To do this, we need to venture much further out—and we need to do so while we still have the ability.

I t's common to see terrestrial projects costing many billions of dollars and taking years to build. In 1948, Leigh Mercer created the famous palindrome "A man, a plan, a canal—Panama!"[11] The creation of the first Panama Canal was a marvel of human achievement and engineering. But building the canal was an onerous and dangerous process; France began its construction in 1881 before abandoning the project in 1894. The United States stepped in a decade later, eventually finishing the canal in 1914. Its construction, connecting the Atlantic and Pacific oceans, is an example of incredible engineering and world-changing infrastructure that streamlined global travel and trade. As such, it is considered by many accounts to be one of the wonders of the industrial and modern world.

Developing adequate infrastructure is never easy, and it does not happen overnight; rather, it requires long stages of planning and collaboration for successful execution. Today, with new investments and activity, there is an accelerating pace of space infrastructure. As business models and use cases are further tested, examined, and refined, more private efforts push out into what is possible for the commercial space sector. Small steps in space now are critical to the much longer and more intensive journeys.

RETURN TO THE MOON

Humans last visited the Moon on December 7, 1972, via NASA's Apollo 17. Nearly five decades later, there is renewed interest on a global scale, led by governments and private efforts alike. There has always been a sizable number of "lunarians" (i.e., lunar advocates) within the space community, but more plans are taking shape today than ever before.

China made history in January 2019 when its Change spacecraft landed on the far side of the Moon and started exploring the area with its Yutu-2 rover.[12] NASA Administrator Jim Bridenstine has been consistently pushing to focus on the Moon and allocate government funds to lunar missions and exploration since he began serving in his role in 2017.

Israel-based SpaceIL sent its Beresheet lunar lander to the Moon in February 2019 via a SpaceX Falcon 9 rocket. This marks the first lunar mission from the private sector, Israel's first lunar mission, and the first organization that competed in the Google Lunar XPRIZE to have a successful launch. Though the spacecraft crash-landed on the Moon in April 2019 (and therefore did not win the title of the first privately funded Moon landing), this mission is only the beginning. Also notable is the cost of the mission: at just under $100 million, this is by far the most inexpensive lunar landing attempt in history.[13]

If we want to do space exploration in the future, we must bring the cost down. To do that, there must be a paradigm shift. The way we did that in SpaceIL is using several clever tricks that are not traditional. Some of them were not accepted before, but they are driving the cost down significantly.[14]

Yonatan Winetraub*

W hy is the Moon suddenly back in the spotlight? As humanity outgrows our Earthly resource constraints, a quest for new economic growth positions us to look toward space for new opportunities. The Moon has an estimated 600 million tons of frozen water at one of the poles, and if you break the Moon down to its core elements, it is composed of 40 percent oxygen.

The Moon turns out to be a resource-rich neighbor of Earth. We now know so much about the Moon that we didn't know even during the Apollo program, or even twenty or thirty years ago. The Moon has six times less gravity than Earth, and it takes 24 times less energy to lift a pound on the Moon than it does on Earth. It's only three days away, and you can have unlimited launch opportunities, so it's logistically a good place to go.[15]

Jeff Bezos | Founder, Blue Origin

★ **Yonatan Winetraub** is the cofounder of SpaceIL, an Israeli nonprofit space organization originally created to participate in the Google Lunar XPRIZE (GLXP). Since GLXP, SpaceIL has been the first private company to attempt a lunar landing, with its Beresheet spacecraft undergoing a crash-landing on the Moon in 2019. In addition to its lunar aspirations, SpaceIL is dedicated to bringing more of Israel's population into the space and STEM industries. Winetraub has a background in electrical engineering and is an International Space University alumnus.

It's possible that nobody has fixated on the Moon more than Jeff Bezos, who has relayed his lunar aspirations for decades—and is the first step of his vision of a trillion humans "living and working in space."[16] Through a white paper in 2017, Blue Origin urged NASA to develop "incentives to the private sector to demonstrate a commercial lunar cargo delivery service." The paper emphasized that "Reaching destinations beyond low Earth orbit takes days, months, or even years, limiting human exploration due to the resource and logistics challenges necessary to sustain life. Fortunately, the Moon provides the resources and proximity to enable human exploration of deep space destinations like Mars, making it the ideal proving ground and rest stop for future exploration."[17] Blue Origin's proposal focused on developing *Blue Moon*: a reusable, uncrewed, robotic lunar lander with the ability to deliver ten thousand pounds of cargo to the Moon.

> *Blue Moon is designed to be a repeatable transportation service, providing NASA with a commercial lunar cargo delivery solution. ... This repeatability ensures low cost and reliable access to the lunar surface for NASA as well as non-governmental activities. With this cadence and substantial payload capacity, Blue Moon can conduct increasingly capable missions over time, such as ongoing pre-positioning of the comprehensive infrastructure needed for a human return. These repeatable missions will be the building blocks of a lunar economy and a key step on the path to millions of people living and working in space.*[18]

Bretton Alexander (Director, Business Development & Strategy, Blue Origin) in testimony before the House Subcommittee on Space, "Hearing on Private Sector Lunar Exploration," September 7, 2017.

NASA listened, and in 2018, awarded Blue Origin $13 million in funding to work on the lunar lander. In May 2019, Bezos held an exclusive press conference where he unveiled a mockup of the Blue Moon, following its three years of design and development.

Blue Origin plans to use the lander to explore the Shackleton Crater in the Moon's south pole, which is predicted to be rich with ice—this ice can be broken down into its hydrogen and oxygen components, which would supply water, oxygen, and rocket fuel. As opposed to most areas of the Moon, which endure two-week long "lunar nights" in total darkness and extremely cold conditions (as low as -300° F), Shackleton is uniquely positioned in constant sunlight—rendering it ideal for solar panels to generate power and offering an environment that is much easier for robots to operate in properly.

Blue Origin also claims that Shackleton holds mineral compounds that can be leveraged to develop new structures, and all these components will contribute to establishing a sustainable lunar presence. Along with the Blue Moon reveal, Bezos announced Blue Origin's new BE-7 engine, which the lander will use. The first engine tests took place in the summer of 2019.[19]

> It's important that we attempt to extend life beyond Earth now. It is the first time in the four billion-year history of Earth that it's been possible, and that window could be open for a long time—hopefully it is—or it could be open for a short time. We should err on the side of caution and do something now.[20]
>
> **Elon Musk | Founder, SpaceX**

As we saw with SpaceIL's attempted lunar landing (and as we've seen throughout history), Moon-focused efforts are difficult—but the challenges don't dissuade ambitious groups from identifying and creating potential commercial opportunities. ipsace is one of many lunar-focused startups, a category that also includes Astrobotic, Masten Space Systems, and Moon Express.

Back in 2014, during a celebration in Mojave for the ten-year anniversary of SpaceShipOne's XPRIZE victory, I met Takeshi Hakamada, a self-described life-long Star Wars fan-turned-aerospace engineer and CEO of Google Lunar XPRIZE's Team Hakuto. He was maneuvering a small remote-controlled rover, which operated similarly to a remote-controlled model car. Over the next few years, I tracked his progress and got to know some of his teammates. Eventually, they formed ispace, a for-profit venture that seeks to commercialize lunar activities.

In an interview, Hakamada-san conveyed several highlights about his company, which successfully raised about $92.3 million for its mission to provide high-frequency transportation and an exploration system for the Moon. ispace initially leveraged advertising opportunities to raise early financing. Hakamada shared that his team worked diligently to identify connections and significance between the company's mission and its sponsors. Hakamada believes that robotics have been and will continue to be a "key enabler in any most space activities," explaining that "robotic technology is a key enabler to open such a new world" and "a focus of ispace's is to miniaturize robotics systems for eventual lunar use."[21]

Our company slogan is 'Expand our planet, expand our future.' Obviously, our planet doesn't expand physically; this is a figure of speech, meaning, we want to extend human presence into outer space. The planet is an analogy of our living sphere. In order to create such a world, I think that creating a space economy is essential, and to create that economy, space mining is going to be a first step.[22]

Takeshi Hakamada | Cofounder & Chief Executive Officer, ispace

In August 2019, the century-old Japanese trading company Sumitomo Corporation announced that as it branches into the commercial space sector, it will serve as a corporate sponsor for ispace's HAKUTO-R, the first lunar exploration program from the commercial sector. The goal of HAKUTO-R is to create a robust lunar economy, leading with resource extraction to ultimately develop the infrastructure and capabilities for humans to work and live on the Moon.[23] Hopefully, sponsorship from a Fortune 500 company and global business leader like Sumitomo signifies the growing support for commercial space ventures—and will help alleviate industry challenges. "The real barrier or constraint restricting the rapid growth of the space industry is mindset. Most people think that it's not real, that space is still a dream. We have to change such a mindset," Hakamada attested.

If most people start thinking, for example, of how to cook something in space— or to cook something, what is necessary—it says a lot about the business opportunities there. I think the key—the very, very essential barrier right now— is about our mindset. I'd like to change such a mindset.[24]

Takeshi Hakamada | Cofounder & Chief Executive Officer, ispace

T he investment sector is exploring similar projects surrounding the Moon—
and ventures consider these options viable enough to begin taking action.
Activities that private investors can support on the Moon to develop the space
ecosystem include prospecting for resources, developing shelter for humans,
moving materials on and off the Moon, supplying water and power, and building
communications systems to link the Moon and Earth.

Back in 2014, Steve Jurvetson organized "Moon Base Alpha—Strategies
for Low Cost Lunar Settlement Workshop," at venture capital firm Draper
Fischer Jurvetson.[25] This meeting of "space experts, entrepreneurs, and venture
capitalists" gathered "to determine an economically viable strategy for building
a settlement of 100 people on the Moon within 15 years"—including "how to
build a core capability supporting ten people on the Moon within five years for
a cost of under 5 billion dollars" and determining the best location for a lunar
base.[26] In 2016, a study by Lynn D. Harper, Clive R. Neal, Jane Poynter, James
D. Schalkwyk, and Dennis Wingo—which includes NASA researchers, private
sector researchers, and subject matter experts—concluded that there were no
showstoppers to a crewed lunar settlement, and it could, in fact, be completed
for a "total development cost of $5 Billion."[27]

Five years after the Moon Base Alpha meeting at DJF, a nonprofit organization
emerged from the shadows.[28] San Francisco-based Open Lunar Foundation spent
years in stealth mode, developing ideas and watching costs drop as technologies
continue to rise. The foundation consists of industry heavyweights who want to
bring civic collaboration into developing a sustainable lunar base—which they
now believe could be accomplished for a mere $2 to $3 billion based on the
industry's evolution. The current team includes project catalyzer Steve Jurvetson,
who provided the initial funding; former astronaut Chris Hadfield, who serves
as the foundation's director; former director of NASA Ames and current chair
of the Breakthrough Prize Foundation, Simon "Pete" Worden, Ph.D.; Planet
cofounders Will Marshall and Robbie Schingler; aerospace software engineer
Jessy Kate Schingler; and nonprofit expert Chelsea Robinson, who serves as
Open Lunar's chief of operations and staff. The group, with a current arsenal
of $5 million in funding, intends to begin efforts focused on robotic missions
while it looks for additional investments, pushes for policy, and develops the
hardware that will lead to the long-term lunar inhabitation plan.[29]

Our highest ambition is catalyz-
ing and enabling a peaceful and
cooperative lunar settlement.
At this time when there are so
many commercial and government actors advancing their
efforts on the Moon, we are
excited to demonstrate a civic
approach to participation.[30]

Chelsea Robinson | Chief of Operations
and Staff, Open Lunar Foundation

The US government also views the Moon as a beacon of promise, and in
May 2019, NASA announced the new Artemis program. The lunar-focused
initiative will provide $45.5 million in total funding to thirteen US commercial
companies: Aerojet Rocketdyne, Blue Origin, Boeing, Dynetics, Lockheed Martin,
Masten Space Systems, Northrop Grumman, Innovation Systems, OrbitBeyond,
Sierra Nevada Corp., SpaceX, and SSL. This funding will go toward developing
new spacecraft and lunar landers to bring US astronauts back to the Moon in
the next five years—and eventually establish a human presence there before
shifting toward crewed Mars missions.[31]

This public-private partnership piggybacks on the Artemis Commercial
Lunar Payload Services (CLPS) contracts, totaling $253.5 million, awarded to
three NewSpace rising stars: Astrobotic Technology, Intuitive Machines, and
OrbitBeyond. These companies will focus on developing lunar landers and
delivering payloads to the Moon.[32] Astrobotic itself received $79.5 million to
deliver up to fourteen NASA payloads to the Moon in 2021, and the company
announced in August 2019 that it will use ULA's Vulcan Centaur rocket to launch
the Astrobotic Peregrine lunar lander.[33]

*We are so excited to sign with ULA and fly Peregrine on Vulcan
Centaur. This contract with ULA was the result of a highly competitive
commercial process, and we are grateful to everyone involved in
helping us make low-cost lunar transportation possible. When we
launch the first lunar lander from American soil since Apollo, onboard*

the first Vulcan Centaur rocket, it will be a historic day for the country and commercial enterprise.[34]

John Thornton | Chief Executive Officer, Astrobotic Technology

In NASA's June 2019 announcement asking for new CLPS applications, the agency stated that the combined maximum contract value of the program from 2019 until 2028 will reach up to $2.6 billion.[35] CLPS also reflects a dramatic juxtaposition with other NASA programs: its proposal request stood at twelve pages, a drastic decrease from the typical multi-hundred-page contract requirements for its other collaborative programs. This signifies something pleasantly out of character for NASA: an emphasis on speed based on a contract structure that minimizes usual delays within the government agency.

Finally, NASA's 2018 Announcement of Collaborative Opportunity (ACO) for Artemis resulted in tapping thirteen companies to work on nineteen different technology-related projects for the lunar program. NASA announced on July 30, 2019, that "NASA centers will partner with the companies, which range from small businesses with fewer than a dozen employees to large aerospace organizations, to provide expertise, facilities, hardware and software at no cost."[36] The participating space companies—Advanced Space, Aerogel Technologies, Aerojet Rocketdyne, Anasphere, Bally Ribbon Mills, Blue Origin, Colorado Power Electronics, Lockheed Martin, Maxar Technologies, Sierra Nevada Corporation, SpaceX, Spirit AeroSystems, and Vulcan Wireless—will each work in various NASA centers across the United States to develop technologies in at least one of the following categories: Advanced Communications, Navigation and Avionics; Advanced Materials; Entry, Descent and Landing; In-Space Manufacturing and Assembly; Power; Propulsion; or Other Exploration Technologies. NASA stated that the work resulting from ACO will help "reduce the development cost of technologies and accelerate the infusion of emerging commercial capabilities into space missions."[37]

NASA administrator Jim Bridenstine anticipates Artemis program costs to clock in between $20 and $30 billion—80 percent less than the first Apollo Moon landing in 1969. If NASA can secure enough funding for this mission, aerospace journalist Rich Smith of *The Motley Fool* predicts that the return on this investment will add between $272 and $630 million in profits to the space sector *per year* that the Artemis program is active.[38]

Space represents what is exceptional about the United States of America. We are characterized by a spirit of adventure, risk taking, and entrepreneurialism. ... It is who we are. This exceptionalism is not genetic. It is born of a competitive, free enterprise, merit-driven culture. Today, American entrepreneurs have revolutionized access and operations in space. In fact, our very way of life now depends on space. We have transformed how we communicate, navigate, produce food and energy, conduct banking, predict weather, perform disaster [relief], provide security, and so much more. The United States of America is the only nation that can protect space for the free world and responsible entities, and preserve space for generations to come. This is our Sputnik moment. America must forever be the preeminent spacefaring nation and the Moon is a path to being so.[39]

Jim Bridenstine | 13th Administrator, NASA

On September 25, 2019, the Japan Aerospace Exploration Agency (JAXA) and NASA released a statement confirming that the two agencies agreed to cooperate on future lunar missions.[40] This partnership makes sense for two countries with serious lunar aspirations.

Japan's space industry now features various consortiums focused on in-space development. Starting in 2018, JAXA partnered with ANA (All Nippon Airways), Japan's largest airline, to begin work on the AVATAR X project—a consortium focused on space development and exploration via Avatar technologies. As the name suggests, the project will use human "pilots" on Earth who are synchronized with robotic Avatar counterparts in space to build, explore, and perform other necessary tasks. While currently testing on Earth, the collaboration plans to begin testing in LEO via the ISS in the coming years, before moving on to the Moon, Mars, and deep space.[41] JAXA, VC firm RealTech Fund, and management consultancy SigmaXYZ came together in 2019 to create a consortium of thirty businesses focused on solving the ever-present question that comes up when we think about humans living in space: how we will feed ourselves. Known as Space Food X, the group will develop technologies to create in-space food production solutions.[42]

AVATAR X will bridge the gap of science fiction and nonfiction ... by making remote operation of Avatar robots on the surface of the Moon and treatment of patients on space stations in Low Earth Orbit by doctors on Earth a reality.[43]

Shinya Katanozaka | President & Chief Executive Officer, ANA HD

P hilip T. Metzger, Ph.D., a planetary physicist with the Planetary Science faculty at the University of Central Florida and former KSC research physicist, has written extensively about the future of "bootstrapping" the solar system. "We are calling this approach 'bootstrapping,'" Dr. Metzger explained, "because of the old saying that you have to pull yourself up by your own bootstraps. Industry in space can start small [and] then pull itself up to more advanced levels through its own productivity, minimizing the cost of launching things from Earth in the meantime."[44]

In the journal article *Affordable, Rapid Bootstrapping of the Space Industry and Solar System Civilization*, Dr. Metzger and his co-authors from NASA argue that if we can effectively bootstrap the Moon, "We can then provide resources back to Earth, clean up the Earth, terraform Mars ... support science and the humanities in a well-endowed institute located in space, and send replicas of our robotic industry to other solar systems where it will do all these same things in advance of our arrival." Simply put, the benefits of investing in a self-sustaining robotic industry in space will yield life-changing resources. "If we begin working on it today," Metzger says, "a vibrant solar system economy will occur within our children's lifetimes or possibly within our own."[45] In a 2014 interview with the Obama White House Office of Science and Technology Policy, Dr. Metzger clarified that "what we need to do is to evolve a complete supply chain in space, utilizing the energy and resources of space along the way."[46]

We are not yet able to model future space industry in much detail, but we can explore some of its main features in this sort of simple model. The modeling looks very optimistic as we vary its parameters to study their relationships, and it indicates that bootstrapping a space-based, robotic, self-sustaining industry is eminently feasible.[47]

Philip T. Metzger et al., "Affordable, Rapid Bootstrapping
of the Space Industry and Solar System Civilization,"
***Journal of Aerospace Engineering* 26 (2012).**

With rapidly depleting resources on Earth and bountiful opportunities off-world, it is important to consider how we eventually treat the in-space environment. As Dr. Martin Elvis, an astrophysicist at the Harvard-Smithsonian Center for Astrophysics, and Scottish philosopher Dr. Tony Milligan wrote in their 2019 paper, "How Much of the Solar System Should We Leave as Wilderness?", we would be wise to approach resources with a long-term perspective.[48] The paper notes that "if a true economy emerges in space it will start to make use of the vast yet finite resources of the Moon, Mars and small Solar System bodies (such as asteroids)." However, while the solar system is so big that "the idea that humans may fully exploit and deplete its resources seems absurd, ... Exponential growth unchecked could have devastating consequences in the future." To that point, the paper urges creation of fixed policy that acts as a safeguard against "Our limited ability to see ahead until such processes are far advanced," particularly because "it may be far easier to implement in-principle restrictions at an early stage, rather than later, when vested and competing interests have come into existence under conditions of diminishing opportunity." For that reason, Elvis and Milligan argue, in-space "development should be limited to one eighth" of the available resources in our solar system, leaving the remaining seven-eighths as space "wilderness." While this may sound like a meager amount, the paper clarifies, "One eighth of the iron in the asteroid belt is more than a million times greater than all of the Earth's currently estimated iron ore reserves, and it may well suffice for centuries." Though we wouldn't reach the one-eighth mark for four hundred years, we must take care not to overly exploit the newly available resources—which is antithetical to the way humanity has operated thus far. To demonstrate why such policy is imperative to consider today, even before a true in-space economy exists, Elvis and Milligan offer our home planet as a cautionary tale: "Population growth and climate change are instances of unchecked exponential growth. Each places strains upon our available resources. Each is a problem we would like to control but attempts to do so at this comparatively late stage have not been encouraging." Space offers us a fresh chance to build a sustainable future—and one that is easily shared, provided we are willing to do so.

t's worth noting that while the Moon holds promising opportunities in the short and long-term, moving to Mars will be a far more difficult endeavor. With a significantly thinner atmosphere, much lower air pressure, and far colder temperatures than Earth, creating a habitable environment on the Red Planet will take far more than buildings and electricity. To adequately terraform the Red Planet, we would need to import and inject carbon dioxide, oxygen, and other gases into the atmosphere to create breathable air, raise the surface temperature for water to exist on the planet's surface, and raise the air pressure.[49] In addition, time spent in much lower gravity has adverse effects on both human physiology and brain function, though we don't have enough studies currently to fully understand how severe those impacts would be on Mars.

Intimidating as that all is, the greatest threat is Mars's lack of magnetosphere. Without a natural shield from solar radiation, the planet is extremely dangerous for humans, plants, and animals. The Mars Curiosity rover reported daily radiation levels of 300 millisieverts (mSv); on Earth, most humans experience between 1.5 to 3.5 mSv per *year*.[50] Radiation exposure on our home planet doesn't tend to result in adverse effects, typically because it is spread out over time. However, receiving more than 100 mSv at once begins to wreak havoc on the human body, with higher levels leading to illnesses including cancer and, in the worst cases, death. (For comparison, the highest radiation dosage reported from the Fukushima nuclear disaster was 180 mSv; the Chernobyl nuclear disaster saw highest levels ranging from 700 mSv to 13,400 mSv, leading to high cancer rates and a considerable number of deaths among those affected.[51]) The infrastructure needed to protect humans from lethal radiation doses would therefore require fully indoor or underground spaces. Radiation also affects the soil, activating chlorine compounds that become toxic perchlorates, so we would need genetically modified plants and hydroponic systems as well—on top of everything else.[52]

Nonetheless, dreams about creating livable worlds on other planets are still strong motivators for many of us on Earth. While safely moving to Mars and beyond may not be a near-term option, the Moon is an excellent training ground to test manufacturing, resource development and management, import-export logistics, space communications, NewSpace business models, and to inform humanity of the benefits of creating economies on other planetary bodies. And, ultimately, if humanity is destined to remain on Earth, we have even more reason to find new ways to preserve and improve our home planet.

CELESTIAL MINING

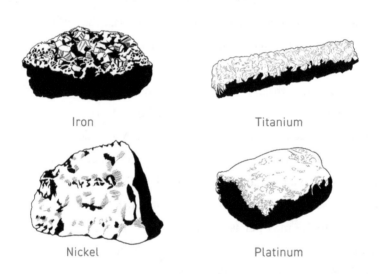

Iron

Titanium

Nickel

Platinum

There's gold in the sky. There's more gold in the sky than here on Earth.[53]

Ian Fichtenbaum | Senior Vice President & Space and Satellite Specialist, American Industrial Acquisition Corporation; Director, Bradford Space

The Moon is not the only resource-rich location. Our solar system already draws out explorers who seek the hidden treasures in shadowed craters, asteroids, and other celestial bodies. Today, select governments and private organizations around the world are rallying to spearhead efforts that can leverage and utilize the various space resources in our current reach.

According to NASA, there are potentially one hundred thousand near-Earth objects (NEO) in our planet's neighborhood. Experts already categorize these near-Earth asteroids and comets in terms of their composition, concluding that NEOs contain a variety of valuable resources, from water to minerals like platinum, nickel, cobalt, and iron, and rare earth elements (REE) used in electronics and security-focused technologies.[54]

Rare earth materials have skyrocketed in use over the past twenty years. They are vital components of modern technologies like computers, cellphones, and communications systems; they are also crucial in the defense sector, from night-vision goggles to armored vehicles. Perhaps most notably today, energy-efficient innovations like electric vehicles and wind turbines depend on neodymium and praseodymium (two REEs) for the magnets they need to operate.[55] As the world creates cleaner and more renewable energy solutions by the year, demand for many of these rare earth materials will continue to increase over the next two decades.

Rare earths are a series of chemical elements found in the Earth's crust that are vital to many modern technologies, including consumer electronics, computers and networks, communications, clean energy, advanced transportation, health care, environmental mitigation, national defense, and many others. ... These elements help make many technologies perform with reduced weight, reduced emissions, and energy consumption; or give them greater efficiency, performance, miniaturization, speed, durability, and thermal stability ... Rare earth-enabled products and technologies help fuel global economic growth, maintain high standards of living, and even save lives.[56]

The Rare Earth Technology Alliance

Multiple studies from MIT predict demand for REEs will quickly eclipse availability, especially as the ability to mine these materials becomes more difficult.[57] Mining itself includes numerous challenges, such as negative environmental impacts and increasing regulations.[58] Another area of anxiety stems from China's present monopoly on the REE market, which many countries around the world are working to mitigate.

MIT research scientist Dr. Randolph Kirchain led a study to examine the necessary resources to power clean energy sources. "The bottom line is not that we're going to 'run out,' … but it's an issue on which we need [to] focus, to build the supply base and to improve those technologies which use and reuse these materials. It needs to be a focus of research and development," Dr. Kirchain explained.[59] There is another level of urgency to this matter. "Developing a new mine, including prospecting, siting, permitting and construction, can take a decade or more," Dr. Kirchain asserted.[60] Barbara Reck, a senior research scientist at Yale University, explained that the MIT study serves as a reminder both "to material scientists to continue their search for substitutes," and "that the current practice of not recycling any rare earths at end-of-life is unsustainable and needs to be reversed."[61] In the short and long term, we will need space's resources for our survival.

There are ample efforts in effect to encourage scientists and students alike to lend their talents to mining asteroids for resources. One example comes from the Colorado School of Mines (Mines) in Golden, Colorado. In August 2018, the Mines Center for Space Resources launched a multi-disciplinary graduate program for space resources, which "focuses on learning the core knowledge in this field and developing design practices in the identification, extraction, processing, and responsible use of available resources in the Solar System."[62]

> *As we spend months, even years, in space, we need*
> *to look at ways to cut our dependency on Earth.[63]*
> **Angel Abbud-Madrid | Director,**
> **Center for Space Resources, Colorado School of Mines**

Luxembourg, which stated that it aims to be in the top ten space-faring nations on Earth, already invests in mining and promotes policy around the commercial exploration of space resources. [64] Though Luxembourg has a small population of under 600,000, it has the highest income per capita on Earth, a history of promoting innovation and entrepreneurship, and an established interest in space. It is also the second-largest investment fund center in the world, the United States being the first.[65] It's no surprise, then, that it directs significant investment power into growing an emerging space sector.

> *Luxembourg will offer an attractive overall framework for space*
> *resource utilization related activities … The government will dedicate*

funding to R&D in technologies related to space resource utilization, in line with our ambition to become a European hub for the exploration and use of space resources. Drawing on its success and proven expertise in the commercial satellite services industry, Luxembourg once again opts for space as a key high-tech sector for the country.[66]

Étienne Schneider | Deputy Prime Minister & Minister of the Economy of Luxembourg

In 2016, Luxembourg launched its Space Resources initiative, allocating $223 million to finance companies focused on resource mining.[67] Luxembourg's Deputy Prime Minister and Minister of the Economy, Étienne Schneider, stated, "Our aim is to open access to a wealth of previously unexplored mineral resources, on lifeless rocks hurtling through space, without damaging natural habitats."[68]

That year, Luxembourg's government invested $28 million into Washington State-based Planetary Resources, as well as an undisclosed amount of funding to California-based Deep Space Industries (DSI) for prospecting missions.[69] Though the ambitious country ended up losing $13.7 million (the total of the direct investment) after ConsenSys acquired Planetary Resources in 2018, and DSI now focuses on propulsion since being acquired by Bradford Space in early 2019, we expect to see Luxembourg—and many others—continue expanding its efforts to develop mining opportunities.

ROBOTICS

Robotics and automation might be one of the most enabling technologies for the growth and acceleration of the NewSpace sector. In the world of small spacecraft, robotic developments span propulsion, computing, machine vision, automation, and manipulation. They will be useful to help establish critical infrastructures, such as in-space communication systems, power systems on the Moon, and even off-world bases. If these capabilities are already up and running, humans can spend their time on other activities when they arrive.

Firmamentum, a division of Tethers Unlimited, Inc. (TUI), develops hardware for in-space manufacturing and has received NASA grants for its various projects. As part of its SpiderFab technologies, TUI's Trusselator device manufactures structures after a satellite has reached orbit, which "allows these components to be significantly larger than if they had to be stowed within a rocket shroud." This in-space capability results in "higher data throughput, higher resolution, higher sensitivity, and higher power than achievable by satellites manufactured entirely on the ground."[70] In terms of scale, SpiderFab can fabricate "multi-hundred-kilowatt solar arrays, large solar sails, and football-field sized antennas" by putting the structures together in space.[71]

TUI is also developing a robotic arm "to enable very small spacecraft to perform challenging missions such as on-orbit assembly, satellite servicing and inspection, and debris capture."[72] Dr. Rob Hoyt of TUI explained in an interview that one of the company's current projects, called MANTIS (Modular Advanced Networked Telerobotic Interface System), uses a robotic arm called KRAKEN "to enable teleoperation of experiments on the space station."[73] While this iteration focuses on operating inside the ISS, the next version—called the KRAKEN X—will operate in space.

In addition, TUI has a DARPA-funded project called OrbWeaver, which will convert space debris into antennas that the KRAKEN can assemble for satellites. Hoyt explained that "the highest value proposition is where you're taking advantage of manufacturing in-space to do things like make components where performance scales with size. So if you can make them much bigger, you can get much more performance out of them." He continued to say that in-space assembly of modular systems is the company's other target area, which would leverage technologies like their KRAKEN Robotic Arm to assemble many small components into a large, reliable, high-performance space system. "The objective is to leverage the low-cost benefits of small satellite technologies but achieve the performance capabilities traditionally associated with the big billion-dollar satellite systems," Hoyt relayed.

In 2015, TUI began developing its Refabricator device with funding from a NASA SBIR grant to help the Agency address ongoing challenges for the in-space economy, specifically on the ISS. Installed on the space station in 2019, the Refabricator device "combines a plastic recycling system with a 3D printer to enable astronauts to recycle plastic waste into high-quality 3D printer filament, and then use that filament to fabricate new parts, medical implements, food utensils, and other items that the astronauts need to maintain their spacecraft and perform their missions."[74] The device's tagline reads "In-Space Recycling for Off-World Manufacturing" and stands as an innovative solution to multiple in-space needs.

NASA is making its own strides in the robotics realm. Most of us are already familiar with the famous Mars Curiosity rover. Other focuses of development include robotic refueling and servicing capabilities to extend the lives of other spacecraft; a self-assembling satellite called Dragonfly; and lunar rovers that will be able to explore the Moon in various lighting conditions as well as drill for ice and crucial resources.[75]

In addition, NASA's Astrobee (aptly named Bumble) became the first robot to successfully free fly "under its own power" in space in June 2019. Plans for Astrobees include aiding the ISS researchers in microgravity, performing maintenance tasks on the space station (i.e., taking care of chores that humans would otherwise be responsible for), and supporting various spacecraft systems on future missions to the Moon or deep space.[76] Robotic cranes and arms are already in use on the ISS to help lift heavy objects, perform maintenance on the station, and help other spacecraft during docking.[77]

Other NewSpace advancements come from Made In Space, which subcontracted both Northrop Grumman and Oceaneering Space Systems to help develop its Archinaut spacecraft. This free-flying robotic spacecraft has many functions, including "3D printing, manufacturing and assembly, all in the harsh environment of space." With additional defense and security capabilities, the full scope of Archinaut "will allow spacecraft to manufacture and assemble unlaunchable structures once on orbit, enabling new mission capabilities, such as large antennas and base stations."[78]

Historically, the commercial space industry has profited off satellite telecommunications—sending ones and zeros back and forth. Made In Space's in-space manufacturing activities expand the commercial envelope to making valuable goods there too. We believe in-space manufacturing of goods valuable to people on Earth will soon drive significant commercial activity in space, perhaps one day creating a space-based economic boom.[79]

Andrew Rush | Chief Executive Officer, Made In Space

SpaceFab is developing a mission to "build a family of robotic mining and manufacturing satellites that can make, form, weld, and assemble metal parts into larger structures," that will reduce the cost of in-space manufacturing, making it more accessible and cheaper than manufacturing on Earth.[80] The company website states that it is "using the latest advances in robotics, electric propulsion, and 3D printing technologies to provide an internet-based service that would allow everyone the ability to manufacture objects in space."[81]

The increase of multi-functional devices focused on space's myriad challenges is slowly but surely transforming the way we understand in-space opportunities. For instance, when we think about humans living in space, biology is an essential component of crewed spaceflight, medical research, and studies around future human settlement off-Earth. In 2016, aerospace engineering graduate student Heather Hava, from the University of Colorado Boulder, developed two robots to win the MIT "Eat It!" contest, focused on food technology.[82] The first robot, called SPOT, grows strawberries, tomatoes, peppers, herbs, and leafy vegetables in a clear container that doesn't use any soil; it waters at the roots in an automatic cycle, allowing it to operate with incredible efficiency. The second robot, AgQ, measures and tracks "the health of plants and astronauts alike." This technology, serving both humans and plants, could also work on Earth to monitor a patient's health remotely, or in robotic farming—an application already being considered in urban environments.[83]

As creative companies solve existing problems and present new capabilities with lower costs and multiple applications, in-space activities will scale more and more quickly. If we think about this in terms of in-space manufacturing, we could soon create fleets of robotic spacecraft to rapidly conduct exploratory missions through the solar system and beyond.

If I were an ambitious space investor, I'd be looking at the value chain of extending the life of assets in orbit. Robotics is going to be a key part of that.[84]

Andrew Barton, Ph.D. | Head of Engineering, Southern Launch

here is, of course, an ongoing dialogue around the concern of robotics and automation putting humans out of work (among other fears). While it is true that this technology will eliminate or reduce the numbers of humans required for some jobs, it's important to understand that robots are specifically designed to solve a challenge or address particular issues. Every spacecraft and rover that we've launched to destinations beyond the Moon has been robotic; they still require human oversight and operation. While we might eventually have robots capable of building or managing other robotic spacecraft in space—that could be anything from tiny robotic clusters sent on interstellar missions to a massive robotic spacecraft that will mine asteroids—for now, we will continue to need people to develop, build, maintain, enhance, and evolve our robotic counterparts.

Consider robots we have on Earth, like iRobot's Roomba vacuum, which makes our lives easier by taking care of an everyday chore. Most robots in space will operate in similar ways, as opposed the to full-capability, sentient AI droids from sci-fi. Robotic systems are crucial assets as we progress in space; they can toil without breaks and conduct repetitive tasks, giving us the freedom to pursue other creative interests that are still uniquely human. Other jobs are far too dangerous for humans, which robots are well-suited to undertake. The unforgiving and harsh space environment is not dissimilar to some places on Earth, such as the bottom of the oceans or near a volcano; these terrestrial locations are valuable for us to develop and test robotic tools and vehicles that might one day have parallel uses in space.

Economics is the system that matches unlimited desires with limited means and resources. Robotic spacecraft don't have desires; we can send as many of them as they want, and they're never going to phone home saying, 'You don't get any more data until you send me another solar panel.' People are an extremely critical part of any economic activity.[85]

**Jeff Greason | Cofounder & Chief Technology Officer,
Electric Sky; Chair, Tau Zero Foundation; Cofounder, XCOR
Aerospace & Commercial Spaceflight Federation**

BUILDING IN SPACE

With space technology borrowing heavily from advances made in other areas, industry benefits range from lower maintenance to more efficient supply chains. Whether manufacturers are looking for innovative ways to leverage microgravity testing or production processes, a field of opportunity exists. In that sense, in-space production could be the holy grail for all of manufacturing. It could allow us to shift less-environmentally-friendly operations off-planet or build new structures with in-space materials. Lower gravity allows us to push new limits.

To do big things in space, we need to use in-space resources. The reason we go to space, in my view, is to save the Earth. We need to move heavy industry off-Earth; it will be way better done in space anyway; access to power is way easier in space.[86]

Jeff Bezos | Founder, Blue Origin

In June 2019, I attended the second re:MARS conference, hosted by Amazon and Jeff Bezos, through my role with Arch Mission Foundation. The conference title serves as a double entendre, both as a nod to the Red Planet and as an acronym for the topics of focus: Machine learning, Automation, Robotics, and Space. Bezos clearly believes these technologies (i.e., MARS) are all necessary to advance different business and strategic interests, and the multi-day conference featured keynotes, technical workshops, a tradeshow, and a simulated Blue Origin suborbital flight. It was a fascinating glimpse into the potential near future of space, industrial, and consumer technologies. "We've sent robotic probes, now, to every planet in the solar system. This [Earth] is the good one. We need to protect it, and we can do that by going to space," Bezos passionately argued during re:MARS.[87] One way

to do this, he has suggested, would be to move all heavy industry into orbit, where
solar energy is abundant and constant.

Extending in-space manufacturing to include current terrestrial activities—particularly those that have significant externalized costs and are challenging to facilitate on Earth—has intriguing potential as well. Could we generate our power in space? Could we move many of our factories to space? While many might see this kind of activity in space as daunting or impossible, Bezos is optimistic about our civilization's ability to expand and explore: "I predict that in the next few hundred years, all heavy industry will move off planet. It will be just way more convenient to do it in space, where you have better access to resources, better access to 24/7 solar power."[88]

Though the ISS is still in the early stages of using additive manufacturing, some argue that "Large-scale manufacturing could be tested and perfected on the ISS, and then implemented in the many commercial carriers that are starting to emerge."[89] Rich Glover, who has over twenty years of expertise in advanced space technologies, believes that space commercialization needs to move beyond its current scope and into the realm of in-space manufacturing and import-export between Earth and space. He argues that the delivery of raw space materials, which would include launch and mining, will be profitable enough to sustain the space transportation industry. "The impact of our microgravity process is just one additional step in a process that already has a sequence of multiple steps. The net result is vastly superior material and improved device performance," Glover attested.[90]

The issue, for Glover, is that nobody prioritizes these opportunities—at least not yet. "The funding required to get the effort moving and show proof of concept would fit comfortably within the IR&D [independent research & development] budget of any one of an aerospace company's many divisions. SpaceX, Blue Origin, and Bigelow could also achieve the same kind of results with small investments," Glover argued.[91] Luckily, there may be other options on the horizon.

E ngineers at NASA and elsewhere are now considering advancements in synthetic biology for in-space uses.[92] By applying synthetic DNA to cells, the original cell grows—much like in organic biology. The benefit of synthetic biology is that it can be used to create food, water, medicines, and structural materials out of basic and inexpensive resources—such as those found in space.

Back in 2015, the Royal Society of Publishing released a report identifying principal areas that synthetic biology could serve: resource utilization, manufacturing, life support, space medicine and human health, space cybernetics (automated control systems), and terraforming.[93] Today, the field has grown significantly, with NASA, DARPA's Engineered Living Materials (ELM) program, and the European Union's Living Architecture program all pursuing solutions via synthetic biology.[94] Furthermore, some of the world's technology leaders (and billionaires) are investing in synthetic biology—such as Microsoft founder Bill Gates, former Google CEO Eric Schmidt, PayPal cofounder Peter Thiel (who invested via his Founders Fund), and Yahoo! cofounder Jerry Yang. In 2018, the synthetic biology industry saw $3.8 billion in investments.[95]

These breakthroughs already exist on Earth. Companies like Ecovative Design, MycoWorks, and Terraform ONE use various forms of synthetic biology to "grow" housing structures that are not only impressive in their ability to self-build and self-repair, but because they are technically alive, their molecular structure benefits Earth by absorbing greenhouse gas emissions. If we consider the potentials for such structures on Mars, which has unsafe radiation levels for human and plant life, synthetic biology could provide safe domiciles designed specifically for the environment.[96] Back on Earth, these capabilities could be used in a variety of capacities, whether to improve existing infrastructure, preserve resources, or respond to existing challenges—like housing crises, areas impacted by natural disasters, or generally harsh environments. DARPA has already contracted Ecovative through its ELM program "to develop living biomaterials which can rapidly grow shelters in any number of challenging environments." [97]

As such, synthetic biology has the potential to produce necessary nutrients and health-related materials for astronauts, and because it can create plastics, synthetic biology's outputs allow for in-situ 3D printing materials. As stated by NASA, "Starting with a few raw materials found in the atmosphere and on the surface of Mars, and using advanced manufacturing techniques such as 3D printing, microbial workers could enable the construction of habitats, tools, and spare parts on-demand."[98] Additionally, this advanced science uses solar energy to grow the engineered cells; combined with the ability to use the limited

EXISTING MARKETS IN THE SPACE SECTOR

1 Spacecraft

2 Communications

3 Space-Based Data

4 Microgravity Research

5 Space Resources & Mining

6 Spaceland

7 Robotics

8 Novel Applications

9 Space-Based Energy

10 Rapid (i.e., Responsive) Launch

11 In-Space Services

resources of, say, the Moon's surface, synthetic biology offers seriously efficient and effective solutions to humans' safety and structural needs in space.[99]

As many areas in and around space advance, there is still a need for more visionary thinking—being able to see a realistic future that moves beyond the structures we have grown accustomed to. For investors and entrepreneurs alike, it's essential to realize that this is a growing, competitive marketplace. It's time to think about how space can—and inevitably will—make Earth different.

> *We often hear about the engineer who was inspired by NASA in their youth and works there now. But what about the bio people who are inspired by these grand ideas? How can they contribute? Now is a chance to transition their ideas to space. ... There is so much opportunity to innovate.[100]*
>
> **Peter Carr | Lincoln Laboratory's Bioengineering
> Systems and Technologies Group**

CHAPTER ELEVEN
THE INTERNATIONAL
SPACE STATION

The International Space Station (ISS) is a unique scientific platform that enables researchers from all over the world to put their talents to work on innovative experiments that could not be done anywhere else. ... We may not know yet what will be the most important discovery gained from the space station, but we already have some amazing breakthroughs.[1]

International Space Station Benefits for Humanity, 2nd ed., 2015.

The benefits of pursuing business opportunities in space are already all around us. The existing and continued dividends made possible on the International Space Station alone are substantial. From data to scientific research to technological developments, the ISS provides abundant opportunities to innovate and create unique solutions.

The ISS facilitates cutting-edge research, tests, medicine, and technologies that can only be produced in the space environment. As Ellen Stofan, NASA's former chief scientist, expressed, "The research we do in the ISS is off the Earth, *for* the Earth."[2] The International Space Station Program Science Forum, a group of senior scientists that represent the ISS's international partners (the Canadian Space Agency, the European Space Agency, the Italian Space Agency, JAXA, NASA, and Roscosmos), also publishes its own book, *International Space Station Benefits for Humanity*. The current edition has over two hundred pages detailing the impacts of the work done on the space station.[3] *International Space Station Benefits for Humanity* states that "While each ISS partner has distinct agency goals for research conducted, a unified goal exists to extend the knowledge gleaned to benefit all humankind."[4]

MICROGRAVITY

Our focus is not necessarily the six people in
orbit, but the 7 billion people on Earth.[5]

Twyman Clements | Cofounder, President, &
Chief Executive Officer, SpaceTango

Conducting experiments in microgravity can change life as we know it. Research from the ISS has resulted in water filtration and purification systems, development of improved vaccines, technology that improves laser eye surgery, and robotics to perform precise surgeries on previously inoperable tumors—the list goes on and on.[6] AiroCide, an ISS-developed technology, uses dry immersion to "preserve freshness of produce during storage and transport, to increase safety in food preparation areas, to kill bacterial contaminants in flowers (botrytis), and to protect against spoilage and contaminants." This is a massive advancement for rural areas that historically face difficulty in receiving food that is safe to eat.

Medicine from space is one of the most exciting areas of progress with clear terrestrial applications. Recent findings suggest that microgravity enables the growth of larger and better protein crystals in space, which are easier for scientists to study. Groups at the ISS have already conducted experiments in microgravity focused on proteins that relate to a wide range of critical medical issues, including "learning how to use proteins in medicines, or finding proteins that cause problems for humans and making drugs to fight them."[7] Work on the ISS also resulted in providing underserved regions with CT scans, MRIs, and X-rays—areas that were previously unable to access those necessary and life-saving technologies.

The World Interactive Network Focused on Critical Ultrasound (WINFOCUS) is a global network organization whose primary goal is to use ultrasound as an enabling point-of-care device in an effort to make medical care more accessible in remote regions.

Using the ADUM [Advanced Diagnostic Ultrasound in Microgravity] methods, WINFOCUS has trained over 20,000 physicians and physician extenders in 68 countries. This includes two crucial holistic healthcare projects: in remote areas of Nicaragua (from 2011) and in Brazil in a statewide healthcare project in partnership with the Secretary of Health of the State of Minas Gerais (since 2012).[8]

NASA, "Bringing Space Station Ultrasound to the Ends of the Earth," 2019.

Because the environment in and around the ISS allows scientists to develop more effective medicines, commercial interests are eager to use the platform. Made In Space's Justin Kugler explained that when conducting the same experiments on Earth, "gravity induces microcrystallization that really ruins the beneficial properties of these materials."[9] Researchers leverage microgravity to look for treatments for Duchenne Muscular Dystrophy, Huntington's Disease, as well as infectious bacteria. Although there are some complaints that NASA's timelines are too slow for pharmaceutical research, the private sector helps to open the ISS to universities, scientists, and others who seek to conduct life-changing experiments in microgravity.

Space Tango, headquartered in Kentucky, provides research and manufacturing labs on the ISS (known as TangoLabs) for commercial experiments. Founded in 2014, the company is driven by the belief that "The microgravity environment is a new frontier for discovery and innovation. ... By exploring it with industries of all kinds, we can improve life on Earth and inspire the next generation to continue to expand the horizon of this new frontier."[10]

Space Tango partners with SpaceX, Northrop Grumman, and Orbital ATK to deliver customer payloads, which focus on various pharmaceutical experiments enabled by the TangoLabs' microgravity environment. Each TangoLab can host multiple CubeLabs: payload modules "that allow multiple biomedical and technology applications to run simultaneously and independently on orbit."[11] Emulate Bio, a company that creates living platforms to emulate the complexities of human biology, has an experiment investigating the impacts of space travel on human brain function, which highlights the ways inflammation affects various parts of the brain; this research can help shed light on brain inflammation's role in neurodegenerative diseases like Parkinson's and Alzheimer's. Micro-gRx, a group performing microgravity experiments on the ISS, conducts studies to improve the safety and accuracy of preclinical drug testing—the lack of which currently leads to a failure rate of 50 percent or more in clinical drug tests.[12] Zaiput Flow Technologies, an MIT spin-out company specializing in flow chemistry tools, works on liquid separation research—a key component of chemical synthesis in drug development. Space Tango notably "designed and engineered flight hardware that allows Zaiput to evaluate separation based on surface tension, a method thought to be independent of gravity but never tested before," according to Gentry Barnett, program manager of TangoLab. Space Tango states that "Zaiput's new system could lead to significant improvements in drug development and production."[13]

By the start of 2020, Space Tango facilitated 135 experiments on the ISS. In addition, the company is working on developing "a fully autonomous robotic orbital platform designed specifically for scalable manufacturing in space," which is planned to launch within the next five years. Given Space Tango's success with its first endeavor, it is a company to watch as the private sector makes serious moves toward commercializing low Earth orbit.[14]

> *You can now fly an experiment on a rocket to the International Space Station for a hundred thousand dollars or fly an experiment on a suborbital vehicle for much less. You may not be able to have your own space program or your own launch company, but you can learn about space and start to practice some of these innovative new space technologies, which is within reach of almost any university on the planet. So, students everywhere can try to do space things—they just have to organize themselves and organize their resources and find ways of doing them. And countries should allocate resources that enable young people with ideas of spaceflight to get smarter, try some experiments, and fly some research.[15]*
>
> **James A. M. Muncy***

Yossi Yamin, cofounder and CEO of SpacePharma, wanted to transform the way space is used for life science and pharmaceutical research.* SpacePharma's solution was to develop free-flying, miniaturized laboratories that would allow companies to place real experiments in microgravity—and its success led *Fast Company* to deem the startup one of the "Most Innovative Companies."[16] The startup's smallsats facilitate a variety of testing in space via free flyers or the ISS, including tests focused on protein crystallization, fluid physics, microbiology, and 3D cell culturing, e.g., organ-on-chips and stem cell cultures.[17]

During an interview, Yamin further shared that most pharmaceutical companies have little idea about the benefits of experimentation and research in space; it's only very recently that a growing number of well-known companies are starting to have more conversations around it and are running some of their own experiments in microgravity. Yamin and SpacePharma want to make it easy for schools and pharmaceutical groups to get their experiments in space.[18]

C hristopher Stott urges astropreneurs to consider the possibilities the ISS creates: "There are so many people, and so many billions of dollars, putting so much hardware into space, providing amazing opportunities and communications bandwidth on the ground. How do you leverage that veritable Library of Congress that's beamed down to the planet every hour?"[19] The ISS is building a new world, or worlds, of possibility—and there is much room out there on the space station for the NewSpace sector to become involved.

★ **James A. M. Muncy** is the president and founder of PoliSpace, an independent space policy consultancy that he formed in early 2000. The goal of the firm is to help commercial space entrepreneurs overcome political, regulatory, and other non-technical barriers to success. He has worked with various government branches, including the US Military, NASA, NOAA, and US Congress. Muncy is a longtime advocate and activist for the space sector who frequently writes and speaks about space policy. In 1988, he founded the nonprofit space advocacy organization the Space Frontier Foundation with Rick Tumlinson and Bob Werb. He served as the Foundation's chair of the board for six years and has also served on the board of directors for the National Space Society.

★ **Yossi Yamin** is the cofounder and chief executive officer of SpacePharma, an Israel-based company focused on developing drugs in the microgravity environment of space. SpacePharma has conducted microgravity missions on free-orbit satellites and onboard ISS mini-labs. Yamin formerly served as the chief technology officer of Israel's Satellite Agency and in the Israeli army, where he commanded the Israel spacecraft in orbit.

*I look at the International Space Station as the most significant labo-
ratory and facility ever given to humanity, and the greatest platform
for entrepreneurial experimentation and growth, ever. Whether it's
material sciences, biotechnology, nanotech, manufacturing in space,
CubeSat design and development, or using it as a port to go to and
from low Earth orbit out to other places, it's there—use it!* [20]

Christopher Stott | Cofounder, Chair, & Chief Executive Officer, ManSat

COMMERCIAL SPACE STATIONS

The ISS is currently only supported through 2028.[21] At an annual operating cost of approximately $4 billion (with NASA typically contributing $3.25 billion), and a total cost of $100 billion since 1994 (with United States taxpayers footing half of that bill), many argue that the expenses outweigh the benefits and that we ought to scrap it after its useful life.[22] Jeffrey Manber, the CEO of Nanoracks, argued further that the ISS itself would probably not be funded today. Although it is a brilliant platform of engineering that engages multiple countries and stakeholders, it attempts to serve too many interests. If we were to look at space stations through the lens of the commercial sector, we wouldn't try to make one size fit all.

As 2028 approaches, there are compelling arguments that the private market could take over portions of the space station. The ISS already serves as a platform to explore new business relationships, developing a vital model that will help the industry shift "from a paradigm of government-funded, contractor-provided goods and services to a commercially provided, govern-ment-as-a-customer approach."[23]

*First, [the ISS] can stimulate entirely new markets not achievable
in the past. Second, it creates new stakeholders in spaceflight and
represents great economic opportunity. Third, it ensures a strong
industrial capability not only for future spaceflight but also for the
many related industries. Finally, and perhaps most importantly,
it allows cross-pollination of ideas, processes, and best practices,
as a foundation for economic development.* [24]

NASA, "Economic Development of Space," 2017.

NASA is also making strides toward a commercial transition, notably with the Commercial Crew and Cargo Program Office, which houses the COTS and Commercial Crew Development (CCDev) programs. CCDev began in 2010 to contract the private sector to bring crew and cargo from Earth to the ISS and LEO. NASA has selected proposals and provided funding to Sierra Nevada Corporation, SpaceX, United Launch Alliance, Boeing, Paragon Space Development Corporation, and Blue Origin to develop these transportation and resupply capabilities.[25]

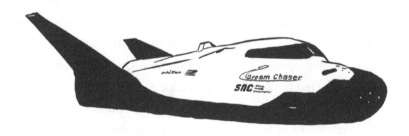

Sierra Nevada's Dream Chaser spacecraft
Developed to transport crew and cargo to the ISS

In June 2019, NASA announced that, starting in 2020, it will allow a minimum of two private astronauts per year to spend up to thirty days on the ISS to conduct "approved commercial and marketing activities."[26] In addition, NASA released an appendix to its Next Space Technologies for Exploration Partnerships (NextSTEP-2) Broad Agency Announcement, calling for commercial proposals to partner with the government agency on future ISS activities via the Node 2 docking port (also known as Harmony). NASA intends to award various task orders to private sector companies that can provide valid, long-term capabilities that serve the Agency's needs on the space station while shifting ISS operations to the commercial sector. NASA stated that part of its goal in this endeavor is to "stimulate the commercial space industry while leveraging those same commercial capabilities through partnerships and future contracts to deliver mission capabilities," citing that a crucial component of this partnership model focuses on "[developing] capabilities that meet NASA human space exploration objectives to support more extensive human space flight missions while also supporting industry commercialization plans for expanding the frontiers of future opportunities in space."[27]

We anticipate that industry will be able to provide the R&D services and technology demonstration services in LEO that the agency needs at a much more efficient cost than NASA currently does with the ISS.

Doug Comstock | Commercial LEO Liaison, Human Exploration and Operations Mission Directorate, NASA

Private companies have begun making plans for the space station, too. Bigelow Aerospace, founded by hotel real estate developer Robert Bigelow, has been working to provide in-space habitats since 2010, when the company licensed intellectual property (IP) from NASA for inflatable structures. In April 2016, SpaceX delivered the Bigelow Expandable Activity Module (BEAM) and attached it to the ISS.[28] The idea behind the company's inflatable space habitats is to send something from the ground in a compact way, inflate in space, and then have a sizable, pressurized interior volume. As NASA explained, these expandable habitats "greatly decrease the amount of transport volume for future space missions" because they "weigh less and take up less room on a rocket while allowing additional space for living and working." While BEAM was only meant to stay on the ISS for two years, the module's performance and capabilities surpassed expectations in the first year, leading to a five-year contract extension. BEAM quickly became a "core facility" on the space station, and in 2019, NASA extended the contract again to keep BEAM until 2028.[29]

Sovereign nations, including the United Kingdom, the Netherlands, Australia, Singapore, Japan, and Sweden, have all demonstrated interest in utilizing the BEAM habitats as on-orbit facilities of the ISS.[30] Habitats like these can help fill multiple industry demands; while a backlog of countries remains interested in sending astronauts to the space station, there is not enough transportation and habitat capacity to meet the demand. NASA noted other benefits of the expandable structures, which "protect from solar and cosmic radiation, space debris, and other contaminants. Crews traveling to the Moon, Mars, asteroids, or other destinations could use them as habitable structures."[31] NASA also touched upon these habitats' terrestrial applications, which range "from infrastructure improvements and repairs to protection of human health and safety." Examples include emergency housing in disaster areas, storm surge protection devices, and plugs to prevent flooding in systems like underground subways.

Bigelow Aerospace also partnered with ULA in 2016 to develop fully functioning space stations—which could be used for research, exploratory missions, and even tourism.[32] In 2018, Robert Bigelow announced that he created Bigelow Space Operations, a sister company of Bigelow Aerospace, to focus on the company's in-space habitats moving forward.[33]

Another effort already in development comes from Axiom Space in Houston, Texas. This initiative, launched in 2016, is led by former NASA ISS Program Manager Mike Suffredini—who spent a decade working with the space station. In January 2020, NASA announced that Axiom had been awarded the first NextSTEP-2 task order, and the company will attach its own habitable, commercial module to the ISS in 2024. In NASA's press release, NASA Administrator Jim Bridenstine noted, "Axiom's work to develop a commercial destination in space is a critical step for NASA to meet its long-term needs for astronaut training, scientific research, and technology demonstrations in low-Earth orbit." Revenue areas for the commercial nodes could include "exploration support, scientific research, and sponsorships," according to Amir Blachman, who heads the strategic development effort for Axiom.[34] Axiom also intends to provide space tourism services and visits to the ISS, the first of which is scheduled for 2021 via a SpaceX Crew Dragon.

Ultimately, Axiom intends to create a commercial space station to replace the ISS after 2028, which Suffredini believes "will help us transition from research and manufacturing and everything else done on ISS on a future platform."[35] Additional Axiom modules will join the ISS in 2025 and 2026; then, when the ISS is retired, the Axiom components will detach to form a separate commercial space station.[36] Until then, other plans include leveraging Made In Space's additive manufacturing capabilities to create and maintain in-space structures.[37] In May 2019, Axiom published images of a sample material being tested on the ISS via Houston-based Alpha Space's MISSE (Materials International Space Station Experiment) facility. The material in question, acrylic that Axiom will use for its commercial module's windows, evolved from conception to in-space testing in only six months—an astounding timeline that indicates both the commercial space sector's agility and Axiom's energetic plans beginning to fall into place.[38]

I n terms of developing a feasible commercial space station, there is precedent— MirCorp, a private space company (created by space entrepreneurs involving the Russian space program), took over the Russian space station Mir in 1999 to use as a commercial platform. Dennis Tito, the first space tourist, visited the space station in 2001 after buying his own ticket. However, due to pressure from NASA for Russia to fully commit to the ISS effort, MirCorp deorbited the space station into the Pacific Ocean in 2001. Jeffrey Manber, who previously worked for MirCorp to develop the business model for the Mir to serve as an entertainment and visitation site, attests that MirCorp remains a critical moment in our history: it proved that a private entrepreneur could commercialize a space station and develop unanticipated markets.

Opening the ISS to companies like Axiom will, most importantly, allow NASA to measure whether commercial companies have enough viable interest, funding, and capabilities to create their own space stations. And yet, as NASA and the ISS open their doors wider and wider for collaboration with the private sector, there is still a need for the world at large to enable the growing NewSpace industry.

CHAPTER TWELVE
SPACE CAN DO QUADRILLIONS

If you look at humanity, we've always been expanding. We've always had a greater appetite for technology. The question is less if there's going to be more going on in LEO and beyond, the question is when—and when do you want to get in?[1]

Shahin Farshchi, Ph.D.*

We have not even scratched the surface of the potential for extreme profits from space. As space-focused investment banker Hoyt Davidson* succinctly stated, "Earth cannot do quadrillions. Space can."[2]

A quadrillion is 1,000,000,000,000,000

Space has the sort of scalability and outsized return possibility that policy experts, science fiction creators, and futurists tend to give their stamp of approval. Could non-traditional companies enter the market and create their own space efforts?

★ **Shahin Farshchi, Ph.D.** is a partner at Lux Capital, a venture capital firm focused on science and technology businesses. A scientist and engineer, Farshchi formerly cofounded Vista Integrated Systems, which built wireless vital sign monitors, developed hybrid vehicles for General Motors, and developed software for multiple Silicon Valley startups.

★ **Hoyt Davidson** is the founder and managing partner of Near Earth LLC, an investment firm working in the satellite, commercial space, and aerospace defense markets. With a physics background from MIT, Davidson worked for Lockheed Martin for six years before returning to MIT for his MBA. He went on to work at DLJ and Credit Suisse before cofounding the Space Finance Group, the first financial group to focus solely on the commercial satellite sector. He previously served on the NASA Advisory Council and is now a board member of Nanoracks and the Pacific International Center for Space Exploration Systems.

Giants such as Google, Microsoft, Dell, and Amazon all started from humble roots. Most of their first offices were in garages, and we're familiar with their stories and how they transformed their respective sectors and the world. Imagine if you, as an investor, were given the opportunity to invest in any of the afore-mentioned companies before they went public: would you invest some of your hard-earned money if only to help the computer sector succeed?

Development of space will improve life on Earth. Access to space is import-ant for agriculture, human-itarian efforts, communi-cations and navigation. Rapid cadence imagery, like Planet is developing, helps us become better, more sustainable stewards of Earth. New opportunities are emerging in space that would not have been possible before. When you lower the cost of access to space, a boom of innovation follows, just as low-cost fiber optics paved the way for the internet and the cloud services that followed.[3]

Steve Jurvetson | Cofounder & Managing Director, Future Ventures; Board Member, SpaceX; Cofounder & Former Managing Director, Draper Fisher Jurvetson

Let's also consider the evolution of email as an analog of NewSpace. In its early days, its use was minimal. Email is now an indispensable form of communica-tion with ecosystems within ecosystems. The mobile phone is another parallel; although Motorola created the earliest version in 1973, it was not until the late 1990s when cellular phone adoption took off. Later, the introduction of smart-phones provided a pocket-sized library with an endless variety of applications to leverage.

When we understand the vast scope of benefits that space provides, many would agree that investing in space infrastructure is a requirement for a successful future.[4] Space has the ability to produce a triple bottom line, or ROIII: Return on Investment, Innovation, and Inspiration. Investing in NewSpace should, therefore, be understood not only as an expectation of future profits and value but as sowing the seeds for not only an extension of the current space system but an entirely new framework for space.

E xisting shifts in budget, workforce, and timelines all help to inform NewSpace's value. For instance, China's 2018 mission to the Moon cost over $2 billion and had thousands of people working on the endeavor. Now compare that with the 2018 Moon landing mission from the privately funded, nonprofit organization SpaceIL, which cost approximately $95 million with forty full-time employees. While the scopes of the missions were different, they both intended to land on the Moon and send data back to Earth. As SpaceIL's cofounder Yonatan Winetraub commented, "This is the *new* space race."[5]

We are poised to see a tidal wave of ideas competing to participate in this new era. Amaresh Kollipara,* chief revenue officer of OffWorld and founder of Earth2Orbit, believes the 2015–2025 period marks the space industry's inflection point, informed by several key developments.[6] First, Google's acquisition of Skybox Imaging (now Terra Bella) in 2014 indicated credibility in the industry, and as the first exit for investors in the NewSpace paradigm, catalyzed the drastic increase of venture capital and investment activities in NewSpace.

Startup grants and contracts from both NASA and ESA grew steadily between 2014–2015. India's PSLV continued to commercialize from 2013–2016, providing inexpensive launch and unprecedented access to space for private companies that opened a crucial door for the commercial market. SpaceX's satellite division in Redmond, announced in 2015, culminated in the first wave of the Starlink constellation in 2019 and effectively created a new satellite-based internet

★ **Amaresh Kollipara** is the cofounder and chief executive officer of Earth2Orbit (E2O), a global satellite launch provider, and serves as chief revenue officer for Offworld, a company developing a robotic workforce. A strong believer in entrepreneurial activity, Kollipara works to develop and grow space applications that will shape the future of space exploration. He pursues his goals through many avenues, including management consulting, financial advising, investment strategies, and as a guest speaker for various space conferences and events. In addition, he is an Emmy-nominated VR producer; his *Mission:ISS* project through Oculus (Facebook) partnered with NASA to create an accurate simulation of the ISS. Along with E2O, Kollipara serves on the board of trustees for both the SETI Institute and the Space Frontier Foundation.

industry from scratch—and helped SpaceX raise an additional $1 billion in financing. Additionally, OneWeb and Virgin Galactic received substantial financing in their 2015–2016 funding rounds, signifying the increasing investment activity in the commercial sector. Finally, Virgin Galactic's plans for frequent space tourism flights (start date still to be announced) and Rocket Lab's plans for two launches per month by 2020 will drive down launch cost and increase access to space—transforming the launch landscape dramatically.

When Henry Ford made cheap, reliable cars people said, 'Nah, what's wrong with a horse?' That was a huge bet he made, and it worked.[7]

Elon Musk | Founder, SpaceX

Think for a moment of Everett Rogers's diffusion of innovations theory (also known as the five stages of technology adoption), which describes how the public comes to support and accept disruptive technologies. Under this premise, the general population will fall into one of the following groups, even when the benefits of new technologies or applications are abundantly clear from the start: Innovators (2.5 percent), Early Adopters (13.5 percent), Early Majority (34 percent), Late Majority (34 percent), or Laggards (16 percent).[8] Those who fall into the earliest groups are responsible for integrating novel capabilities into society; they are also the ones who benefit from their investment. How will we each fall into these categories when it comes to the space sector?

We are right back at the beginning when Christopher Columbus was trying to persuade the monarchs in Iberia to fund expeditions to faraway places, with almost no plausible direct means of value coming out of that. What Made In Space and others on the cutting edge of spaceflight are trying to put together today is the equivalent of that first ship (or the first few ships). And, of course, the technology involved in space exploration is quite different; it's a three-dimensional problem now, not just a two-dimensional problem on the oceans. But there are many similar challenges; it's unfamiliar to people, so it's difficult for them to grasp the opportunities. And it's expensive without a near-term return on investment. That means the amount of money that's available for space ventures in the foreseeable future is going to be limited, and the number of people who believe that it's worthwhile investing in is going to be very limited until space becomes more a part of the everyday experience of ordinary people.[9]

Andrew Barton, Ph.D.*

There are hundreds of burning questions that need research, validation, and answers. With this ever-growing need for actionable intelligence, as well as new and varied data sets, there is a massive opportunity in the near- to mid-term. Space is one of the best grounds to prove that interdisciplinary work and collaboration can yield exceedingly positive results for human knowledge and wisdom, economic and technological progress, and even cultural advancement—all contributing to our evolution.

Unlike Columbus's expedition to the New World, space does not require displacing others, waging war, or erasing cultures and their history. This conquest is one of spirit, inspiration, knowledge. As we explore, we may one day find ways to inhabit other celestial bodies—but it will happen without colonization. If we can work together collectively and globally, it can be a peaceful adventure with a common goal: to expand.

As we see some ambitious companies partnering with the space sector, whether they are startups or Fortune 500 corporations, we can begin to broaden our thinking to consider the best ways to collaborate for our future. Capital might be the fuel to power astropreneurial efforts, but behind the money is intelligence with vast options to weigh. The area that still needs more road to travel on is the investment thesis.

★ **Andrew Barton, Ph.D.** is the head of engineering for Southern Launch, a NewSpace smallsat launch provider in South Australia focused on polar orbit, and a venture partner with NewSpace accelerator Syndicate 708. Dr. Barton formerly served as the chair and the director of technical operations for the Google Lunar XPRIZE and as the chief technology officer and director of launch & US operations for Fleet Space Technologies, a telecommunications company that leverages satellite constellations and the Internet of Things.

What's interesting about the space industry now is that it's a Moore's Law industry—which is because sensors, computation, display, communications, radios, and so forth are directly relevant to building smaller and smaller, and more and more capable, spacecraft or satellites. The reason that the Moore's Law advances matter is that you are either doubling the capability or power, for instance, every eighteen months. A satellite needed to be the size of a school bus twenty years ago and is now the size of a toaster, and in another five to ten years, it will be the size of a Rubik's Cube. So, without doing anything, your launch cost per unit of capability keeps getting cut in half every eighteen months. And when you couple that together with very dramatic improvements that are being made on the launch side, led by companies like SpaceX and Rocket Lab and others, it means that a typical venture-backed startup can actually build a fleet of small satellites and launch them using venture dollars.[10]

Rob Coneybeer*

Space is the backbone of the digital economy; this is how we have to see it. How you connect the last three billion people to the internet? It will be by space. And we all know 'internet' means connectivity, which means education—and education is the base of everything. It is the source of fighting poverty. Education means democratization. So, space helps to democratize the world.[11]

Return on Investment, Innovation, and Inspiration

Frank Salzgeber*

★ **Rob Coneybeer** is the managing director of Shasta Ventures, an early stage investment firm focused on ambitious entrepreneurs. He focuses on emerging capabilities spanning space, robotics, AR/VR, and the connected home.

★ **Frank M. Salzgeber** is the head of the Technology Transfer and Business Incubation Office of the European Space Agency, where he supports entrepreneurial space efforts in Europe. He serves on advisory boards for multiple organizations, venture capital funds, and startups. His previous experience includes founding an IT startup in Germany and seven years with Apple.

PART IV

INVESTING IN THE COSMOS

CHAPTER THIRTEEN
AN INDUSTRY IN ITS OWN LEAGUE

O ur Earth is the product of stars, making us at least one-part stardust. What's keeping us from our star-faring origins? Investing in space has traditionally existed as a niche interest, and many of the same principles from technology investing hold true for space investing. Early investors in space startups, although hoping for a return, invested in part out of passion, with the hope that the sector will ultimately succeed. They sought to help the tadpole-sized industry move to the next stage in a growing, thriving way.

Space is still in its own league. The sector is vast, intricate, and fraught with market, regulatory, and technological risks. Most investors typically only want to deal with one of these risks; space has all three. And given most venture-oriented investors' preference for returns on their investment in less than seven years, it's no surprise that investors in the past shied away from in-space investments outside of the more traditional satellite communications subsector. Exit activities that would activate large numbers, like an initial public offering (IPO) or merger and acquisition (M&A), are infrequent—at least for now.

Compared to other sectors, investing in space can be intimidating, if not difficult to manage. As a result, space is under-discovered and still suffers from tremendous underinvestment. As Jeff Greason remarked, "This is a problem that goes way beyond space: how do you invest in worthwhile projects that are tremendous growth agents to the economy but don't have a three to five-year time scale?"[1] Fortunately, with new models, space is becoming more venture-scalable: new funds emerging with longer terms—fifteen years—will allow many space projects to realize their vision.

Dr. Steve Goldberg,* operating partner at venture capital firm Venrock, shared that "In the venture community, you're trying to quantify risk. There's market risk and then there's technology risk, and most of the time, what we take is market risk."[2] Now that space-focused technology is widely proven and understood for its myriad values, bold frontier investors view space as a growing market with incredible potential that will influence future technology developers, entrepreneurs, culture, and more.

Seraphim Capital is a London-based investment firm that specializes in commercial space opportunities. *When I spoke to Mark Boggett, Seraphim's CEO and managing partner, I was surprised to learn that he became interested in space purely by accident.* Boggett explained that in the early 2000s, he and his partners suddenly started hearing about the space industry left and right—and that the sector was not only going through a rapid period of disruption but was underserved by the venture community. "From that point on, virtually every interesting company that I read about or saw or discussed linked back to the space industry. It was amazing—it just seemed to be absolutely everywhere I looked," Boggett recounted. "So, I did an analysis of the market, the deals, the deal flow, the exits, who the players were, and it really helped me understand what the opportunities were within this market. The more that I dug, the more intrigued and excited my peers and I became."

While space initially appeared slightly too niche to take seriously, Boggett began to consider the sector through a different lens. "I looked back at all of the technology investments that the team and I had made, and I sort of evaluated them, trying to determine whether we had historical relevance to the space sector. I started to recognize that many of the things that we'd done in the past—which were in areas like artificial intelligence, new materials, robotics, Big Data,

★ **Steve Goldberg, Ph.D.** is an operating partner at Venrock, a venture capital and private equity firm that focuses on technology and healthcare companies. Dr. Goldberg's background is in electrical engineering, and through Venrock he works on investments in connectivity, M2M and IoT, robotics, and embedded systems.

★ **Mark Boggett** is the chief executive officer and managing partner of Seraphim Capital, a venture capital and private equity group based in London and the first venture fund in history dedicated to supporting the NewSpace sector. He joined Seraphim in 2006, its founding year. Boggett has worked in the investment sector since 1995 and is the director of UK Space Tech Angels.

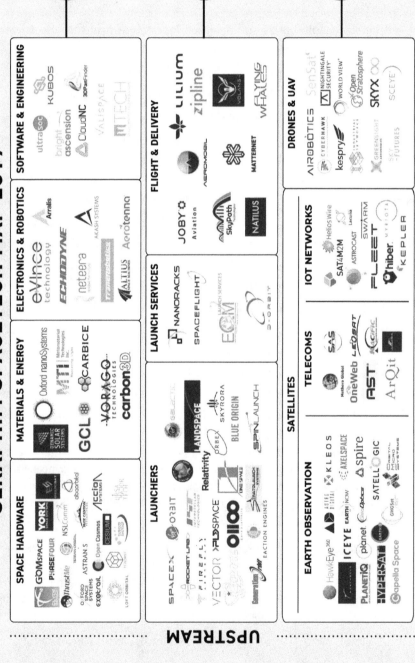

SERAPHIM SPACETECH MAP 2019

Source: www.SeraphimCapital.com

DOWNLINK

STORE

ANALYZE

PRODUCT

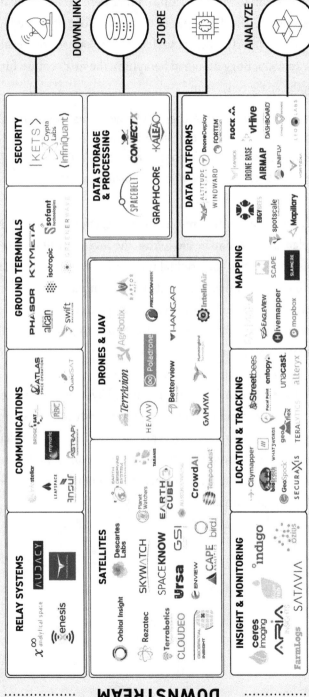

DOWNSTREAM

BEYOND EARTH

SECURITY
KETS
Crypta Labs
InfiniQuant

GROUND TERMINALS
PHASOR   KYMETA
alcan   isotropic   sofant technologies
swift   GREENERWAVE

COMMUNICATIONS
stellar   ATLAS SPACE OPERATIONS
BRIDGESAT   mynaric   RBC   QuadSAT
LEAFSPACE   ansur   ASTRAPI

RELAY SYSTEMS
analytical space   AUDACY
enesis   TRANSCELESTIAL

DATA STORAGE & PROCESSING
SPACEBELT   CONNECTX
GRAPHCORE   KALEAO

DATA PLATFORMS
ALTITUDE ANGEL   DroneDeploy   FLOCK
WINDWARD   DRONE BASE   FORTEM
AIRMAP   vHive   DASHBOARD
UNIFLY   LEO LABS
VORTEXA

DRONES & UAV
RAPTOR MAPS
Agribotix
Terravion   Poladrone   PRECISIONHAWK
HEMAV   Betterview   vHANGAR   IntelinAir
Hummingbird   GAMAYA

SATELLITES
Descartes Labs
Rezatec   SKYWATCH   EARTH OBSERVING SYSTEM
SPACEKNOW   ursa   GSI   Planet Watchers   EARTH CUBE
CLOUDEO   ENVIEW   CAPE ANALYTICS   birdi
ORBITAL INSIGHT
Terrabotics   DIGITSATIAL INSIGHT   CrowdAI   TempoQuest

MAPPING
SCAPE   EBIGYDREES
EAGLEVIEW   SLAMCORE   spotscale
Hivemapper   mapbox   Mapillary

LOCATION & TRACKING
Streetbees
Citymapper   Focal Point   entopy
WHAT3WORDS   geoflex   unacast.
bigspace   GeoSpock   TERAVITICS   alteryx
SECURAXIS

INSIGHT & MONITORING
indigo
ceres imaging   OZIUS
ARIA
FarmLogs   SATAVIA

SPACE INFRASTRUCTURE
ORBITFAB   ASTROFETIC
ASTROSCALE   INFINITE ORBITS
ATOMOS   EFFECTIVE SPACE

SPACE RESEARCH
SPACE TANGO
SPACEPHARMA   CEPLANTFACTORY

SPACE EXPLORATION & RESOURCES
TEAM INDUS   SPACEVR   MADE INSPACE
MAANA ELECTRIC   AXIOM
ispace

sensor technology, graphic image recognition technology, telecommunications, mobile—were directly relevant to the opportunities that were presented by the space industry," he recounted. The decisive step was when Boggett created his own graphic to measure the opportunities for various technology sectors related to the space industry. In 2006, Boggett joined Seraphim, the first venture fund dedicated to growing the space ecosystem.[3]

> *This exercise really convinced me that there were just so many technology areas that had high potentials to converge with space applications or space services that weren't already doing so.*
> **Mark Boggett | Chief Executive Officer, Seraphim Capital**

nvesting to date is about contributing resources—time, effort, and financial capital—with the plan that one day in the future, the investor will receive a financial return that is greater than the original input. Investing in innovation and out-of-this-world opportunities take a bit more stamina and patience. However, despite space's challenging nature and steep path to access, there's already a quarter-trillion-dollar industry behind it. With each passing month, enabling technologies from other areas make the possibility of creating space startups easier, faster, and less expensive than ever before.

As more private efforts come to fruition—influenced by new policies, new ideas, and energy (both time and money)—new saplings are steadily emerging from the soil of the industry, and fund managers are more willing to take calculated risks to test the waters in a blossoming sector. Currently, technology-focused investment funds, some angel investors, very wealthy individuals (also known as super-angels), and a few governments pave the way.

CHAPTER FOURTEEN
INCREASED INVESTMENTS

*Space is no longer a billionaire's playground. Because of the
technological advancements that have occurred, the average
person can access space, either to invest in it or to build
a business. So, those who want to get involved in what is
becoming a trillion-dollar economy need to get started today—
because space is Internet 2.0., and it's happening right now.*

Lisa Rich[*]

nvestments in NewSpace increased substantially over the past decade. In 2015, the private space sector received $1.8 billion in investments, equating to more than double the investments over the past fifteen years *combined*. The US Chamber of Commerce reports that global revenues in the private sector totaled $175 billion in 2005 and have grown at a 7 percent increase since, with nearly $385 billion in revenue reported for 2017.[1]

Goldman Sachs released a 98-page report in 2017 speaking favorably about NewSpace, particularly the areas of mining and utilization of resources in space. We can interpret this act as signaling on several levels. First, given that the IPO market is soft (if not drying up, by some analysts' standards), Goldman Sachs

★ **Lisa Rich** is a lifelong entrepreneur and prolific venture capital investor. She is a managing partner of Hemisphere Ventures, an early-stage venture capital firm focused on frontier tech—synthetic biology, robotics, drones, and space—which she founded in 2014 with her husband, Jeff Rich. Hemisphere has invested in over 200 companies, including seventeen private space sector investments—making Hemisphere the second most active venture capital investor in NewSpace (Space Angels currently has twenty-two investments in NewSpace). Additionally, Rich and her husband founded the private space exploration company Xplore in 2017, where she serves as the chief operating officer. In 2000, she and Mr. Rich created BrainyQuote, the internet's largest quotation website.

is looking to expand into new markets—i.e., space. Second, it sees accelerated investment activity in a previously slow-moving sector. Finally, it could gain insight into new entrants and potentially raise money for later-stage groups in public markets.

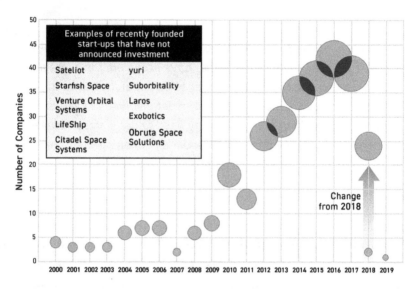

Over 310 angel- and venture-backed space companies have been founded and funded since 2000. *Excludes companies that have not announced investment, including many founded in the last few years. In the 2019 Start-Up Space report, only two angel- or venture-backed startup space companies were reported as having been founded in 2018. In the 2020 Start-Up Space report, the 2018 number increased to twenty-four companies. This suggests that the number of reported startup space companies founded in 2019 (one) will likely increase in the future.*
Data for inset reflects publicly reported investments through December 31, 2019.[2]

Space Angels, the most active angel investment and venture capital firm in the space economy, called 2017 "The Year of Commercial Launch," pointing to "Launch receiving over 72% of capital deployed and commercial launch capacity rivaling that of government."[3] Total private investment into NewSpace totaled $4.7 billion in 2017, and the Kensho Space Index (which tracks public companies with any exposure to the space industry) increased 27 percent over that year, while the S&P 500 only increased 12.5 percent.[4]

The year 2018 saw $3 billion more, as capital continued to flow into the sector and its many subsectors.[5] Space Angels attributes a majority of that increase to the rise in small launch vehicles—led by the likes of Rocket Lab, Vector (now defunct), and Virgin Orbit—and dubbed 2018 "The Year of Small Launch." Space Angels CEO Chad Anderson noted that they "see the entry of small launch vehicles as a specialization within the sector and an indication that commercial launch is maturing."[6]

Morgan Stanley analysts predicted that 2019 would be "the year for space," based on increased activity from SpaceX, Blue Origin, Boeing, small launch providers, and more government focus on the United States' proposed Space Force.[7] Based on more specific rising industry trends, Space Angels anticipated 2019 to be "The Year of Commercial Space Travel," with $1.7 billion invested into space companies within the first quarter of 2019—almost double the amount invested in the last quarter of 2018.[8]

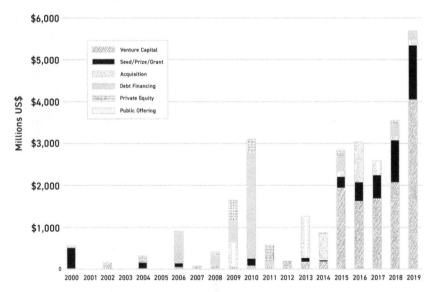

The mix of types of investment in space companies varies from 2000 to 2019.
Data and table courtesy of Bryce Space and Technology[9]

Traditional venture capital firms now lead investments in NewSpace. Mark Boggett of Seraphim Capital confirmed in 2018 that, "It's really difficult to identify a top-tier VC that hasn't yet made a space investment." He further relayed that this increasing trend is "very different to what it looked like 18 months ago."[10] Chad Anderson reinforced this assertion. "Venture capital investment in space is now a generally accepted theme," Anderson said, adding that forty-one of the one hundred largest VC firms have invested in at least one space startup. "Given all this, we expect significant investment in space to continue in 2019," Anderson concluded.[11] And as predicted, 2019 received $5.7 billion in total investment funding.[12]

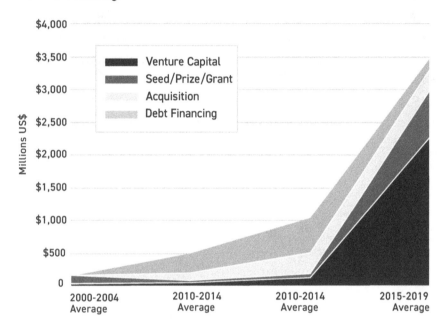

Considering multi-year periods, average annual startup space seed funding, venture capital, and acquisitions have increased.

By number of investors, VCs are the largest investor group for space startups. *Note that angel investors and altruists are combined into the angel investors category in this chart.*

Data and visuals courtesy of Bryce Space and Technology[13]

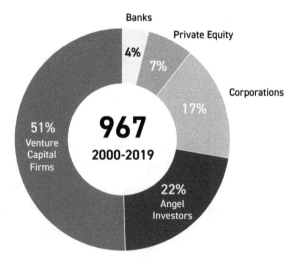

Mithril Capital Management, cofounded by Peter Thiel, provides growth capital to later-stage companies in "industries long overdue for change."[14] Mithril provided $18 million in Series B financing to Spaceflight in 2016.[15] In January 2017, Mithril closed financing on a second fund for $740 million.[16]

SoftBank's Vision Fund, which funds late-stage startups, reached $100 billion in 2019.[17] Softbank invested $1 billion in OneWeb in December 2016 and another $1.25 billion in 2019.[18] In a company statement, OneWeb CEO Adrian Steckel confirmed that the 2019 funding will help the micro-satellite startup reach its goal: increasing production to deploy 650 satellites in the coming two years, based on its ability to churn out more than one satellite per day for one-tenth of the traditional cost. OneWeb's ambitions make it a prime candidate for SoftBank, which states its goals are served by a strategy to "concentrate its operations in the information industry, and advance the Information Revolution with leading technologies essential to the times and superior business models."[19] SoftBank's funding adds to OneWeb's total of $3.4 billion in investments since being founded in 2012; additional investors include Virgin Group, Coca Cola, Airbus, Bharti Enterprises, Intelsat, and Echostar.[20]

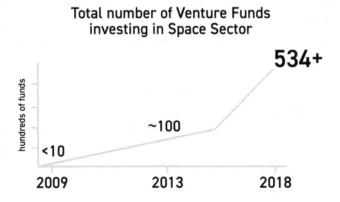

Total number of Venture Funds investing in Space Sector

We are delighted to see a lot of venture capital coming in, stirring things up, and questioning assumptions we have held for decades.[21]

Anthony Freeman, Ph.D. | Innovation Foundry, NASA Jet Propulsion Laboratory

In March 2019, Swiss investment bank UBS published a report showing that it expects the $400 billion global space industry market to double by 2030, with space tourism representing a projected $3 billion market by that time.[22] Morgan Stanley published a report titled "Investment Implications of the Final Frontier," which proposed that the space sector will grow into a $1.1 trillion industry by 2040—a sentiment echoed by Goldman Sachs.[23] And both United Launch Alliance and Bank of America Merrill Lynch envision a $2.7 trillion space economy by 2045.[24]

> *While space tourism is still at a nascent phase, we think that as technology becomes proven, and the cost falls due to technology and competition, space tourism will become more mainstream. ... Space tourism could be the steppingstone for the development of long-haul travel on [Earth] serviced by space.[25]*
>
> **Jarrod Castle and Myles Walton, quoted in "Super Fast Travel Using Outer Space Could Be $20 Billion Market, Disrupting Airlines, UBS Predicts," by Michael Sheetz, *CNBC*, March 18, 2019.**

Between 2017 and 2019, we didn't see any major M&A activity in the space sector—unlike in previous years when Monsanto acquired Climate Corporation (2013),[26] and when Google acquired SkyBox in 2014 (which Google renamed Terra Bella and later sold to Planet in 2017).[27] There was, however, a moderate amount of smaller M&A activity in and around the edges of the space sector, including Northrop Grumman's acquisition of Orbital ATK for $9.2 billion in 2017,[28] Planet's acquisition of Boundless Spatial in 2018,[29] and UrtheCast's acquisition of GeoSys in 2019.[30] We should probably expect significant M&A activity as the industry progresses and as investments continue to increase.

> *Our complementary portfolios and technology-focused cultures will yield significant value creation through revenue synergies associated with new opportunities, cost savings, operational synergies, and enhanced growth.[31]*
>
> **Wes Bush | Chair & Former Chief Executive Officer, Northrop Grumman**

Virgin Galactic became the first space tourism-focused company to go public after its IPO on October 28, 2019. With a valuation of $2.8 billion, the company closed its first day at $11.75 per share, trading under the ticker symbol SPCE.[32] The IPO follows a merger with Social Capital Hedosophia (SCH), which holds a 49 percent stake in the company; SCH's founder, venture capitalist Chamath Palihapitiya, now acts as the new chair of Virgin Galactic.[33] "By embarking on this new chapter, at this advanced point in Virgin Galactic's development, we can open space to more investors and in doing so, open space to thousands of new astronauts," Branson commented to CNBC.[34]

To date, commercial space visits, or "space tourism," have been minimal, mostly through privately funded trips on Russian Soyuz rockets. However, there is little doubt that the market has potential. Though there have only been seven "space tourists" so far, and their flights have cost up to $80 million apiece, Virgin Galactic alone has reportedly sold over six hundred seats for trips to suborbital space.[35] (Their tickets cost a much more reasonable $250,000 each—though there's a huge difference between orbital tourism for a week and suborbital for a few minutes.) Virgin Galactic's SS2 vehicle, called VSS Unity, flew three crew members in a successful suborbital test in February 2019. Beth Moses, the company's chief astronaut instructor, was on the flight to survey the experience from a commercial customer's standpoint. According to the spacecraft's pilot, Dave Mackay, the company is now on track to perfect its commercial experience—and the next flights will host a full cabin of space tourists.[36]

It still remains to be seen when these flights will begin or how frequently they'll occur; Virgin Galactic has pushed the start dates for its commercial flights numerous times. The company did announce in October 2019 that the first flight, planned for 2020, will shuttle researchers from the Italian Air Force to space.[37] Virgin Galactic also said it aims to have sixteen flights in 2020—and scale up to 270 per year by 2023.[38] What *is* certain is that once there are more humans visiting space, new challenges and needs will emerge.

Perhaps more significant is that many in the investment and space industries see the Virgin Galactic IPO as a strong indicator of things to come. Peter Platzer, CEO of Spire Global, commented in September 2019 that after its recent funding round, the satellite company has crossed the threshold into profitability and now expects to IPO in two years.[39]

At a top-level, I think things that expand our planetary perspective are the things that my heart's in. Whether it's movies, television, competitions, or different ideas where people can either go to space themselves or virtually with others, it's exciting, because it gives more people the chance to experience the wonder of our own planet.[40]

George T. Whitesides | Chief Executive Officer, Virgin Galactic

New investment options also indicate broader avenues for sector-wide growth. SpaceFund, a tokenized venture capital firm based in Austin, Texas, believes that their funding model could lead the industry's future. Meagan Crawford, the managing partner of SpaceFund, used the tech industry to illustrate space's investment challenges.* While tech startups tend to take fourteen years to IPO, space's timelines are typically even longer; as a result, most funding comes from governments or billionaires—both of which can realistically afford to take on both the financial risk and very long road to a return on investment. "The idea behind our fund was figuring out how to fix that—how to change that dynamic such that we can get the capital inflow into the industry that it needs to be successful. We looked at a lot of different technologies and jurisdictions with different laws, and our research concluded that, by far, security tokens were the absolute best way to solve that problem," Crawford said.[41]

SpaceFund operates in a standard venture capital structure, and the tokens themselves are simply digital representations of stock—exactly the same as a paper

★ **Meagan Crawford** is the managing partner of SpaceFund, an investment group that uses blockchain to finance NewSpace efforts. She has a successful entrepreneurial record, having sold her first company before the age of thirty, and formerly served as chief operating officer for Deep Space Industries and as principal of Ramsey Financial Group. Crawford is also the cofounder of Eden Growth Systems (a farming technology company), Delta-V (a marketing agency focused on NewSpace), cofounder and board member of the Center for Space Commerce and Finance, and an advisor for Esprit Data.

stock certificate, "but safer, because the token lives on the immutable blockchain ledger, meaning it can never get lost, destroyed, or stolen," Crawford explained. The primary reason for the tokenization is early liquidity. "The only difference with us is the way that you hold your interest, either via token or a whole piece of the share certificate. Obviously, the tokenized version gives you the option for liquidity. And because the tokens are all based on open source blockchain technology, with wide interoperability, they're also extremely inexpensive to maintain," she said.

Aside from early liquidity, tokenization opens the door to previously unreachable foreign investments. This partially stems from a new Financial Industry Regulatory Authority (FINRA) regulation, passed in 2018, which allows US-based venture capital firms to accept foreign funds as long as they don't supply American IP and technology. The blockchain system makes that kind of transaction possible. Crawford even echoed an argument I've made in the past: "I've always thought that there are probably legitimate sources of investment from overseas that would want to invest in US space opportunities, but until now it's been fraught with challenges." As tokenization is also moving quickly in international markets, United States space companies can now take advantage of more investment options.

Overall, this business model gives SpaceFund high hopes for the industry's future. "The problem SpaceFund is fundamentally trying to solve is providing data that proves that NewSpace is a credible investment opportunity," Crawford said, pointing to the SpaceFund database. In addition to its funding model, SpaceFund is developing a comprehensive database to track industry changes— companies and their evolutions, sector-wide trends, investment activity, and more. SpaceFund will provide the database for free to the public based on the belief that it will help drive the sector—which is the ultimate goal. These metrics, hopefully, will allow investors and entrepreneurs alike to gain an understanding of NewSpace's potentials to the point where they will feel comfortable (and excited) enough to get involved.

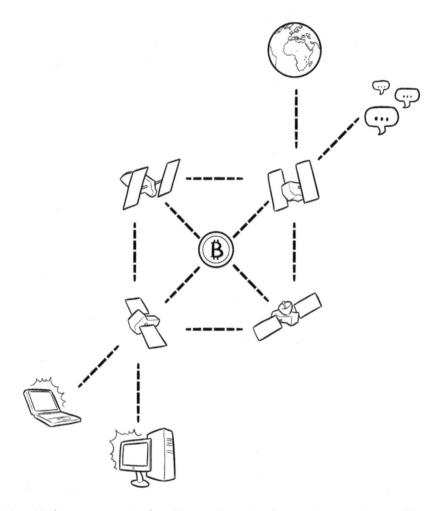

Yes, they're new, yes, they're different, yes, there are still a lot of questions, but we've made a big bet on that direction because we really see that train taking off out of the station already. We're seeing a lot of the legal background that you need, we're seeing the first trading platforms open, we're seeing clarity around legal regimes. We strongly believe that these tokens will create near-term liquidity for our investors. Somebody can invest in a ten-year fund and know that they don't have to wait till the end of the ten, fourteen, or eighteen years that it's going to take for the funds to return the capital. You're obviously not going to get 100 percent of the value when you exit something early, but to get investors a large amount of the value appreciation available for them to exit with, at any time, means that this is now a legitimate, reasonable investment opportunity for your average accredited investor.[42]

Meagan Crawford | Managing Partner, SpaceFund

CHAPTER FIFTEEN
SIGNALS FOR SUCCESS

We take for granted the amount of space infrastructure that goes into making our day-to-day lives so convenient, like through our smartphones. And now, other platforms that are dependent on that space infrastructure—that have been primarily used by intelligence agencies and other government defense needs—are becoming common use for other sectors. Whether you're a hedge fund manager looking to make a short against oil in China using synthetic-aperture radar or trying to bring internet to the world, the public is just starting to become familiar with those layers of infrastructure that make commercial space possible.[1]

Van Espahbodi*

There's clear signaling and receptivity today that space is an essential area for governments, academia, and various industries to continue to focus on. The natural upshot of the ubiquitous use of space will be a much larger industry, with wide-ranging applications from personal and corporate to entertainment and infrastructure plays—just like any other medium of commerce. We live in a time where there is reasonable access to capital, abundant talent, emerging innovations, and—best of all—an authentic interest in opening space up to the rest of the world.

★ **Van Espahbodi** is the cofounder and managing partner at Starburst Aerospace Accelerator, an aerospace innovation hub for startups in collaboration with government, industry, academia, and the tech community. He has over sixteen years of experience working in the space sector, with roles spanning government, corporate, defense, and commercial markets; as an entrepreneurial futurist, Espahbodi has helped identify and shape future industry trends, product strategies, and investment trade policy.

Dr. Simon "Pete" Worden is a stalwart for the private space sector. He has an excellent pedigree, including a doctorate in astronomy. He is a retired US Air Force General, a former director of NASA Ames Research Center, and a chair of an innovative private foundation focused on science. Worden believes that there are three key considerations that make the space sector and exploration, together, crucial for a vibrant and prosperous society today: expanding opportunities, the chance to make Earth into an ecological paradise, and the human imperative to settle other worlds.

First, we're not making any more land on our planet—clearly—or resources. If you're going to have a long-term expanding opportunity-base for humans, which I think is essential for us to be human, we have to go to space to do that. Second, if we really want to make Earth into a sustainable paradise, the fact that you can remove some waste and bring in some resources from outside is a really critical thing—and it's far better to do heavy industry deep in space rather than on Earth. In more humorous terms, I saw a bumper sticker that said, "Save the Earth. Let's strip mine the other planets first." And you might laugh, but it makes sense. The last point is a biological imperative, where humans have evolved to expand and reproduce. It's similar to the argument that Elon Musk is making, which is that we need both the opportunity and the backup—and I think going to the Moon and Mars are really important now. I'd even say that we really need to go to interstellar distances.[2]

Pete Worden, Ph.D.*

★ **Simon "Pete" Worden, Ph.D.** is the chair of the Breakthrough Prize Foundation for Breakthrough Initiatives, a science-based organization founded in 2015 with the mission of searching for extraterrestrial intelligence. He served as the director of NASA's Ames Research Center for nine years, before retiring to pursue opportunities in the private space sector. An expert in space issues, Dr. Worden has co-authored over 150 scientific papers and helped lead two NASA space science investigations; for his role in the Clementine Mission (1994), Dr. Worden was awarded the NASA Outstanding Leadership Medal. He has been a leader in small satellite development and implementation through his government roles; he also served in the US Air Force for twenty-nine years, where he was instrumental in various space-related strategic plans.

This human imperative to settle other worlds, in addition to the opportunities afforded by going to space and improving life on Earth, is arguably what will push us to take the necessary steps off our home planet. As humans, we certainly have a history of wanting more, needing more; we have a history of curiosity, a desire to discover, and an internal calling to create a better life for ourselves.

What can yield from a stronger investment in space in the near to mid-term? Lower-cost access to space. Cures and treatments for a variety of diseases. Faster terrestrial communications through high-performance cables. New meta-materials that are stronger, lighter, and more durable than ever before. Better, faster, and more accurate weather forecasting. Precision agriculture. Remote sensing and Earth observation. New advanced manufacturing. Debris mediation and tracking. Space resource mining. Disaster relief. Smarter farming and water conservation. Advanced maritime. All of NASA's technology spinoffs—and much more.

The supporting industries around NewSpace make investment increasingly attractive, with variables like the miniaturization of electronics, NewSpace-enabled applications coming online, machine learning, increased research and development of new launch options, and artificial intelligence bolstering many of these launch efforts. We could soon begin extracting viable water from the Moon and asteroids to use for fuel, radiation shielding, human consumption, and more. Imagine having continuous real-time visual coverage of ships traveling across the ocean. That kind of data is useful to analysts monitoring globally shipped goods for trading intelligence and economic trends. There are already cases today where companies sell similar data sourced from in-space assets. As new capabilities and business models roll out, there will be myriad new opportunities that will make this trillion-dollar industry possible much sooner than most analysts suggest. What we need is a movement.

A major and often overlooked generic advantage of space technology transfer deals is that space technologies are proven—contrary to many new technologies in Silicon Valley. They have flown in the harshest environment of space; they are durable, compact, lightweight, and often autonomous—and hence superior technologies by nature, so that the technology risk is eliminated, and focus shifts to commercialization.[3]

Joerg Kreisel*

★ **Joerg Kreisel** is the chief executive officer of JKIC, an independent space business and financial advisory firm located in Germany. JKIC focuses on space commercialization, developing global partnerships between the private space industry and investment entities, and supporting space-related businesses around the world.

PART V

JOINING THE MOVEMENT

CHAPTER SIXTEEN
MOONSHOTS

The opening of the space frontier is a really, really big deal. It is potentially as important as the industrial revolution, or even the agricultural revolution. Combining the nearly unlimited energy and material resources of our Solar System with emerging technologies will change everything about human civilization. It will profoundly affect the way we live, work, and play. This is not the task of a single generation or even a single century, but the choices this generation makes—both for the good and the bad—will have impacts that last for millennia.[1]

Bob Werb*

I tend to be attracted to moonshot initiatives because I want to make a difference, directly or indirectly, in everything I do. In 2017, I joined the founding team of Arch Mission Foundation, a nonprofit organization based in Los Angeles with a vision to "place enough backups in enough places around the solar system, on an ongoing basis, that our precious knowledge and biological heritage can never be lost," as explained by cofounder Nova Spivack.[2] Why? Historically, most civilizations fail—even the most prosperous and impressive (think of Ancient Maya, the Roman Empire, the Vikings, or Macedonia). After learning about Arch Mission, I realized my personal interest in developing and safeguarding personal and professional archives.

I see Arch Mission's social role in helping to preserve Earth's civilization and beyond as a potential bridge to build more understanding and empathy in our

★ **Bob Werb** cofounded the Space Frontier Foundation, a space advocacy nonprofit, in 1988 with Rick Tumlinson and James A. M. Muncy. He served as the Foundation's chair for many years before retiring in 2014. Werb is credited as being one of the creators of the term "NewSpace" as a movement and philosophy.

world. I recognize how fragile our cultures, knowledge, biological systems, and more are, and it's impossible to predict what information will be crucial in future years. As such, Arch Mission does not designate any data set as more valuable than another; while there are still limitations in data storage, it works as a neutral provider of safe storage for all of humanity.

The first successful effort was the Solar Library. In December 2017, we at Arch Mission provided the disc containing Isaac Asimov's *Foundation* trilogy to Elon Musk. The disc is now orbiting the Sun for the next thirty-million years, inside the glove compartment of Musk's Tesla Roadster—the famous SpaceX payload from the first Falcon Heavy flight, launched in February 2018. The launch generated massive attention, and the library—described in the launch webcast as one of the Easter eggs—piqued curiosity around the globe. After that launch, we would go on to complete several more space missions.

As individuals, we will all die in blink of an eye on a galactic timescale. What can live on for long time is civilization. Those who first go to other planets will face far more risk of death [and] hardship than those who stay. Over time, space travel will be safe [and] open to all.[3]

Elon Musk | Founder, SpaceX

On February 1, 2019, Arch Mission and Singapore-based SpaceChain announced that their partnership to launch a data archive into space had delivered its first payload: The Orbital Library (also known as the LEO Library). The Orbital Library contained an encrypted copy of *Wikipedia*; Nova Spivack explained in a press release that this library is "beginning a ring of backup data orbiting around the Earth, and constitutes the first extraterrestrial archive and first step in establishing more Arch libraries that will preserve human knowledge and culture."*

★ **Nova Spivack** is an entrepreneur and investor who has founded various startups and venture firms in the span of his successful career. He cofounded Arch Mission Foundation in 2015, a nonprofit organization with a goal to preserve humanity's history through data in space. To date, Arch Mission has developed various space libraries, launched via partnerships with NewSpace companies like SpaceX, SpaceIL, and SpaceChain.

The library marks an essential milestone for Arch Mission's goals: "Through massive replication around the solar system we will be able to guarantee that the Arch Libraries will never be lost—even millions to billions of years in the future," Spivack wrote.[4] In an interview with *GeekWire*, SpaceChain CEO Zee Zheng illuminated how space-based blockchain systems add new levels of security to transactions and information. "We are envisioning applications like ultra-secure encrypted messaging, a space-based distributed data center, etc. And of course, we will be able to facilitate blockchain transactions in rural areas, oceans and places that terrestrial network is not available," Zheng explained.[5]

T*he 2019 Lunar Library was our team and my moonshot—literally and figuratively. We struck a deal for SpaceIL to carry the first installation of the Lunar Library, "a 30-million-page archive of human history and civilization, covering all subjects, cultures, nations, languages, genres, and time periods."[6] In December 2018, I took a red-eye from Los Angeles to our partner lab in Rochester, New York, where we used a few limited, precious hours to finish the processing for the Lunar Library. Once we completed the work, I took two consecutive flights, traveling overnight to Israel, where I hand-delivered the payload to SpaceIL for integration on the Beresheet lander. SpaceIL then transferred the Beresheet to Florida, where SpaceX integrated it on a Falcon 9 rocket.*

The Falcon 9 launched smoothly on February 22, 2019 and arrived in lunar orbit on April 4, 2019. During that journey to the Moon, Beresheet was able to take some fantastic photos, including a few selfies with Earth in the background. Once again, humanity fixed its attention on an amazing moonshot. It's worth recounting SpaceIL's origin story. It began with three engineers in a pub who wanted to enter the Google Lunar XPRIZE and inspire the youth of their home country, Israel. They created SpaceIL as a nonprofit and became the last entrant to competition—and the only private, lunar-focused effort to date that has successfully made it to space and into lunar orbit. The Beresheet mission also put Israel on the map as one of seven nations to place an object in lunar orbit.

On April 11, 2019, Beresheet made a hard landing on the Moon, destroying the landing vehicle. The analysis indicated that the Lunar Library likely survived, although its specific location is unknown. Even if the library shattered, it would be similar to broken pottery shards; there would still be analog and compressed digital data in the broken pieces that could be read and extracted. It is now a treasure to one day be discovered.

The Arch Mission Lunar Library includes:

- 25 stacked, thin nickel films that Arch Mission insists can resist radiation, extreme temperatures, and other harsh conditions found in space for billions of years

- 60,000 pages of tiny analog images that can be viewed with optical microscope technology

- A full copy of *Wikipedia*

- More than 25,000 books

- Data for understanding over 5,000 languages[7]

In May 2019, Blue Origin flew the "Moonwalker Capsule," an archive of the 2018–2019 student submissions to the Conrad Challenge. Arch Mission's partnership with the Conrad Foundation celebrates the fiftieth anniversary of the Apollo Moon landings and "highlights the innovative spirit of today's young minds" along with past Conrad Challenge innovators.[8] Upcoming Arch Library missions include further installments of the Orbital Library satellite constellation and Lunar Library payloads; missions in development for the coming decade include the Mars Libraries and the Lagrange Libraries.

Lagrange points in space, often described as "parking spots," are prime locations for space stations, asteroid-hunting spacecraft, and astronomy alike. These points exist in a gravitational equilibrium between the Sun and Earth, which allows objects to remain almost completely still—meaning spacecraft in a Lagrange point require minimal fuel to maintain their position. Data communications speeds also remain high because the spacecraft never moves too far away from Earth. The physical conditions in Lagrange points are unique as well; shielded from the Sun, spacecraft don't experience light and heat interference from our parent star, nor do they need help staying cool. For these reasons, the planned James Webb Space Telescope will station in the Lagrange point known as L2.[9] Arch Mission intends to place a series of libraries in Lagrange points L4 and L5 "for long-term safekeeping and discovery" in the coming years.[10]

One might wonder why we do this at all, if the return on time and investment may not occur for lifetimes. On a personal level, it's fascinating to collaborate with those whose work legacy is intended to last billions of years. Universally, we understand that human culture and knowledge is as fragile now as it ever was before.

INNOVATING

Futurists are people who specialize in lots of different disciplines and the focus is not to predict what might happen next, but instead to forecast given what we know to be true today and doing extensive modeling using evidence and data, what might be the possible scenarios tomorrow and what do we do about it?[11]

Amy Webb | Quantitative Futurist

nnovations and discoveries are often a serendipitous business. When working on large, complex projects, we often end up inventing something else—in the process, we make an unexpected connection, and a lightbulb goes off. Suddenly, a solution to a past problem becomes evident, or you realize that there is a new way to think about your challenge. As Don Brancato, chief strategy architect at Boeing* attests, "I expect bursts of special activity, or special capability, in any projects that I do."[12] Let's put things clearly to make sure we're on the same proverbial page: disruption comes from the outside, while innovation usually comes from within.

Anytime you have humans thinking about something perceived as hard, complex, and far away, you have ancillary, serendipitous products, services, and capabilities that sort of show up. You're searching for something, and you discover penicillin—that's probably the most serendipitous thing that can happen.[13]

Don Brancato

Exploring our ideas can pay off in multiple ways, whether we reach our goal, create something new, or become inspired to connect dots that seem entirely unrelated. We must be ready and willing to take chances on our ideas. Opening our minds to the endless realms of possibility, envisioning what could exist—even if we don't know exactly how to make that happen quite yet—is, at the very least, a crucial starting point.

> Instead of innovating out from the present, what you
> want to do is invent the future from the future.
> Go out and live in the future and bring the future back.[14]

Alan Kay, "How to Invent the Future I," Lecture at Stanford University Center for Professional Development, 2017.

As we navigate forward, into the unknown, we can think about prominent innovators and the keys to their success. Boeing is a massive player in the space sector; its consistent progress in the industry has made it a leader in spaceflight. Peter Hoffman, Boeing's vice president of intellectual property management, shared in a *Washington Post* interview that Boeing's success depends significantly on creating a culture of innovation. Employees receive rewards for their innovative ideas and inventions every year, and the company has a technical fellowship program to help propel the top minds forward.

The company has an entire division called Boeing Research and Technology to pinpoint and develop the best technologies to benefit the company and its goals. Hoffman explained, "although it is only now becoming mainstream, we have been researching the use of 3D printing or additive manufacturing (AM) technologies in aircraft production for decades."[15]

Boeing also invests in fringe technologies and innovations. "Staying at the cutting edge of technology is very expensive," Hoffman said. "At Boeing we try to mitigate these costs by striking up business relationships with companies and researchers trying to solve the same problems we face. We co-invest in this research and share the results, which makes it more affordable for both parties."[16]

★ **Don Brancato** is the chief strategy architect at Boeing and was formerly the chief technologist at Hewlett Packard Enterprises. He has twenty-five years of experience as an enterprise architect, and his extensive skill set includes domain experience in advanced aerospace and security applications, space and aviation modeling/simulation, Big Data, and IoT. Brancato is also a standards author and keynote speaker, and he serves as a board adviser for Arch Mission Foundation, bioTope Project, and Xplorico.

Technology has a shelf life and we sometimes have the opportunity to share technologies that help less developed aerospace industries develop while we continue to invest in pushing the technology envelope on our new products. As long as we keep investing in the future, and keep a lead on our competition, we can remain competitive.[17]

Peter Hoffman | Vice President of Intellectual Property Management, Boeing

Collaboration within and outside of the space sector is crucial to innovation, especially because addressing the complex challenges that exist in space often requires multiple areas of expertise. For instance, we now know that there are Earth-like worlds within 1,500 light-years from us, and privately funded efforts are looking for ways to make interstellar travel a reality. Groups such as Positron Dynamics work on developing new types of propulsion that could allow humans to travel to Mars in less than one month, or to Kepler-452b—also described as Earth 2.0—in a trip lasting approximately twelve years (Kepler-452b is almost the same distance from its sun as Earth is to our Sun, which makes it highly desirable for researchers as a place to visit).[18] And yet, even if we had Positron Dynamics' proposed propulsion, we would need to address a multitude of advances in other areas. Communicating with spacecraft is different from communicating with aircraft on Earth because of the speed of light, physics, and the distance of our various spacecraft from Earth—and therefore requires scientific insight paired with advanced technologies. In the case of Positron, developing those solutions could mean better performing spacecraft, or new ways to supply power to remote bases in places such as Antarctica or the bottom of the ocean.

Every challenge has many solutions. One idea, project, or problem has the potential to result in numerous discoveries, and any of those discoveries could change the world as we know it. Space investor and venture capitalist Will Porteous attested that the benefits of an innovative mindset resulted in massive shifts within the satellite industry.* "It's what you've seen with these satellite constellations: people fundamentally rethinking how to build a space base capability. Part of it is to distribute that capability across what are essentially the nodes of a network, and part of it is putting out different technologies that the legacy satellite industry would consider riskier."[19] Prior to these shifts in mindset, the satellite sector suffered from stagnation—resistance to change and an unwillingness to try new things—for decades. "If you look at some of the architecture that is going on in a lot of our satellites, you will see technologies on those satellites that were introduced in the commercial market twenty-five years ago, and it's taken this long for the satellite industry to get comfortable with putting them on a spacecraft," Porteous pointed out. Ultimately, true progress only resulted from an ability of new entrants to look beyond industry traditions and envision another way to leverage the technology.

We could use this tactic to solve challenges within the launch sector, too. As Porteous explained, solutions will result "when we look at launch differently and ask what happens when launch is not this rare, elusive experience. When it's something that's much easier to access, and when you can launch a lot more frequently, you can start to rethink not only the resilience of that spacecraft—you can start to open your design envelope up to taking more risk technically and trying new things."

Above all, the critical component of the innovation process is mindset. Ask questions. Look at a challenge from new angles. Some of today's and yesterday's pioneers in this sector might not fully realize their plans—but it may not always be due to their initial idea or technology. Mismanagement, funding gaps, founder blowups, and burnouts are all possible. The reality is that much of today's attention focuses on marginally improved consumer technology iterations. The ability to see a challenge as open-ended, or to rethink the existing obstacles, can lead to the most impactful solutions.

★ **Will Porteous** is a general partner and chief operating officer of RRE Ventures, a venture capital firm based in New York. Porteous has over eighteen years of experience as an investor and has served on the board of more than twenty companies. He is currently a director of Breather, BuzzFeed, Nanit, Paperless Post, Pilot Fiber, Spaceflight (chair), Spire Global, and Ursa.

CHAPTER SEVENTEEN
FAILURES AND THE FUTURE

When I first started with the USC Rocket Propulsion Laboratory, we flew a bunch of tests. We failed many times, and I would argue that that's the only way we actually made progress. We learned so much by doing that, and the cost was nothing compared to launching into space over and over again and hoping it works.[1]

Dave Barnhart | Research Professor, Department of Astronautical Engineering, University of Southern California

One of the biggest obstacles for NewSpace is fear of failure. There is no denying that there's an almost infinite number of issues that can kill a startup—and the majority of startups fail. Though the exact percentage varies depending on whom you ask—some will say it's 60 percent, while others claim it's closer to 90 percent—the odds are intimidating. Whether you are an investor, entrepreneur, or policymaker, it's worth taking a moment to recognize that business is complicated. However, failures are a crucial component of progress. They teach, inspire, and often create foundations for success.

The SpaceIL lunar mission in 2019 serves as a strong example of learning from failure. A week after the crash landing, SpaceIL founder Morris Kahn announced via a video on Twitter that, "In the light of all the support that I've got—from all over the world—and the wonderful messages of support, and encouragement, and excitement," he and the company would be meeting first thing the next day to assemble a task force to begin working on Beresheet 2.0.[2] Six weeks later, SpaceIL tweeted, "Beresheet's journey to the Moon was already received as a successful, record-breaking journey. Instead we will seek out another, significant objective for Beresheet 2.0. More details to follow…"[3] This second effort will use the failures of the lunar mission to improve SpaceIL's odds for success. Kahn also relayed that Beresheet's crash did not deter him; rather, it encouraged him: "This is part of my message to the younger generation: Even if you do not succeed, you get up again and try."[4]

> I would say that 'to fail' is not to achieve the objective that the organization had. The research and development may create long-term value for the field, but not the value the company was originally after.[5]
>
> **Dezsö Molnár***

There are, in fact, many aspects of a "failure" that can hold value and potential. The key is to assess these efforts with the scientific method: determine what didn't work and *why*, figure out what went wrong, find what may have been missing. Figure out what could improve and what should change. Pinpoint the successful aspects—what *did* work—and take those learnings into the next pursuit.

> We're not here to make a profit. We're here to create an impact; this is how we set up SpaceIL at the very beginning. We could have set it up as a company, but we wanted to do this for the impact of it. We wanted to show the kids that they can dream big and that there is a way of achieving that. If you study hard and you understand your science and math and physics, you can achieve whatever you want. It's not just a dream.[6]
>
> **Yonatan Winetraub | Cofounder, SpaceIL**

Masten Space Systems, founded in 2004 by David Masten, has a long history of bouncing back from failures. From a botched first test flight to nearly shuttering after running out of funding (and being saved at the last second by an investor), to moving to the Mojave Desert, the first five years in the company were riddled with challenges and setbacks. Still, founder David Masten and his lean team of fifteen pushed forward with an unyielding determination to develop effective rockets that would help lower the barriers of entry into space.[7]

★ **Dezsö Molnár** is a licensed airplane and gyroplane pilot, flight engineer, and mechanic. He is a former transport jet pilot for the US Air Force and once served as crew chief for Craig Breedlove's "Spirit of America" land speed racing team. He was on the crew that built and tested rocket planes for the Rocket Racing League, and he was a judge for the original XPRIZE. At Truax Engineering, Molnár helped build the X1, the first private rocket ship intended for manned flight. He is now a staff inventor at WET Design in Los Angeles, California.

In 2009, Masten Space Systems scored the second-place prize for Level 1 of Northrop Grumman's Lunar Lander Challenge (funded by the NASA Centennial Challenges), a competition in which participants attempted to mimic a Moon launch and landing on a flat surface. The Masten Space Systems Xombie rocket's successful landing raked in a $150,000 prize. Level 2 of the competition was based on the same idea, except that the landing in this case would be on a rough surface comparable to the Moon's cratered topography. Masten opted to fly the Xoie rocket, which encountered various setbacks during the first Level 2 flight (including the oxygen tank bursting into flames after landing); however, Masten received an option to re-do the flight the next day. In a spectacular display of camaraderie that seems to occur frequently in the space sector, members of other participating teams rallied to aid Masten in troubleshooting and repairing the rocket. They completed the work only minutes before the designated launch—and the flights were successful. Masten walked away with a $1 million prize and a boosted reputation.[8]

In 2018, NASA selected Masten Space Systems as one of the nine companies to participate in its Commercial Lunar Payload Services program—an effort focused on delivering to-be-determined cargo, and eventually humans, to the Moon. NASA tapped the company again in 2019 to develop a crewed lunar lander prototype as part of the new Artemis program. Masten Space Systems then partnered with P3 Technologies, a propulsion company based in Jupiter, Florida, to develop electric pumps which will be used in the Artemis program. Masten and P3 explain that these e-Pumps, as they call them, provide multiple benefits compared to turbine-driven pumps. "They don't have the pressure drop associated with the turbine, and enable rapid engine starts and throttle changes, which are advantageous to in-space and lander propulsion systems," P3 president Philip Pelfrey relayed in a Masten press release.[9]

Masten CEO Sean Mahoney provided some insight into the company's activities during an interview, explaining that while they (and other space

★ **Sean Mahoney** is the chief executive officer of Masten Space Systems, an aerospace R&D and flight services company focused on reusability. Mahoney formerly served as the director of operations and then as the chief operating officer of Masten before becoming CEO in 2013.

startups) wait for the world to catch on to what they're doing, they look for ways to create value, remain viable, and stay relevant.* "The difference between being wrong and being early is virtually indistinguishable," Mahoney said. But Mahoney believes that there are ways to help enable industry progress: once more people think about how to leverage and use space, or how it affects them and their businesses, more and more opportunities will emerge. "Companies who spend time *now* to factor what space can do for them could benefit highly," Mahoney attested.[10] This also means that incumbents, startups, and governments alike need to make more noise regarding the importance of space—and to do that, they need to demonstrate value for people outside of the industry.

Another key theme at Masten is remaining realistic: "Balance the vision with the understanding of what you can actually do," Mahoney said. Don't rely on miracles to make your plan work. The lunar mission, for example, will be bumpy—therefore, those at Masten build the company to be gritty, resilient, and able to push through the rough areas ahead.

As a rocket engineer, [David Masten] has long advocated for relentlessly testing and tweaking reusable machines rather than trying to nail designs on the first try. This means that even though Masten is tiny, it can lay claim to forms of experience that larger companies lack. Xombie, Masten's first operational rocket, has flown 227 times— which the firm claims is a record for any rocket-powered airframe.[11]

Haley Cohen Gilliland, "The World's Smallest Rocket Company," *MIT Technology Review,* **June 26, 2019.**

Failures enable us to not only make new mistakes but to create genuine and lasting innovation. If you are not occasionally failing in what you do, you are unlikely to achieve great things.

- *The more great people you hire, the easier it is to hire great people. Positive feedback can be powerful.*
- *The better the quality of your existing shareholders, the easier it is to attract new high-quality shareholders.*
- *Having smart, talented and accomplished lead investors is invaluable in raising funds.[12]*

Tren Griffin, "A Dozen Things I Learned Being Involved in one of the Most Ambitious Startups Ever Conceived (Teledesic)," *25iq,* **July 23, 2016.**

Not all innovations happen at the right time, and often, progressive ideas and technologies don't receive the support and financial backing needed to survive. Failures don't mean that the entire sector is doomed, nor that specific subsectors are unworthy of investment. When failures occur, human talent can move to other projects and opportunities.

Game developer John Carmack, known for his role as the cofounder of id Software and for video games such as *Doom*, spearheaded a reusable suborbital effort called Armadillo Aerospace for several years. Carmack paid for gear and hardware while volunteers ran the team. In August 2013, Carmack put the initiative on ice saying, "I've basically expended my 'crazy money' on Armadillo."[13]

Two years later, in the spring of 2015, John Quinn and David Mitchell revived the effort under a new name, Exos Aerospace, with the same mission: to develop crewed suborbital space vehicles. Quinn explained, "The Exos team is taking what John Carmack's ethos was and proceduralizing and formalizing it." The team's reusable rocket, the Suborbital Active Rocket with Guidance (SARGE), "can serve payloads that were previously not feasible to experiment with in space" with their ability to "bring those payloads directly back to the launch area about 20 minutes after launch."[14] SARGE intends to facilitate new in-space discoveries, from research to manufacturing capabilities and beyond.

Beal Aerospace is another classic failure-turned-opportunity. In 1997, entrepreneur and bank owner Andrew Beal founded Beal Aerospace with the intent to create a private rocket vehicle to launch communications satellites. Unfortunately, NASA was not ready to take on commercial partners like Beal Aerospace—at that point in time, NASA saw them as a competitive threat. Despite having invested substantial resources and making admirable progress, Beal shut down the company in October of 2000, "citing the difficulty a private company faced in competing with NASA's subsidized space programs."[15]

Beal's efforts were the rights ones; unfortunately, they occurred at the wrong time. On the bright side, Beal's failure helped set some of the industry's evolution in motion. SpaceX ended up acquiring some assets from Beal; this initial access to crucial information and inexpensive assets may have contributed significantly to SpaceX's early success, which included procuring NASA as one of its first customers.[16]

There's a silly notion that failure's not an option at
NASA. Failure is an option here. If things are not
failing, you are not innovating enough.[17]
Elon Musk | Founder, SpaceX

M ost failures in the space sector result from at least one of the following issues: market, timing, leadership and management, technology, or funding. In some cases, failed efforts can be either revived or built upon in future endeavors.

In the late 1980s, engineers from Motorola conceived of Iridium. They then spent the first half of the 1990s developing the plan for a constellation of seventy-seven satellites that would serve the globe with telecommunications, using the company's own proprietary handsets. By providing a new type of mobile phone that used satellite constellations to receive cellular signal in remote areas of the world, Iridium seemed poised for massive success.

However, Iridium quickly became a notorious example of stellar technology that failed to align its business plan with a viable target demographic. Throughout the eleven years it took to develop the technology and product, the rise of digital mobile phones (and their widespread adoption) stripped Iridium's initial target markets. Although the constellation launched successfully, the revenue was not enough to cover the debt. Iridium secured just 55,000 out of the 600,000 customers needed in its guarantees to debt holders, and the promising company went on to become one of the largest bankruptcies at that time in history.[18]

Iridium's failure can be attributed to several factors, including a vastly inadequate level of customer demand validation, adoption of a "too big to fail" approach by the main companies instead of a step-by-step development approach, and an absence of interest in a more affordable minimum viable product (MVP) that could have been achieved in a shorter timeframe and with a lower budget.

The most crucial component to this failure was how quickly other companies responded to the gaps in the cell phone market during Iridium's long development time, filling the spaces that Iridium assumed would still be waiting for its expensive (and niche) service. Iridium thus failed in large part *because* it took so long to enter the market. Business conditions never stay static for long—there is a good reason why investors prefer ventures with a brief time to market. As industry expert Jeff Greason attested, "Speed is life."

The Iridium saga was a valuable learning experience for the investors and technical managers in the space industry today. At the time of Iridium's development, the world was accustomed to seeing gargantuan, NASA-style moonshots. Now, space projects can exist in many different forms and sizes. For example, a company like OneWeb attempting such a big project today would use a healthier approach and progressively develop the product-market fit by taking onboard customer feedback earlier.

Iridium itself even ended up learning from many of its mistakes. After the effort was brought out of bankruptcy by private investors, the company went through a restructuring and proceeded to achieve relatively strong business, focusing largely on its initial demographics where the having a satellite phone is necessary or very helpful, such as in the military, energy exploration, and journalism.

You have to take risks and be willing to take risks. If you come up with a business idea and there's no risk there, it's probably already been done—and done well. So, you have to have something that might not work, and you have to accept that your business is going to be, in many ways, an experiment—and it might fail. That's okay, that's what risk is. At Amazon, we still take risks all the time—we encourage it, we talk about failure. We should be failing. Our failures have to grow with the company. We need big failures if we're going to be moving the needle; we need billion dollar-scale failures. If not, we're not swinging hard enough. Everybody knows that if you go to the plate and swing hard, you're going to hit more home runs, but you're also going to strike out more often. When you're inventing something—the difference with baseball is that you have a max amount of four runs—in business, every once in a while, when you swing hard, you get a thousand runs. So, the risk is capped on the downside, and for all practical purposes, it's unlimited on the upside. As a result, because of that probability distribution, you really should be swinging hard—and you are going to fail a lot, and it's okay—and you need to have a culture that supports that.[19]

Jeff Bezos | Founder, Blue Origin

The he possibility of failure should not act as a deterrent for risk-taking and creativity. Let's consider an example from another industry. The American business Radio Shack, a retail supplier of electronics supplies for home and hobby use, is now a shadow of its former self. A longtime leader in sales of radio and telecommunications equipment, Radio Shack began its long decline after peaking in 1999. Management issues on the corporate and retail levels, an inability to keep up with market trends and customer demands, and the emergence of big competitors like Best Buy and Amazon all led to its demise. Radio Shack filed for bankruptcy first in 2015 and again in 2017.

Overall, it's difficult to say if a downfall like Radio Shack's could have been avoided (as the saying goes, hindsight is 20/20). However, it is worth considering missed opportunities. Back in 2001, Radio Shack and the Russian space program co-created a chance to work on a space-related project through Jeffrey Manber (the NewSpace pioneer who previously worked for MirCorp and is now the CEO of Nanoracks).[20] Unfortunately, there were some missteps, in part due to NASA preventing American astronauts from participating, and the project ultimately failed.

As Radio Shack went back to business as usual, new subsectors of commercial space were emerging. Had Radio Shack kept its eye on space activities and entered one of those markets, even in a limited way with something like CubeSat technology, it may have discovered viable business opportunities; perhaps it would have evolved into "Satellite Shack." Like we saw with Iridium, when there are gaps in a market, it's only a matter of time before someone—whether the government, a large company, or a passionate startup—finds a way to capitalize on the opportunity. The idea of a "Satellite Shack" is now an industry of its own, led by NewSpace companies around the world that include Clyde Space, AWS Ground Station, Gom Space, Planet, Astrobotic, SpaceIL, and Surrey Satellite Technology.

Ultimately, understanding who has innovated before and identifying the potentials for success can lead to spectacular accomplishments. Investors, entrepreneurs, startups, established companies, students, and everyone in between benefit from failures and the gaps they leave. Let's consider another one of the most notable NewSpace failures: XCOR Aerospace.

XCOR existed for eighteen years as a startup specializing in rocket engines and suborbital flight. When I co-led an investment in XCOR in 2008 through my investment entity, Desert Sky Holdings, the company was taking various contract work to keep the lights on. As XCOR came closer and closer to running out of money (for the last time), it also lost a critical contract to develop ULA's Vulcan engine, and the business was left with few options. I, along with acting CEO Michael Blum and a board member, went into overdrive to find potential solutions. However, private equity groups want companies with revenue, and XCOR was out of contracts; other aerospace companies passed on acquiring XCOR. Members of the board were helping to fund payroll. After a final private investment opportunity didn't work out, XCOR filed for Chapter 7 liquidation bankruptcy in November 2017.

While developing fantastic technologies throughout its lifespan, XCOR suffered from management issues that eventually became insurmountable. It also took various forms of financing from economic development groups in Midland, Texas and Florida, which proved to be unnecessary distractions. Additionally, XCOR was forced to put its main project, the Lynx rocket, on the backburner because there wasn't enough financing to support the full development. Throughout the many issues, management insulated itself from what was happening, both internally and externally.

Henry Vanderbilt, a former XCOR employee and stakeholder, penned his thoughts on the company's failure after the bankruptcy. "The company's technology was not the problem. Quite the opposite. ... The company's expertise at flying winged rockets at ridiculously high op rates and low op costs was very real, and [was] thoroughly embedded in the design," Vanderbilt said.[21] He posited that mismanagement, specifically "founder's syndrome,"† was the primary issue.

Jeff Greason, one of XCOR's founders, shared some of his own ideas about the failure during an interview.[22] From Greason's perspective, there were two main problems; first, the Lynx rocket took more time to develop than XCOR ever imagined. Greason noted that, in retrospect, they should have pivoted and

---

†**Founder's syndrome** is a phenomenon often cited in the tech and nonprofit worlds wherein a company's founder is resistant to change in organizational structures (specifically, in relinquishing any of their own power or the key roles they have appointed), such that the leadership becomes stifling and damaging to the company and other employees.

done something easier: "We should have taken a smaller step to a product and told the investors that we were changing plans to do so." The other paramount factor was that "when our major customer shorted our contract in 2008, we should have just gone out of business rather than limping along and bringing in investors with conflicting agendas to stay alive," he said—even adding his speculation that, had this not happened, XCOR might have survived to this day. Overall, the big lesson to learn is a rather simple one: if things are too difficult, find a way to take smaller, easier steps.

Despite its various obstacles, XCOR achieved great significance in its lifetime, both as a business and in its effects on the space industry. In an email written to the investors and shareholders, Michael Blum relayed the news of the company's closing after failing to secure viable investments. He also shed light on the positive impacts of startups taking risks. "The advent of entrepreneurial endeavors has led to significant cost reductions in recent years. ... This trend will continue[,] and with it[,] low-cost access to space for humans will arrive. I am certain of this," Blum wrote.[23] Vanderbilt also noted, "XCOR getting all this technology done ... for a total burn over the years that I'd estimate at about $50 million, is nothing short of a miracle of technical vision and skill by a LOT of very smart, dedicated people."[24]

Planetary Resources, which was acquired by ConsenSys in October 2018, is another case of failure's long-term benefit. The splashy, Seattle-based startup was formed in 2009, though it remained quiet for its first three years before finally announcing its plans for mining space resources in 2012. In 2016, Planetary Resources received substantial funding from Luxembourg for space resource mining prospecting and capability development. The country itself provided $13.7 million in direct investments, and public investment bank SNCI provided an additional $14.5 million in grants.[25] By 2018, Planetary Resources had completed tests on its in-orbit asteroid prospecting technology. However, after the company suffered funding setbacks and was forced to lay off many of its employees, it began to lose steam.[26]

The company initially invested too much into promoting its investor and advisor ties without sound customer and user development. In 2018, ConsenSys acquired the company's assets, with nothing else left but the Planetary Resources attorney and CEO.[27] Sources close to the company claim that it spent close to $49 million in capital before its acquisition. It's also worth mentioning that Deep Space Industries (DSI), Luxembourg's other space mining investment, was acquired by Bradford Space in 2019 and now focuses primarily on propulsion.[†]

The long-term strategic value of NewSpace startups like Planetary Resources and DSI, founded with bold visions, is not whether they themselves achieve their objectives, but whether they help humanity push forward toward those objectives. Viewed through that lens, both companies were immensely successful. They promoted a global discussion about private sector deep space exploration, developed innovative technologies along that road map, and played vital roles collaborating with Luxembourg toward a viable legal regime.

Even if each individual company took a different path to maximize value for its shareholders, we are now much closer to making deep space resource utilization a reality because of their audacious visions, their investors' commitment, and their teams' hard work. They paved the way for other astropreneurs to pick up the mantle and carry humanity to the next step in that long road toward deep space exploration and permanent off-world settlement.

This is all to say that if, as a culture, we can better embrace failure and be of better support to those failing, we might be able to grow and inch ourselves upwards in our collective, emotional intelligence. This emotional intelligence, combined with ingenuity and creativity, sets the stage for more successful opportunities, endeavors, and leaders. As a civilization, we will all benefit from adopting better ways to support, rather than penalize, those who fail.

The problem I've seen in companies with big aspirational goals, like XCOR and DSI, is that there's an internal tension between that long-term aspirational goal and the mere terminality of the business world

---

[†]*For transparency, I was a minor stakeholder in DSI, and now Bradford.*

and financing. Everyone has to be comfortable with claiming success if all you did was get through the first part of your roadmap. Maybe you won't be providing the reusable access to space like XCOR was trying to do, or maybe you're not going to be doing the asteroid mining that Deep Space Industries and Planetary Resources were trying to do, but at least you're doing your part towards that aspiration. You've got to see that you're pushing the ball forward for humanity while still making sound business decisions and finding ways of creating value for the shareholders.[28]

Guillermo Söhnlein*

We are in a new age: an age of possibility. As the nebulous nature of the space sector becomes clearer over time, formerly impossible ideas appear more and more tangible. There is also a generation—possibly multiple generations—in this current era that believes in progress and thinks that we should increase risk. Why not experiment, fail fast, and then take those learnings to continue pushing forward? This is the scientific method at its core.

Don't be afraid to get fired. I've been fired a number of times, and when you're trying to change things—it's like the old quote from Machiavelli about how the hardest thing to do is not to become discouraged; you just have to keep pushing forward. In fact, one measure that you're on the right track is the measure of who's opposing you.[29]

**Pete Worden, Ph.D. | Chair, Breakthrough Prize
Foundation for Breakthrough Initiatives**

★ **Guillermo Söhnlein** is an entrepreneur and investor who has played a strong role in NewSpace development. He founded the International Association of Space Entrepreneurs (IASE) in 2003 to encourage private space sector activities around the world, and then Space Angels Network in 2006, an angel investor group focused on early-stage space ventures. He has also created numerous successful technology companies and ocean exploration ventures. He currently serves as CEO of Blue Marble Exploration (which he also cofounded), an exploration company that organizes submersible expeditions in deep ocean, polar, high altitude, and space environments. Söhnlein is also the founder and managing member of Fortivo Holdings, a partner with Nexxus Ventures, a board member of SynapseMX, the chair of the board of directors at WayPaver Foundation, and an advisor for Kubos, Orbit Fab, and Spike Aerospace.

CHAPTER EIGHTEEN

BETTER BUSINESS MODELS

What we need is to have some core discovery, some breakthrough, something that just turns the eye of every operator in any industry—and by virtue of that, that'll turn the eye of every investor. That's a little bit like what happened with Terra Bella. Because in any frontier industry, what we need to see next is investment dollars that have been attracted into the existing part. And by the way, space has been around for eons, it's just the fact that the privatization has really begun to increase.[1]

Brandon Farwell*

Along with investment growth and innovative forms of funding, space startups are catching up with industry standards (i.e., profit margins and operating ratios)—and beginning to surpass expectations. There are, however, still many obstacles.

One common issue for startups, particularly in the space industry, is the basic business model—in other words, combining value with sustainability. Kartik Kumar, an interplanetary scientist and aerospace engineer, aptly illustrated this challenge. "The key thing that we've learned over the last couple of years is that a space business in its mechanics is largely not defined by being 'space,' but rather by being a business. If you're building a space business, the first thing you need to get right is how to build a business," Kumar said.

★ **Brandon Farwell** is a partner at XFund, an early-stage venture capital firm based in Silicon Valley that partners leading venture capital firms with universities around the world to enable the strongest minds and ideas. Prior to XFund, Farwell served as an investor focused on software for Draper Fisher Jurvetson and Rothenberg Ventures. His passions lie in emerging technologies, specifically machine intelligence, robotics, space, autonomous vehicles, VR/AR, and drones.

The two aspects that are typically overlooked, but nonetheless critical, for NewSpace are financial development and market viability. As Kumar* pointed out, "Most if not all companies are missing, from what I've seen, a strong chief financial officer (CFO). And that's not accidental; that's because these businesses are not built around a CFO. But, in a lot of ways, the CFO is the most important person in the company."[2]

Many NewSpace startups typically comprise mostly engineers—who are no doubt necessary to thrive—but these organizations also need smart financial discipline and strategy in the beginning stages. Lisa Rich, frontier tech investor and a founder of space-focused investment firm Hemisphere Ventures and private space exploration company Xplore, noted in an interview that "It's important to understand that space is a highly intricate field that requires more sophistication, more diligence, and a higher level of accountability. The engineers are not the ones who succeed in space; the successes come from those with a business mind and who understand how to build markets in this new era of space exploration."[3] She made clear that while space is now available for anyone to access, it's not a sector for the faint of heart. "It requires time and exposure to understand the sector, and the level of expertise requires industry veterans who can supply a 'shortcut to knowledge,'" Rich explained. But, she said, a dedicated entrepreneur or investor has a massive opportunity in front of them. "Space has a higher barrier to entry, but it's a feasible pathway to extraordinary revenues for those who take the time to understand the sector and create strong business models," Rich emphasized.

Frank Salzgeber, head of the Technology Transfer and Business Incubation Office at the European Space Agency, reiterated some of the main roadblocks for the growing sector. "Space's problem right now is not the technology; it's the business model," he said. "The key to space development today is building

---

★ **Kartik Kumar** is an aerospace engineer and planetary scientist. He cofounded satsearch in 2015, a space industry marketplace dedicated to indexing the products and services of the global space sector—with a goal of democratizing access to space by expanding the global supply chain. Kumar also serves as the National Point of Contact (Netherlands) for the Space Generation Advisory Council and as an analog astronaut for the Austrian Space Forum (OeWF).

the infrastructure. That costs a lot of money, but it's how all the big industries were able to grow—energy, telephones, and so on. And investors know that if you have the right infrastructure, you can then make a lot of money." Salzgeber sees a world of potential for the space economy, from creating new markets to bringing education and equality to the world, all depending on how the industry shifts its mindset to become more aggressive and innovative. "The problem is scaling up, and this is a thing where the US model is moving—it's about making things grow quickly. First growth, then revenue. The rest of the world is first revenue, then growth," he noted.

Astro Digital is one NewSpace startup pursuing such new methods to scale their satellite and data services. In an interview, cofounder and CEO Chris Biddy explained that they focus on a model that they refer to as "Mission as a Service," which is "essentially providing a full turnkey mission to a customer, including the regulatory licensing, logistics, and infrastructure that comes with operating a satellite."* This process counters the typical venture capital standard of receiving a large chunk of funding and then building a system before generating revenue; instead, Biddy said, "we're moving into a context where we can build the system out in phases where the customer goes on the journey with us." Biddy expects effective and faster results from this strategy, emphasizing that "When you can get to low, single-digit millions per satellite built and launched, and then have kind of this subscription model with monthly recurring payments, the economics start to work out where your revenue becomes $10 million or $15 million a year over five to seven years."[4]

★ **Chris Biddy** has a background in mechanical engineering and over a decade of experience working in NewSpace. He is currently the cofounder and chief executive officer of Astro Digital (formerly known as Aquila Space), a startup based in Silicon Valley that provides data monitoring via imaging satellite constellations as well as logistical support for clients that spans licensing and regulations to launch and operations. He previously served as the vice president of engineering for Stellar Exploration (an aerospace product startup) and as vice president of research and development for Canopus Systems US (a Silicon Valley satellite startup).

Understanding the market is another integral element for startups to survive; it can also serve as a key differentiator that catalyzes success. Jason Dunn, cofounder and director of Made In Space, recounted that his startup used this technique to great avail: "We built the entire company on exponential thinking, on forecasting technologies using some highly accurate models to predict where the technologies would be headed. So, we completely understood where 3D printing and robotics were headed in 2010 and were able to build a company based on that."* Dunn also clarified that market forecasting set Made In Space apart from other companies who looked at robotics, providing a further edge for the startup.[5]

You want to invest in people who are looking at integral solutions—not just the machine but the design and the material, the whole package. Because if I can make a machine that prints things out super-fast but can't integrate with other software, or can only use a limited amount of material, then it isn't terribly valuable. So, try to look at the entire solution, because you may come across something that is bigger and more valuable than you initially expected.[6]

Federico Sciammarella, Ph.D.*

The other vital point for Made In Space was a future-focused mindset, both in terms of its own business and the entire industry landscape. "You have to create companies that can get us from A to B, and companies getting started in the space industry need to identify a first step they can take that can be monetized and commercialized," Dunn said, adding, "My biggest piece of advice is to *think big, but start small.* For us, our small step was a 3D printer on the International Space

★ **Jason Dunn** is the cofounder and director of Made In Space, a US-based company that develops innovative space manufacturing technology in an effort to establish sustainable, in-space infrastructure.

★ **Federico Sciammarella, Ph.D.** is a metallurgical and materials engineer. A champion of the advanced manufacturing field, he is currently the president and chief technology officer of MxD, a nonprofit focused on innovative manufacturing solutions. A strong supporter of STEAM studies, he also teaches at the Northern Illinois University College of Engineering and Engineering Technology. Sciammarella has authored numerous peer reviewed journal articles and has received various professional honors for his work.

Station that is useful today, even with current 3D printing technology. And a 3D printer on the space station was not the purpose of our company—the purpose of our company is that one day, nothing is launched from Earth, everything is manufactured in space." Dunn concluded by reiterating the point that the company's initial model was "a very small step compared to the big vision, but it's one that we could build a business around."[7]

While the business side of NewSpace may require a more pragmatic approach, there is still ample room to combine creativity with critical thinking—and the companies that synthesize practical business sense with cutting-edge execution are leading the race.

Sector forerunner SpaceX is well known for crushing timelines, traditions, and building new avenues for industry-wide progress. Musk and his trailblazing space effort undoubtedly have many variables behind their success; the one worth looking at now is their strategic ethos. In an interview following a public update on the Starship spacecraft in October 2019, Musk shared one of the business's most valuable secrets: spending the time and energy to figure out what questions are worth asking. Musk explained that this approach is the true game-changer, because "product errors reflect the organizational errors. One department will design to the constraints that the other department has given them, without calling into question those constraints or saying 'those constraints are wrong,'" Musk said. "You should actually take the approach that the constraints you are given are guaranteed to be, to some degree, wrong—because the counterpoint would be that they're perfect."[8] For SpaceX, this may in fact be the golden rule for truly groundbreaking achievements.

Salzgeber, who is passionate about the private sector influencing the industry's future, substantiated Musk's mindset. "Startups are what space needs because they can take risks, they can ask the tough questions and develop the right solutions. This is how innovation works," Salzgeber said. "This the ability to take risks. The big corporations and the government space agencies aren't willing to take risks."[9]

Question your constraints. It doesn't matter if the person who handed those constraints won a Nobel Prize—even Einstein was wrong some of the time.

Elon Musk | Founder, SpaceX

These passioned arguments about business constraints relate back to many of our other success stories and insights. As Kartik Kumar reminds us, "Space is a place, and space technology is a tool or a suite of tools. What you're still trying to do is solve problems on Earth." He further stressed that "Space is exciting because it offers an opportunity to solve a bunch of problems that maybe we were not able to solve before, or could only solve poorly, by current solutions."[10] NewSpace is a special corner of the global industry which must understand the rules in order to break them—and as we've seen, many of its leaders are equipped with both the fervor and the talent to disrupt the way we understand the world.

There's no magic pixie dust—there's nothing that special about the space industry. You have to have the fundamentals right: focus on customers, make sure the business model works and that you have a product that people want, and find people who are better than you are at everything that you need done. Then, execute—and execute well. That's the way to build a business.[11]

Daniel Faber*

★ **Daniel Faber** is a seasoned entrepreneur in aerospace and mining with a background in growing startups into successful, profitable companies. He is the chief executive officer of Orbit Fab, an in-orbit fuel supply startup based in Silicon Valley; on the board of advisors for the National Space Society, a nonprofit focused on creating a spacefaring civilization; and the chief executive officer of Space Arena, a space entertainment company in development. Faber is also the president and chief technology officer of Heliocentric Technologies (which he founded in 2005), a research, technology development, and commercialization company focused on various space industry subsectors, including satellites and asteroid mining. Additionally, he served as the chief executive officer of Deep Space Industries for five years, where he built a viable technology business and grew DSI's revenue from zero to $10 million.

SUPPORTIVE SYSTEMS

I think it's very important to have a feedback loop, where
you're constantly thinking about what you've done and
how you could be doing it better. I think that's the single
best piece of advice: constantly think about how you could
be doing things better and questioning yourself.[12]

Elon Musk | Founder, SpaceX

As a space startup grows and expands, it's necessary to attract new talent, new partners, and potential customers. Advocacy groups, incubators, and accelerators are therefore crucial in NewSpace development. These organizations encourage larger companies as well as space sector incumbents to invest directly into smaller, non-traditional startups as a way to work together, bolster the emerging private sector, and provide new opportunities.

Advocacy groups (*such as the Aerospace & Defense Forum, which I cofounded in 2010*), actively seek to facilitate conversations between the space sector, other industries, and government through events and conferences that merge cross-industry interests. Some of these conversations have been ongoing for years, but with increased investment activity now bolstering NewSpace-enabled applications and infrastructure, it may soon become easier for non-space industries to justify partnerships.

Incubators and accelerators play important parts to support innovation and enable business growth in emerging sectors. While the two models are often considered interchangeable, they have several distinct differences. Incubators focus primarily on developing new ideas that can be evolved into a minimum viable product and functional business or company. They tend to have flexible timelines and loose constraints, providing the startup or individual with ample room to experiment and grow. This is where a seedling idea is set with ideal conditions; from there, the incubator can try to match some of those conditions to help spur growth. They can be run by separate organizations, government groups, investment groups, or corporations.

Accelerators, on the other hand, are designed for rapid development of early businesses and their product. There is an application process to join an accelerator (Y Combinator is a very selective one, for example); they also require businesses to have a minimum viable product. Accelerators often have short, defined timelines (somewhere between two and six months) and provide seed funding (in exchange for equity), along with mentorship, networking, and business resources to get the startup off the ground quickly. The process ends with a demo day where the startup pitches to investors, often angel groups and venture capital firms.

I'm a huge proponent for corporate venture, and I was always really frustrated—there's Facebook ventures, Google ventures, Intel ventures—there are all kinds of technology ventures, but none of them are for space. Most of the time, what the startups need most is someone helping them through the steps and the problems that they don't have experience in, whether it's investment or product markets. We've got to progress this to the point where it's easy to create something. We're still a step or two away from that, but it's happening.[13]

Monica Jan*

O ver the years, I have had several distinctly different experiences with accelerators of varying models. My first experience was a collaboration with Aeroinnovate (which came out of the University of Wisconsin) through my involvement with Space Angels Network. Oshkosh, Wisconsin is the headquarters of the Experimental Aircraft Association, which hosts AirVenture, the largest (and one of the oldest-running) airshows in the world. While mostly aviation-focused, AirVenture also features space-related exhibitions and activities. I was connected to Aeroinnovate via angel investor Richard Leamon, a longtime attendee and supporter of AirVenture. I participated along with other teammates from Space Angels Network in a hands-on event where we worked on identifying sponsors and organized entrepreneurship-focused programming to get startups in front of aerospace-interested investors. Much of this experience centered on building

★ **Monica Jan** is the senior director of strategy and customer experience for Virgin Orbit, the satellite division of Virgin Galactic. She is a cofounder and former managing partner of Syndicate 708, an accelerator focused on deep-tech and space-related startups. During her time at Northrop Grumman, Jan's work on a satellite switching subsystem won the Chairman's Innovation Award. She is a graduate of the University of Pennsylvania's Wharton School and serves as the vice chair of the Wharton Angel Network.

connections within the space network, and the process culminated in a pitch event where entrepreneurs presented their efforts to investors.

Several years later, I participated in the Starburst Accelerators pitch events as an attendee. These events, which took place around the United States, centered on entrepreneurs pitching (in person) to investors, strategic organizations, and other professionals. The unique aspect of this effort is that Starburst works with corporate partners to help matchmake for the startups (a form of what I call "external business development"). Audience members also provided feedback and a "score" during and after the pitches, which offered useful metrics for the startups to measure how their businesses were received by a larger and more diverse group.

I n 2016, Starburst announced a $200 million fund to invest in startups. A strong proponent of collaboration and future-focused initiatives, Starburst now stands as the number one space startup accelerator. Van Espahbodi, Starburst's cofounder and managing partner, commented that today they see "an unprecedented number of technologists and innovators that are being connected to the business enablers." Starburst currently has eight locations across the globe and has accelerated over two hundred startups.[14]

> *We don't want to ignore who else might be out there. By opening that door, we're entertaining other challengers into that frame, which defensively forces the established suppliers to think differently about how they want to work within the sector. Previously, there's been more of a positive discrimination model that forced set-aside contracts for small businesses. However, I don't think that's been an effective model; what it basically does is create this vicious cycle of people who know how to play the procurement game with the government rather than become a competitive threat and productize in ways that established suppliers can't. In other words, there are more doors opening for the non-traditional players to fan the fires that are shaking up the established way of doing things.[15]*

Van Espahbodi | Cofounder & Managing Partner, Starburst Aerospace

Syndicate 708 (formerly LightSpeed Innovations), is an accelerator that focuses primarily on deep tech startups in sectors with high barriers to entry, such as space and AI. The program provides a large network of experts, mentors, and industry-specific investors during an intensive business boot-camp, and is centered on creating an ecosystem for astropreneurs "to mature to the point where investors actually want to have them in their portfolio," explained cofounder Monica Jan.[16] Efforts like these have been crucial for educating both individual and corporate corporate investors, and helping create a stronger environment for investment funds to flow.

For some context, Jan is a former satellite engineer turned MBA consultant who was looking at ways to help grow the aerospace market in Southern California. To assist the process, I provided leads and introductions to help inform her business model research and development. The result was the creation of LightSpeed Innovations with Ellen Chang. Both Ellen and Monica earned their MBAs from the University of Pennsylvania, and the accelerator follows a cohort model which, from my understanding, is influenced from their time in business school.

In 2017, I served in an advisory role for LightSpeed, participating in the cohort from January to May as a mentor. The process included both live and online events and meetings, with the startups working remotely for the majority of the five-month experience. (This accelerator operates heavily on the "lean" principles advocated by Steve Blank.) At the end of the cohort, the startups pitched their opportunity to a group of investors and professionals (who I describe as "strategics") in a meeting that included both in-person and virtual participants.

Our primary mission is to build up the aerospace entrepreneurial ecosystem, where the focus of the companies is primarily private/commercial space. We believe founders who have taken on the challenge of building a space startup need tremendous support and guidance. Success would be touching more and more astropreneurs to help them understand the need to balance market and technology perspectives. We believe this will provide the foundation for a successful space industrial base supported by commercial revenues, witnessed by these companies being purchased or going public.[17]

Ellen Chang*

★ **Ellen Chang** is a cofounder and board member of Syndicate 708, an accelerator focused on early-stage deep tech startups. Chang spent twelve years at Northrop Grumman as a systems engineer and project manager. A graduate of the University of Pennsylvania's Wharton School, she now serves as co-president of the Wharton Aerospace Community and as chair of the Wharton Angel Network (SoCal).

Shaun Arora,* managing director of MiLA Capital, noted that space tech is a big focus for their group. MiLA, a venture capital firm focused on supporting and building out venture-scalable technology, originated as a hardware- and software-focused accelerator known as Make in LA in 2015. After four years of accelerator cohorts and investments in nineteen different startups, Arora and team evolved the accelerator into MiLA Capital, which leverages its accelerator roots to create turbocharged investment strategies for "tech you can touch" companies. In an interview, Arora said, "The entrepreneurs entering space tech are motivated not by financial outcomes but by a greater belief that amazing feats in engineering are possible," and that MiLA Capital realizes "that ambitious quests necessitate the invention of new technologies for established and emerging markets. Those founders know that there are many problems on Earth that need to be solved."

Arora also pointed to the vital role of accelerators in a time where many companies lack the opportunity to test at NASA facilities, which many startups complain are bottlenecked and expensive. Arora explained, "Since there are pains, we have come across founders looking to resolve some of those bottlenecks. There are new and exciting ways to de-risk space startups with and without NASA resources."[18]

I wish we competed more with the federal government. Only 0.57 percent of our federal budget is spent on "General Science, Space, and Technology." Angel investors and, increasingly, venture capital, are being deployed into space due to the federal funding shortfall. We are excited that there are more accelerators also embracing the new space race. However, despite [the new] Space Force, we have political stakeholders without a singular space focus and an industry struggling to attract and retain the best talent in an incredibly competitive hiring market.[19]

Shaun Arora | Managing Director, MiLA Capital

★ **Shaun Arora** is the managing director of MiLA Capital, a venture capital firm based in Los Angeles. MiLA leverages its origins and experiences as a former accelerator to create turbocharged investment strategies at the pre-seed and seed stages for startups developing high-potential technology in sectors like aerospace, climate tech, and automation.

M oonshot Space Company (Moonshot), based in Melbourne, Australia, is another organization focused on developing a space-faring community. Since its creation in 2016, the company has been building an international space economy framework by bringing entrepreneurs, students, researchers, investors, and industry experts together to participate in space ventures. Founder Troy McCann relayed that Moonshot now has investments in space startups from Australia to the United States, is currently building a larger venture capability with two new funds, and offers space entrepreneurship resources through its numerous community chapters across the globe. Moonshot refers to its business model as the "Space Elevator," which begins at outreach and progresses through an accelerator program all the way to investment. Moonshot offers training programs, investment opportunities, business development, supply chain growth, project execution, and talent recruitment.[20]

W ith contemporary methodologies and best practices, entrepreneurs can more quickly test ideas in the marketplace and iterate ideas which, when adequately vetted, evolve into successful products. How do you put a value on a potential cure for a disease derived from medical research in space or the creation of platforms which enable human settlement off-Earth? Space, in this sense, is the unlimited business plan. Space can transform the world in ways not possible by the bounds of terrestrial business endeavors. If you can dream it, it may be possible in this space-future.

> *Space isn't just a location above the sky. Our planet—the cradle of humanity and, as far as we know, the only location of life—is an astoundingly tiny dot in the infinite abyss of the universe. We are a part of space. Humanity, representing life that is sentient and sapient, for the first time has greater power than any of the gods of our ancient stories.*[21]
>
> **Troy McCann | Founder, Moonshot Space Company**

★ **Troy McCann** is the founder of Moonshot Space Company, an international network of NewSpace organizations and individuals. Moonshot provides consulting, business development, investment, and accelerator services.

CHAPTER NINETEEN
SPACE IS NOT A MONOLITH

This sector will keep expanding because it has to.
Eventually, more and more people will want to expand
into the space economy. It's just going to be a part of
what people desire to do going into the future.[1]

Ian Fichtenbaum | Senior Vice President & Space and Satellite Specialist,
American Industrial Acquisition Corporation; Director, Bradford Space

I n the early-to-mid-2000s, some industry insiders predicted that space tourism would open the floodgates for funding, business activity, and interest in NewSpace. Others speculated whether humans should return to the Moon, visit Mars or its moons, or land on an asteroid as the next great accomplishment. Space experts such as Jerry O'Neil envisioned space cities with artificial gravity, while others imagined in-space factories, spaceports, access to space resources via mining, or new medicines created in microgravity.

A presentation by the Science and Technology Policy Institute, titled "Global Trends in Civil and Commercial Space," shared one phrase which is essential to understand what we're dealing with: "Space is not a monolith."[2] Given that space can support numerous kinds advanced technology, and is in many ways being attractive to a variety of disciplines, industries with difficult challenges can identify new solutions with space in mind.

Certain investors will suggest that the industry's leaders are already selected and that there are few well-priced opportunities for those looking to make investments in the space sector going forward. However, while we each have our own biases and preferences, nobody can predict what new efforts will arise from this burgeoning sector, and no one place should be the defining prize for the twenty-first century. It's impossible to understand the future path of our current technology and the advances it will bring—but many see this uncertainty as an open highway of potential, not a roadblock. What we *can* predict is that investing in and improving space-derived or adjacent technology will benefit us here on Earth. The questions to consider are how these efforts will all work together and how the individual will find ways to become involved.

> *It is important that people understand that the true believers are driving this field; they are investing their money because they believe that humanity and life should expand into space. That doesn't sound very business-y, and we spend a lot of our time in the field trying to sound like legitimate businesspeople, but we have to admit that we are doing this because we believe this is what humanity should do. That is not an illegitimate reason for doing important work like opening the frontier; in fact, many civilizations and economies began with people who had a belief. And there have been thirty-plus years of engagement and sometimes conflict, changing work to change the conversation from a national federal-driven status space program to a frontier-opening agenda—it's particularly important to understand that.[3]*
>
> **Rick Tumlinson***

Dreams might drive astropreneurs, but they realize how their business could help the world and act as a catalyst. If we continue to allow individuals and organizations to take calculated risks on space ventures, we increase the probability that the space future many of us dream of could be a reality in our lifetime.

★ **Rick Tumlinson** is a founding partner at SpaceFund, a tokenized space venture capital firm headquartered in Austin, Texas. Hailed by *Space News* as one of the "most influential people in the space industry," Tumlinson has cofounded various space organizations and startups, including Deep Space Industries (a startup focused on space resource mining), the Space Frontier Foundation (a space advocacy nonprofit), Orbital Outfitters (a NewSpace manufacturing company), and the Earthlight Foundation (a nonprofit organization focused on expanding space exploration and settlement efforts through education, advocacy, and events). Tumlinson's expertise and record of space advocacy has led him to testify before the US Congress six times on space-related issues.

PART VI

POLICY AND POLITICS

CHAPTER TWENTY
GLOBAL DEVELOPMENTS

O ver the past decade, countries lacking a strong stake in space worked tirelessly to establish themselves in this expansive industry. With growing interest from the intelligence, defense-security, and commercial sectors, all will compete for essentially the same space-terrain.

Countries in the Middle East, including the United Arab Emirates (UAE), Saudi Arabia, and Israel, are investing further into the space sector, completing milestone missions, and working to further their domestic space programs. Saudi Arabia and UAE, in particular, are allegedly looking to alternative ways to slowly reduce their exposure to oil as their respective economies transition. One energy analyst from Navitas Resources even commented to *Bloomberg* that resources in space could be "the new oil."[1]

UAE launched its first satellite in 2018, has established national laws for space, and is developing a Mars mission with plans to launch in 2020. In early 2019, the UAE announced its National Plan for the Promotion of Space Investment, which "will include creation of business accelerators, funds and specially designated economic zones."[2]

Australia, with a historically small role in space, joined the new race after establishing its domestic Space Agency in July 2018. The agency raised $41 million in funding over four years and is headed by Megan Clark, former chief executive of the Commonwealth Scientific and Industrial Research Organisation (CSIRO).[3] The new agency has big goals, including growing the Australian economy, becoming a key player in the sector, and taking on a leadership role in international space legislation.[4]

Latin America and the Caribbean (LAC) are starting to get involved in space with LATCOSMOS, a four-year space development program established in 2017 by the International Astronautical Federation (IAF) Latin American and Caribbean Regional Group (GRULAC). LATCOSMOS invests in space-related education first and foremost as a way to remedy LAC's lack of local technology,

R&D, testing facilities, and startups.[5] LATCOSMOS partners with companies like Blue Origin and Orbit Muse, and ultimately aims to generate enough funding and interest to establish its own space program and economy.

Even in less developed parts of the world, space plays a significant role. Take Indonesia—composed of 17,000 islands, installing fixed-line internet (like fiber optics or broadband wiring) is geographically challenging and incredibly expensive, particularly in the many sparsely populated rural areas. The development of telecommunications brought connectivity to the whole country—and yet, most people don't realize the profound impact that space had there. In 2019, Indonesia partnered with global satellite company SES to bring further connectivity to their remaining population.[6] And nations that weren't heavily involved in space in the past, like Lithuania and Nigeria, are gearing up for the future.[7] Kyu Hwang,* a space industry consultant with a background at DARPA and at the FAA Office of Commercial Space Transportation, shared in an interview that while Africa cannot yet afford space programs comparable to the United States or China, he predicts that "Africa will emerge in areas such as manufacturing in space and will utilize innovations created in NewSpace."[8]

ASIA

The people of Japan have such a keen interest in space that being a space tourism fan isn't regarded as fringe. There are clubs, meet-ups, and other societies dedicated to space tourism. Japan is also famously strong in robotics, one of the most essential space-enabling technologies. Most of Japan's space activities revolve around the Japan Aerospace Exploration Agency, the country's government space agency. In June 2010, JAXA spacecraft Hayabusa returned a

★ **Kyu Hwang** is a space industry consultant for DecisionBox, a management consulting firm focused on data, decision science, and digital capabilities. He formerly served as the vice president of EarthNow, a space startup funded by Softbank, Airbus, and Bill Gates. Prior, he worked at DARPA on the Falcon Program (small launch vehicle and hypersonic technology vehicle), for the FAA Commercial Space Transportation Office, and then at Orbital Sciences, Schafer, Paragon, IDair, and Stratolaunch (formerly Vulcan Aerospace).

sample of an asteroid to Earth—a first in human history. Another more recent accomplishment includes the development of Kibō, a module on the ISS. In 2019, Japan Airlines Corporation (JAL) announced its partnership with Japanese lunar exploration startup ispace to focus on lunar commercialization and exploration. JAL provided financing in ispace's 2017 Series B funding round, which raised over $90 million for the robotic tech company.[9]

In addition, Japan has a robust roster of space startups, and the country's commercial space economy is growing. Infostellar, a network provider for satellites founded in 2016, raised $7.3 million from investors (including Airbus Ventures, WERU Investment, Sony Innovation Fund, and FreakOut Holdings) in its Series A round. Infostellar uses a cloud-based satellite antenna sharing platform, called StellarStation, to allow satellite operators and antenna holders around the world to connect and maximize data transmission.[10] Japan's Interstellar Technologies, which began as a launch service provider for small satellites in 2003, now also develops small launch vehicles. The company, which is dedicated to lowering launch costs, had its first successful launch in 2019—and at one-tenth the cost of a JAXA launch, Interstellar plans to become a competitor of SpaceX in the coming years.[11] Such startups are also helping to prove that private sector efforts do ultimately pay off, and the Japanese government is committed to developing the country's NewSpace sector. In 2018, Japan announced it would dedicate $940 million to space startups via investments and loans in an effort to stimulate the country's space economy.[12]

China is now focused on long-term space activities with the intention of creating a permanent presence in space, and the global superpower is moving forward with serious momentum. China was responsible for one-third of the 103 global satellite launches in 2018, surpassing Russia and the United States for the first time in history.[13] Along with the historic Change lunar mission, the China National Space Administration (CNSA) launched communications, science, weather, remote sensing, and Earth observation satellites into orbit in 2019. Its Long March rocket family had its 300th launch in March 2019 and launched another Long March rocket from the sea in June. As CNSA works further to make those rockets reusable, we'll likely see China's rockets increase in volume and capability in the coming years.[14]

Although China's space program is dual-use, meaning that it has close ties to its military, the country publicly stated it would like to collaborate more on peaceful efforts with the international community. In 2017, China and Russia announced a planned bilateral agreement to work more closely together in several areas in the space sector. In 2019, we saw the first collaboration between Chinese and US space programs when China shared data with NASA about its Chang'e spacecraft landing on the far side of the Moon.[15]

Since 2014, China has also been active in the startup sector and is now home to over eighty private space companies. The majority of these startups focus on satellites and software, including small satellites like CubeSats, though the launch market is growing as well.[16] Launch company OneSpace focuses on affordable microsatellites and nanosatellites. LandSpace intends to build a medium-size rocket launcher for both crewed and uncrewed uses, and founder Roger Zheng noted that SpaceX was the startup's "role model" in its launch endeavors.[17] Shenzhen Yu Long Aerospace Science and Technology is currently focused on building a small sounding rocket—but intends to make much larger vehicles. China clearly recognizes that investment in the aerospace sector benefits the public. With over $230 billion raised by venture capital and private equity funds in 2017, which includes $180 million raised by Chinese space-focused company ExPace, we should expect more commercially oriented, space-related efforts developing in China.[18]

India is an excellent example of a homegrown space industry. The Indian Space Research Organization (ISRO) formed in 1969 and began developing the Polar Satellite Launch Vehicle in 1978—though it didn't fly the rocket until 1993. Now, India accounts for a considerable portion of global launches each year, mostly because it provides low-cost access compared to the rest of the world. As a result, government-subsidized efforts out of India attract many customers with their low costs; ISRO has provided launch for governments, private initiatives, and students from over fifty countries to date.[19] In 2017, the Polar Satellite Launch Vehicle launched 104 satellites into space—which remains the highest amount of satellites launched simultaneously in history.[20]

India has more aspirations for space beyond acting as a launch provider. In 2018, India's Prime Minister announced that the country plans to have its own astronauts in space by 2022.[21] ISRO also stated that it would create an organization to help transfer intellectual property to the commercial sector.[22]

EUROPE

T he European Space Agency, which consists of twenty-two member states, seems to recognize that even modest amounts of government funding can be positive signaling for entrepreneurs and other commercial efforts to tackle challenges. In interviews, a few ESA representatives shared insights around the agency's plans and ethos.

First, ESA thinks of space as an economy rather than merely as a tool for exploration and therefore works hard to expand its position in the global industry by following the trends of new and emerging technologies. It encourages the spin-off and spin-in effects, noting the value of learning from other sectors—particularly the digitalization and design processes, which the space industry needs to stay receptive to in order to remain competitive. This includes opening the doors wider for private efforts and responding to the decreasing costs enabled by latest technologies in the market—without losing sight of the member states.

ESA thus looks for ways to incorporate more types of activities with NewSpace players and programmatic elements while showing the value of basic research, scientific activities, and space infrastructure behind the various outstanding core activities. Luca del Monte, ESA's head of Industrial Policy and SME Division, noted that one area of focus is attracting known industry verticals with heritage competence to the space sector: ESA's Grand Challenge—a competition similar to the Google Lunar XPRIZE—which the agency hopes will encourage other industries to participate in alongside space startups and small to medium-sized enterprises (SMEs). "ESA is trying to stimulate new areas, one by one, entrepreneur by entrepreneur. By understanding their niche, we can demonstrate mutual benefits and then showcase the successes as examples of value creation for the taxpayer," del Monte explained.[23] By identifying common challenges that encourage participation from outside of the space industry, ESA believes it will create a new class of space entrepreneurs in Europe.

Frank Salzgeber, head of the Technology Transfer and Business Incubation Office at ESA, relayed that the ESA business incubation center selects startups for two-way contracts and helps them grow via business coaching, advising, technical support, and workspace. In addition, ESA is developing tools to help with early financing for startups via joint projects with investment banks in Europe—a model that has proven effective in countries like Finland, Ireland, and Spain. ESA also works toward providing institutional support for SMEs to penetrate markets outside of Europe and establish a global reach. Overall, the private and public aspects of the industry work toward ESA's core mission for the European players to grow and have a stronger presence in the global market—and, hopefully, they will both receive the support to take calculated risks to push the sector forward.[24]

L uxembourg has been a famously strong leader of the space industry, both on a civil and commercial level. Though a member of ESA since 2005, the tiny country has wielded significant influence over the private space sector and continues to promote the industry through advocacy, regulation, and investment in a future space resources market— including mining. It is also one of the leading countries to develop legal frameworks for NewSpace.

Marc Serres, Ph.D., CEO of the Luxembourg Space Agency (LSA), explained in an interview that space is a key sector for the country.* "What we do here is really driven by the need to diversify our economy," Serres said. Noting the success the country has had with SES so far, "Space represents approximately a bit less than 2 percent of GDP [gross domestic product], which is already really significant if you compare that with other countries." Serres continued by saying, "I think our goal is really to continue increasing that portion of GDP in the future."[25]

As a pioneer in the industry, Luxembourg has spurred private sector activity effectively. LSA's website proudly states that "For more than three decades,

★ **Marc Serres, Ph.D.** is the chief executive officer of the Luxembourg Space Agency, where he also heads the Luxembourg Delegation at the European Space Agency and represents Luxembourg in the Council of ESA. He formerly worked at the Ministry of Higher Education and Research as an industrial policy officer, where he managed Luxembourg's relationship with ESA. Prior to his government roles, he worked in the commercial satellite communications industry.

Luxembourg has been at the forefront of commercial and co-operative initiatives, shaping a vibrant space economy in pragmatic and progressive ways."[26] Serres shared further, "What we have been doing is trying to create awareness with the private sector." One example, he said, was that "we saw immediately the parallel with the terrestrial mining industry—we already have a system on Earth where the whole economy depends on the resources we find on Earth—and this is something that, in a certain way, you can replicate in space." To establish that kind of infrastructure, of course, will require earnest effort.

Étienne Schneider, who served as Deputy Prime Minister from 2013 to February 2020, is considered the "architect" of Luxembourg's strong foray into NewSpace and responsible for establishing Luxembourg "not only as a hub for the New Space and space resources industry in Europe, but also as a hub for companies and organisations in the industry from all over the world," as reported by *SpaceWatch.Global*.[27] Since his tenure as deputy prime minister began, Schneider has stood as a progressive dynamo for space industry policy and politics, building on Luxembourg's global leadership role in the space sector by pushing for new regulations and legal frameworks on a domestic and international level. As to his decision to step down from his position as deputy prime minister in 2020, Schneider's successor will hopefully continue the Luxembourgian legacy of spurring the space sector forward.

Luxembourg possesses a rich history and experience in space technology, communications and innovation, backed by unswerving public commitment to entrepreneurship and business development. With government support, the country's space businesses have been instrumental in building a high-value European and global broadcasting, communications and connectivity infrastructure.[28]

Luxembourg Space Agency

From competitive advantages to establishing oneself as a global power, the influence that rests on a country's space presence is undeniable. Space is strategic, supporting nations and their respective military forces with insights, communications, timing and navigation and access that it alone can comprehensively provide. With conversations and plans developing around eventual space resource utilization, mining, and inhabitation, nation-states that are serious about maintaining their strength and leadership must continue to keep space a high priority item. This includes regulation and policy—areas that, at the moment, are in dire need of attention and action.

CHAPTER TWENTY-ONE
THE REGULATORY LANDSCAPE

I was in a meeting with one client, and when they told the FCC that they were looking to build and launch within a year, jaws hit the table. The law and licensing timeframe that the FCC is used to is a minimum of three years. We have to change the speed at which the FCC can do this—and it's not just a matter of layering on more people, it's a matter of revising and restructuring the way we regulate these activities.[1]

James Dunstan*

NewSpace's rapid advances have resulted in outdated space-related policies and regulations. The vast disparities between the civil and commercial industries present ongoing difficulties, and most governments struggle to address and solve for them adequately. Some of the most glaring issues include gaps in commercial space regulations, slow approval processes for NewSpace companies, data and mining resource ownership rights, an absence of comprehensive international standards and policies for space, and inconsistencies between the existing regulations of space-faring nations.

On the technological side, we can chalk these inconsistencies up to the emergence of digital technology, where our machines are ever more interconnected, capable, and resilient. There is also the increasing adoption of more renewable and sustainable energy sources. Yet, as the public and private sectors are ready to shift in new, more valuable directions, red tape threatens to constrain our advancements.

★ **James Dunstan** is the founder of Mobius Legal Group, a private law firm that provides legal services to clients in the communications, high-tech, outer space, and computer game industries. Dunstan has been practicing law for more than twenty-five years.

A s the leading NewSpace power, let's focus on the United States to understand the current regulatory challenges. Commercial space activities require jumping through rigorous regulatory hoops and spending excessive amounts of time on inefficient, redundant licenses. The various requirements currently span crew notification, medical qualifications, environmental control systems, hardware and software testing, crew training, and licensing.

There are four separate governing bodies that companies must deal with for commercial licenses: the FAA, which manages licenses for launch, re-entry, and spaceports; the NOAA, for remote or Earth sensing capabilities licenses; the FCC, for satellite communications licenses; and the Departments of Commerce and State, for space technology exports licenses. On top of all that, the US Air Force awards numerous contracts to private companies and has its own plethora of regulatory requirements to meet.[2]

Regulatory neglect has resulted in an antiquated, slow permit process for U.S. firms, putting them at a disadvantage to companies in countries with more laid-back regulation. Still, the effects of inadequate regulation are likely to intensify in the future. If the United States fails to tackle comprehensive space policy before a major civil, commercial, or international dispute occurs in space, legal fallout could be widespread.

Because the future of space policy seems far-off, many of its complex issues are often brushed aside as abstract. However, each individual challenge must be tackled, and the vague authority of documents like the Outer Space Treaty must be refined into specific policies before unfortunate externalities occur.[3]

Amir Siraj, "Why Congress Must Act Quickly to Reform U.S. Space Law," *Harvard Political Review*, September 28, 2017.

To complicate things further, the existing challenges in regulating the space sector in the United States are often paradoxical. While many current regulations function as red tape rather than as enablers, there is also a lack of adequate policies and regulations to push the industry forward safely and efficiently. This combination adversely affects startups, technologies, and the overarching economy alike. With progress evolving far more quickly than policy, government agencies lack the resources to keep up with demands for licenses—resulting in long and cumbersome licensing processes. The fact that the new technology outpaces regulatory and policy advances makes it difficult for the commercial sector to operate in compliance and be safe stewards of the space environments.[4] Jeremy Conrad, a cofounder of early-stage investment firm Lemnos and current cofounder and CEO of software and hardware startup Quartz, voiced frustration about the major flaws in the government procurement system. "Let's say you have a $100 million program in the government—that's like a four-year budget process. Then there's a competitive bid process, and then everyone sues each other. It's really like this—a fucking nightmare."[5]

Rex Ridenoure, who spent eleven years at NASA and now runs a space-tech firm in the private sector, relayed similar sentiments.* "Our government-influenced procurement systems, whether at the government level per se or as flowed down to the aerospace ecosystem at large, are significantly mismatched with small business and commercial business practices—and are borderline dysfunctional," he lamented. Ridenoure continued, "These processes are the prominent source of stress and hassle in our company, and we by and large despise them—but are forced to work with them anyway. The dysfunction of Congress and the policy apparatus is also very disappointing."[6]

> The U.S. regulatory environment needs to accommodate the new era of commercial activities in space and the technology developments that are on the horizon. ... This committee has an opportunity to steer commercial space activities through legislation authorizing NASA and the FAA Office of Commercial Space Transportation (AST).†
>
> In the case of expendable rockets, FAA and Air Force requirements are nearly identical. When launching from a federal range, a company can create a single set of deliverables for the Air Force and provide the

---

★ **Rex Ridenoure** is the cofounder and chief executive officer of Ecliptic Enterprises Corporation, a company that specializes in space avionics and sensor systems designed for the space environment. He has over twenty years of experience as a space-mission engineer and systems architect, and much of Ridenoure's background includes developing low-cost spacecraft and missions. Prior to his tenure in the private space sector, he spent eleven years at NASA's Jet Propulsion Laboratory as a mission and systems engineer, where he worked on projects including Deep Space One, the New Millennium Program, and the Voyager Neptune encounter. For his contributions on the Deep Space One project, he was a co-recipient of the AIAA Space Systems Award in 2002.

same information to the FAA to satisfy launch license requirements. It is duplicative, but not onerous. In contrast, Air Force and FAA licensing requirements for reusable rockets are completely different from each other, necessitating two entirely different but equally rigorous sets of deliverables. This is duplicative and onerous, and will increase costs, delays, and uncertainty.

We want FAA as the single point of contact for any commercial space-flight company interactions with the government with sole authority over launches and reentries, without regard to location or type of launch, consistent with the National Space Transportation Policy.[7]

Bretton Alexander (Director, Business Development & Strategy, Blue Origin) in testimony before the House Subcommittee on Space, "Hearing on Private Sector Lunar Exploration," September 7, 2017.

G iven the space sector's rapid progress and interdisciplinary nature, it needs flexible regulations to support its long-term goals *and* allow it to grow in different directions. James Dunstan has extensive experience in high-tech and outer space law and confirmed that the regulatory landscape is both severely outdated and in need of revision: "The entire regulatory structure of space was designed essentially thirty to forty years ago. It assumed that we would have about ten commercial launches a year that would put up about twelve to fifteen satellites—we're now doing ten times that on all fronts." In order to facilitate industry growth, rather than stagnate activity, Dunstan argued that "We're going to have to completely revamp the way we do licensing on all levels—for launches, for payloads, for payload reviews, for spectrum licenses—all of that is going to have to be changed and sped up."[8]

A s enabling technologies and infrastructures continue to evolve, it is crucial that new regulations do not inherently slow the (often) unpredictable advancements that drive the industry forward. If we look at the high level,

---

[†] **The Office of Commercial Space Transportation** (OCST) was created in 1984 and was originally part of the Department of Transportation's Office of the Secretary. When OCST was transferred to the FAA in 1995, the acronym changed to "AST" per FAA routing symbol standards; "A" is the routing symbol used to identify subdivisions of the FAA and is followed by two letters that identify the subdivision itself (as prescribed by the US Department of Transportation, Federal Aviation Administration Order 1100.87F).

there are two addressable areas: regulation of launch and regulation of space-craft (including satellites). The latter includes radio spectrum, operations, and licensing. Moreover, space is one area along with nanotechnology, additive manufacturing, artificial intelligence, and uncrewed aerial vehicles, which are all being pursued globally at an unprecedented rate.

For instance, satellites alone require incredible coordination and operations acumen to function, let alone succeed. Besides developing the spacecraft, there are communications licensing issues that must be resolved before flight and operations. Satellite communications companies' complete business models also depend on getting dedicated spectrum for their service, whereas Earth observation companies can use shared resources—which led to a more granular ecosystem with the emergence of companies like KSAT and Infostellar. Still, Earth observation companies need imagery licenses. As space resource mining companies and other new space activities continue to emerge, they will each require their own licenses, too.

> *I do believe that we need a managed, controlled, and disciplined regulatory environment. However, as the regulatory environment evolves, it needs to be within reason—business-safe, probusiness—it can't be so restrictive that it stifles entrepreneurism and new business growth and new opportunities. You've got to allow for companies to get into the business, maybe to make some mistakes, have some losses and problems. And, of course, they need to choose to act responsibly and be held accountable for their actions—but you've got to give them the freedom to act.*[9]
>
> **David Livingston, Ph.D.***

★ **David Livingston, Ph.D.** is the founder and host of *The Space Show*, an internet radio broadcast focused on current space-related issues. Dr. Livingston is also an adjunct professor at the University of North Dakota Graduate School of Space Studies, a frequent lecturer at national and international space conferences, and has published numerous papers, chapters, and a code of ethics for off-Earth commerce.

U nfortunately, government space-derived security, intelligence, and other agencies tend to look down on private efforts. Granted, the requirements and capabilities of government spacecraft can be deep and complex, and the government operates in a completely distinct way from the private, for-profit industry. For some historical context, the first commercial use of space was communications. In 1962, AT&T and Bell Telephone Laboratories sponsored the launch of Telstar 1, the first truly commercial satellite. This effort helped pave the way for other communications and weather satellites such as Syncom 3, Television Infrared Observation Satellites, Intelsat, Anik A, and Iridium. However, the Kennedy Administration banned the privatization of space in an attempt to prevent private sector monopolies. Kennedy passed the Communications Satellite Act in 1962, which prevented the involvement

Telstar 1
Launched by NASA
on July 10, 1962

of many groups such as AT&T, GTE, Hughes, and others who were ready to invest in satellites. Instead, in 1963, the United States formed COMSAT, which was a public satellite organization co-owned by the public and private sectors.

There has been a tug-of-war between support and opposition for commercial space efforts in the United States since the 1960s. The first government effort to support more commercial activity came from the Commercial Space Launch Act of 1984, under President Ronald Reagan. However, NASA quickly pushed back with excessive red tape to prevent private efforts. The Launch Services Purchase Act, signed into law by President George H. W. Bush in 1990, attempted to remove the NASA restrictions and Space Shuttle monopoly that kept the space industry in a chokehold; this led to incumbents Lockheed Martin and Boeing receiving government launch contracts. The Commercial Space Act of 1998 aimed to promote commercial activity further, but again was met with resistance from NASA and other government agencies that continued to keep the private sector locked out of space.

While regulating the commercial space sector has long been complicated, it was not originally intended that way. When the Reagan Administration created the Office of Commercial Space Transportation (OCST) in 1984, there were arguments about which government department would oversee it; the main case around keeping it out of the Department of Transportation (DOT) stemmed from the fear that if it fell under the jurisdiction of the Federal Aviation Administration, the FAA's proclivity for heavy-handed regulations would stagnate the purpose of the new Office. OCST was thus placed in the Department of Transportation only after the agreement that it would be part of the Office of the Secretary of Transportation (OST).[10]

In its first year, OCST adopted the motto "Blue Skies, Not Red Tape," and the concerted effort to sustain relaxed regulations was successful for the Office's first decade in operation—so much so that OCST conducted studies in its early years that considered whether the commercial space sector should be self-regulating, largely based on how low-risk commercial launches were for public safety. But as Norman Bowles, OCST's Associate Director for Licensing and Safety from 1984 to 1994, penned in an article outlining his role in the office before it transferred to the FAA, the mismatch between needed resources and what the Office was provided has long been an issue. "I believed that OCST was about to go on a wild ride. We didn't know how many rocket launches we would see, but I knew for sure that we didn't have the capability to handle very much," he recounted.[11]

As Bowles and his colleagues worked to develop OCST into a strong enough operation to function as an independent organization within OST, the FAA made several attempts to absorb the Office. Bowles noted why this change was so problematic: "If the program ever moved to FAA, the days that the industry could count on an enlightened regulator were numbered. After all, Tony Broderick, the FAA Associate Administrator for Regulation and Certification had personally told me he was going to eliminate the failures in rocket launches via strict regulations." Bowles further explained that "Tony was a friend and his comment was made in a serious, factual, non-threatening way, but it exemplified FAA culture."[12] When Stephanie Lee-Miller became Director of OCST in 1989, she began pushing for the Office to become a separate agency, arguing that because of OCST the Department of Transportation was already responsible for more launches than NASA, and that "$2.5 billion worth of satellites are now scheduled for launch by companies which are subject to DOT's regulatory authority." Furthermore, OCST "develops safety regulations, issues operating licenses and approvals, and conducts an active inspection and enforcement program," Lee-Miller said, adding that "DOT's legal regulatory influence over space exceeds that of NASA or DOD [Department of Defense]." She noted that DOT was responsible for the insurance requirements for NASA's Kennedy Space Center, as well as the sole regulating authority for space debris in the commercial sector. She concluded by emphatically advising against merging OSTP with the FAA—or any other agency.

Unfortunately, when President Clinton took office in 1992, the transition into a new administration derailed much of OCST's momentum to become an independent agency. The newly elected Congress that took office in 1995 created further obstacles, and soon, the FAA was finally successful in taking over OCST—and its firm regulatory grip commenced.

As Bowles explained, the overall problem reflected in OCST's trajectory is that "The Office is headed by a political appointee. The vision for this Office needs to be set externally, and the person chosen to head the Office has to have the ability and openness to carry that vision forward." Such a process works with many government offices, he noted, but commercial space is different: "It needs a consistent, lasting vision that won't waiver. It needs political heads that understand that vision and carry it through."[13] As Bowles concisely wrote, "Simply, when first conceived[,] the regulatory program was designed to facilitate the pathway to the stars[,] not hamper it. The problem with 'visions' is that they are only good as long as someone knows, follows and/or remembers the 'vision' and its foundations."[14]

> Commercial space travel is our future, and the regulatory process shapes its direction. If done correctly[,] we humans get to those stars in the shortest time possible. However, done in the wrong way, the pathway to the stars will never materialize or will be rocky indeed. Aviation and automobiles went 50 years or more with no serious government regulation. The regulatory program for the space industry should not be more than a framework that allows all possible futures.[15]
>
> **Norman Bowles | Former Associate Director for Licensing and Safety, Office of Commercial Space Transportation (OCST)**

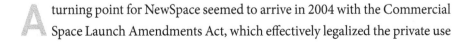

A turning point for NewSpace seemed to arrive in 2004 with the Commercial Space Launch Amendments Act, which effectively legalized the private use of space. The act included an eight-year "learning period" that prevented the FAA from placing safety restrictions on private spaceflight with passengers; instead, it required commercial launch operators to adhere to safety, operational, and informed consent procedures. The bill also included government indemnification for the same period (up to 2012) on third-party damages or losses over the amount of $3 billion.[16]

In 2006, the FAA rolled out its mandated requirements (to be effective in 2007), with a summary stating the following: "The requirements should provide an acceptable level of safety to the general public and ensure individuals on board are aware of the risks associated with a launch or reentry. The rule also applies existing fiscal responsibility and waiver of liability requirements to human space flight and experimental permits. Experimental permits are the subject of a separate rulemaking."[17] The FAA further noted that "Recognizing that this is a fledgling industry, the law required a phased approach in regulating commercial human space flight, with regulatory standards evolving as the industry matures."[18] While this act allowed more private sector activity, the FAA refused to grant licenses for commercial passenger flights.

With calls from the private sector and Congress alike to increase commercial efforts, President Obama signed the Spurring Private Aerospace Competitiveness and Entrepreneurship (SPACE) Act into law in 2015. The SPACE Act, which is effectively a continuation of the 2004 launch legislation, extended the third-party launch indemnification and the FAA learning period to 2025 in order to provide the private sector with more time to build up experiences that could inform future regulations. It also opened the door for space resource mining and experimentation. The response from the private sector was celebratory. Eric Stallmer, president of the Commercial Spaceflight Federation, commented that "By removing the regulatory unknowns that suppress and repel investment, this bill unleashes and incentivizes the creativity that leads to unknown breakthroughs in innovation."[19] Others referred to the SPACE Act as an industry milestone and the start to an effective legal framework for commercial space.

Frustration is still rampant throughout the rest of the commercial industry, however. Despite a presidential directive in 2018 to streamline regulatory requirements, which "instruct[ed] the secretary of transportation to devise a new regulatory regime for launch and re-entry activities, and to consider requiring just a single license for all such commercial operations," the resulting FAA/AST Notice of Proposed Rulemaking (NPRM) appears to create even more barriers for smaller commercial companies. While its title, "Streamlined Launch and Reentry Licensing Requirements (SLR2)," sounds progressive, NewSpace players contend that the new rules are precisely the opposite; meanwhile, incumbents like ULA have lauded the new regulations. *The Lurio Report* states that SLR2 "could be fatal to much entrepreneurial growth while enabling these high cost, high overhead, traditional companies to artificially maintain their 'markets.'"[20]

Eric Stallmer provided testimony before Congress on July 25, 2019 to address many of the issues in the new NPRM. Stallmer stated that while "The goal of SPD-2 [a government policy known as Space Directive Policy-2] and the NPRM is only to streamline the regulatory process and create a performance-based approach to regulating an innovative, evolving industry while encouraging it to become even safer," the results are disappointing. "Unfortunately, instead of a giant leap forward, the FAA seems to have taken at best only a cautious half-step towards the regulatory regime America needs to enable the growth and diversity of new space transportation providers and their current and prospective users," Stallmer said in the testimony.

The Commercial Spaceflight Federation further illuminated the specific issues within the NPRM. First, that it "is not performance-based" and instead "includes highly-prescriptive requirements, such as for software and flight termination systems, that might undermine industry efforts to implement innovative approaches to improve safety." Second, that it "adds burdens and cost" via "new regulations and requirements that do not appear to replace existing rules, but will increase the cost and effort necessary to comply rather than reduce and streamline the process." The NPRM also "lacks flexibility" that would allow new applicants to pursue specific efforts or integrate new technology, and overall is risk-averse, which means the regulations will be "quickly outdated and discouraging [to] innovation." Stallmer's testimony also points to the NPRM being "anti-competitive," both in "[lacking] the clarity for even experienced launch operators to understand their purpose" and by favoring established incumbents. Additional issues include regulations that "attempt to 'fix' things that were not broken," such as a process for collision avoidance that conflicts with licensing processes. Finally, the regulations are both "confusing" and reliant "on missing documents," resulting in a lack of "adequate justification of new prescriptive regulatory requirements."[21]

Others who have critiqued the NPRM include Blue Origin, SpaceX, and Sierra Nevada Corporation. Jeff Greason, who was instrumental in creating the Commercial Space Launch Amendments Act of 2004, also offered some scathing commentary on the new rules, citing that "none of the industry's or AST's goals will be accomplished by this proposed rulemaking." Greason told *The Lurio Report* that "detailed technical requirements should have no place in the proposed rules; instead, as the field progresses, AST could provide advisory circulars, and industry should update 'best practices.'"[22] These FAA rules reflect the ongoing battle between NewSpace capabilities and the crippling restrictions that prevent new entrants from progressing. The space sector as a whole will be unable to function at its full capacity without revised regulations across the board.

IMPROVING THE REGULATORY ENVIRONMENT

While the consensus from the space sector is that some regulation is positive and helpful, creating a viable balance is crucial. Improving these processes would benefit both the commercial and civil sector; reducing restrictions has proven economic payoffs.

Countries that present fewer restrictions, such as the Isle of Man and Luxembourg, reap the benefits of attracting substantial business from other countries. In fact, Luxembourg adopted the Isle of Man's business model *because* it was so successful.[23] As a result, the NewSpace sector has appealed to the various government agencies to streamline the licensing processes—which would save time, money, energy, and other resources.

The Isle of Man is now the world's largest offshore finance center for satellites. There are now over fifty-one satellite and communications space companies choosing to work from the Isle of Man in everything from leasing procurement all the way through to manufacturing. The first launch vehicle was also done on the Isle of Man, for over a billion dollars. And why? Because of its good laws and good regulations. It's politically stable, economically stable, part of the North Atlantic

Treaty Organization (NATO). It has proper regulations, so it is a perfect place to do space business.[24]

Christopher Stott | Cofounder, Chair, & Chief Executive Officer, ManSat

M
any in the space community believe that we are five years from a radical reduction of launch cost, which will result in a drastic increase in launch frequency. Already, companies are manufacturing more space satellites than at any time in history, and these satellites are intended to serve new and existing markets—however, there is not enough launch for them all, despite the dozens of emerging launch efforts underway around the world. And reusable launch vehicles face additional scrutiny versus launches and flights that are payload-only. Absence of policies that enable the launch market means that providers might only schedule flights as quickly as the slowest part of the chain—which is the regulatory side. With both orbital and suborbital providers thinking about reusability and higher flight frequency, it remains to be seen if and how the government will influence the overall architecture and development of these systems.

One of the few steps in the right direction came when the FCC created streamlined licensing procedures for the smallsat industry. This change results from an understanding that smallsats have different capabilities, lifespans, costs, and development times compared to the traditional satellite industry.

The Commission's satellite licensing rules, in particular those applicable to commercial operations, were generally not developed with small satellite systems in mind, and uniformly impose fees and regulatory requirements appropriate to expensive, long-lived missions. ... Therefore, in 2018, the Commission adopted a Notice of Proposed Rulemaking that proposed to develop a new authorization process tailored specifically to small satellite operations, keeping in mind efficient use of spectrum and mitigation of orbital debris. ... Applicants qualifying for this process would have a streamlined application, would be exempted from the Commission's processing round procedures, and could take advantage of a one-year grace period from posting of a surety bond.[25]

US Federal Communications Commission, "FCC Fact Sheet: Streamlining Licensing Procedures for Small Satellites," August 2, 2019.

Transforming regulatory systems so they can keep up with the pace of business as well as current technology trends is a continuing challenge in need of a solution. Though there are exhaustive lists of suggestions to bridge these gaps, we haven't seen much in terms of results. Part of the issue stems from government standards being military and defense-focused, which makes regulations inherently complicated.[26] The other part of the issue is a willingness to adjust protocol to reflect market needs. As Dr. T.X. Hammes wrote in the *National Defense University Press*, "It is essential to remember that institutional biases can keep investment focused on the dominant technology even as multiple emergent technologies clearly challenge it."[27]

Conventional past and recent practices involve the use of political lobbying to enable government budgets that support sponsorships or funding—whether for commercial crew, space resource mining, or research. Often, US Congress leads these efforts; they hold both the purse strings and carrot stick, enabling and facilitating billions of dollars in non-dilutive funding via contracts, loans, and grants while creating the laws that influence the industrial and business sectors.

Let's consider other sectors for comparison. The oil and gas industries spend many years and billions of dollars developing new energy projects, from refineries to fields and beyond. Underwater submersibles guided by telepresence regularly inspect underwater energy infrastructure. These projects rely heavily on advanced technology to exploit and derive future returns for investors; they also have business plans with time horizons that can extend beyond the range of technology or other startup venture-oriented investors. These energy-focused opportunities leverage institutional investors, government incentives, bonds, and other investment vehicles. Barclays bank estimates that energy bonds compose 15.7 percent of the global $1.3 trillion high yield debt market. It makes one wonder what could be possible if just 1 percent of that went into the space sector.[28]

A simple example of a sizable private capital outlay is the $37 billion spent on a single natural gas terminal offshore of Western Australia. A typical large-scale industrial project today ranges from the single-billions to tens-of-billions of dollars. The problem is not availability; it is the direction of capital flow.[29]

Dennis Wingo | Founder & Chief Executive Officer, Skycorp Inc.

T here is ample room for the government to help remove existing barriers for the commercial sector, invest in fundamental scientific research, and make it easier for commercial providers to take over products and services and execute them better than government providers. Rex Ridenoure believes that the government could implement a few crucial strategies to improve the status quo: only take on the actions or projects that the commercial world cannot; procure what it needs from commercial business and not compete with the private sector; and significantly increase the use of firm-fixed-price procurements while holding procurement officials in both government and business accountable for consequences of poorly negotiated or executed contracts.

One growing argument posits that the US Air Force, which currently monitors the space environment, should focus on military assets and allow other areas to handle commercial traffic in space. The Federal Aviation Administration, which monitors airline traffic, is one potential solution—though it is already spread too thin when it comes to its role in the space sector. There is, however, an opportunity to help automate the processes by which the FAA and private sector handle launches. Improved software and streamlined requirements could help manage the slow, tedious process for launch providers attempting (and expecting) to fly repeatedly and rapidly.

Changes in direction between leadership poses yet another problem. Given space's complexity, dependence on hardware and interdisciplinary specialties, and long timeframe for exploration, administration-based decisions have the power to influence the industry's subsectors dramatically—whether in a positive or negative way. Overall, reliance on a presidential administration's whims does not enable a continuum for success. How can we expect to make meaningful progress if one president funds a Mars-focused effort and his successor pulls the plug, opting instead for a mission to the Moon?

While it might be impossible to preclude changes in administrative direction, Dennis Wingo argues that "A business-friendly administration can help to foster commercial space enterprises across the spectrum, from launch, human spaceflight, and in-space manufacturing to exploration and even lunar or Mars activities. At the end of the day," Wingo said, "space must be more than a government-focused and government-directed enterprise, and companies that are able to make revenue and profits will continue to seek such opportunities. Thus, this path is the best way of buffering change in government space policies."[30]

Many NewSpace subsectors are too embryonic to survive on their own; it will take sound economic growth policy and community building to improve the ability for more players and new entrants—and not just the ones with strong marketing and lobbying resources—tomore effectively participate and to develop fundable space-tech startups outside of the top-tier markets. That said, the point of contention is around timing. While technology and management are key, timing plays a significant role in the rise and development of any entrepreneurial effort—and is often the variable with the greatest impact.

> *We are still not at a point in time where a single company or organization can create and close the chain from product development and service to end-user development in space beyond GEO.*[31]
> **Jim Keravala | Chief Executive Officer, OffWorld**

The policies of our nation ought to reflect bold, exciting, vision-based leadership. Although new forms of communication might help create new advocacy areas and help unify the populace around future-forward aspirations, it's the tight fist of the political, elected leadership that yields significant change-making power. It will take smart policymakers who can aptly listen to the cues and needs of the private sector to address tomorrow's challenges today.

> *Policymakers need to make sure they understand the value in creating jobs and enabling new automation for industries that have historically relied on coal for energy. So, moving forward, don't just look at biotech, and don't just look at clean tech. Take the lessons learned from those experiences to ensure that as this technological shift happens and the investments continue to exponentially grow, you curate that technology so that it protects your citizens and allows them to have a role in pushing that frontier and creating new economies.*[32]
> **Van Espahbodi | Cofounder & Managing Partner, Starburst Aerospace**

CHAPTER TWENTY-TWO
INTERNATIONAL ISSUES

On a global scale, the space environment suffers from a glaring lack of sustainable, functioning space regulations as well. Lower altitudes of space remain an at-risk resource; with no clear way to regulate spacecraft, debris, and space weather, we're heading toward problematic and challenging situations.[1]

Integrating spaceflight with commercial airliners in our airspace is one issue growing more ominous by the day. Airlines already push back when it comes to sharing that airspace, which is increasingly limited and congested. On June 29, 2018, over two hundred thousand flights flew, which was the highest number of aircraft flights in a single day, as tracked by Swedish tracking company FlightRadar24.[2] July 29, 2019 saw 225,000 flights, setting a new record. With air traffic at an all-time high and increasing by the year, it is crucial to create solutions that allow spacecraft and aircraft to coexist safely and effectively. We need new software that integrates with air traffic control (which is currently unable to connect to other data sources). Effectively streamlining the communication between these two industries will be imperative to enable safe scheduling, quicker launch turnaround, and higher launch frequency. On a global scale, it will be impossible to resolve the growing airspace problems without international diplomacy.

We also need better methods to track and control dead or retired spacecraft, which can have potentially ruinous consequences if they collide with other objects or spacecraft. Although experts contend that LEO can handle much more traffic and activity from new satellites and other spacecraft, that doesn't account for retired spacecraft or debris that isn't controlled remotely from Earth. There are already more than 23,000 pieces of large orbital debris (objects larger than 10 cm) tracked by NASA and the US Space Surveillance Network; there are an estimated additional 500,000 pieces of debris between 1 cm and 10 cm, and over 100 million pieces between 1 mm and 1 cm. This debris spans various Earth orbits, and the current challenges increase when we consider that mass-produced spacecraft will inevitably appear over the coming decades.[3]

It's also important to understand that the higher the orbit, the longer space-craft can survive. For instance, in LEO, atmospheric conditions degrade orbit over time and eventually pull objects back down to Earth, typically within a few years (if the object is not being piloted and steered from Earth). Spacecraft in GEO, which accounts for most telecommunication and weather satellites, is far more unpredictable; objects in GEO can remain in orbit for millions of years.[4] Though space debris has not yet caused any significant or severe pain to the sector, it will cause issues in the future if steps are not taken to curb its effects. The unknown is not if, but *when* such incidents will occur.

> *If we're not careful, we face the potential of the*
> *'tragedy of the commons,' where companies will focus*
> *on near-term business success rather than long-term*
> *sustainability and shared safety of operations.*[5]
> **Scott Kordella | Space Systems Director, The MITRE Corporation**

The risk of collision between errant spacecraft or debris is not the only loom-ing danger; space weather and electromagnetic pulse (EMP) attacks pose problems as well. Both occurrences can destroy electronics and electrical grids, which would result in catastrophic effects on the economy and military alike.

Adverse space weather, including solar storms, can disrupt satellites on a minimal or debilitating scale. In the case of the latter, our communications and navigation capabilities reliant on satellite data would be destroyed. Professor Robertus von Fay-Siebenburgen, an expert in the matter, explained in an inter-view, "A worst-case scenario may cause the setback of the economy of a country even up to a decade."[6] The American Geophysical Union's journal *Space Weather* included a paper in 2017 estimating that the daily economic impact would likely see losses between $40 billion and $50 billion.[7]

EMP attacks, which affect Earth's magnetic field, result in power blackouts in the affected areas. Such attacks can derive from naturally occurring phenomena such as solar flares and lightning, but the more significant threat comes from nuclear EMP attacks as part of nuclear warfare. In today's world, one of these attacks would have crippling effects on communications systems, hospitals, our access to food and water, and everything else in between powered by electricity.

These attacks can also destroy satellite capabilities, which is what happened with AT&T's Telstar satellite in 1962.[8] The ability to anticipate these naturally occurring threats and to protect ourselves from human-made attacks grows increasingly urgent, despite the fact that EMP attacks have historically garnered minimal attention.

There are startup efforts underway to forecast space weather events, which could be valuable to organizations managing spacecraft. In March 2019, US President Trump signed an executive order to protect against EMP attacks, citing that "The vulnerability of U.S. critical infrastructure to cyber, physical, and electromagnetic attacks mean that adversaries could disrupt military command and control, banking and financial operations, the electrical grid, and means of communication."[9] The order instructs multiple federal agencies to prioritize identifying high-risk systems and determine how to protect them from potential attacks.

Unfortunately, society tends to work reactively rather than proactively on crafting and enabling intelligent solutions. As we know, our quality of life on Earth depends on these structures and technologies; preserving them is of the utmost importance. Governments can slow down or speed up the pace of these activities, but can government act and support in smarter ways?

While some individuals in Congress have tried to pass space-related bills concerning the above areas—one as recently as December 2018—disagreements from others have blocked the efforts.[10] Whether these are political issues or results of a lack of education, we all need to push for change in these high-risk areas to ensure that our representatives understand them and care about them enough to take effective action. It is crucial that we consider these variables and begin to solve for them while they are manageable—not after they become threatening to our infrastructure and activities, both in space and on Earth.

KEEPING SPACE SAFE

Given that some space technology—such as rockets—can be weaponized, the argument consistently arises that not every nation ought to have access to space. In some cases, specific technology is not permitted to be shared or sold out of its origin countries. Some have called for a type of "space police," possibly created by the United Nations. However, our civilization has not yet reached a point where it can tolerate policing structures in space; treaties exist, but many of them don't include the critical space players, and signatories can leave them quite easily. Instead, countries with a strong stake in space, especially in the defense realm, are exploring options to solve this problem on a national level.

The prohibition of various activities in and around the space sector is representative of the ongoing high degree of mistrust between different nation-states. However, space is fair game for anyone willing to pay for launch. With that in mind, the power that's available in space comes with serious implications, whether a nation puts a tracking satellite or an armed rocket into space. The private sector also has a considerable amount of autonomy despite existing regulatory gaps. While the United States is today's leading space power, it is unrealistic to expect every other foreign power to submit to precisely what the United States wants and needs. The real longevity of the space ecosystem requires looking beyond national interests. If we are going to develop more infrastructure and economic opportunities in space and beyond, we need more collaboration between domestic and foreign organizations, both private and public.

For instance, the official view from the United States government is that until the People's Republic of China cuts back on its espionage against the United States and improves its human rights record, it will make it almost impossible for American organizations to collaborate with Chinese interests. As such, NASA is prohibited from any bilateral collaboration with China without prior approval from Congress.[11] Nevertheless, US company Nanoracks received sign-off of approval in 2017 to take a Chinese scientific experimentation to the ISS (to operate on the Japanese module of the station).[12] In 2018, Nanoracks partnered with Chinese NewSpace company KuangChi Science on its Traveler spacecraft, a high-altitude helium balloon.[13]

The space arms race is another looming problem; the consequences of in-space warfare, satellite destruction, and more would be far more severe. Japan planned and developed a space-specific military branch over recent years, while Russia and China steadily increased and fortified their in-space military capabilities.[14] In 2019, India launched its third and fourth radar imaging reconnaissance satellites (RISAT), which will be used on a civilian level for disaster relief and to improve the agriculture sector—but India will also use its imaging data for intelligence and defense surveillance.

This is not the only military use that India has in the works for space; in April 2019, ISRO conducted an anti-satellite test, becoming the fourth country to do so (the others are, of course, the United States, Russia, and China).[15] The resulting debris, among other implications, sent shockwaves throughout the industry. Reactions ranged from mild concern to calls for boycotting the country's PSLV. Planet, which has a successful and longstanding relationship with ISRO as its launch provider, was one company that condemned the test. Brian Weeden of the Secure World Foundation commented that "the commercial sector should be concerned about where the space arms race is heading and how it may impact their business, and they should have a voice in the debate."[16]

Business implications are certainly one thing, but security and safety are more significant issues. As Weeden noted, "Coupled with increased reliance on space for military purposes by many countries, it means there's a greater chance a future conflict may include attacks on satellites. And that could have devastating consequences for all, including commercialization and investment in space." India also plans to simulate a space warfare exercise, called IndSpaceEx, to explore the potential threats that space could hold in the future and to help determine how to develop its capabilities moving forward.[17] While this exercise certainly has pragmatic intentions, it also sheds light on the urgency to create global policies around the uses of space.

The United States has over seven hundred military bases around the globe, and taxpayers pay close to $1 trillion annually for this global infrastructure. The more we distribute defense spending to put some of those dollars into space infrastructure and technology, the more the United States will increase the complexity of its reach. Shifting Department of Defense capabilities from a few large military satellites to co-hosted payloads on many commercial satellites would also make the United States much less susceptible to a surprise first-strike in space. That in itself provides diversification of resources, new tech development, new career opportunities, and a safer, more robust space

presence—which will make the nation stronger, more resilient, and continue its status as a global space power.

Unfortunately, government space programs have a history of looking at things in narrow ways. Given the security and secrecy issues around government space efforts, many interests and ideas aren't exchanged properly or correctly. As aerospace engineer Michael Clive* explained, "We have the resources. What we don't have is the allocation of those resources."[18] What Clive is describing is a call for collective action and a cohesive vision of the future. We must motivate ourselves to do something with what exists in front of us.

GLOBAL FRAMEWORKS

With space activities growing by the day and new developments on the horizon, countries such as Luxembourg and the United States are slowly

★ **Michael Clive** is an engineer with extensive expertise in high pressure systems. With an early background in digital animation, Clive worked at NASA as an animator before moving into the aerospace sector. He then worked as an engineer for both XCOR Aerospace and SpaceX, specializing in high-pressure fluid systems, and now serves as the director of engineering, high pressure systems, for a stealth startup in San Francisco.

creating frameworks that will provide more security for the industry. US Congress finally made progress after decades-long debates and established the US Space Force (USSF) on December 20, 2019 as the country's sixth military branch. As part of the Air Force, the USSF will operate primarily in a military defense capacity, and a four-star general, with the title of Chief of Space Operations (CSO), will head the branch.[19] The first CSO is Gen. John W. "Jay" Raymond, who formerly served as Commander, Air Force Space Command, Peterson Air Force Base, Colorado. This new branch and its developments will be critical to watch over the coming years, both in how the branch responds to continued advances in the global space sector and how it navigates its evolution as a separate service within the US military.

Creating a new space agency branch is but one small step to ensure the industry's ongoing safety and success. In Luxembourg's push to create adequate space regulations, Marc Serres shared, the LSA found that establishing comprehensive national law is impossible without facing the other industry challenges—which include technical, financial, and business or market challenges. "Even though we saw that [the national law] may be a radical game changer in the space economy, we saw that we needed a lot of things to be done in parallel to make all this possible," Serres explained.[20]

Another essential aspect of Luxembourg's plans for space depend on international cooperation—this is crucial. "What we try to do here is raise awareness, to convince people to cooperate on these topics for the future. And I must say that the situation, in regard to where we started three years ago, is radically different," said Serres. He noted further that, "If you look at the agenda of the United Nations in the last two years, the space resources topic was again on the agenda of the COPUOS (The United Nations Committee on the Peaceful Uses of Outer Space). And informal groups have started working on aspects related to regulatory frameworks; for example, there is an initiative from the Netherlands. It shows that something is now evolving."

Serres also shared that the LSA has engaged in ongoing discussions with countries like Japan, Portugal, the Czech Republic, Poland, Belgium, and ESA, and has agreements with the United Arab Emirates and China to help shape the future of the space industry.

I think we've got a couple of good models to look at. Certainly, what the Isle of Man has done—what Chris Stott has done there with ManSat— is a good example of a small nation essentially throwing its doors open and saying, 'Hey, come do business here. We'll cut through all the red tape.' That's the model that Luxembourg is now using. I think we'll see more models like that, but at the same time, there needs to be some level of regulation to protect the country itself.[21]

James Dunstan | Founder, Mobius Legal Group

The critical component in the future of space will be aligning our values to develop international frameworks and solutions for the industry. Whether this framework results from an all-encompassing treaty or from establishing industry standards each piece one at a time until a robust structure exists, regulating space will require international collaboration and collective agreements.

Space is a domain that we all benefit from and share. It is too crucial to our world and holds too much potential for disaster if mishandled; we need to determine common, global interests and concerns if we want to create solutions that are favorable for all. While this kind of cooperation might be antithetical to the way most nations or even companies inherently operate, seeking proactive, collaborative solutions will result in a stronger, safer industry. Basing decisions off of rigid self-interests will only result in unfavorable compromises—and might eventually cause other issues as well. When our species stops focusing solely on nationalistic initiatives and begins to move toward actions that enable a functional space economy, we'll be on the path to amazement, discovery, wonder, and prosperity. As autonomous beings, these decisions belong to us. We will inevitably determine the future of our involvement in space in expanding our horizons. Now is the time to pursue your wildest dreams, turn your passions into profits, and maybe even change the world.

CHAPTER TWENTY-THREE
THE SPACE RUSH

*Both exploration and development are necessary components
to ensure we have a sustained path to the bright future
we all want to see—a future worthy of our species.*[1]
Armin Ellis, Ph.D.*

hroughout the ages, throughout all the trepidations and skepticism, it remains abundantly clear that space holds immense potential. It's no wonder that countries around the globe seek access to space as well as leadership there. Space is difficult, complicated, and majestic. If you can leverage space, you have access to power and dominion that most countries on Earth—even prosperous ones—aspire to obtain.

To better inform our understanding of the potentials for NewSpace, we can look to history to see who excelled economically and militarily through exploration. Support for such activities came from governments, whether it was the Ming Dynasty ordering ships to explore the Indian Ocean in the 1300s, Lewis and Clark's Corps of Discovery Expedition to the Northwest portion of the continental United States in the early nineteenth century, or the United States' Voyager spacecraft exploring the outer planets in the twenty-first century. And today, we know more about the planet Mars than Marco Polo, Leif Ericson, Alexander the Great, or the entirety of Europe during the Age of Discovery knew about the various areas of the world they each explored.

★ **Armin Ellis, Ph.D.** is a scientist, engineer, and explorer with a long history in the space sector. He worked on Mission Systems Concepts at NASA's Jet Propulsion Laboratory for eight years, spearheading missions from the International Space Station to Mars. Dr. Ellis later founded the Exploration Institute, a think tank based in Los Angeles County that uses its trademarked "i2i" (idea to implementation) method to develop breakthrough strategies across various sectors, primarily the aerospace, new tech, and marine industries.

Let's think back to the Gold Rush in the nineteenth century to understand the possibilities within an emerging sector. Beginning in 1799 in North Carolina and spanning across the globe in Australia, New Zealand, Brazil, Canada, South Africa, and the United States, millions around the world were inspired by the opportunities and potential resources that the Gold Rush held, often risking everything they had for a chance at the benefits.[2] What might be different between a "space rush" and a gold rush is that today, we have the wisdom and benefit of over 150 years of advances in finance and technology. We have more specialized knowledge and tools than those nineteenth-century gold miners could ever imagine; to the Gold Rush era, many of our more recent innovations, such as Earth observation satellites or the internet, would look like magic. Another key difference is that space initially existed as an exclusive activity, requiring specific expertise along with high capital investments (and, by extension, larger organizations). Yet the initial focus of a movement does not mean that there is only one way to gain value from it or to become involved.

As Dr. Armin Ellis, founder of the Exploration Institute, emphasized, "Exploration for its own sake pushes us to the edge of our comfort zones." Exploration is about growing as individuals, as a society, and as a civilization. This is undoubtedly true in the case of space exploration and of the NewSpace revolution. It also means that, ultimately, better understanding the universe can yield a better understanding of ourselves—and each other. The universe is big enough for us all, but the countries that take leadership positions stand to gain the early benefits—economically, culturally, politically, and socially. They will also be the leaders who shape the future. Consider Gavin Menzies's disproved theory that the Chinese circumnavigated the planet in the fifteenth century and sailed to America.[3] If, from the fifteenth century onward, the Chinese *had* continued in their explorations rather than decide to focus within their borders, it would be a very different world today.

Humanity also requires goals—challenging goals—to keep us moving forward and pushing the boundaries. Look at sports: we've all heard of unbreakable records, yet at some point, a determined athlete would shatter the pre-existing belief of what is possible. Space is similar. People said it would be impossible to send any living creature to space and return safely to Earth, yet we've done it. The same was said about visiting the Moon, then about reaching Mars, or leaving our solar system—yet we have accomplished all those things, and more. Perhaps there is evolutionary wiring deep within us that requires us to try, test, experiment, and push the limits when we hear, "No, it can't be done." Or, perhaps we know there is more to learn, more to discover, and more to create beyond the familiar.

It's time to dispel the myth that space is an esoteric subject to be dealt with only by astrophysicists, rocket scientists, government space programs, and a few wealthy individuals. Space's success has been built on dreams, persistence, and creative minds coming together. Space is only 100 kilometers above sea level. That's incredibly close—about an hour's drive on most United States highways (at speed limit, of course). It's frequently stated within the space community that once in space, you are halfway to anywhere. Whether you dream of a future Earth that looks like a park or envision lunar sports and recreation facilities, every dream of space has its place.

PART VII

THE BLUEPRINT OF EVOLUTION

CHAPTER TWENTY-FOUR
SPACE IS EVERYWHERE

Now it's time to leave the capsule if you dare
This is Major Tom to Ground Control
I'm stepping through the door
And I'm floating in a most peculiar way
And the stars look very different today
David Bowie, "Space Oddity," 7-inch single, July 11, 1969.

Five days before the Apollo 11 Moon landing, David Bowie released his acclaimed single "Space Oddity," singing from the perspective of an astronaut alone in the universe, observing the small blue dot that is Earth before a space-walk. The Apollo program ran from 1960 to 1972, cost over $25 billion ($200 billion in today's terms), and inspired countless innovations—both quantifiable and unquantifiable.[1] The inspiration for the song, however, was unrelated to the Apollo mission; Bowie wrote "Space Oddity" after watching Stanley Kubrick's 1968 film *2001: A Space Odyssey*.[2]

Those familiar with David Bowie are aware of his fascination with and love for space; evidence appears throughout his performances, personal aesthetic, albums, and lyrics. Bowie is widely considered an unparalleled icon, his influence affecting music, pop culture, visual style, fashion, social issues, sexuality, personal identity, and an overall understanding of the world. Bowie is but one example of space's impact on individuals, which then transfers onto art and culture. Eventually, this impact spreads over each and every one of us, whether in profound moments or in the small, precious details that gently shape our experiences as humans. In 2013, forty-four years after the release of "Space Oddity," astronaut Chris Hadfield performed a rendition of the world-famous song from the International Space Station—which Bowie said was "possibly the most poignant version of the song ever created."[3]

For centuries, investing in space through arts and culture has proven to be a profoundly effective way to win hearts and minds. Space touches and inspires nearly every industry related to art, design, and entertainment. We see it everywhere we look, from the silver screen to the screensavers on our computers. We covet futuristic appliances; different versions of cosmic apparel emerge every year as we dream of what we would wear if we lived on another planet or among the stars; we wonder when our cars will finally fly. We see both overt and subtle nods to space in architecture, automobiles, furniture, fine art, theme parks, video games, children's toys, and the vast amount of technology at our disposal today. Designers around the world craft expansive, visionary ideas that push traditional and terrestrial boundaries, fueled by wonder and imagination. We receive these creations with appreciation and awe, our minds and spirits stimulated by these small tastes of exciting potentials yet to come.

A GATEWAY TO PROGRESS

Star Trek was an attempt to say that humanity will reach maturity and wisdom on the day that it begins not just to tolerate, but take a special delight in differences in ideas and differences in life forms. ... If we cannot learn to actually enjoy those small differences, to take a positive delight in those small differences between our own kind, here on this planet, then we do not deserve to go out into space and meet the diversity that is almost certainly out there.[4]

Gene Roddenberry | Creator, *Star Trek*

I s it possible through entertainment to not only make money but create Apollo-sized returns on inspiration? Can entertainment and "infotainment" experiences become the gateway for future explorers, technologists, inventors, and other pioneers? At first glance, the imprint of science fiction reaches us on individual and cultural levels. But its effects are also visible on humanity as a whole, from technological advancements to economic prosperity.

Star Trek, known worldwide across multiple generations, gave rise to countless technology developers and leaders. It inspired people to study hard sciences and to invent, love, and devote their lives to space-related work.

Gene Roddenberry, creator of *Star Trek*, notably employed a consultant from the RAND Corporation, Harvey Lynn, Jr., to help develop certain technological aspects of the show.[5] Back in 1965—before *Star Trek* was even picked up— Jeffrey Hunter (who famously played Captain Pike) relayed in an interview that for him, the most interesting aspects of the show were "actually based on the RAND Corporation's

projection of things to come," and explained that the show "will be like getting a look into the future" as "some of the predictions will surely come true in our lifetime." An *MSNBC* article from 2002 explored Lynn's role in shaping the series: "[Lynn] contributed indispensable insights that helped shape ideas like the ship's computer (he suggested that it talk in a woman's voice), the sickbay (he suggested that beds be outfitted with 'electrical pickups' that monitor the body) and teleportation."[6] Though the show may have "predicted" certain technologies already in the pipelines, it also provided the blueprints for countless other innovations across a wide variety of industries. The relationship between science fiction and science fact, in this case, has been an incredible two-way street.

More recently, television shows and movies such as *Westworld*, *The Expanse*, *The Martian*, *Gravity*, *Interstellar*, and *Arrival* all portray their own versions of where the edges of science, space, Hollywood, and reality converge. Visibility from entertainment has the power to guide public perception and even garner support for future space programs and missions. *The Martian* (2015) helped cement a renewed interest in Mars, a longtime passion of SpaceX and Elon Musk. Bert Ulrich, NASA's media liaison for film and television, noted that *The Martian* helped put NASA back on the public radar since the 2011 Space Shuttle program ended; it certainly helps that many of the technologies featured in the film actually exist today, are used on the ISS, and were developed by NASA.[7]

If seeing is believing, seeing a movie about an astronaut growing their own food, creating their own oxygen, and surviving the harsh conditions of the Red Planet led the public to believe that life on Mars is genuinely possible. In 2016, a year after the film came out, NASA received over 18,000 applications from prospective astronauts—by and far the highest record of applicants in history. One of the missions that the twelve selected astronauts will embark on is a journey to Mars.[8]

Global technology leaders such as Intel and Google invest in science fiction to aid their internal developments and help them stay competitive. Intel employed futurist Brian David Johnson (who is also a science fiction author) from 2009 to 2016.[9] Eric Schmidt, longtime Google CEO and current chair of the US Department of Defense Innovation Advisory Board, noted in his opening speech at CeBIT in 2012 that science fiction affects "present and future technology."[10]

There are also groups investing in cutting-edge ideas inspired by sci-fi. One such example is venture capital firm Lux Capital, which explains that those in the company are "strong believers in the symbiotic relationship between science fiction and science fact and the ever-shrinking gap between them." Lux Capital scientist Sam Arbesman pointed to key examples that drive its mission to build the future: "*Star Trek* predicted both the flip phone and the iPad; Neal Stephenson and William Gibson imagined cyberspace and virtual online worlds, such as Second Life; Isaac Asimov even anticipated Big Data-driven quantitative social science."[11]

Competitions such as the Breakthrough Prize and the XPRIZE Foundation enabled people to turn science fiction into reality. Peter Diamandis, the founder of XPRIZE, played a crucial role as an effective advocate to renew interest in private spaceflight in the 1990s. He could even be considered the archetype for the advocates, leaders, and change-makers who leveraged ideas from both science fiction and history to create a better future.

CHAPTER TWENTY-FIVE
INSPIRING THE FUTURE

Humans have always wanted to know what is over the next hill. We have never been satisfied by the status quo—we have always had a drive to do things better. It is said by some that this impulse is driven by the DRD4-7r gene, and though the true source is likely more complex than a single gene, it is this desire to explore—our refusal to be satisfied with existing conditions—that has separated our species from other humanoid species.

Major General Thomas D. Taverney, US Air Force, Retired*

S cience fiction itself works as a catalyst for science creation. It plants seeds of imagination in our brains and pushes forward the ideas that we spend time thinking about, dreaming of, and actually creating. To understand the extent to which imagination and art have influenced humanity, industry experts offer a glimpse into the worlds and ideals of science fiction—and the realities they enable.

★ **Maj. Gen. Thomas D. Taverney** was the Vice Commander, Headquarters Air Force Space Command, Peterson Air Force Base, Colo. He retired from the USAF in 2006 after thirty-eight years of service in space operations and space systems development. Since 2001, he has been the senior vice president of space systems development at Leidos (a US defense, aviation, information technology, and bio-medical research company). At Leidos (formerly Science Applications International Corporation (SAIC)), he led the Commercially Hosted Infrared Program (CHIRP), which received awards for its groundbreaking capabilities from *Aviation Week*, C^4ISR *Journal*, and NASA. Taverney has been recognized numerous times for his many achievements, notably with inductions into the Space Operations Hall of Fame in 2010 and the Air Force Space Command Hall of Fame in 2016; he received the General Bernard Schriever "Lifetime Achievement Award" in 2014 and the von Braun Award for Excellence in Space Program Management at the AIAA Space and Astronautics Forum (SPACE) in 2018.

THE VAST UNKNOWN

Ray Podder

Ray Podder is the founder of GROW, a company that focuses on a whole systems approach to decentralized technologies for humanity. The organization designs and integrates full-circle technologies and strategies, with an eye toward universal sustainability.[1]

I believe that the evolution of humanity and the advancements in progress are directly related to how we see ourselves in relation to the cosmos. The space economy and space represent where we are today as a global society. It's always a work in progress. Historically, ideas that captured people's imaginations regarding the possibilities that the future holds, or what that vision looks like, have directed societies and civilizations.

If you look at the existing space narrative and its connotations, it's a derivative of twentieth-century industrial-economy culture, which presented a new way of being where everyone had an opportunity, and you could move forward and create your own path. We tend to view the artifacts of space exploration—the rockets and the technology—as an extension of going forward from that factory-building, industrial-era mindset. What has perpetuated that perspective to this stage, however, is something else: the desire to explore the unknown. Few narratives from the 1950s and 1960s touched on that, *Star Trek* being one of the critical exceptions. Then there was *Star Wars* telling the hero's journey, and later breakthrough sci-fi films, from *Blade Runner* to the more recent, impressive films [like *The Martian*]. It's starting to mirror the cultural zeitgeist that's going on at the moment.

If you focus on the thread of culture, what are the set of social agreements that allow humanity to move forward, and what does that look like? What does that feel like? One of the more striking aspects in sci-fi, fantasy, and other space-related things is that they are becoming more about perception, or our conscious reality. *Arrival* touched on non-temporal use of language and what that does to our understanding of time and space. *Doctor Strange* tapped into the visible reality that we believe in versus the quantum reality that we may or may not be able to navigate. There were some films, such as *Contact*, where we looked at space exploration very much from a consciousness perspective rather than from the physical, mechanistic way of achieving those ends. I think that's an indicator of things to come and a sign of new narratives that could be created to support the cultural shift that's happening in the world right now.

A ll cultures embrace fiction; the creation myths of any culture are rooted in fiction. Fiction itself defines the metaphors that we construct our reality against, and we evaluate our technical, physical reality against those narratives. In the United States, for example, there's the underlying narrative of the explorer and the maverick; that's always been embedded in American culture. Now the underlying narrative has shifted a little bit.

Our historical understanding of science, even from the time of Galileo or Descartes, is going down a cause-and-effect reductionist path, looking at things in isolation, hoping that they would add up to a whole. Currently, what we're seeing in scientific communities everywhere is cross-pollination: looking at whole systems, understanding interconnectedness of parallel disciplines or even unrelated innovations or unrelated data points, understanding how the human animal plays into that.

This is the case even in how we look at industrial design—we look at human factors now more than anything else. We look at things less from a mechanical point of view and more from psychological and behavioral understandings of our inner and outer worlds. That changes how we frame science, because the line between art and science is starting to blur. What part of it is quantitative, measured, and progressive? What part of it is open, curious, and all-encompassing? Quantum computing is a good example—state change versus binary change.

These shifts in mindset are evolving into a scientific field: a new iteration of the alchemical tradition, what alchemists were to the original life sciences and the applied sciences that branched off the holistic understanding of nature. We're coming back to that full circle, with everything from Big Data to data visualization, to understanding human psychology or human behavior relative to technology, to understanding the interconnectedness of the environment and technological impact. We're starting to connect the dots.

As we start to connect the dots, the definition of science becomes a bit broader. Then, what defines fiction, coming off those understandings, is something else entirely. We're seeing some cultural markers in newer sci-fi/fantasy works in that they are incorporating the idea of consciousness, which is something we didn't see in the sci-fi narratives of the twentieth century. That said, new kinds of fiction will play a critical role in evolving our existing cultural sensibilities and will have a massive impact on how we explore space and what that means for humanity going forward.

Geopolitically and socioeconomically, we are seeing a disruption in the type of linear thinking that considered gross domestic product as the primary measure of growth. The monetary system has always been a way of measuring wealth, but what does that mean if your resources are being depleted and you aren't able to replenish them?

As we run into limits with these kinds of things, it's natural for us to reimagine alternate scenarios. Where are the alternatives open for exploration? There is an interesting relationship between humans and how we perceive and imagine when looking at the sky versus how we perceive and imagine when looking at Earth. One is directly connected to the other. For example, our date and time system, from the Gregorian calendar to the modern calendar system, is based on lunar cycles. We inform all kinds of things that are physical Earth phenomena by how we relate to the skies. That's always been a part of human existence; we're the translators between those two worlds.

Space is a critical narrative used to reimagine things from the perspective of a new, conscious awareness of what we understand today on Earth. Then, we can reflect that perspective back to how we organize our societies, how we classify our resources, how we determine what has value, how we prioritize, and how we create contextual hierarchies. Space shows us the way to figure that stuff out. What we see, what we understand, and what we can imagine by looking at the vast unknown impacts what we think is known and how we approach what is known.

We aren't necessarily breaking *limits*—we're breaking *preconceptions* of limits. There are, absolutely, limits—but we're widening our perceptual lens. The technology that we use to talk to one another right now, for example, is made of materials that have existed on Earth for hundreds of years, but no one thought of putting them together in this particular configuration to create this telecommunication technology that we use to communicate virtually. That is interesting because it's just expanding the limits of perception that produce these things. Space represents infinitely more—or is at least asymptotic toward—ways of perceiving and creating in ways we never before imagined.

In the twentieth century, at least in this country, John F. Kennedy made a decree of putting a man on the Moon, and the quest for that set into motion a brand-new socioeconomic reality—including the way NASA moved toward that goal and all the technologies that came out of it. That dream, or that projection of a new storyline, took it to this level.

Dreaming is part of the human experience, part of our existence. It's like training for our psyche: we go through these subconscious simulations that help us process whatever we're observing or whatever our perceptual abilities are picking up in the natural world. Now is a fascinating time because our conscious existence is media-saturated. To me, this signals that we are searching for a new dream—we are continuously trying to figure out which stories resonate with us. We don't really like what's going on in this reality, so we need time to contemplate, think, dream about alternate realities, and escape our current reality daily.

The visible reality is that we are consuming more and more media all the time, and we are spending more and more time in dreamlike states (i.e., interacting with the digital world rather than the physical world). Consumer culture is pretty much trying to get us into a dreamlike state of consumption—hypnosis if you will. More than any other time in history, we're living in a hypnotic, transient reality for many of our waking hours. I see that as a fascinating signal in the noise, because we are now working with new tools to imagine a new reality. But the truth that opens our minds for expansion is the vast unknown—it is looking up at the sky.

The things we think about now when we look up at the sky versus what humans thought about when they looked up at the sky one hundred years ago are remarkably different; what's going on in your mind is quite different from what happened when you had less information and less media-inundated experiences. So, what's next? What does that look like? How do we expand into that space both literally and metaphorically, and what does that mean? To look into the skies and see infinite possibilities starts to open up those questions and those conversations. That's why space is always going to be critical moving forward, and it certainly is now more than ever before.

THE VIRTUOUS CIRCLE

Daniel Abraham

Daniel Abraham is an author, comic book writer, screenwriter, and television producer. He is the co-creator and author of science fiction book series *The Expanse*, which the Syfy network adapted as a television series in 2015.[2]

The deep history of *The Expanse* started off many, many years ago as a pitch for a massive, multiplayer online game. By the time I came to it, it was already this well fleshed-out world. Then I thought, we could write this as a book and sell it for pizza money and giggles. But the vast majority of this is just because [Ty Franck and I] were science enthusiasts.

Daniel Abraham |
Author, *The Expanse*

The kind of 'virtuous circle' with this specific artistic endeavor is that when we're kids, we read these books and see these movies and television shows that have these amazing, weird, gorgeous technologies and vistas and this wide-open imagination. That's our first opportunity to imagine what a future could be like; then, as we get older, we find out how much is *actually* possible. We basically have that as our grand strategy as we figure out innovations in various sciences and technical problems, until we wind up with some new approximation; next, the science fiction writers come and say, '*What if we extrapolated that?*' Then, we have a new round of imagination and technique—what's genuinely possible or what's totally implausible and improbable (but awesome to look at or imagine). They all feed into the same kind of soil.

I think there's always a feedback loop between science fiction and actual science and engineering. We've had great interaction with folks in the commercial space industry. Here's what excites me most about the commercial space industry: the ideas of building permanent stations on Mars or the Jovian moons, or mining the asteroid belt. What drives that, to begin with, is the sense of wonder that comes with science fiction, followed by visions for exactly what it would take to have an awesomely cool future. The returns that we see on that process are almost always more profound and unexpected. I look at the Space Program from the sixties and seventies, and I look at the return that we've had on that—that's digital photography, that's new kinds of heart valves—this entire wealth of things that we figured out while we were working on these incredibly hard problems.

I look at the threats and challenges that are coming to Earth, to our lived environment, very quickly—the difficulties of living on a hot planet and trying to control the environment and systems that are so gigantic. Then I look at what we need to solve to have a Mars colony, and these two issues are in conversation with each other. The tremendous payout that we're going to get is not just domes on Mars; it's all the other things that we figure out as we try to build them. Worst case scenario, if we invest a tremendous amount of time and effort and capital in expanding out into the solar system and we fail, we will still wind up richer and smarter as a species, and better prepared to deal with things on Earth from making that effort.

We are in extraordinarily strange times. The ways in which we are understanding how to control and encode and preserve information—and have information that carries enough of its own context so that it remains legible—is a deep issue and a deep project. So, I would love to see this kind of expansive future, but even more than that, I would love to see what we learn and what we create as we reach for it. That's the process of science fiction. That's Jules Verne writing about the Nautilus and the United States then having nuclear submarines. We've been doing this for decades, maybe centuries, and it's been part of what has driven us to achieve miracles.

THERE IS ALWAYS A TOMORROW

Michael Clive

Michael Clive is an engineer with extensive expertise in high pressure systems. With an early background in digital animation, Clive worked at NASA as an animator before moving into the aerospace sector. He then worked as an engineer for both XCOR Aerospace and SpaceX, specializing in high-pressure fluid systems, and now serves as the director of engineering, high pressure systems, for a stealth startup in San Francisco.[3]

Science fiction, to me, has always been a way to see the spectrum of possibilities of human society through people whose whole life fixates on the concept of speculating. I dabble in writing science fiction from time to time; I use it to unpack a lot of my thoughts about the interlocking complexities of our modern technological age.

People like Bezos and Elon grew up watching the space program. Because Musk watched the space program unfold, and because he was a science fiction reader, he decided to create this world that he wanted to inhabit—the 'Mars Oasis.' That is one example of a particularly well-known entrepreneur using science fiction as a template for reality. We need science fiction.

I think one of the most significant issues that we face in society right now—specifically in America, but also more generally—is a lack of a vision. The American Dream was one vision of the future, kind of a personal future for American citizens to be able to support a family, have a home, and all the material goods you want. That was *a* vision of the future, but that vision existed because, during that period, it was still mostly an agrarian society. Now that many people live within the 'American Dream,' they don't know what's next. Politically, spiritually, or whatever, it feels like people have stopped looking beyond the five-year horizon. I've noticed this a lot amongst my peers as well as in society at large: long-term planning makes many people nervous and uncertain. A lot of people are uncomfortable talking about where they see themselves in five years; very few people actually think through the spectrum of possibilities for their life. Take that society-wide, and I think what we're lacking right now is a vision of the future.

At this point in history, we need *utopian* science fiction. It's extremely easy to write dystopian science fiction; we have an obsession with the destruction of things. We like to watch buildings collapse, cities get nuked, asteroids hit Earth. For some reason, there's a perverse incentive to watch these types of events. What I haven't seen is a significant amount of utopian science fiction in film, print, or media. Even ones that could be utopian end up being very dystopian.

Science fiction is a blueprint for society; science fiction is how we see ourselves in the future. One of the major things I was thinking about a couple of years ago was that we're in a post-science fiction age. What more science fiction can you write, now that we're living in this kind of science fiction world? But then I realized that was tremendously short-sighted of me—because there is always a tomorrow.

What I would hope is for some science fiction authors to have the audacity to dream and to present a world in which things are going well—even better than now—so that when our children get to read it, they will see a picture of reality and a way to go *forward,* rather than something to cower away from.

A GUIDING LIGHT

Christopher Stott

Christopher Stott is the chief executive officer and chair of ManSat, the world's largest commercial provider of satellite spectrum, which he founded with his father in 1998. ManSat is a pioneering success story of the private space sector, and established the Isle of Man, where it is based, as a hub for commercial space efforts. Stott is a space entrepreneur with experience in government policy and regulation, a fellow of the Royal Astronomical Society and the International Institute of Space Law, an alumnus and faculty member of the International Space University, and a founder of the International Institute of Space Commerce. He continues to support NewSpace through his involvement in space and STEM education by serving on several boards and by contributing to multiple space-related publications.[4]

'm a science fiction devotee; it is what I call 'research and development' for the company. You have some of the finest minds in human history who make a living out of predicting the future, of the impact and implications of different technologies upon human society. How can that not be fascinating? How can it not be relevant?

Science fiction is a guiding light. It is thought-provoking, mind-expanding. It challenges every assumption you can make in life, and it makes you stop and think about what is truly possible in space. It is the most politically subversive literature in all of human history; it's still banned in some countries. Growing up when everyone else was talking about pop stars and soccer, I was reading about nanotech, biotech, atomic warfare, and political upheaval—all through science fiction.

There's a reason why Elon Musk, Burt Rutan, and Jeff Bezos all flew sci-fi books on their first-ever flights. Elon Musk talks about how, growing up, one of the greatest books he ever read was *Foundation* by Isaac Asimov. Paul Allen said that when he was thirteen years old and completely lost as a child, he went to the library, and the library gave him a copy of Heinlein, and that's what got him into technology and computing. Same with Jeff Bezos reading Heinlein, Niven, and Pournelle. It's astounding. All those authors give you the alternatives and let you pick and choose the future you want to aspire to.

Look at Konstantin Tsiolkovsky and Sergei Korolev (the great Russian rocket scientists), Wernher von Braun (aerospace engineer and space architect), and Robert Goddard, and ask why they all got involved in space. They all said, quite simply, *'We read Jules Verne and H.G. Wells and Conan Doyle. We were inspired by their work.'* Then you find out that Clarke and Asimov and Heinlein all knew each other—Asimov and Heinlein shared a lab during World War II. Then you find out that Heinlein guided Pournelle and Niven. Pournelle and Niven are the team that literally came up with the Strategic Defense Initiative (SDI) program and pitched it to Reagan—*two Ph.D. sci-fi guys pitched the SDI program to Reagan.* There's a whole stream of these thinkers, going all the way back to Aristotle.

The Baltimore Gun Club's projectile, which travels into space in books *From the Earth to the Moon: A Direct Route in 97 Hours, 20 Minutes* (1865) and *Around the Moon* (1870) by Jules Verne

S ci-fi embraces our love of science, and the impact of science upon society can be matched almost page-by-page to science fiction literature. How do you envision space? When you watch *2001: A Space Odyssey*, how do you envision artificial intelligence? Do you think it's a coincidence that your iPhone looks like the Monolith? What about Google—what was their operating system called? Android. What was the first Google phone called? It was Nexus One. Think of *Blade Runner*, think of Philip K. Dick—what were the androids called? They were Nexus androids.

Let's look at people talking about settling Mars—that idea comes from science fiction. Look at Kurt Vonnegut, who was a science fiction writer, same as Ray Bradbury. William Gibson and Neal Stephenson came up with cyberpunk [a sub-genre of sci-fi] and the whole internet revolution. Neal Stephenson was a cofounder of Blue Origin with his friend Jeff Bezos, who invented the Kindle after reading *The Diamond Age*—Stephenson's book! Look at the impact of Stanley Kubrick with *2001*, who obviously had a visualization of Arthur C. Clarke's book, when you talk to the founders of human spaceflight in our industry. Clarke was the founder of geostationary satellite communications, of open source. Talk about artificial intelligence—how about HAL 9000 [from *2001*]?

It's a guiding light. You have a whole bunch of people who are into science, technology, engineering, and space, who grew up reading science fiction that gives them ideas—very subversive ideas, mind-blowing ideas. It expands the horizons as to what could be possible, and they then make that world a reality. This is the first case in human history of life imitating art, not art imitating life. It's the first time because life is *actually* imitating art, absolutely, without compunction.

Jerry Pournelle and I collaborated on many, many projects.
Heinlein and Clarke were in the team that generated SDI in
my house, and Jerry shaped the final pitch. Those who predict
the future are in a conversation stretching back centuries.[5]

Larry Niven* | Award-winning Science Fiction Author

★ **Larry Niven** is one of the world's most celebrated science fiction writers. His best-known work is *Ringworld* (1970), which received Hugo, Locus, Ditmar, and Nebula awards. A significant amount of his work resulted from collaborations with other sci-fi writers, notably Jerry Pournelle and Steven Barnes.

SPACE IS CLOSER THAN WE THINK

Nahum Romero

Nahum Romero is a space artist, composer, and multi-instrumentalist. He also works at the Committee for the Cultural Utilizations of Space (ITACCUS) within the International Aeronautical Foundation.[6]

My father bought me *The Cosmos* DVDs, and the effect that Carl Sagan had on me was profound—I realized that he was talking about space through poetry. When I meet people from the space community, everyone tells me that they got interested because of *A Space Odyssey,* or Jules Verne, or Carl Sagan. That's the power of culture and arts in these people.

Something great about the private sector is that we see a very bold series of companies taking crazy risks—because the profit is uncertain, because that technology is complicated, because it's expensive—and yet they're doing it, and they're embracing these risks. These companies can take risks more easily, they can be more experimental than space agencies. This is a fantastic opportunity because it'll be easier to work with all these new companies than with space agencies.

Space is not distant. It's closer than we all think. That's a big concern for me, how we perceive space. When we talk with people who aren't working in the space sector, we see how people feel distant—like it's such a faraway topic. Space is about us, it's about being human, it's about benefiting and contributing to our societies in economical ways, in planning, in understanding. We're using space for us—when we use our phones, every time we look up an address, to know the weather. We use it for so many things, so it's vital that we get involved. In any field, we don't want to have a single discourse. We want to have as many voices as possible. As artists, as free souls, as anyone working with space topics, we have the responsibility of being actively involved in shaping space agendas.

When I say that space is my medium, it is because it allows me to have a unique perspective of this moment and this place—and I mean physically, but also metaphorically. Before there were space activities or before we had rockets, there were artists, writers, and musicians that were already thinking about this. Before science and technology, artists were able to take us there.

Our role is also to envision the future, the impossible things, and to create new, imagined possibilities.

I think it is a privilege to be able to look at ourselves with that perspective and that distance; that is when we are able to understand ourselves better. How do you know what light is if you have never experienced darkness? How do you describe gravity if you have never experienced weightlessness? That's a beautiful thing about space—it leads to this extreme alternative perspective and experience.

THE FUTURE IS TODAY

Penn Arthur

Penn Arthur is the cofounder and chief executive officer of Inhance Digital, one of the largest and most cutting-edge digital media agencies in the United States. Throughout his career, Arthur has successfully provided marketing concepts for technically complex industries and products, including aerospace and telecom.[7]

When we started the company, my business partner Maziar Farzam and I were huge science fiction fans. We would always watch these movies, like *Minority Report,* and say, 'We need to build that.' And honestly, I can say that we really have been building the stuff that we see in movies. We love to use rendered face designs; we love how some of those things work. We are always trying to build those types of things; we're always thinking about those things.

It's a fantastic time to be in this business, because the computing power and the hardware and the devices are finally starting to catch up to what our original vision was. When I put that HoloLens[†] on outside of the aircraft and had things popping up around me, depending on where I walked around the [virtual] aircraft, it just screamed that this is totally the future. It was like something out of *Back to The Future,* where you're walking around and seeing these advertisements and things popping up around the airplane. It's amazing. It's incredible.

[†] **The Microsoft HoloLens** is a pair of smart glasses that features mixed reality technology (i.e., a combination of real and virtual worlds). Here, Arthur refers to the software application that Inhance Digital developed as a proof of concept for the US Air Force Research Laboratory, which simulates various aircraft and their technical aspects in order to help train Air Force maintainers.

BUILDING THE FUTURE

Jeremy Conrad

Jeremy Conrad is the cofounder and chief executive officer of Quartz, a San Francisco-area startup focused on reimagining construction via new robotics, hardware, and software applications. Previously, he was a founding partner at Lemnos, a venture capital firm focused on hardware in industries including aerospace, construction, agriculture, and manufacturing.[8]

To this day, I do ideation sessions with entrepreneurs where we watch science fiction movies, and we write down everything in it that doesn't exist, and then we debate what's possible today. Using science fiction as inspiration is something that people have done forever. If you go back and look at certain books of science fiction, you realize that most of Silicon Valley today is built on people making the future they wanted. Between space, science fiction, and what we can do today, now is the time to go do it.

SPARKING IMAGINATION

Shahin Farshchi, Ph.D.

Dr. Shahin Farshchi is a partner at Lux Capital, a venture capital firm focused on science and technology businesses. A scientist and engineer, Dr. Farshchi formerly cofounded Vista Integrated Systems, which built wireless vital sign monitors, developed hybrid vehicles for GM, and developed software for multiple Silicon Valley startups.[9]

My dad was a huge science fiction fan and an engineer, so I grew up watching *Star Trek*, seeing grown men traveling the galaxy in their pajamas, and people talking to their cars in *Knight Rider*. They got me excited about engineering; I became enamored by technology and understanding how things work as a result of watching science fiction. I think those shows sparked imagination and made me passionate about pushing the frontier of technology, which is even why I got a Ph.D. Then I fell into venture, and I'm glad that now my role is to empower those founders who are on the forefront of technology.

A VIVID SHIFT

Richard Godwin

Richard Godwin is the president of Space Technology Holdings, a strategic development group focused on commercializing and bringing to market intellectual property related to government and private space research. He is also the founder of Starbridge Venture Capital, a venture capital fund that invests in dual-use advanced technologies derived or designed for spaceflight.[10]

can remember, vividly, the day when I first got into the whole space thing. I was eight years old, watching TV in England, around the time when Project Mercury [NASA's first human spaceflight program] ended. Suddenly, *Fireball XL5* comes on the television, and it's about spaceships going to other planets. I watched it and I thought, *Holy moly, how cool is that?* I got into it from that point on. Then *Doctor Who* came on the air in November of '63; it later became *2001: A Space Odyssey*, and that was always my favorite film because it was just so realistic.

You know all the people who watch *Star Trek* and then say, '*Oh, I can make that. I can make a tricorder, let's figure it out.*' Science fiction does tend to lead our thinking, and I think to a great extent it's philosophical as well—we look at it from a philosophical viewpoint.

GLOBAL UNITY

Peter Platzer

Peter Platzer is the cofounder and chief executive officer of Spire Global, a data analytics company in the United States that designs, builds, launches, and manages a network of small satellites for Earth observation. Platzer and his cofounders met while attending the International Space University and created Spire in 2012, which is now considered one of the most successful NewSpace companies to date. Spire has successfully deployed more than one hundred Earth observation CubeSats into low Earth orbit, which it uses to monitor our planet 24/7.[11]

read a large amount of German science fiction—serials that were published once a week in magazines and then compiled into novels. I read a couple hundred thousand pages of those types of science fiction series. One called *Perry*

Rhodan had an underlying theme of unity—unifying people across external boundaries such as skin color, religion, and sexual preference, and focusing instead on the internal qualities of individuals.

When I was a teenager, I had a passport, but I didn't understand the whole border thing. I wanted a passport that said, 'Peter Platzer, Citizen of Earth.' I think the idea of borders is kind of silly, which is partially driven by me growing up literally thirty minutes west of the Iron Curtain. I was very close and could see that, as a physicist, and from a rational perspective, it's entirely random that I was born on the left side of the Iron Curtain rather than the right side—and my life would be entirely different if I had been born on the right side of the Iron Curtain.

That concept of unity is something that deeply resonates with me, which is why the first and most important value of Spire Global is 'global.' It is a global company that was set up early to have offices across the world. Satellites are global, outside of country boundaries. Space is extraterritorial: it has a different set of laws. There are a lot of things about satellites that, by definition, make them global. Our customers are global, our product is global, our data collection is global. We have people across the world; we travel all over the world. If you work with space, you're working with something that unifies the planet across borders, and that is something not unique just to Spire Global, but to all space companies.

PROFESSIONAL DEVELOPMENT

Mandy Sweeney

Mandy Sweeney is the vice president of operations at the Museum of Science Fiction. She previously worked as a deputy program manager at NASA where she acted as the lead consultant for developing NASA's strategic plan.[12]

was working at NASA, helping with communications to Congress. Everybody sort of 'spoke' science fiction at NASA. For instance, if they needed a metaphor, they would draw from science fiction. If there was a joke, it was coming from science fiction—and I didn't get it, I was kind of out of the loop. So, I had colleagues who put me on a science fiction diet; every other week, there was a new book on my desk or a set of DVDs.

It was really part of my professional development to immerse myself in science fiction so that I could relate to my colleagues and be able to tell NASA's story better. It sounds kind of ridiculous, but my ability to succeed in communicating the NASA story to Congress and justifying their budget was, in large part, thanks to science fiction—like reading Arthur C. Clark and watching *Star Trek*, and then being able to explain to people why it was worth investing in what essentially was the replicator. There was a lot of early-stage technology, so we would draw metaphors from science fiction when we talked to people because they could understand it, and then think it was cool, and *then* understand why it was important. I think you would have to search quite hard for technology and engineering that wasn't wired by science fiction.

DISNEY AND THE MOON

John Spencer

John Spencer is the founder and president of the Space Tourism Society, an organization focused on establishing and expanding a space tourism industry. Spencer is also an outer space architect, internationally renowned for his design and creation of in-space structures and facilities and for space-themed structures on Earth. For his innovative architectural design work on the International Space Station, NASA awarded John with the Space Act Award and a Certificate of Recognition.[13]

There's a true link between entertainment and real space, and between real space and entertainment—they've always paralleled each other. Disney was a key player in the early days of the American [crewed] space program, with his *Man in Space* television show and other things, even with attractions at Disneyland. He actually had Wernher von Braun and Willie Ley create storyboards for their TV series that they showed to President Kennedy. They laid them out in the Oval Office to explain a space system where you had reusable rockets and space stations with Mars missions. That gave Kennedy the confidence to do the Moon speech—he had great admiration for Disney. So, there has always been an intimate connection between storytelling, myth, mythology, exploration, and space, because those are all exploration tools.

CONNECTING THE DOTS

Lynette Kucsma

Lynette Kucsma is the cofounder and chief marketing officer of Natural Machines, a company focused on using technology and design to provide fresh and healthy 3D-printed food. In 2015, CNN named Kucsma one of seven "tech superheroes to watch."[14]

'm sure there is a subconscious thing to it, or if you look back where you can connect the dots. I watched the *Jetsons* as a kid, I watched *Star Trek* and *Star Wars*, I was into the whole science fiction thing. You look at it and think, *'Can that happen?'* You start seeing things from science fiction coming to reality in many other areas, not just 3D printing, obviously. It can also be a challenge because when people hear about 3D food printing, they automatically tend to think *Star Trek* replicator or *Jetsons*—press a button and something comes out. The replicator on *Star Trek* did everything: the ceramics, the tea, the food. We're not quite there yet, but this is the stepping-stone to getting there.

CHAPTER TWENTY-SIX
SCI-FI AND SOCIETY

S pace as a subject in art, literature, film, and television goes back to each of their earliest respective origins. There's no shortage of topics in and around space that have potential intrigue, whether one wants to look at hard science fiction stories or explore the growing areas of focus that are part of the greater space movement.

T here is a deep well of literary science fiction dating all the way back to the second century, and the genre has existed on a global scale throughout numerous different civilizations and cultures. Notable examples include "The City of Brass," a folk tale that features robots, from Islam's Golden Age collection *One Thousand and One Nights* (ninth century); Mary Shelley's *Frankenstein* (1818); Edgar Allen Poe's short story "The Unparalleled Adventure of One Hans Pfaall" (1835); Jules Verne's novel *Around the Moon* (1872), which includes artistic renderings by Émile-Antoine Bayard and Alphonse de Neuville; and countless others that are part of the literary canon.

Science fiction has also influenced the film industry since its beginnings. Auguste and Louis Lumière, the French brothers who are widely regarded as the inventors of the moving picture, created the first science fiction film in 1895: *The Mechanical Butcher*, which features an imagined, rapid-manufacturing technology. A few years later, Marie-Georges-Jean Méliès made *A Trip to the Moon* (1902) and *The Impossible Voyage* (1904) as inspired by Verne's novels; the former is the first sci-fi film to depict space and considered one of cinema's most influential films. In *Science Fiction Directors, 1895–1998*, Dennis Fischer deems Méliès "the first great science fiction filmmaker."[1] Méliès is still hailed for his profound impacts on film as an artistic medium, best known for developing new visual and technical styles. He constantly experimented with his camera, leading him to invent a variety of special effects—such as making objects change in size or vanish altogether—that augmented his many sci-fi and fantasy-driven films. Indeed, the influence of science fiction in inspiring dazzling new creations and capabilities can be seen throughout cinematic history.

In more modern times, sci-fi films have been a consistent catalyst for advances in special effects, beginning in particular with Kubrick's *2001: A Space Odyssey* (1968). *Star Wars* and *Close Encounters of the Third Kind* (both 1977) led to another boom in cinematic innovations, resulting in the ultra-realistic effects—like computer generated imagery (CGI)—that we see in film and television today. It should be unsurprising, then, that science fiction accounts for some of the most financially lucrative entertainment in history. *Avatar* (2009) retained the title of the top-earning film worldwide[†] at $2.78 billion for ten years, until *Avengers: Endgame* (2019)—which employs sci-fi elements of time travel, alternate realities, advanced technologies, and life on other planets—pulled in $2.8 billion.[2] In 2015, *Star Wars: The Force Awakens* beat the *Avatar* box office record with over $764 million in revenue during its release—the only two films in North America to pull in more than $700 million—and pushed the film industry's domestic economy to a record-breaking $11 billion in 2015.[3] The *Star Wars* franchise itself is valued at over $43 billion.[4] Other sci-fi films from the last decade have seen huge numbers as well, like *Gravity* (2013), *Interstellar* (2014), and *The Martian* (2015), with worldwide gross sales of over $723 million, $677 million, and $630 million, respectively.[5]

Science fiction illuminates the possibilities of the space frontier; it also shapes these ideas on a societal scale. On the recommendation from my trusted friend and resident science fiction critic Adi Tantimedh, my wife and I ventured out to Monterey Park on a rainy February night to see Chinese film The Wandering Earth *(2019). The film is a strong statement of science fiction that borrows elements from other renowned films such as* 2001 *and* Armageddon. The Wandering Earth *is about our Sun going supernova in the future, and humanity's attempt to save the planet by physically moving it to a location 4.2 light-years from Earth—a journey that will take approximately 2,500 years.*

[†] There are numerous arguments that because of inflation, these modern figures of "highest-grossing film" are misleading (with correct inflation adjustment, *Gone With the Wind* is actually the highest-grossing film in history). So, to keep things simple, let's just agree that *Avatar* made a lot of money.

There are some significant aspects of *The Wandering Earth* that are worth pointing out. First, the film was partially funded and promoted by the Chinese government, which gives an insight into the country's aspirations and intentions.[6] As Tantimedh observed, "*Wandering Earth* is China's declaration of intent" to expand its activity and power into space. Historically, China did not venture far to explore or conquer lands, as other major countries did—this film helps lay the foundation for China to become a global leader, both on and off Earth.

In addition, the film consistently allows its characters to develop solutions based on science rather than magic or unobtanium. While many aspects lean more toward fiction than science, the film rests primarily on rationality—i.e., what is possible in reality. This is important particularly because the Chinese population lacks the late-nineteenth-century science fiction references that profoundly influenced and informed technological developments and vast areas of innovation. Although China has its own, more modern, indigenous sci-fi culture, it has been heavily influenced by Western science fiction created in the last forty years—mainly via movies. Consider the magnitude of sci-fi in the United States, Europe, and Japan—these are the countries that continue to surge forward technologically. Now, it seems that China is following that lead, drawing its own roadmaps of the future and using compelling sci-fi narratives and media to promote an innovative societal mindset.

Finnish director Renny Harlin, who now lives and works in China and is currently working on a sci-fi space adventure film called *Solara*, remarked in a March 2019 interview that he anticipates a surge of sci-fi films in China: "Traditionally, I think the Chinese filmmakers and audiences felt like it wouldn't be believable to put a Chinese actor in a space suit. … We're used to seeing Americans in space suits, but for the Chinese it would feel forced. But *Wandering Earth* definitely proved that to be wrong." What's more, he continued, "I know that every studio now has science fiction projects in development."[7] *The Wandering Earth* grossed nearly $700 million worldwide in box office sales in 2019—becoming China's second-highest-grossing film of all time, and one of the highest-grossing sci-fi films in history.[8] It will undoubtedly be fascinating to see how China expands its domestic sci-fi culture, and what will yield from its investment into space-based art and culture.

CHAPTER TWENTY-SEVEN
IMAGINING NEW ECONOMIES

L ike space, economics affects each of us on both a personal and global scale, regardless of whether we're aware of those effects. Science fiction consistently provides new and different versions of potential economies, whether the economy focuses on currency or something else entirely.

Take the iconic science fiction franchise *Alien*, which portrays a future where for-profit organizations are a focal point. While most recall certain notorious scenes, *Alien* is worth reviewing for its subplot on ethics within business operations. As explained in an article from *Slate*, the film "raises important questions about the future balance between the public's interest in outer space and whatever businesses can be built out of publicly funded space exploration."[1] Like many other forms of fiction, sci-fi includes critical understandings of our world and the questions or concerns that plague us.

I n a wonderfully insightful interview, renowned fiction writer Jo Lindsay Walton explored the relationship between science fiction and economics; one of the most compelling points he made compared the foundation for both disciplines. Of economics, he shared that "by far the most influential definition, by Lord Robbins in the 1930s, puts scarcity at the heart of economics. Robbins says economics is the science of human behavior, considered as a relationship between ends and scarce means, especially scarce means which confront us with some kind of choice … things that could be used in this way or that way, but not both." He goes on to explain that "ends" refers to human "[needs], desires, hopes dreams. And this 'ends' side of things is so important. We have to remember that scarce isn't just a synonym for finite."[2] The present-day model of economics, though, is inherently limited and flawed. It does not encompass the complexities of human needs; rather, it assigns a monetary value to our needs, i.e., what do we want, and how much we are willing to pay for what we want.

Science fiction, in contrast, can envision alternate economic models—ones that are more comprehensive, more socially based, more effective. As Walton attests, "science fiction—and other kinds of literature—is obviously extremely interested in getting inside people's heads and hearts, and figuring out not only what people desire, but also why and how, and what it feels like. And how desires might *change*."[3] This focus on the flexible nature of humans—even of the world itself—is of paramount importance. What might feel important one year can completely change, and often does, as a society, our resources, and our desires evolve. "Maybe that's one reason [why] the meeting between science fiction and economics can be quite fruitful. Science fiction has the same love for abstraction and modelmaking, and shares a certain sense of what 'rigor' is," Walton observes, "but it's fundamentally about actual human experience in a way mainstream economics just isn't."[4]

A more recent example with economics as a central theme comes from *Artemis*—the latest novel from Andy Weir, author of *The Martian*. Set within a lunar settlement called Artemis, with humans visiting from all around Earth, Weir developed a lunar currency (known as "soft landed grams" or "SLGs") that is universal and, more importantly, reflective of the most prominent value on the Moon: cost of travel from Earth. One SLG is therefore equivalent of the cost to transport 1 kilogram from Earth to the Moon, and humans who visit Artemis exchange their home currency for SLGs, which they can spend similarly to store credit while on the Moon. [5] While this kind of economy seems pragmatic, it also offers an interesting insight: by establishing a specific resource as the basis for everything else, each SLG spent is a representation of using the core resource. Were we to shift our own economic models that way—being able to quantify exactly what amount of precious Earth resources we depleted with each purchase—perhaps we, as a global society, would begin to prioritize making sustainable, rather than destructive, choices.

The span of science fiction is, for all intents and purposes, unlimited. Its role in speculating better worlds, better lives, and better interactions between humans often eclipses our realities on Earth. Walton argues further that "science fiction is more than interdisciplinary: science fiction can be meta-disciplinary, it can make up its own little disciplines and fields. There's something I don't think

I've really seen, but would be very interested in, and that's imaginary economics, as opposed to imaginary economies or imaginary economic laws."[6] So far, the economic aspects embedded in science fiction exist, predominantly, below the radar—especially compared to technology or remarkable subject matter. The resulting impact on shaping our Earth economies, compared to tech innovations, is similarly less clear or concrete. That does not mean, however, that its impact does not exist, or that we shouldn't pay attention to economic themes in sci-fi.

Economics is deeply rooted in government, and as most would agree, much more difficult to alter (let alone transform completely). And yet, the disruptors that change life as we know it—from FaceTime to Uber to Spotify—transform our economies. They satiate specific needs, create new demands, result in new aspirations, destroy previous desires, and change the way we see ourselves and each other.

Economic influence may not be immediately obvious or clear, but it is a critical part of the equation when we think about science fiction, space, and their effects on humanity. If we were to take a closer look—and act with more deliberate intentions—we could, collectively and individually, begin to push our economies toward a model that is more positive and more beneficial for all.

CHAPTER TWENTY-EIGHT
ASPIRING TO EVOLVE

I came to the conclusion that we should aspire to increase the scope and scale of human consciousness in order to better understand what questions to ask. Really, the only thing that makes sense is to strive for greater collective enlightenment.[1]
Elon Musk | Founder, SpaceX

We're in the first quarter of the twenty-first century. We have access to our mobile applications; we can talk to virtually anyone in the world via one of our communications platforms and reach almost every place on the planet in a day. We have robots on Mars, a few people living and working on the International Space Station, and a spacecraft outside of our solar system. However, if we only benchmark our progress with past events, we as a civilization of beings are short-changing ourselves.

A paper published by Soviet astronomer Nikolai Kardashev in 1964 suggested that there could be a scale to measure a civilization in terms of its "level of technological advancement, based on the amount of energy a civilization is able to use for communication."[2]

THE KARDASHEV SCALE HAS THREE DESIGNATED CATEGORIES:

A Type I (planetary) civilization can harness all the energy available on its home planet as received by its parent star (for us, that would be the power Earth receives from the Sun).

A Type II (stellar) civilization can harness the total energy of its planet's parent star (i.e., all the Sun's power. The Dyson sphere is an example of this model, in which the sphere encompasses the star and sends its energy to the planet).

A Type III (galactic) civilization can harness the energy of its entire host galaxy (i.e., all the power within the Milky Way).[3]

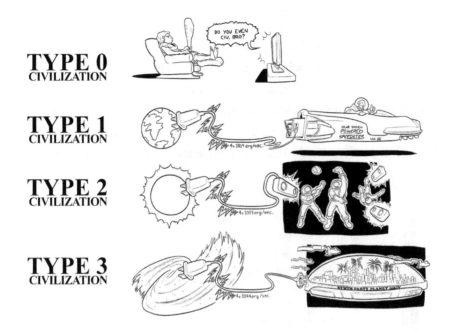

Humanity does not even reach Type I; Kardashev's calculations find that the total energy we receive from the Sun is five magnitudes higher than what we currently leverage. While the Kardashev scale is a hypothetical model, it does offer a chance to reflect on where we stand in our evolution—and how much farther we could potentially go. Today's efforts and innovations will prove foundational for our collective development, and our progression into becoming a space-faring society is one component of this massive, long-term effort. While many of these advancements will not happen overnight, that does not mean they aren't directly in our reach.

We have reached a threshold where we can address significant and substantial challenges. Space can make these theoretical realities possible, and that is only the tip of the tip of the tip of the tip of the iceberg. Space is the only sector that could bring billions out of poverty. It can help us preserve our Earth. It can create innovations and applications that improve the way we live. We have the potential to become a Type I civilization—possibly even beyond—and that means we need sharp minds to enable creative solutions for these questions, and passionate entrepreneurs to lead these efforts. We as a species must adopt an individual and global mindset that we are not only residents of Earth and this solar system, but of this entire galaxy.

Space is the springboard for our individual and collective imaginations. It inspires, kindles, and magnifies the most incredible aspects of humanity. It's time we take the absolute best and most useful ideas, expertise, and scholarship from terrestrial entrepreneurship and apply them to space startups. The future depends on what we decide today. Let's take our aspirations and run with them.

As an engineer on the Apollo 11 mission, I can say that when we challenge ourselves with the impossible, it sharpens our thinking and gives us the ability to foresee all the countless eventualities from a technical perspective. We then have to imagine the experimental tools that we will need to measure the impossible—and it is then that we arrive at the possible without loss of life or mechanical failure. As engineers all over the world know, it is through experimentation, trial, and error that we arrive at success.[4]

Cesar Sciammarella, Ph.D.[*]

NASA Saturn V rocket,
Apollo Program (1969–1973)

★ **Cesar Sciammarella, Ph.D.** is a world-renowned scientist and engineer who has contributed significantly to various fields of experimental mechanics. As an engineer for Apollo 11, he helped develop the spacecraft's third stage Saturn V liquid fuel tanks; his contributions were critical components to the mission, ensuring the spacecraft would reach lunar orbit and return, with the astronauts, safely to Earth. For his achievements, Dr. Sciammarella has received numerous awards from the Society for Experimental Mechanics (SEM), including the Hetenyi, Lazan, Frocht, and Theocaris Awards, the William M. Murray Medal, and in 2013 received the Honorary Membership of the Society for Experimental Mechanics. Dr. Sciammarella has also served as a consultant for corporations including Chassie System Railroad, General Electric, General Motors, Goodyear, Honeywell Corporation, Rand Corporation, Rockwell International, IBM, and Samsung. In addition, he has lent his expertise to various government agencies, including NASA (Langley Research Center), the US Air Force (Wright Patterson), the US Department of Energy, and the US Department of the Interior.

EX ASTRIS,
AD ASTRA

FROM THE STARS, TO THE STARS

Clearly our first task is to use the material wealth of space to solve the urgent problems we now face on Earth: to bring the poverty-stricken segments of the world up to a decent living standard, without recourse to war or punitive action against those already in material comfort; to provide for a maturing civilization the basic energy vital to its survival.[1]

Gerard K. O'Neill, *The High Frontier* (1976).

AFTERWORD

The global space sector currently hovers annually around $350 billion. My interest is in supporting the industry to become an even more outstanding enabler for worldwide economic growth. How will that happen? In anticipation of breakout applications derived from space, how can investors, policymakers, and business leaders encourage more terrestrial companies to experiment with space in a sustained way? How can we help improve conditions to help the space sector to flourish? What are the enablers that would allow space to move humanity forward and eventually become a Type I Civilization?

All ecosystems need sustenance, and the emerging NewSpace ecosystem is no exception. Both the private and public sectors need to convey clear models of the tangible and intangible benefits that the space sector can provide. NewSpace's economic growth depends on the ability of new markets to flourish and reach their potential. Whether our existing infrastructure promotes or slows down that progress will determine when the industry makes its inevitable strides. Smart policy, technology and innovation adoption, increased space-entrepreneurship, and timing will all affect the industry's trajectory. We also need collaboration within and outside of the sector. It will take all of us, regardless of age, location, or profession, to become advocates in changing the world for the better.

Given the space sector's complex ecosystem and interdependent areas, it took me years to get a handle on it. In some ways, I have still only scratched the surface. My original thesis was that the space sector has a unique ability to provide prosperity, wealth, and sustainability for billions more here on Earth. Today, that belief has only grown stronger. My intention is to continue to help facilitate and lead the sustainable growth of the space industry through smart collaboration. This sector can benefit from your contributions—in whatever shape or form. The remainder of the book is therefore broken down into sections dedicated to readers interested in helping to advance NewSpace, including insights from the book's sponsors, Hypergiant and SpaceChain; a case study of NewSpace startup

Planet; my thoughts on how to grow the space sector to a trillion-dollar industry within a decade; and space industry resources.

During my time at the International Space University Space Studies Program, we regularly heard the motto, "Dream It, Build It, Launch It." This is an exciting time. Perhaps nothing captures the hope and optimism of the future like space, and we are at a unique juncture when space is now finally starting to open for us—today. The wait is over.

Ad Astra,
Robert C. Jacobson

If you enjoyed this book, please consider writing a review with your honest impressions on Amazon, Goodreads, or the platform of your choosing. Your feedback is incredibly valuable for helping independent authors like me to reach a wider audience.

To learn more or participate in the expansive space sector, visit my website to connect, find ways to work together, and stay in the loop by joining my mailing list. The website also features unpublished bonus material from the book, NewSpace resources, and *Brave New Space*—my space podcast for investors, entrepreneurs, and business leaders.

RobertJacobson.com
SpaceIsOpenForBusiness.com
SpaceAdvisors.com

#RobertJacobson
#SpaceIsOpenForBusiness

INSIGHTS FROM OUR SPONSORS

BEN LAMM | HYPERGIANT

Ben Lamm is the founder of Hypergiant, a startup that leverages AI to create improved capabilities both on Earth and in space. A serial technology entrepreneur who builds intelligent and transformative businesses, Lamm was the chief executive officer and founder of various other successful startups prior to Hypergiant, including Conversable, the leading conversational intelligence platform, and Chaotic Moon, a global mobile creative technology powerhouse acquired by Accenture. During his time at Chaotic Moon and Accenture, Lamm spearheaded the creation of some of Fortune 500's most groundbreaking digital products and experiences in the emerging tech worlds of IoT, VR, Connected Car, mobile, tablet, and wearables. In addition, Lamm is active in angel investing, incubators, and startup communities, with investments in the software and emerging tech space. He is also passionate about mentoring fellow entrepreneurs, lending his expertise and guidance to build disruptive businesses through accelerators and corporate programs.

What is Hypergiant's mission and how did it originate?

At Hypergiant Industries, our mission is to create emerging AI-driven technologies and develop commercial products and solutions that improve the world around us and advance humanity's position in the universe.

Hypergiant is working on AI infrastructure for space. What this means is that we are not just looking at the hardware to get to space or improving satellites in space; rather, we are looking at the entire ecosystem of data transference from Earth to space to other planets and back to Earth. This means we own satellites, and we collect and analyze the captured data for our own products and services. It also means that we think about critical infrastructure projects like interplanetary internet, which is fundamental for data transference and requires AI to power it. There's a lot at play here.

I started Hypergiant because I could see the huge possibility in AI across space, defense, and critical infrastructure, and I knew that now was the moment to use AI to solve these huge problems that underlie the foundational structures of what it means to be human. We are building the world of tomorrow, today, by applying AI to hardware to solve problems. That's fun; it's more a question of imagination than it is of technology—and that's the promise AI holds: it is limited only by one's imagination. Luckily, my team and I have huge imaginations.

What is AI's role in the space sector?

AI is the technology that will make it possible for us to live in and truly explore space. There are other technologies that will be essential, but AI is the big computing advantage that will allow living outside of Earth to be possible

Space is the next new API [application programming interface]. From outer space, we can gather Earth data in a way we've never been able to do before. There is still data from space missions we did in the '70s that hasn't been fully reviewed. This is where AI steps in: we need AI to review and interpret our space data so that we can take actions based on that knowledge set. That data can help us tackle big global challenges like defense, climate change, ocean health, and critical infrastructure. That understanding of our own Earth system will then help us develop systems and accurate mathematical computing tools to help us understand non-Earth systems, which will be critical as we explore new systems and new planets.

Finally, our ability to gather information in space and interpret on Earth will help us better understand and improve the space sector. AI is a tool for handling Big Data. There is no place that has more and greater data than space. The better our tools can be, the more we can begin to take on bigger and more aggressive missions in space—like travel outside our galaxy or creating a habitat on another planet. Longer missions will require even more intelligent systems and automation to make the long travel distance and life support systems possible.

What is not commonly known about AI for business?

The big thing we need to remember is that none of this is new. This is not the first AI revolution or even the first Big Data revolution, nor is it the first time we've actively looked at commercial opportunities in space. In fact, we've been talking about all of this for a long time, with research dating back into the late 1800s. The thing is that now there are a lot of market conditions that make it possible to have expansive growth into AI for business that haven't existed before, including the diminishing price of computing power and sector-specific advances in computation. Like all industries, we are coming up on an inflection point that is also a tipping point for a massive acceleration of opportunity.

Still, some people worry that we are in a bubble. That's absolutely likely, but it's a bubble that's predicted to be worth $3 trillion by 2024. The reason we are in a bubble, though, is that AI hype has yet to meet AI reality—but not because the market isn't there for the implementation of AI. As the math improves, the case studies improve, and the applications improve, we will see AI start to match the hype. Realistically, some of the companies that don't have the tech aren't going to make it. Those that do, though, are going to fly through the bubble and accelerate rapidly.

This is where the orbital AI and intelligence comes in. The winners here, and ultimately the winner overall, will be the one who gets that [orbital] data. This satellite-based Earth observation market alone is predicted to hit $6.9 billion annually by 2027, and $54 billion cumulatively over the next decade.

What do you think is the greatest challenge facing the world/ humanity today?

Climate change. I want to go to space because exploring space is exciting; I don't want us to have to run away from our home planet because we have destroyed it.

How can AI benefit daily life on Earth?

So many ways: how about helping to stop our CO_2 problem? Or protecting us from space junk falling into the atmosphere? But, also, there are small things we might not even notice. AI can be used to help control robots everywhere, from surgery to warehouse inventory management. Or, AI can be used to help improve traffic patterns in cities. Or help make urban farming efficient and effective. Or help us learn how to create oceanic agriculture farms that change the shape of our coastline for the better. This year, we launched a program focused on creating interplanetary internet, a helmet that uses AI to improve the ability of astronauts to operate in space by adding haptic feedback and various layered data on top of their visors—a bioreactor that sequesters four hundred times the carbon of an acre of trees.

The public needs to learn to not be afraid of AI. AI is not inherently bad or scary. People can be bad and scary—but people can also be good. Allowing our fear of unknown technology to limit its adoption hurts all of humanity. Instead, we should focus on understanding AI so that, as a public, we can make informed decisions about where and how to regulate the industry.

What does the AI sector need to reach its potential?

We need to continue to push for technological and mathematical improvements in the industry, but we also need to pull in experts from other industries (like biology, psychology, and neuroscience) to help us—and we need to overlay that with creativity and imagination. AI now operates based on pattern recognition. AGI (artificial general intelligence) will operate based on an inherent child-like learning capacity. Children aren't just pattern-recognizers, they are truly creative innovators. We need to make the switch at this fundamental level to get AI to the place that will make it increasingly impactful in the future.

Why do you believe now is the time for investors to invest in AI and/or space?

The gold rush is starting. Data has already surpassed oil in value. Hardware was the costly issue with space, i.e., physically getting there. Now that it is becoming easier and easier to launch things into space, we have the opportunity to think about what we do in space: this means software, new products, people, travel. Everything we have on Earth, we need in space, and those companies are just starting to pop up.

I personally invest in emerging technology primarily because I already know a fair amount and I find it exciting. Being at the vanguard of an industry keeps me involved in new and nascent industries that are developing. I'm fascinated right now by data visualization companies, because that's a major pain point at the moment. We have a ton of data, but few high-quality ways to see the data. Because we can't see it, a lot of people don't know how to wrap their heads around it. I recently invested in Molecula, an Austin-based data visualization company, because of this specific reason. Molecula's software reduces the risk of errors in data and helps prepare it for complex analysis by making data from a variety of sources and locations instantly available through a virtualized access layer. Everything that allows people to analyze data faster and then act in a timelier manner is powerful.

What is NASA's role in space and innovation today, from your standpoint?

I love NASA, and we are fortunate to get to do a lot of work with them. The various teams at NASA are incredible, and the work they are doing will benefit humanity forever. Many people don't realize how many things in our lives that we take for granted exist because of the amazing innovation from men and women at NASA over the years. NASA is a critical partner in all space and space innovation work. I believe as a civilian-focused agency, NASA has our best interest in mind and is a force for science and exploration in the world today.

How do you plan to improve the internet and our relationship with it?

I am not very focused on Earth internet, but I do think interplanetary internet is critical to exploration of space and our future. We have come to rely on the internet for everything, and we will need that infrastructure in space to create a habitable environment and also a safe one. The interplanetary internet will allow us to reach out for medical advice, or historical advice, or rapid translation of languages. This isn't central to our business model right now; Hypergiant won't succeed or fail as a business based on the success of this project. We're doing this because we see it as central to our core mission. The progress and stability of human existence are entirely dependent on what we call the three core Elements of Civilization: Space, Defense, and Critical Infrastructure & Resources. When in balance and harnessed by the forces of good, life on Earth advances, as does the economy underlying it all. The pursuit is to preserve the longevity of our species and the habitability of our environments. There is no greater example of these principles in action than this communications network. We want humanity to become an interplanetary species, and we see the interplanetary internet as a fundamental human right and need.

How did you get interested in AI?

I grew up on pop culture: sci-fi, adventure, *Indiana Jones,* you name it, and those stories inspired in me a deep and unending curiosity about this world and the universe around us. After selling my previous companies, I started to contemplate what else I could do to improve the world around me, and I started to think about all those stories I had been obsessed with. I realized there was a real disconnect between the future we had talked about in the 70s and 80s and the future we were talking about now. I wanted the future we were promised, not the dystopian narrative of our current dialogue.

I joined the advisory boards of the Planetary Society and the Arch Mission Foundation. I started to speak with the leading experts in space, in AI, and in defense. And what I learned was that I had a unique set of skills that could help lead a company that would use AI to transform the world around me. I have a deep understanding of emerging technology, but more than anything, a passionate curiosity about how it works, combined with an understanding of how to break down complicated problems and bring products and solutions to market.

When did your interest in space become serious?

After selling my other companies, I was able to spend more time reflecting on what really fascinates me. I spent a year thinking, reading, and learning, and I begin to see space for all its potential: economic, philosophical, inspirational, and otherwise. We have an opportunity within our lifetime to live in space for the first time ever. That is one of those things that's utterly unique in the growth of humanity, and I started to understand that I could be part of this moment in a big way. The moment I realized my role, I became incredibly serious about space and began to hire the leading thinkers on the topic to help me grow my company.

I think there is a lot we can learn from better exploration of the world around us that we can then overlay with science to really understand how things work. I'm always fascinated by how little we know about our oceans and the potential to harness the oceans to make substantial changes. AI was the best technology to do what I wanted to do: use technology to solve the world's biggest problems.

What has your approach been in running successful startups?

I believe in brand first and foremost. You must create a company that has a personality and a vision. People should immediately get what you are trying to do and emotionally respond to that. So, I start there. Then I hire the best of the best to do the jobs they want to do, even if they aren't jobs that they have done in the past. Then we deliver great products and solutions to the markets.

If you could tell your younger self anything, what would it be?

More is more: it never hurts to have more ideas, more time, more money, and more opportunities. Chase them all.

What is your vision for the evolving space economy?

Space is the new frontier, and with it comes all the opportunities of any new frontier: there will be big booms and busts but also great achievements for humanity. Right now, the space opportunities are three-fold:

- LEO – which is quickly becoming saturated from a hardware perspective.
- Data – which is about a.) getting data from space, b.) sending that data to Earth, c.) analyzing that data, d.) making that data useful, quickly, for real-time decision making.
- Software – which is about updating the systems and services that are being used in the hardware race.

Eventually, the space frontier opportunities are going to grow in a variety of other ways that democratize the opportunities for non-technology companies to profit. These include areas like:

1. Water (e.g., supply, safety, distribution, etc.)
2. Food (e.g., supply, safety, storage, preparation equipment, etc.)
3. Textiles & Body Protection (e.g., clothing, shoes, etc.)
4. Consumer Health and Safety (e.g., equipment, nutrition supplements, ensuring and aiding sleep, medications, hygiene, prevention of illness, accidents)
5. Living Spaces (e.g., cooking, sleeping spaces/furniture/equipment, beds, desks, etc.)
6. Connectivity and Communication

How can newcomers get involved with the space industry?

The space industry is growing rapidly, and there are lots of ways for people to get involved—and not just technologists. We need people to think about political structures, the law, investments, agriculture, and more. Join a local meet-up, read everything you can, and talk to people who work in the sector. Like any industry, the best way to get involved is through having a curious mind and connecting with people who are already involved.

How should individuals and companies alike shift their mindsets to create a successful future?

We must simply believe that changing our future is possible. Most people only think about the small problems in front of them; what more people need to do is think about how we can address big global problems together. Nothing will change unless people believe they can be the change they want to see in the world.

JEFF GARZIK | SPACECHAIN

Jeff Garzik is the cofounder and chief technology officer of SpaceChain, the first open source, blockchain-based satellite network that has developed a community platform that allows its users to create their own space applications—from anywhere in the world. Garzik is known as a pioneer in software engineering and development, playing crucial roles in the 1990s to first integrate CNN.com with the internet, followed by creating open source projects like the Linux kernel—the operating system used by the five hundred most powerful supercomputers, all Android devices, and endless other computing devices. After discovering Bitcoin in 2010, Garzik went on to become a global blockchain leader—the number three bitcoin developer (and the most active for many years) before transitioning from building software to building companies. He founded Bloq in 2015, a Chicago-based blockchain technology company that provides open source, decentralized blockchain infrastructure, applications, and solutions to the business world.

What is SpaceChain's mission?

SpaceChain's vision was always to democratize access to space. It's really a grassroots approach of getting to the point where we have sufficient satellites to provide an API [application programming interface] so that developers can literally spend a dollar or two, get a couple of tokens, and then use them to actuate spacecraft sensors, motors, cameras, store things on the spacecraft, and store data encrypted for signed transactions on the blockchain networks. That means there's some low-cost way to deploy a mobile app on your phone and then talk to our servers on Earth, which talk to the various satellites (first around Earth and then eventually around other bodies of the solar system), and then talk to an API (programmer-speak for making a computer somewhere do something). These APIs are really the lingua franca of the modern cloud, the modern realm. So, it's that sort of touchpoint where, from your personal computer, you can talk directly to one of the satellites in a carefully controlled sandbox environment—that's part of what blockchain provides for us. A space API is something that, given the right pricing and the right economic model, will enable university students to experiment with satellites in their spare time, for pocket change.

How does SpaceChain plan to achieve its goals?

The internet was built around standards, and that's how we have, for example, two large companies like Cisco and Juniper, which are competitors, but at the same time they speak the same protocols in the hardware that they manufacture and sell. Those protocols are what allow the internet to inter-operate, they allow my Mac to talk to your Windows PC or to an Android phone. SpaceChain wants to see the same thing happen in space. We have about five years of runway, which is a lot for a startup, but at the same time, we can't write a check and put up a multi-billion-dollar constellation by ourselves. So it's all about creating a set of standards where anyone can manufacture a satellite and plug it into this shared constellation where it's not one leader (i.e., SpaceChain) who says what happens on the network—it's multiple owners that sort of form a consensus about what can and can't happen on the network, or what capabilities are in that network. That's how the internet was built.

Why is blockchain valuable for the economy?

We can talk all day about blockchain technology, but one of the aspects is providing security for money and providing some new "shapes" of money. For the first time in thousands of years, money can come with strings attached. With blockchain technology, you can attach tiny computer programs to each Bitcoin or each Ethereum, and these can be arbitrarily complex rules for how you can spend that money. The digital signature is simple case, and that's what most people use today. A more complex case is something called a "smart contract," which is like an English language contract but written in a language only a computer would love.

For example, let's say you and I are on the board of directors of a charity; the smart contract would be the one who acts as the treasurer of the charity. If you and I agree that we spend some of the charity's funds on a certain philanthropic endeavor, then the treasurer transfers those funds to the blockchain technology; if we don't agree, then the funds don't get transferred. The notable part in that whole transaction is that neither you nor I can just stick our hands in the cookie jar and embezzle funds or spend funds in a way that's not prescribed. It's like a banker who always dots his I's, crosses his T's, and makes you follow the rules to the letter—and that's an enormously interesting potential for space. You can have space-based businesses where some of the capital—the investment capital or the capital expenditures—are doled out through these smart contracts. So, someone like the XPRIZE could dole out specific milestones for any company that builds the first apartment building on the Moon. You can dole out funds for specific rideshares and fractionalize a rocket launch and sell it to 1,000 investors; when that rocket launch makes a profit, those 1,000 investors get a share of the investment profits—and quite legally, according to all securities laws.

All of this is enabled in the backend, by this new plumbing or re-plumbing of economics, by blockchain technology and smart contracts. Basically, it's reinventing money. We are seeing some efforts this year with security tokens, which are regulated, equity-style blockchain tokens to fractionalize space missions. I think you'll see some space STOs (security token offerings) in the next six to twelve months. It's kind of like a mini-IPO for a single space mission, like an asteroid sample return mission.

How is SpaceChain democratizing the world?

With near-Earth satellites and constellations, the economics are such that it's now, for the first time, really cheap to throw a bunch of hardware up in the air. Inter-satellite linking (ISL) is a big technical point in current research, which is thousands of satellites in low Earth orbit that are linking together and talking to each other, and they're talking to the ground at higher speeds and in more locations than any other internet provider has ever been able to reach before. I call it 'the other five billion,' as in the other five billion who, even as we're running on 5G phones, are still barely getting 1G or 2G. Their experience connecting to the global village is radically different from people in the modern, developed world.

The vision for SpaceChain, and what OneWeb and SpaceX are pursuing, is the 'this many plus T' model, where you throw thousands of satellites up into the air, and the launch costs and per unit costs are very, very low, so you can tolerate a significant minority of these satellites failing completely—and ultimately, the constellation itself continues to provide internet service cheaply at very high speeds to the end consumers. That's one way to provide inexpensive networking that enables us to become a global village, enables emerging markets and developing countries to have the kind of internet access that we have in the developed world.

How does cooperation influence progress?

It's cheaper to do a flight test now, so you can do many more iterations actually in space, and there's a lot of parts-sharing among space startups—the, 'I'll fly your part on my spacecraft and, and you help me out in six months by testing the board,' type of camaraderie and cooperation, so that we're all getting to space, not just once every five years but multiple times a year.

How has NewSpace changed the traditional industry?

The biggest highlight is economic change: the old players are getting out, new players are getting in, costs are falling through the floor, and so there's never been a better time to get into space travel, space business, space science. I've never been more excited than I am right now for space as an industry, especially as a space enthusiast and activist. Really, the economics drive everything in this world. If it's too expensive, it's not going to happen; if it's cheap enough, it is going to happen.

We're definitely headed in the commodity direction. The overall cost approach is radically different; you can get common, off-the-shelf parts quite cheaply, and at this point, even space-hardened, flight-tested hardware is essentially a sunk cost. For example, the SpaceChain approach: the satellite we launched earlier this year was all off-the-shelf except for the one board that is custom. So, it's not a completely custom rig each time you're going, with 90 percent off-the-shelf and 10 percent being your mission-specific hardware that maybe hasn't been flight-tested, and that helps you quantify and draw a circle around the risk. That's part of the economic story as well.

The cost of getting mass to orbit is what's falling the most, so it's already cheap to build or even 3D-print a CubeSat, and that's what SpaceChain has been doing. Creating a spacecraft has evolved quite a bit, and it's now very simple. The barrier to entry was always launch, and since the cost of getting one kilogram to low Earth orbit is now in the realms of a small startup with, say, $100,000 of venture capital, they can put a spacecraft into orbit. Previously, you had to be a large consortium that had hundreds of millions, maybe billions of dollars, and either venture capital or debt or some combination thereof, so only a couple companies could swim in those waters. Now, a small startup funded on credit cards can compete with the big guys, and that is a game changer. For instance, Planet had a great success with their first official payload. So, we're going to see self-funded pop-up efforts increase in frequency, and it's not even going to have to be a group of millionaires doing this stuff. It can be a group of buddies with $25,000 credit card limits; they're the ones who are going to be sending the interesting projects to space.

What do potential investors need to know?

I think that knowledge is always power, and in this case, you'll have to engage in a lot more legwork, because the space funds these days are few and far between, and they're small. There are some space hedge funds spinning up, but having been on both sides of the table, there's not a lot of space investment infrastructure right now. There's Space Angels and a couple of private networks, but that's really it; especially compared to, say, enterprise software or mobile apps or something, where there are hundreds of VC firms that are very familiar with those particular industries and have whole teams devoted to micro-parsing every aspect.

I'd say it's a good time to enter if you're a CEO, and it's a good time to enter if you want to create a new fund and have that knowledge advantage over other funds. If you're an investor, I would say that you're still going to have outside returns by doing direct research into the portfolio companies themselves. I think that there are a lot of entry points for institutional money that's coming online, but there's also a lot of opportunity. The more you know, the better your investing is, and there are some amazing plays coming online now.

What do we need to understand about today's space economy?

It's such an untold story about how much and how fast costs are dropping. Even the military is going to the many-plus-cheap approach. They're still spending tens and hundreds of millions on satellites, but that's down from the billions, and they can have a forest of satellites up in space providing real-time battle data for pick-your-specific-battlefield. I can't repeat the country, but that was used in one conflict in the past twenty years. The US military did not have coverage over a certain battle space, and the cheapest and quickest and most effective way to get better pictures of this country was to launch a bunch of cheap CubeSats. It's all about being quick, small, nimble. On-demand, just-in-time production-type principles that apply to software are increasingly applying to hardware with 3D printing and rapid assembly of off-the-shelf parts.

Things are changing so quickly that the only thing you can be sure of is that the old reliable customer, meaning a large government, is no longer the old reliable customer. That said, the industry will need to be far more creative. We have people who are exploring business plans that fuse industrial assembly-type techniques with zero gravity and low Earth orbit, people who fuse art and space, people like us who want to fuse software and money and financial technology and space. It's going to be new products and new markets. The old products are too expensive, and the old markets are drying up—that's how much the landscape is shifting. But the good news is that it's going to be a lower cost, volume-type market rather than a hit-or-miss, multi-billion-dollar contract once every five years.

How do these economic and industry shifts affect us on Earth?

With the cost falling through the floor, people around the world are going to be enabled and empowered in new ways. That was always the motivation, the headline, and the biggest point of interest. The more focused point that's interesting is that we are changing the way satellites work. Traditionally, satellites just bounce signals around; they were repeaters, and now they're becoming computers in space. That opens the door to AI and autonomous entities, which is very science fiction-y. AI and drones are coming to space. Sadly, there's a little bit of nationalism coming to space. We're getting, in the United States, the Space Force, and we will eventually see weapons in low Earth orbit, and we will have to deal with those. But, in general, just like how the previous space programs—Apollo, the Space Shuttle programs—unlocked so much economic activity, innovation, and new developments, what we do in space all trickles back to everything that we do in our modern lives. We wouldn't have mobile phones and these tiny supercomputers in our pockets if it weren't for the space program. What we don't necessarily see around the corner will be an outcome of space exploration and space technology. It really is going to help us live longer healthier better lives.

How did you become interested in space?

I have always been a computer nerd and science fiction aficionado, and have always, from when I was a little boy, thought about outer space—what it's like to live in space, what it would take to get to space. Growing up, space was never a dystopia, it was always more of a utopia—there's all this cool stuff, all this advanced technology, advanced thinking, and advanced political structures. That was how most of the fiction presented leaving the planet: as the graduation of the species to a higher plane or more advanced version of safety. So, that, combined with computer programming since age eight. I've always been highly technical and wanted to know how the physics of the rockets work, about the computers that ran the Apollo program, things of that nature.

How might one get involved in NewSpace today?

There are a number of ways that individuals can get involved with the NewSpace sector. The first step is to educate yourself on the companies, governments, and leaders that are pushing space forward today. Join social media related to NewSpace. Join one of the NewSpace companies, either as a volunteer or paid worker. Start a company. Write. Contribute knowledge, designs, and ideas in written form. Get involved in STEM programs at the local middle, high schools, or university—or start a STEM program.

Why do we need to develop infrastructure in space?

I think humanity needs a backup plan. We're naturally explorers, and the best way to continue to evolve is interplanetary settlement. Why you want to wire the solar system is presumably the same reasons why they laid railroad tracks in the 1800s into new lands. We now need digital railroad tracks and efficient lines of communication between various planetary bodies. Right now, what we have is a few large, slow, government-owned sites. The industry infrastructure is not really built for small, agile, commercial startups, the type of which I predict we're going to see dozens or maybe hundreds of in the next five years.

CASE STUDY | PLANET

Planet Labs Inc. (Planet) was founded in 2010 by Will Marshall, Robbie Schingler, and Chris Boshuizen, three NASA scientists with a goal to use space to help life on Earth. The cofounders met at the UNISPACE-III conference in 1998 and eventually worked together at NASA Ames. In 2011, the founders and a small group of physicists and engineers began building Planet's first satellite in a garage in Cupertino, California. As of early 2020, Planet has more than 200 satellites in orbit capable of imaging all of Earth's landmass every day, making global change visible, accessible, and actionable.

An Agile Approach

Planet took a new, agile approach to building, designing and manufacturing satellites. Since 2012, Planet has completed fourteen major iterations of the Dove spacecraft design with new generations being released at a steady rate. 'Agile aerospace' is a philosophy of spacecraft development that encourages rapid iteration, where the aim is to make small improvements to every spacecraft design instead of exhaustively trying to perfect each one on the first try. The goal of this approach is to continue to optimize spacecraft architecture through an evolution of capabilities. At Planet, this means frequently releasing new spacecraft designs, testing them in space, and making changes based on the results.

New Space Industry

NewSpace is a movement that encompasses the emerging private aerospace industry, and Planet is a leader of innovation in this field. As a private company, Planet collaborates with private launch vehicles through a diversified launch manifest. In December 2018, Planet was the lead payload on Spaceflight's SSO-A launch, otherwise known as the SmallSat Express, a rideshare on the SpaceX Falcon 9 that included sixty-four satellites from thirty-five different organizations across seventeen countries. This launch was a notable example of how Planet and SpaceX have collaborated to define the new space age: SpaceX with reusable rockets and Planet with agile development to build and deploy hundreds of satellites. Further, this launch on SpaceX was one of three that Planet executed with different launch providers on three different continents in less than forty days. This series of spacecraft and launch milestones would have been improbable just ten years ago.

Disaster Relief Efforts

Planet's Disaster Response Program offers government, commercial, and non-profit organizations flexible monitoring options to deliver useful data when disaster strikes. Planet is uniquely equipped to aid in natural disaster response at all scales—from state and local to national and international.

Planet's daily, global monitoring (PlanetScope) enables entities to monitor areas of interest as recent as the day before an event occurs. Recent and timely pre-event imagery disrupts the industry standard. When officials are working with out-of-date contextual information, where imagery is months or even years old, it can be a detriment to emergency response. Daily monitoring allows near real-time access to imagery while an event is ongoing and eliminates the need to task satellites before an event. Continuous coverage then allows the observation of long-term recovery efforts post-event.

SkySat's high resolution (.72 m) imagery compliments PlanetScope, providing stakeholders a closer look at damage or impact from a disaster. While there are commercial opportunities for disaster response, Planet makes disaster imagery and data available at a highly reduced cost, with the aim of supporting the company's mission to encourage transparency and help life on Earth.

In 2018, Planet became the first direct, private sector data provider to the International Charter: Space and Major Disasters, a consortium of international space agencies that provide rapid access to satellite data in the event of a natural or humanmade disaster. At present, the Charter has been activated for 624 disasters in 126 countries since its inception in 2000.

SmallSat Market

The types of new satellite missions that are emerging include optical imagery, multispectral imagery, weather prediction, and AIS ship tracking—with more missions under development. This "SmallSat Revolution" was enabled by the advancement of commercial electronics, lower cost and more frequent access to launch services, and cloud-based infrastructure to store, process, and deliver the terabytes of data being generated from space.

Small satellites have been flying since the launch of Sputnik, and CubeSats have been flying since the early 2000s—but it has only been over the last three to five years that we've seen companies with commercially viable business models deploying operational constellations and making an impact on the market. The industry has also seen an influx of VC funding, enabling new companies across the entire value chain, which in combination with government-funded Earth observation missions like Landsat and Sentinel, have created a robust commercial ecosystem that continues to grow.

ENABLING A TRILLION-DOLLAR SPACE INDUSTRY

A non-exhaustive list of the immediate, necessary changes needed
to help propel NewSpace forward and achieve its unlimited potential.

(1) IMPROVE DOMESTIC POLICY

I. **Revise (or eliminate) the rules regarding "government purpose rights"
    license for startup grants and small company contracts.**

    > Recent legislation requires the Commerce Department to evaluate controls
    > on 'emerging technologies.' ... This included tech in the sweet spot of the
    > bat for venture: AI/ML, robotics, 3D printing, and biotechnology to name
    > a few. ... It is an open question as to which of these technologies will
    > ultimately be subject to controls and to what degree.
    >
    > Imagine the government decides to control artificial intelligence as an
    > emerging technology and that a U.S.-based AI company employs an engi-
    > neer on an H-1B visa. Under these facts, it seems the company would
    > need an export license for the foreign national to work at the company. ...
    > Obtaining these licenses would present a tremendous burden for small,
    > high-growth startups that often build teams by attracting the best and
    > brightest from foreign countries.[1]
    >
    > **Jeff Farrah | General Counsel, National Venture Capital Association**

II. **Create a dedicated department for commercial space activities
    and regulation.**
    - Reduce restrictions for the commercial sector
    - Streamline licensing for private sector launch
    - Improve satellite spectrum and licensing challenges.

    > Spectrum is probably the scarcest resource that we've got. There is a finite
    > amount of radio frequency spectrum to be shared across these systems.

One of the big issues becomes how to share what little spectrum there is amongst the existing systems and future systems.[2]

John Paffett, Ph.D. | Founder & Managing Director, KISPE; Managing Director, Applied Space Solutions; Member of the Board, Swedish Space Corporation

Price per kilogram is no longer the relevant question to ask. It's a throwback to the (very recent) age of enormous, multi-ton satellites where price per kilogram was the critical business metric for launch. Today, everyone is building constellations of satellites that weigh between 3 and 30 kg; all that matters to these operators is time to orbit. They are burning millions per month while their revenue hinges upon deployment of systems delivered to specific orbits. Planet, Spire, or OneWeb would gladly pay an extra $10,000 per kilogram if it means they can launch quickly, on schedule, and on target, instead of waiting months and years for a rideshare to the wrong altitude and inclination.[3]

David Cowan | Partner, Bessemer Ventures Partners

III.   Create sustainable regulations for sharing airspace.

- Improve software to integrate with air traffic controls.

    On June 29, 2018, over 200,000 flights flew, which was the highest number of aircraft flights in a single day, as tracked by Swedish tracking company FlightRadar24; July 29, 2019 saw 225,000.[4] The FAA monitors over 44,000 flights every day. With air traffic at an all-time high and increasing by the year, it is crucial to create solutions that allow spacecraft and aircraft to coexist safely and effectively. It will be impossible to resolve that kind of issue without international diplomacy.

    The FAA uses decades-old analysis and air traffic control tools to segregate the airspace around a launch or reentry.[5]

    Eric Stallmer | President, Commercial Spaceflight Federation

Right now, the Air Force's Joint Space Operations Group gets updates on launch times over the phone or by email and then sends that information, on paper, to the FAA, according to the agency. This can result in what happened during the first Falcon Heavy flight: planes have to divert over airspace that doesn't need to be cleared. That's why the FAA is working on a new technology called the Space Data Integrator, or SDI. ... When deployed, SDI will enable the FAA to safely reduce the amount of airspace that must be closed to other users and more quickly release airspace that is no longer a risk as a mission progresses.[6]

Wayne Monteith | Associate Administrator for Commercial Space Transportation, Federal Aviation Administration

While there has been great progress in traditional aviation and commercial space transportation, like new entrants, drones, and personal air vehicles —all good and desirable developments—that progress is highlighting the need to improve the hardware, software, and human systems that manage the NAS [National Airspace System]. In particular, the way that we restrict airspace around launch or reentry events—an approach called "segregation"—is an inefficient use of the airspace.

While these tools are being developed, there are things that space operators can do to help aviation operators minimize system delays during launch and reentry events. If FAA/AST were to create an integrated schedule of licensed or permitted launches and reentries, industry could authorize FAA/AST to share much of that information a few months, rather than about ten days, with aviation operators. The benefit of earlier notice is that aviation operators can still reallocate their crews and airplanes to create some slack in higher value scheduled flights that are more vulnerable to delays.

Ultimately, however, the challenge is getting the FAA to the point where it can adapt, move, and innovate quickly enough to keep up with the advancement of aviation, commercial spaceflight, and new NAS entrants. Given the importance of aviation and space to our economy, our freedom, and our national security, we have to find a way to help the FAA to move much faster and get ahead of industry, rather than struggling to catch up.[7]

Eric Stallmer | President, Commercial Spaceflight Federation

IV.   **Continuously prioritize commercial efforts for domestic space activities.**

- Government to take on only the projects that the commercial sector cannot

- Government to leverage commercial capabilities without competing with private efforts

- Increase the use of firm-fixed-price procurements, and hold procurement officials in government and business accountable for the consequences of poorly negotiated and/or executed contracts.

There is no way to preclude changes in administration direction regarding government expenditures on space projects. However, a business-friendly administration can help to foster commercial space enterprises across the spectrum, from launch, human spaceflight, and in-space manufacturing to exploration and even lunar or Mars activities. At the end of the day, space must be more than a government-focused and government-directed enterprise, and companies that are able to make revenue and profits will continue to seek such opportunities—thus, this path is the best way of buffering change in government space policies.[8]

Dennis Wingo | Founder & Chief Executive Officer, Skycorp Inc.

V. **Balance the industry playing field for startups by reducing certain advantages that favor established incumbent companies.**

- Limit lobbying activities and, by extension, revolving door positions between government and commercial space
- Preclude any officer over the rank of Major from working as a Department of Defense contractor for five years after retirement.

Over three-fourths of Defense Aerospace lobbyists are former government employees (76.14% in 2019 and 79.56% in 2018). Incumbents Northrop Grumman and Lockheed Martin spent $13.4 million and $13 million, respectively, on Defense Aerospace lobbying in 2019. In 2018, Boeing spent $15.1 million, Northrop Grumman spent $14.3 million, and Lockheed Martin spent $13.2 million on Defense Aerospace lobbying.[9]

Data sourced from the Center of Responsive Politics

In a little-noticed provision of the 2018 National Defense Authorization Act (NDAA), Congress imposed new 'revolving door' restrictions on senior Department of Defense (DoD) personnel. Section 1045 applies new one and two-year cooling off periods prohibiting former high-ranking military officers and their civilian counterparts from conducting any 'lobbying activities with respect to the Department of Defense' ... including conducting behind-the-scenes research, advice and strategy with others ... contact with 'covered executive branch' officials within DoD and contact with 'covered executive branch officials' in any Department if it concerns DoD matters.[10]

Caleb B. Burns, Sarah B. Hansen, and Robert L. Walker, "2018 NDAA Imposes Sweeping New Revolving Door Restrictions on Lobbying Activities by Former Senior DOD Officials," Wiley Rein LLP, January 12, 2018.

(2) COLLABORATE GLOBALLY

VI. **Create flexible international frameworks that can be revised as the industry shifts.**

- Maintain a peaceful space environment and prevent weaponizing space
- Track and manage debris (including retired or dead spacecraft)
- Take steps to protect against EMP attacks
- Establish data ownership rights
- Establish space resource and mining ownership rights.

> Managing innovative and privately-run space ventures does require a certain element of privacy, but this doesn't stop companies from collaborating and working together to ensure the progress of commercial space industries. Trust between industries is being strengthened and built upon every day through relationships in organizations such as CSF [Commercial Spaceflight Federation]. Many in industry, as well as government and academia, are currently participating in the development of industry consensus standards through the American Society for Testing Materials. This requires a lot of teamwork and compromise, oftentimes working around limits regarding privacy, but results in trusted relationships. Although proprietary information will always exist in the aerospace industry, we are working every day to share best practices and lessons learned.[11]
>
> **Jane Kinney***

VII. **Continue to keep the International Space Station open and available to all.**

- Continue private sector access and increase support of private efforts
- Increase funding and grants for private sector research.

> I look at the International Space Station as the most significant laboratory and facility ever given to the human race, and the greatest platform for entrepreneurial experimentation and growth, ever. Whether it's material sciences, biotechnology, nanotech, manufacturing in space, CubeSat design and development, or using it as a port to go to and from low Earth orbit out to other places, it's there—use it![12]
>
> **Christopher Stott | Cofounder, Chief Executive Officer, & Chair, ManSat**

(3) INCREASE ENTREPRENEURSHIP

VIII. Increase internal technology transfer and IP licensing.

> London Economics estimated the value of the [non-space applications] technology transfer market opportunities by adopting a 'ripple effect' multiplier. Previous research and analysis by London Economics showed that a factor of 2.0 times the initial technology investments could be used to estimate technology transfer sales to non-space sectors. To quantify the total investment by GLXP [Google Lunar XPRIZE] teams, a long-tail distribution was assumed for all registered teams with the maximum investment per team set at US $31 million (with launch costs removed). This resulted in a total investment across all teams of $98 million. Applying the estimated ripple effect multiplier to this investment suggests a potential total of technology transfer value of GLXP technology of $197 million, over a period of up to 10 years.[13]
>
> **London Economics, "Google Lunar XPRIZE Market Study," 2014.**

> By making these technologies available in the public domain, we are helping foster a new era of entrepreneurship that will again place America at the forefront of high-tech manufacturing and economic competitiveness.[14]
>
> **Daniel Lockney | Executive, Technology Transfer Program, NASA**

IX. Encourage the private sector and government to continue initiating and sponsoring strategic innovation competitions.

- Triple the corporate sponsorship space incentive prize competitions to $100 million
- Create a "double dip" tax incentive for corporate sponsors of space prize competitions.

★ **Jane Kinney** is the assistant director of the Commercial Spaceflight Federation (CSF), a private space industry association dedicated to growing the commercial space sector while improving regulations, safety standards, and best practices. Prior to her role at CSF, Kinney worked at the United Launch Alliance and Ball Aerospace.

Ultimately, the ability of prizes to mobilize participants and capital, spread the burden of risk, and set a problem-solving agenda makes them a powerful instrument of change. They offer a valuable form of leverage to sponsors that use them as part of a well-designed strategy.[15]

Jonathan Bays, Tony Goland, and Joe Newsum, "Using Prizes to Spur Innovation," McKinsey & Company, July 2009.

As of July 2018, agencies have sponsored more than 840 incentive prizes. Over time, agencies became willing to sponsor prizes that are larger, more ambitious, and more important. ... For example, DARPA is sponsoring a $10 million prize for a team that can launch payloads to orbit, with no prior knowledge of the payload, destination orbit, or launch site, and accomplish that goal twice within days. This could dramatically expand access to space, with important applications in Earth observation and global communications.[16]

Thomas Kalil and Jeff Ubois, "The Promise of Incentive Prizes," Stanford Social Innovation Review, Winter 2019.

Prizes help build social economic legitimacy. Prizes forces organizations to show off products to the public sooner rather than later.[17]

Kenneth Davidian, Ph.D.*

★ **Kenneth Davidian, Ph.D.** has worked for the FAA Office of Commercial Space Transportation since 2008 and currently serves as the agency branch's director of research and as the program manager for the FAA Center of Excellence for Commercial Space Transportation. He began working for NASA at the Lewis Research Center and from 1997 to 1999 was assigned by NASA to serve as the assistant director of operations for the International Space University. From 2001 to 2004, Davidian worked in the private space sector in various roles for Paragon Space Development and the XPRIZE Foundation before returning to NASA to work on the agency's Centennial Challenge prize program. He also serves as the co-chair for the International Academy of Astronauts (IAA) study group called "Public/Private Human Access to Space – Earth Orbit and Beyond," as a member of the Ohio State University Aerospace Engineering Advisory Board, and as the associate editor of the *New Space Journal*. He formerly served as the vice president of strategic communications for the American Astronomical Society (AAS) and also led the Commercial Space Group of the American Institute of Aeronautics and Astronautics (AIAA).

"To Encourage Innovation, Make It a Competition"
Frame the competition around a specific need.
Break up challenges into manageable, implementable steps.
Provide company resources and internal mentors.
Draw value from the competition process, not just the results.[18]

Anil Rathi, "To Encourage Innovation, Make It a Competition," *Harvard Business Review,* **November 19, 2014.**

The Google Lunar XPRIZE, which ran from 2007–2018, was an unprecedented incentive competition that challenged privately funded teams from around the globe to be the first to land a rover on the surface of the Moon, drive it 500 meters across the lunar landscape, and send HD video and imagery back to Earth. Ultimately, GLXP ended without a winner, but the competition certainly helped kick off a new era of private space exploration. Several of the world's most relevant lunar startups today were born from GLXP, including ispace, SpaceIL, Moon Express, and Astrobotic.[19]

Yasemin Denari*

X. Allow free access to NASA test facilities and geographically convenient government labs for small companies and startups.

Industry is developing new technologies rapidly, using new tools and methods in software development and other areas. ... It's incumbent upon us to learn from developments in industry and contribute our vast expertise in technology as we prepare to use them in our future missions.[20]

Tom Cwik | Manager, Space Technology Office, NASA Jet Propulsion Laboratory

We actively support our entrepreneurial researchers through our New Venture Office, strong intellectual property protection, information, mentoring, guidance, and networking. Startups are frequently the best avenue for early stage technology commercialization and may require the active involvement of the JPL scientists and engineers in order to launch.[21]

NASA Jet Propulsion Laboratory Office of Technology Transfer

★ **Yasemin Denari** is the former marketing manager for Google, where she led the marketing efforts for the Google Lunar XPRIZE, including co-creating the *Moon Shot* docuseries for GLXP. She is now an investment, strategy, and branding consultant through her firm, YSD Consulting.

XI.   Provide loan forgiveness for space physicists and engineers after seven years of working in the industry.

> In an effort to keep more engineering students in the field, foundations, states, and companies are offering debt repayment as an incentive.[22]

Robert Farrington, "Student Loan Forgiveness for Engineering Majors," *College Investor*, February 2, 2018.

> This bill amends title IV (Student Assistance) of the Higher Education Act of 1965 to include as a public service job for purposes of the public service loan forgiveness program a full-time job as an employee of a management and operating contractor of a national laboratory owned by the Department of Energy.[23]

Fairness in Forgiveness Act of 2017, HR 2992, 115th Cong., 1st sess., _Congressional Record_ 164.

XII. Create new makerspaces across the United States to support entrepreneurial innovations, especially in non-ideal geographical areas.

> I think it's no exaggeration to say that if you head a startup, makerspaces have the potential to change the future of your company. A makerspace can give you access to the technology you need to get your idea off the ground. It can connect you with collaborators. And with entities like corporations and government getting in on the excitement, a makerspace can help you find funding for your ideas. Once your startup is off the ground, a makerspace inside it can help you recruit talented employees who are attracted to the idea of being able to spend time in a makerspace working on cool new ideas.
>
> A makerspace is about more than just being in the same space with other creators. It's about having access to the specialized tools and talent required to build the thing you want to create—and then taking advantage of those tools and talent to actually do it.[24]

H.O. Maycott, "How Makerspaces Are Inspiring Innovation at Startups," *Forbes*, February 2, 2016.

> When you move the cost of entrepreneurship from $100,000 to $2,000-$4,000, you completely change the operating terrain for entrepreneurs and inventors.[25]

Mark Hatch | Former Chief Executive Officer, TechShop

- Establish local, regional, and national grant systems along with federal tax incentives to promote the continued success of makerspaces within the United States.

> TechShop was the leader in the 'build it and they will come' model—with large facilities, and a huge catalog of tools. TechShop raised over $11M in investment—but in the end, still could not make their business model work—and was transitioning to a licensing model before finally running out of cash. ... We work to keep our nonprofit spaces operating with a safe amount of cash in the bank—and yet we don't have to generate a return for investors, we don't pay for labor, we don't pay taxes on member income, we don't pay sales taxes, AND we benefit from nonprofit pricing, grants, and more. While some might believe that size or scale and focusing on startups provides enough income to overcome these additional costs, I haven't seen it work in a way that supports a for-profit model.[26]
>
> **Ian Cole | Founder, The Maker Effect Foundation and Maker Faire Orlando**

- Adopt makerspaces as a nationwide educational standard.

> The U.S. ranks 25th in science and is below the PISA [Programme for International Student Assessment] mean score in math, with this score showing a negative trend from the last PISA report in 2012. In reading, the U.S. is only four points above the mean and ranks below many European and Asian countries. Educators will need to take these results into consideration as they look for new ways to engage students and teach STEAM subjects. One of the tools that educators can employ to help bridge this disparity in math and science is the use of makerspaces and hands-on learning techniques. These methods have shown promise for moving students from being typical consumers and brought them towards creative innovation.
>
> In addition to the focus on STEAM subjects, the recent changes in the economy and job market have impacted education. According to a recent Pew research Study, the education and training needs of today's employees have changed drastically in the last ten years, and many positions require constant learning and adapting to new technologies and methodologies. In this study, *The State of American Jobs,* researchers found that computer/technology, soft skills, and communication/writing skills were ranked as being integral to success in the job market, with 85 percent of respondents reporting that these skills were either extremely or vital to success in the market.

The study also compared the skills needed today to those from 1980 and found that overall there has been a 68% increase in the amount of education and training necessary to succeed in the workforce. With the market's increased demand for talented workers who are skilled in technology and communication, the opportunities that makerspaces generate for learning many of these skills are more important than ever before.[27]

Matthew Lynch, "Why Makerspaces Are the Key to Innovation," *Tech Edvocate,* **January 19, 2017.**

We're entering the twilight of the automobile era. We now have the ability to build a spacecraft for relatively low costs—it's even happening regularly at the university level. Wouldn't it be wise and forward-looking to start seeding space-themed makerspaces at a local level? This is the perfect time to develop modest infrastructure that can inspire and prepare future aerospace engineers.

XIII. Allocate 2 percent of NASA's budget to startup grants.

The [NASA FY2019] Budget supports the Administration's new space exploration policy by refocusing existing NASA activities toward exploration, by redirecting funding to innovative new programs that support the new policy, and by providing additional funding to support new public-private initiatives.[28]

Robert Pearlman | Space Historian; Founder & Editor, collectSPACE

XIV. Include a minimum of one (1) space-related project in part of the US Presidential Innovation Fellows (PIF) program.

The PIF program was established by the White House Office of Science and Technology Policy (OSTP) in 2012 to attract top innovators into government who are capable of tackling issues at the convergence of technology, policy, and process. ... PIFs have worked in tandem with federal agencies to solve critical governance issues including accelerating speed to service, developing new methods of procurement, and encouraging risk-taking in public-private partnerships.[29]

Davar Ardalan | Deputy Director, Presidential Innovation Fellows Program

"This new initiative will bring top innovators from outside government for focused 'tours of duty' with our best federal innovators on game-changing projects. Combining the know-how of citizen change agents and government change agents in small, agile teams that move at high speed, these projects aim to deliver significant results within six months."[30]

Todd Park, "Wanted: A Few Good Women and Men to Serve as Presidential Innovation Fellows," The White House, May 23, 2012.

XV.   Increase federal and state financial support for STEM initiatives involving space.

- Promote global adoption of STEM initiatives, which will increase students' capacity for innovative thinking, collaboration, and creativity
- Create new grants for students to work on space-focused projects
- Expand programs like the Space Integration Module

> In our Space Integration Module, our students learn about space missions, teamwork and the science of space. We have impacted four hundred teachers in training with that program and twelve thousand students. One student who participated in the Flight Centers program later interned at Boeing and worked at NASA—she just recently passed the test required for piloting the International Space Station.[31]
>
> **Colleen Howard***

- Increase funding and support for nonprofits like Teachers in Space

> Teachers in Space has been working since 2011 to build research equipment, procedures, data and skills together with relationships with flight providers, to build a path towards flying our teachers as researchers and research payload specialists as flights become available. The mission of Teachers in Space is to send teachers safely and affordably to space, then return them to the classroom to inspire students to pursue educational and career opportunities in the new space industry.

★ **Colleen Howard** is a STEM professional development educator who has worked in the public school system in Mesa, Arizona since 1987. For her outstanding work, she has received the PBS Teacher Innovation Award and the National Science Teachers Association's "Making a Difference" Award. She is an elected advocate with the Space Frontier Foundation, the National Space Foundation's Teacher Liaison for Arizona, and a member of the American Institute of Aeronautics and Astronautics (AIAA).

Much of our data on student impact is anecdotal but strongly encouraging; schools aren't allowed to track the progress of students once they leave, but the successful ones do report back to their teachers to thank them. The stories that come back from these students to their teachers are: 'I didn't know I could do experiments in space. You gave me an amazing opportunity to do my own research, and my essays and photos from that got me the interviews at the schools I wanted.' For example, the team of seventeen eleventh-graders from Melbourne, FL who won our first Flight Experiments competition all went on to STEM studies in college, and two continued to medical school to continue their research into ALS disease, inspired by their high school work on this experiment.

Most importantly, our teachers get to build their expertise by continuing to fly experiments with us year after year, learning recent technologies, getting new flight opportunities, and working with their students and communities to improve their own capabilities.

The Kansas teachers helped us get a contract at Cosmosphere in KS, which had a grant to produce an 'Engineering Day Out' for middle school girls; we conducted a half-day of hands-on workshops for one hundred girls there. Three of the teachers who've come through our workshop have established ongoing balloon programs at their schools. At Forest Hills High in NYC, teacher Joel Jackel credits his ongoing participation in Teachers in Space with enabling his assistant principal to get increased STEM funding for the school. He's now working with a physics teacher and with Gloversville High to bring a version of the High-Altitude Achievement balloon club to Forest Hills.[32]

Elizabeth Kennick*

★ **Elizabeth Kennick** is the executive director of Teachers in Space (TIS), a nonprofit educational organization that develops student interest in STEM studies by providing space experiences and industry connections to its students and teachers alike. Kennick previously served as a board member of the Space Frontier Foundation, where she directed the TIS program before incorporating it into a nonprofit. She also worked at Morgan Stanley as the VP of client technology, cofounded New York City's Software Process Improvement Network, and has produced Yuri's Night, the annual space-themed party in New York City, since 2008.

(4) ENABLE NEW MARKETS

I think the most important thing we need to do is not try too much to define the roadmap. There's going to be some really unexpected detours, and it'll be interesting to see what they are.[33]

Greg Autry | Marshall School of Business, University of Southern California

XVI. Provide incentives for commercial companies to develop reusable launch vehicles and drive down launch costs.

You cannot start an interesting space company today from your dorm room; the price of admission is too high, and the reason for that is the infrastructure doesn't exist. So, my mission with Blue Origin is to help build that infrastructure, that heavy lifting infrastructure, so that future generations will be able to stand on top of it the way I was able to stand on top of the US Postal Service and so on. That's critical, and that's all about reusability.[34]

Jeff Bezos | Founder, Blue Origin

XVII. Enable infrastructures for the economic development of solar system resources.

Our goals include protecting the Earth's fragile biosphere and creating a freer and more prosperous life for each generation by using the unlimited energy and material resources of space. Our purpose is to unleash the power of free enterprise and lead a united humanity permanently into the Solar System.[35]

Space Frontier Foundation

We're convinced that there's a market for space resources, and not just for such things as hard materials like aluminum or iron, but we think the initial products are going to be water and volatiles, like fuel. ... Then there's the sheer amount of material in the asteroid system—our solar system is mind boggling! It's roughly enough material to rebuild everything that we've built on Earth three thousand times over.[36]

William Miller*

XVIII. Create new incentives for the private sector to develop cost-effective solutions and innovations around technology, energy, and other pressing challenges.

In November 2019, the US Air Force hosted a Space Pitch Day for Phase 1 winners of the 2019 Small Business Innovation and Research program with space-focused technology and products. The two-day event, which was "designed to find new partners, innovative technologies and products while fast-tracking development," resulted in $22.5 million in on-the-spot contracts (paid in full) for thirty non-traditional startups. These new partners of the USAF have two years to develop their prototypes; eight of the companies were selected to compete for an additional contract of up to $3 million. These pitch days are unique signals for the future: such initiatives offer new avenues for bold ideas and risk-taking, and are crucial developments that will aid the NewSpace industry's growth. As explained by the Air Force, "The goal is to break free from the traditional paper-heavy, bureaucratic process for assessing products and signing contracts. Instead, the Air Force aims to take better advantage of existing commercial expertise and technologies while also serving as a catalyst for innovation and partnership with companies based in the United States." [37]

"'Space Pitch Day' Yields Innovative Technologies and New Partners for the Air Force." US Air Force, 2019.

Technology drives exploration, and the selection of these [SBIR] projects represents an investment in achieving our space exploration goals and supporting the United States innovation economy, as well.[38]

Steve Jurczyk | Associate Administrator, NASA

XIX. Enable a technology-based growth policy by dedicating 10 percent of the national R&D budget for space and the development of advanced nuclear generation capacity.

Monetary and fiscal policies to stimulate the economy are no substitute for the national research and development investment needed to spur

★ **William Miller** is a principal with SpaceCap Investments, a private equity firm focused on NewSpace startups. He was previously the chief executive officer of Deep Space Industries (DSI), a private space company that worked on space resource mining before being acquired by Bradford Space in 2018 (and now develops and builds spacecraft technologies for the commercial and civil sectors).

productivity growth and create high-paying, high-skill jobs. ... logically, as a society, we should be increasing research and development (R&D) spending to extend leadership in the current technology epoch and to prepare for the next one. ... the dominant target of such funding is to support social missions (defense, space, clean and domestic-sourced energy, etc.). Conservative factions have not bought into the concept that technology development for economic growth purposes has any substantive role for federal funding.[39]

Gregory Tassey, "A Technology-Based Growth Policy," *Issues in Science and Technology,* **March 6, 2017.**

The [United States FY2019] Budget provides $4.2 billion for the Office of Science to continue its mission to focus on early-stage research, operate the national laboratories, and continue high priority construction projects.

The ability of entrepreneurs and businesses to commercialize technologies that take full advantage of those resources [oil, gas, coal, nuclear, and renewables] is paramount to promoting US economic growth, security, and competitiveness. That is why the Budget provides more than $1.7 billion across the applied energy programs at DOE, which support early-stage R&D that enables the private sector to deploy the next generation of technologies and energy services that usher in a more secure, resilient, and integrated energy system.[40]

US Office of Management and Budget. *Budget of the United States Government, Fiscal Year 2019.*

XX.   Create better to tools to measure space-derived benefits.

- Advocate for and educate the public on the various impacts from space.

Every single business on the planet can benefit from space-related applications. There's an infrastructure side on the left, which is hardware-focused, and there's applications on the right. If you look at the companies on the left, these are hardware-centric companies. On the rights are companies that utilize the infrastructure on the left and make money. The companies on the right—Facebook, Google, Amazon—would not exist without the companies on the left; the companies on the left would not have a market to sell to without the companies on the right. It's a mutual, symbiotic relationship. The infrastructure-application relationship has existed for decades now, since the early 80s when the PC market was launched.

That fundamental distinction between infrastructure and applications has not changed when we come to the space industry. So, this symbiotic relationship, I think, definitely exists; the space industry, as we proceed forward, will see more companies follow that pattern—if our industry is healthy. I think most disruptive business models that we're talking about will have a strong understanding and strong connection to actual applications.[41]

Amaresh Kollipara | Chief Revenue Officer, OffWorld;
  Board of Trustees, SETI Institute and Space Frontier Foundation;
  Founder, Earth2Orbit

I think the general population doesn't fully appreciate how much space impacts their daily lives, and there's so much more potential, so many things that we haven't even thought of yet in terms of applications.[42]

Karina Drees | Chief Executive Officer, Mojave Air and Space Port

XXI. Create an advisory group of retired DoD and NASA "fellows" who can advise the venture capital industry in technical due diligence of potential space companies.

- Include Zero G, Zero Tax (revenue neutral legislation) for investments and revenue on all space-related ventures

The tax holiday on the internet was one of the crucial factors enabling its growth from a few hundred academic computers in the 1980s to the global force that it is today. This is also the potential for space.[43]

Dennis Wingo | Founder & Chief Executive Officer, Skycorp Inc.

XXII. Develop tax incentives to increase risk-taking and entrepreneurship.

Within the New Space market, many good ideas are housed in younger companies that lack sufficient funding and experienced management teams; they just need a little help in some of these areas. Small groups of smart, talented, and properly motivated people can accomplish great things when compared with large groups who have bureaucratic hurdles.[44]

Bill Miller | Principal, SpaceCap Investments;
  Former Chief Executive Officer, Deep Space Industries

Previously, there's been more of a positive discrimination model that forced set-aside contracts for small businesses. However, I don't think that's been an effective model; what it basically does is create this vicious cycle of people that know how to play the procurement game with the government rather than become a competitive threat and productize in ways that established suppliers can't. In other words, there are more doors opening for the non-traditional players to fan the fire of the established way of doing things and allow for faster ways of things getting done.[45]

Van Espahbodi | Cofounder & Managing Partner, Starburst Aerospace

Enterprise Investment Schemes (EIS) and Seed Enterprise Investment Schemes (SEIS) are investment schemes designed to encourage investment in small or medium sized companies. They do this by offering tax reliefs to individual investors who buy new shares in your company. To access them, you need to invest in the shares of a small, unlisted company.

Obviously, investing in small companies is generally riskier than buying shares in giants like HSBC or Shell. And the fact that the companies are not listed on the stock market means that there's no easy way to sell your shares. But small companies can grow very quickly because they are coming from a low base. With a small company, you're more likely to lose your money, but you're also more likely to make double, treble, or an even bigger multiple of the amount you invested.[46]

David Thorpe, "Investment Schemes Offer Tax Relief to Encourage Small or Medium-Sized Companies," *What Investment,* **October 5, 2018.**

XXIII. Focus more efforts on strategic business development in the commercial sector.

I firmly believe that the space market is missing basic business fundamentals. It's being driven by technology purists who lack the skills for commercialization. Until the sector changes to the extent where NewSpace companies are set up as strong sales organizations, rather than technology organizations, the market is likely to stagnate.

In addition, I think that we're doing a pretty poor job in the space industry of mapping out real value chains and understanding who the end-customer is. A lot of ventures seem to be predicated on the idea of, 'Let's build it and they'll come.' There needs to be dramatic shift toward market focus to drive value and money from a real end-customer upstream.[47]

Kartik Kumar | Cofounder, satsearch

The real space revolution has yet to begin in earnest. Most of the current revenues from space activity accrue to industries, such as direct-to-home television and geolocation, navigation, and timing services. The next development phase will be decidedly different, potentially shifting into new product development, additive manufacturing in low Earth orbit, and new activities like space mining. It is not speculation to suggest the future development will see new markets, new industries, and new sources of innovation.[48]

**Brian Higginbotham, "The Space Economy: An Industry Takes Off,"
US Chamber of Commerce, October 11, 2018.**

BREAKING INTO NEWSPACE

The following resources represent a sampling of the NewSpace ecosystem and are meant to provide direction for readers who aspire to enter the industry or become involved in NewSpace.

TIPS FOR ENTREPRENEURS WHO WANT TO BECOME ASTROPRENEURS

Collaborate with other entrepreneurs and connect with the industry
- Seek guidance from successful mentors and peers
- Identify indigenous incubators that might be supportive of space-focused initiatives
- Reach out to advocacy groups to help raise funding and support
- Take evolved ideas to accelerators to develop your visions into realities
- Locate makerspaces to work in an innovative environment with potential collaborators
- Attend conferences and events to connect with other astropreneurs
- Look to university labs for potential collaborative opportunities
- If you are in an area with less mature or active space activities, seek to create your own community of allies and supporters

Leverage existing resources
- Technology transfer
- Open source hardware and software
- IP transfer

Develop an innovative mindset
- Use the scientific method to test ideas
- Learn from failures to create viable solutions
- Rethink what exists to improve capabilities

SPACE ECOSYSTEM TOOLS

*The following organizations are a sample
of digital NewSpace resources.*[†]

Aerospace & Defense Forum – Global community that provides extensive online resources as well as monthly forums and meetings for its members. Resources include news, insights, analytics, and business and partnership opportunities in the space sector.

ESA Industry Portal – Tool providing educational materials as well as business opportunities at ESA.

NewSpace Hub – Global updates of new and lesser-known NewSpace startups, organizations, products, events, and tools; aimed toward entrepreneurs, business professionals, investors, and analysts.

satsearch – Search engine for space products and services.

Society of Japanese Aerospace Company Directory – Japanese space products, services, organizations, and contact information.

Space Industry Map – Digital map of NewSpace companies around the world.

Space-Industry.com – Database that connects space-faring organizations and individuals interested in partnerships, research, parts, and services.

Space Frontier Foundation's NewSpace Directory – Non-exhaustive list of NewSpace companies and their business models.

[†]Direct links for all organizations and resources mentioned can be found on Robert Jacobson's website, **tools.spaceisopenforbusiness.com**

ASTROPRENEURIAL COMMUNITIES

The Space Foundation
- Space Commerce Business Growth Workshops
- Space Commerce webinar and speaker series

Moonshot Space Company
- Not-for-profit chapters around the world that bring entrepreneurs, students, researchers, investors, and industry experts together to participate in space ventures
- Space Elevator framework: training programs, investment opportunities, business development, supply chain growth, project execution, talent recruitment
- Monthly newsletter with updates and events from the Moonshot community

Make: Community – Makerspaces map, directory, events, projects, job board

Hackerspaces.org – Global hackerspaces map, directory, mailing lists

The Astropreneurs Space Startup Accelerator (Europe) – Space startup accelerator; mentoring and training; space events database and news

WOMEN IN SPACE

Rocket Women – Online platform and resource focused on bringing more women into space and technology careers.

The Space Gal – Online platform and resource focused on bringing more women into STEM careers.

Space Foundation's Women's Global Gathering – Brings together women in the aerospace sector and features senior industry speakers as well as networking events.

Women in Aerospace (WIA) – Professional development resources for women in the space sector (includes programs, conferences, and networking events).

CONFERENCES

Earthlight Foundation –
  New Worlds Space
  Settlement Conference

International Space Development
  Conference

International Symposium for
  Commercial and Personal
  Space Flight

MIT New Space Age Conference

Next-Generation Suborbital
  Researchers Conference

Reinventing Space (Europe)

Satellite 2020

Small Satellite Conference

SmallSat Symposium

Space Symposium

Spacetide (Japan)

SpaceCom

DUE DILIGENCE

Reading up on the space sector.

Ad Astra – Periodical published by the National Space Society; acts as a bridge for those less interested in the purely commercial aspects of the sector.

The Lurio Report – Electronic newsletter published by Dr. Charles Lurio of Massachusetts; contains highly nuanced and excellent journalism focused on primary sources.

Parabolic Arc – Electronic publication from Doug Messier (another excellent journalist).

Spaceflight Now – Online news portal focused on aerospace.

Spacetoday.net – Online portal that compiles and summarizes space-related news from around the internet, daily.

The Space Review – Online platform providing in-depth essays, commentary, and reviews of the entire space sector.

The International Institute of Space Commerce – Online nonpartisan think-tank dedicated to space commerce, business, and economics.

NASA & GOVERNMENT RESOURCES

NASA Innovative Advanced Concepts (NIAC) Program

Presidential Innovation Fellows

Small Business Innovation Research (SBIR)

Small Business Technology Transfer (STTR)

White House Office of Science and Technology Policy (OSTP)

NASA Prizes & Competitions
- Asteroid Grand Challenge
- Centennial Challenge Program
- Center of Excellence for Collaborative Innovation
- Challenge.gov
- Innovation Pavilion
- NASA@work
- Open Innovation & Prize Competitions
- Tournament Lab

ACCELERATORS

Syndicate 708

Starburst Aerospace

Moonshot Space Company

ANGEL GROUPS

Angel List – A virtual network with no focus sector.

Propel(x) – A virtual investment group focused on science-based startups.

Space Angels – A virtual network focused on the space sector.

STEM EDUCATION

Base 11 – Nonprofit dedicated to entrepreneurial development that provides STEM accelerators to underserved high school and college-level students around the United States.

Space Integration Module – Immersive STEM and space experience program for sixth graders in Mesa, Arizona public schools.

Stages – Education center focused on developing the next generation of talented and innovative techies, artists, economists, and scientists.

Teachers in Space – Nonprofit educational organization that sends teachers to space, then returns them to the classroom to inspire students to pursue educational and career opportunities in STEM and NewSpace.

LICENSING

Early astropreneurs need to think globally, but they will often lack the resources of larger, global companies. If one is having difficulty identifying potential astropreneurial opportunities, one easy way to start is tracking IP licensing offices. licensing is a smart way to help jumpstart new opportunities.

Types of Intellectual Property
- Copyrights
- Trademarks
- Patents

IP Licensing and Technology Transfer Sources

Universities

Public and Private Research Facilities

Licensing Firms and Offices

Government Labs

Indian Space Research Organization (ISRO)
- Technology transfer for commercial companies

NASA

- Technology Transfer Program – patented NASA technology available for patent licensing
- Patent Portfolio – online database of NASA technologies with commercial potential
- Spinoff – publication tracking all benefits resulting from the Tech Transfer program
- Software Release – free NASA software, searchable via online catalog

A 2011 data survey of the tech transfers over the five-year period of 2003–2008* revealed that commercialized NASA technologies:

- Created over 9,200 jobs
- Generated over $1.2 billion in revenue
- Created more than $6 billion in cost avoidance
- Saved more than 12,000 lives
- Significantly improved quality of life for more than 86 million people

*Data represents the responses from 103 of the 250 companies (representing 274 tech transfers) that NASA contacted for this survey.[1]

OPEN SOURCE RESOURCES

Licensing can still have drawbacks: it is expensive and can come with various strings attached. Licensees must be meticulous about details and ownership rights. Another option is to leverage space-focused open source software and hardware.

Collaborative Space Travel and Research Team (CSTART) – Open source spaceflight hardware (OSSHW)

Mach30 – OSSHW

Radio Amateur Satellite Corporation (AMSAT) – Satellite software and Gpredict tool

SpaceGAMBIT – OSSHW

One thing I always tell startups who want to work with us is that we also have a lot of IP that we are not interested in taking to market; that's another reason to engage with us. There are some things that Caltech will want to work on, but there is still a lot of other IP that we developed here that we have moved on from, and we're more than happy to license it, to do a technology transfer to get it to the outside world.[2]

**Anthony Freeman, Ph.D. | Innovation Foundry,
NASA Jet Propulsion Laboratory**

We empower companies with their intellectual property. We help them evaluate their IP, ascertain where the market may be, and determine if there is a white space for their products and who their competitors are. There may be a competitor who already has a share of the marketplace, for example, and can move faster than you can. New market entrants can deal with that in two ways: either by out-licensing their technology through these companies or by actually partnering with them. We facilitate those connections.

Working with many Fortune 50 companies over the years, we've found that optimization is an important aspect. They want to avoid internal R&D by looking outside for IP from people who have already maneuvered all the hurdles and now just need some muscle, some help (often monetary), to gain entrance into the market or to strengthen their place in it. The services that IP Technology Exchange offers are critical to big companies and small companies alike. Big companies are often looking to in-license technology. Small companies are normally looking to out-license their technology and take it to the marketplace."[3]

Sam Reiber*

★ **Sam Reiber** is the general counsel for Cognis Group, a global research firm focused on intellectual property. He is also the director of IP Technology Exchange a Cognis subsidiary firm that specializes in intellectual property analytics, licensing, and marketing for creators of modern technologies.

We started Equipois by licensing the technology from Garrett Brown. During the venture, we filed numerous patents, but we also bought a patent that we thought was relevant from a university in Canada. So, you can find your ideas in a number of places. You can develop technology yourself or through your engineering team. But if you don't do that, you can license it or buy it, especially from a sector that's adjacent. They may be using the technology for something different and be willing to let you take a shot at using it for space or aerospace.[4]

Eric Golden*

INFLUENCING POLICY

For those who wish to engage more regularly with their elected leadership, I'd recommend following and joining some of the more pressing, urgent issues via advocacy organizations and efforts. The following groups do a reasonable job summarizing issues into manageable and digestible chunks, which can then be relayed to Congress.

Space Frontier Foundation

National Space Society

March Storm

Commercial Spaceflight Federation

★ **Eric Golden** is the managing director of Armory Securities, an investment bank where he advises clients across many industries, including technology, media, business services, manufacturing, and transportation. Previously, Golden was the president and chief executive officer of Equipois, a company that designs and manufactures products that support the musculoskeletal system to encourage full spatial and rotational freedom of motion.

GLOSSARY

accelerators: mentorship and business development programs for promising start-ups (i.e., small teams that typically have a product). Accelerators generally provide seed funding to the startup (in exchange for equity) with an aim to scale the business up and attract investment by the end of the process, which is normally three months long. The accelerator ends with a pitch or demo day with potential investors.

additive manufacturing or **3D printing:** technology that creates a three-dimensional object using a computer-aided design (CAD) model (i.e., digital file) by adding the printed material layer by layer.

Advanced Diagnostic Ultrasound in Microgravity (ADUM): experiments on the ISS that led to development of ultrasound technology that can diagnose internal injuries and illnesses, and can be operated with little training—making the tech valuable in areas of the world where access to medical facilities is limited.

advocacy groups: informal (i.e., non-government) groups that focus on a subject of interest and work to improve public interest and perception, with an ultimate goal of influencing political, business, and/or social systems.

agribusiness: the commercial industries focused on agriculture and farming, particularly those that leverage advanced and modern technologies.

Air Force: the US military branch responsible for aerial warfare, established in 1947.

The USAF is housed within the Department of the Air Force, which is one of three military branches within the Department of Defense. The USAF has long been a key contracter of commercial space companies.

airspace: the area of atmosphere above a given territory that is controlled by that territory's country, and is subject to the laws of that country.

anti-satellite or **ASAT:** weapons designed to damage, disable, or destroy targeted satellites for military or strategic reasons. The United States, Russia, China, and India are the only countries to have conducted ASAT tests (shooting down their own satellites) to demonstrate their capabilities; ASAT weapons have not been used against other countries or in warfare to date.

Apollo 11: the fifth crewed mission of NASA's Apollo program, which became the first in history to land humans on the Moon (July 20, 1969) and the first to result in humans walking on the Moon (astronauts Neil Armstrong and Buzz Aldrin, July 21, 1969). The successful Apollo 11 mission signified the completion of the Space Race, fulfilling President John F. Kennedy's promise of "landing a man on the Moon and returning him safely to the Earth" within a decade, and remains one of the greatest and most celebrated accomplishments in spaceflight history.

Apollo program or **Project Apollo:** NASA's third human spaceflight program, which ran from 1961 to 1972 during the height of the Space Race between the United States and the USSR. Apollo resulted in major spaceflight milestones, including sending a crewed spaceflight beyond low Earth orbit (Apollo 8), orbiting a celestial body (Apollo 8, 1968), and landing humans on the Moon (Apollo 11, 1969). The Apollo program accomplishments range from scientific to cultural, resulting in lunar samples for scientists to study, advances in various areas of technology (and nearly 2,000 spinoff technologies over the half-century that followed), major impacts on popular culture, and increased funding for NASA facilities and programs.

application programming interface or **API:** a computing toolset that allows users to access and use functionalities of other systems.

Arch Mission Foundation: a nonprofit organization that works to create an archive of human civilization on and off-Earth. To date, Arch Mission has completed three successful missions that leverage the in-space environment: the Solar Library (2018, launched by SpaceX), Isaac Asimov's *Foundation* trilogy encoded in 5D optical storage in quartz and is orbiting the Sun for 30 million years; Orbital (LEO) Library (2018, launched by SpaceChain), an English copy of Wikipedia stored in a CubeSat now located in low Earth orbit; Lunar Library (2019, launched by SpaceIL), a thirty-million-page archive of human history housed in a nanotechnology device designed to survive for billions of years (stored in the Beresheet lunar lander, which crashed on the Moon in April 2019).

Artemis: US government-funded lunar program announced in 2019 and led by NASA. Artemis will partner with commercial companies to develop new spacecraft, robotic landers, payload delivery, and various new technologies for future Moon missions. Artemis is planned to allocate between $20 billion and $30 billion in funding for its various initiatives. NASA is working with private sector companies (thirteen so far) and international partners (e.g., ESA, JAXA) as it moves toward the program goals of landing US astronauts on the Moon by 2024, establishing a sustainable presence on the Moon, and setting the stage for human settlement and a lunar economy. NASA's Commercial Lunar Payload Services (CLPS) also supports the Artemis program.

artificial intelligence or **AI:** computer science technology that attempts to mimic human "intelligence" via "smart" machines. Most AI that exists today is based on machine learning, in which technology is programmed to perform specific functions and uses algorithms to optimize said functions. The AI we see in science fiction, otherwise known as artificial general intelligence (AGI), "true" AI, or "hard" AI, in which technology is fully sentient and capable of thinking, feeling, and acting on its own accord, is not the AI we have today. Our AI, also called "soft" AI, is extremely limited and can only perform its programmed functions. However, soft AI has revolutionized many industries with its capabilities and will continue to improve as research continues.

AST or **Office of Commercial Space Transportation:** the US government branch responsible for overseeing all commercial space activities (i.e, any space activity that is not "by the government, for the government"), currently housed in the Federal Aviation Administration, and commonly referred to as FAA/AST. Originally, this branch operated under the Department of Transportation from its founding in 1984 until 1995 (and was known as OCST), during which it emphasized relaxed regulations for the commercial space sector. Since the rise of NewSpace, AST has struggled to adequately keep up with the increasing number of launches, requests for licenses, and overall shifting landscape of the commercial space sector.

asteroid mining: the practice of extracting resources, such as metals, minerals, and water, from asteroids, comets, or other near-Earth objects.

astropreneur: an entrepreneur involved in the space industry, particularly NewSpace.

Atlantis: NASA Space Shuttle that operated from 1985 until 2011 and completed the last mission of the Space Shuttle program. Atlantis notably deployed probes to Venus and Jupiter, and aided the assembly of the ISS, among many other accomplishments.

Beresheet: the lunar lander co-developed by Israeli nonprofit space company SpaceIL and Israel Aerospace Industries for a record low of $100 million. Beresheet launched on a SpaceX Falcon 9 on February 22, 2019 and crash-landed on the Moon on April 4, 2019. The lunar lander's payload included the Lunar Library, an archive of human history created by the Arch Mission Foundation, which is believed to remain readable even if broken into pieces during the crash landing.

Big Data: large data sets (structured or unstructured) categorized by at least one of the following characteristics: high volume, high velocity, high variety, or high veracity.

Such data sets are analyzed in order to extract valuable insights that help businesses make better informed decisions. Big Data is a nearly $140 billion global market and continues to grow by 10 percent every year as the demand for precise and profitable business analytics increases.

blockchain: a digital ledger for cryptocurrency that is notably decentralized and distributed—and therefore extremely secure. As blockchains are typically public, users are prevented from altering records or transactions, thereby creating an inherently transparent system that enables the users to verify information easily. The digital structure offers added security benefits for users to secure their payments using "smart contracts," which are exchange agreements that only process payment when specific requirements have been met.

booster: a rocket or engine that helps a launch vehicle reach low Earth orbit by providing additional thrust and power during the early stages of launch. Boosters typically detach from the launch vehicle once their fuel has been used up, at which point they fall back to Earth (and often can be used again on other launches).

burnouts: overwhelming stress, exhaustion, lack of interest, or even depression caused by running one's own business. Often resulting from "burning the candle at both ends" for too long, factors like work style, employees, and passion for the job can all contribute to burnouts.

bus: the main infrastructure of a satellite, responsible for housing the computer (and software), payload, sensors, transponders, and other hardware; it is also where the power of a satellite generates that allows "driving" via propulsion and steering.

C band: the segment of the electromagnetic spectrum with a frequency range of 4 to 8 GHz (gigahertz) and a wavelength range of 7.5 to 3.75 cm. The C band is most notably used for satellite communications and was the first frequency band allowed for commercial satellite telecommunications.

CASIS: the Center for the Advancement of Science in Space is a nonprofit organization that manages the ISS US National Laboratory (which is NASA-funded but not a NASA asset). CASIS develops research opportunities for science, medicine, and technology, offering seed funding and access to space to select organizations in the private sector.

Challenger: NASA Space Shuttle that experienced structural failures during the launch of its tenth mission, resulting in the spacecraft breaking apart and the fatalities of its seven crew members, one of whom would have been the first teacher in space. The Challenger launch and disaster, which occurred 73 seconds into flight, was televised live in the United States, leading to extensive media coverage and attention on both NASA and the safety of spaceflight. As a result of the Challenger disaster, NASA paused all Space Shuttle missions for the next two and a half years.

Chang'e: a lunar orbiter for the China National Space Administration's (CNSA) lunar exploration program. There have been four Chang'e orbiters so far, which have completed the first two phases of the lunar exploration program (orbital missions and soft landers/rovers); future Chang'e orbiters are planned to complete lunar sample returns and eventually establish a robotic research station on the Moon. Chang'e 4 landed on the far side of the Moon in January 2019, where it deployed a lunar rover.

Commercial Crew & Cargo Program Office or **C3PO:** NASA program focused on expanding the commercial space transportation industry in the United States. Formally established in 2005, C3PO invests in commercial space companies in various ways (partnership agreements, contracts) in an effort to establish commercial space transportation services that are safe, reliable, cost-effective, and available to both the private sector and the government. C3PO manages the Commercial Orbital Transportation Services (COTS) program, the Commercial Resupply (CRS) program, and the Commercial Crew Development Program (CCDev).

Communications Satellite Act of 1962: an act signed into law by President John F. Kennedy on August 31, 1962 in a controversial effort to regulate the emerging satellite sector.

COMSAT: the Communications Satellite Corporation is a global, primarily satellite-based, communications company that was created with JFK's Satellite Communications Act of 1962. While federally funded and regulated, COMSAT was publicly traded and its creation hoped to prevent satellite communications monopolies in the private sector, primarily by AT&T.

constellation: a group of satellites (artificial) that are typically much smaller than traditional satellites, but that work together as one cohesive system in order to match the power and performance of a much larger, much more expensive satellite. One notable feature of constellations is that the individual satellites can be replaced or swapped out without costing very much, making constellations a more sustainable alternative to a traditional, singular satellite performing the same functions.

COPUOUS: the United Nations Committee on the Peaceful Uses of Outer Space, established in 1958, aims to create international policies and agreements for the space environment such that it does not become weaponized, militarized, or misused by any country. COPUOUS is responsible for overseeing the five space-related treaties created by the UN: Outer Space Treaty (effective in 1967), Rescue Agreement (effective in 1968), Liability Convention (effective in 1972), Registration Convention (effective in 1976), and Moon Treaty (effective in 1984).

Commercial Crew Development or **CCDev:** NASA program that contracts private sector companies for various technology and vehicle developments aimed at creating new crewed spacecraft. Early on, CCDev adjusted its requirements to focus on vehicles that will specifically transport astronauts to and from the ISS. The program's benefits include lower-cost, reliable spacecraft and launches for NASA, a shift back into domestic launch (versus using Russian rockets), and supporting private sector growth. CCDev is a program within the Commercial Cargo and Crew Program Office and is currently in its fifth development phase.

Commercial Lunar Payload Services or **CLPS:** NASA program established in 2018 to contract private sector space companies to develop lunar transportation,

robotic landers, in-situ resource utilization, and more generally to support the Artemis program. CLPS has issued ten-year general contracts to various commercial companies and has so far awarded task order contracts to three of those companies to develop lunar landers. Other program goals include reducing the cost of lunar exploration, extracting samples of the Moon's surface for scientific examination, scouting resources in the south pole, and supporting the innovation and growth of the private space sector.

Commercial Orbital Transportation Services or **COTS:** former NASA program (2006–2013) that contracted private sector companies to develop and build spacecraft for the purpose of delivering cargo and supplies to the ISS. When COTS was created, NASA's ISS resupply missions were growing too expensive for the Agency to continue funding; the options were either to use another country's spacecraft or to involve the commercial sector. SpaceX and Orbital ATK ultimately designed, built, and launched their own spacecraft and launch rockets per the COTS parameters, supplying NASA with cargo resupply options at a fraction of the previous cost—and concluding the program successfully.

Commercial Resupply Services or **CRS:** NASA partnership project with the commercial space sector to resupply the International Space Station. The two companies contracted for CRS are SpaceX and Orbital ATK, which developed spacecraft through the COTS program and have been successfully supplying cargo to the ISS under their CRS contracts since 2008.

Crew Dragon: SpaceX's reusable spacecraft capable of safely transporting humans and expected to serve as a shuttle for NASA astronauts to and from the ISS. As one of two models in the Dragon 2 class of spacecraft, the Crew Dragon is able to self-dock at the ISS.

CubeSat: a class of small satellite characterized by its cube shape and weight being less than 1.33 kg, which typically places it in the category of "picosatellite." The CubeSat design was created in 1999, and over 1,200 CubeSats have been deployed as of the start of 2020. They are particularly inexpensive to create, generally costing around $100,000 each, though very basic models can cost as low as $50,000, making them accessible to universities and students. CubeSats are frequently used for microgravity testing as they are small enough to transport as cargo and then deploy from the ISS.

DARPA: the Defense Advanced Research Projects Agency, an agency within the United States Department of Defense, was created in 1958 by President Eisenhower as a response to the USSR's launch of the Sputnik 1 satellite. DARPA's purpose is to develop technology for military use and has worked with academic, government, and commercial industry partners to conduct research and development, and ultimately creation, of leading-edge science and technology.

data processors: the entity that collects, organizes, summarizes, analyzes, classifies, or otherwise manipulates specific data in order to produce meaningful information.

data providers: the entity (e.g., individual, company, software) that collects and supplies relevant data to an end-user.

data purchase: companies can buy data specific to their needs from third-party data providers rather than spend the time, money, and other resources compiling accurate data. Instead, the providers sell precise and actionable data for companies to leverage based on their business goals.

deep tech: highly advanced science and/or engineering technology on the cutting-edge. Deep tech often requires significant time and funding compared to mainstream tech, especially because of the time needed for proper research and development. Deep tech's end goal is focused more on developing a functional and advanced ecosystem rather than user sales; examples include blockchain, robotics, artificial intelligence, and quantum computing. In recent years, progress of deep tech efforts has led to increased investments and is considered a rising sector that will have a wider reach and impact on industry, particularly as the technology continues to offer solutions for the complex and difficult problems of our world.

defense surveillance: the use of satellites and other aerial vehicles or technology—such as high-altitude balloons, remote sensing, radars, hyperspectral imaging, and Earth observation—for strategic tracking in near-real time. Such satellite reconnaissance helps detect nuclear weapons, ballistic missile launches, border security, and enemy communications. Defense surveillance is used to gain insights on potential threats, whether domestic or foreign, across land, sea, air, and space.

Delta-v: the energy (more specifically, the change in velocity) required for a spacecraft to successfully perform a maneuver in flight (e.g., land on a planet, launch). The Delta-v budget refers to the total energy required for a full spaceflight mission and is the measure that tells us how much propellant is needed.

diffusion of innovations: a theory proposed by Everett Rogers (published in his 1962 book of the same name) that attempts to explain the way new technologies or ideas spread in a given culture. By Rogers' theory, successful innovations diffuse in five stages, represented by the adopters: innovators; early adopters; early majority; late majority; laggards. Factors like social status, education, financial liquidity, social mindset, and proximity to scientific information all play a role in determining which category an individual falls into.

DoD or **Department of Defense:** an executive branch within the United States federal government responsible for national security and the country's armed forces. The DoD oversees the US Department of the Army, Department of the Navy, Department of the Air Force, and various defense agencies, including the Defense Intelligence Agency (DIA), the National Security Agency (NSA), the National Reconnaissance Office (NRO), and the Defense Advanced Research Projects Agency (DARPA).

dual use: equipment or technology designed or able to be employed for both civilian and military purposes.

Earth observation or **EO:** the use of remote sensing technologies to compile information about Earth; EO data typically focuses on physical, chemical, or biological systems, and is helpful for detecting changes in weather and the environment. Long-term EO data is used to illustrate changes of a given area over time, which offers insight into causes for the change,

impacts of the change, and then allows for informed responses to the change.

edutainment: entertainment with educational merit or an educational aspect, such as science-focused channels and programming (including science fiction).

EELV or **Evolved Expendable Launch Vehicle:** a US government program that began in 1994 in an effort to create more cost-effective launch vehicles for the US Department of Defense and led to the creation of the Delta IV and Atlas V launch families. In 2019, the program name was changed to the "National Security Space Launch" (NSSP) program.

electromagnetic pulse or **EMP:** a brief burst of electromagnetic energy that causes surges in voltage and electric currents. EMPs can damage or destroy electronic devices or systems, depending on the magnitude and location of the pulse, and are therefore highly dangerous events as their effects can disable the electronic systems we rely on. EMPs can be natural, resulting from lightning or solar flares, or they can be created artificially via nuclear explosions or other weapons designed to generate an EMP.

energy harnessing: controlling or directing an energy source in order to convert said energy into usable forms. For example, the wind's kinetic energy causes wind turbine blades to spin around a rotor and into a generator, which converts the kinetic energy into electricity. Other forms of energy that can be harnessed include solar, tidal, geothermal, nuclear, and via fossil fuels (such as coal or oil).

European Space Agency or **ESA:** the intergovernmental, multi-national space agency for twenty-two European countries (member states). ESA was established in 1975 and focuses on maintaining a peaceful European presence in space, cooperation between European countries, and the pursuit of scientific and technological research—all aimed at improving quality of life, the economy, safety, and knowledge for European citizens. In recent years, ESA has created programs and initiatives to support NewSpace startups in Europe. ESA is one of the five participating space agencies on the International Space Station and has contibuted various technological systems along with five modules: Columbus, a laboratory to conduct scientific research; Harmony, the station's "utility hub"; Cupola, an observatory module; Leonardo, a perma-nent multipurpose module; and Tranquility, a support systems module. ESA also offers educational materials from the ISS that are available to students online.

ESA's member states are Austria, Belgium, the Czech Republic, Denmark, Estonia, Finland, France, Germany, Greece, Hungary, Ireland, Luxembourg, the Netherlands, Norway, Poland, Portugal, Romania, Spain, Sweden, Switzerland, and the United Kingdom; Canada and Slovenia are partial members. Each member state participates in varying degrees, and most have their own national space programs as well; ESA also cooperates with the European Union and receives funding from both the EU and from the member states."

exit activities: in business, an exit activity or exit strategy refers to liquidation of one's invested assets or stake in a company, either because the profit objective has been reached (in successful cases) or in order to limit losses (in unsuccessful cases).

expandable habitats: structures that can be transported compactly and then expand or inflate once they reach their target destination, making them easy to carry as payloads. Once expanded into their full structure, the habitat should be pressurized such that it can sustain human life. Currently, Bigelow Aerospace has an expandable habitat attached to the International Space Station; while the habitat was originally implemented in 2016 as a two-year test, it has "exceeded performance expectations" so significantly that NASA has extended its contract with Bigelow to keep the habitat on the ISS until at least 2028, where it is used as a critical storage space.

expendable launch vehicle or ELV: spacecraft launch vehicles that are used only once; after launch, the various rocket stages detach from the spacecraft (and are either discarded in space or destroyed on Earth). To date, most rocket launches have used ELV, as the design is simpler than reusable launch systems; however, compared to reusable launch vehicles, the cost-per-launch of ELVs is significantly higher, and both uses and wastes more materials.

exponential technologies: refers to the pattern of technological progress increas-ing at an exponential rate (rather than the standard linear rate) while costs, in compar-ison, drop. More specifically, "exponential technology" is when the tech's power and/or progress doubles every year, and/or the cost of the tech drops by half. Examples of exponential technology include artificial intelligence, biotech, nanotech, robotics, and network and computing systems (for instance, consider the power and cost of a personal computer in 1980 compared to today, or the cost and computing power of a cell phone two years ago compared to today).

FAA or **Federal Aviation Administration:** a governmental agency within the US Department of Transportation. Created in 1958, the FAA is responsible for overseeing all civil aviation in the US, the airspace above the country's surrounding international waters, air traffic control, and commercial space transportation (notably launch and re-entry of spacecraft). The four lines of business within the FAA are Airports (ARP), Air Traffic Organization (ATO), Aviation Safety (AVS), and Commercial Space Transportation (AST).

Falcon 9: a two-stage, medium-lift rocket designed and built by SpaceX; the Falcon 9 family consists of three versions: v1.0, v1.1, and v1.2 "Full Trust." The Falcon 9's first stage booster is reusable and undergoes a controlled landing after it separates from the rocket. Design for the Falcon 9 began in 2005 and received a boost in development when NASA awarded SpaceX with a Commercial Orbital Transportation Services contract and seed money in 2006, and then with a Commercial Resupply Services contract for missions to the ISS in 2008. While the NASA contracts helped SpaceX develop, build, and test the Falcon 9 more quickly, the success of the rocket benefited NASA greatly with its cost being a fraction of typical NASA costs for development. In Falcon 9's first decade in operation (beginning in 2010), there have been 87 launches and a 97.7 percent success rate. SpaceX plans to replace all Falcon 9 rockets with the reusable Starship models in coming years.

Falcon Heavy: a two-stage, super-heavy-lift rocket designed and built by SpaceX; the Falcon Heavy is a derivative of the Falcon 9 rocket and is designed for its boosters to be reusable. Falcon Heavy currently has the highest payload capacity of any rocket in operation; its first flight occurred in 2018 (which launched Elon Musk's Tesla Roadster into heliocentric orbit). Falcon Heavy has been contracted by the Department of Defense, the US Air Force, and NASA, as well as commercial clients. SpaceX intends to replace the Falcon Heavy class with the reusable Starship rocket in coming years.

FCC or **Federal Communications Commission:** an independent government agency in the United States, created in 1948 by the Communications Act. The FCC houses seven bureaus and eleven staff offices, has five commissioners, and is responsible for regulating all domestic communications by radio, television, wire, cable, and satellite. Within this role, the FCC regulates all commercial spectrum and requires licenses for individuals or companies to use dedicated spectrum—and thus requires commercial space companies with any communication features in their technology to obtain an FCC license.

fixed-price contracts: a type of contract where the payment or fee for completed work is agreed upon and does not change based on costs incurred to complete said work. Typically, fixed-price contracts will anticipate all expenses (materials, labor, etc.) in determining the set amount to be paid.

flags and footprints: the period of space missions during the Space Race, until the end of the Apollo program (1958–1972), in which Cold War rivals the United States and the Soviet Union attempted to achieve "firsts" in space. While the two government space programs' objectives were to prove technological prowess and assure their citizens of security and national capabilities, the objectives themselves were mostly symbolic. This period culminated with US astronauts walking on the Moon and planting an American flag on the Moon.

founder's syndrome: a phenomenon often cited in the tech and nonprofit worlds wherein a company's founder is resistant to change in organizational structures (specifically, in relinquishing any of their own power or the key roles they have appointed), such that the leadership becomes stifling and damaging to the company and other employees.

funding gap: the amount of money a business needs in order to continue current and/or future operations or development. Funding gaps occur most often in early-stage companies that require long periods of R&D (such as tech, pharmaceuticals, or space) and costly prototype development; at some point, the company runs out of money and cannot continue without a cash injection. Funding gaps can be closed by outside investment or financial vehicles like bank loans.

GDP or **gross domestic product:** the total financial value of a country's finished products and services over a specific amount of time (typically annual or quarterly). GDP reflects both the government and public sectors, and includes all industries, investment activities, and foreign trade balances. GDP offers a broad view of a specific nation's economic health and growth rates, which is valuable information for investors, policymakers, and businesses alike.

GEO or **geostationary orbit:** also known as geosynchronous equatorial orbit, GEO occurs 35,786 km above Earth's mean sea level (in GSO) and notably remains fixed with Earth's equator while also matching Earth's rotational period; objects in GEO therefore appear stationary in the sky. Satellites in GEO provide consistent and broad coverage, without the on-Earth provider needing to adjust its receivers; its location above the equator gives GEO satellites the largest coverage of any position in space: 42 percent of Earth's surface—making GEO satellites particularly suited for communications and weather monitoring.

geospatial Big Data: Geospatial data is information with a geographical component and is often culled using Earth observation satellites and remote sensing technologies. Geospatial Big Data (or "spatial Big Data") refers to data sets that exceed the the capacity of a computing system; at least 80 percent of all data is geospatial (i.e., has a locale component) in nature, and such data is growing exponentially. While the growth rate presents its own challenges, geospatial Big Data is unique in its ability to detect complex global challenges and develop proper solutions.

government purpose rights: the United States government's legal ability to perform any action, without restriction, to data or computer software within the government (including using, modifying, disclosing, and distributing the data), including activities in which the government is a party (e.g., government contracts with commercial companies, international cooperative agreements, and international sales or transfers). While purpose rights allow the government to use the aforementioned data for any government purpose, such data cannot be used for commercial purposes. For commercial companies, such purpose rights extend to IP related to technology or software developed under a government contract, grant, or other funding.

GPS or **Global Positioning System:** a US government-owned navigation system that uses satellites to provide global navigation, positioning, and timing information. GPS is dual-use technology, used by civilians and for defense purposes alike, and accessible for free use by anyone with a GPS receiver, although the government is able to selectively deny or degrade access.

GSO or **geosynchronous orbit:** the orbit that occurs at an altitude of 35,786 km (22,236 miles) above mean sea level on Earth. In GSO, satellites orbit exactly in sync with Earth's rotational period and therefore always monitor a specific area—allowing them to detect changes in that region over time, which is useful for military insights, agriculture, satellite radio, and communications. Geostationary orbit is a type of geosynchronous orbit.

Hayabusa: JAXA spacecraft that returned an asteroid sample to Earth—a first in history—in 2010.

HAPS or **high-altitude pseudo-satellites:** uncrewed aerial platforms—balloons, airships, or planes—stationed in the stratosphere (an altitude of about 65,000 feet or 20 km), above commercial air traffic and below traditional satellites. HAPS are increasingly valuable for their ability to remain stationary for very long periods of time, which offers a middle ground between uncrewed aerial vehicles (UAV) and satellites in space; HAPS have the mobility and flexibility of UAVs

and the remote sensing and monitoring capabilities of a satellite. They are sometimes called high-altitude platform stations.

hybrid engines: a rocket engine that uses solid fuel as well as liquid or gas fuel in an effort to avoid the disadvantages of using one sole fuel type, notably reducing dangers associated with solid rocket engine failures and mechanical complexities associated with liquid fuel rockets. Hybrid engines are far safer than liquid or solid engines, and recent improvements in additive manufacturing technology have made creating helical engine structures that are ideal for hybrid fuels possible. Hybrid engines are still uncommon and lack the research and development of solid or liquid engines.

hyperlocal weather monitoring: the use of various sensors—from satellites, weather stations, and electronic sources close to the ground (e.g., cameras, airplanes, smartphones)—to provide near-real-time weather conditions (e.g., temperature, wind speed, precipitation, humidity, atmospheric pressure) in a specific location. Hyperlocal weather monitoring thus provides extremely accurate and timely information that is not only convenient for daily weather checks but for industries that rely heavily on weather conditions for their operations (e.g., airspace, agriculture). Hyperlocal weather services also tend to leverage machine learning and/or the internet of things with historical weather data and real-time data to make more accurate predictions.

hyperspectral imaging: an advanced form of imaging technology that uses sensors to capture and analyze a very wide spectrum of light; while spectral imaging can process a few wavelength bands of light, hyperspectral imaging uses spectroscopy (the study of objects based on the colors they emit, absorb, or reflect) and can capture and process tens or hundreds of bands for each pixel of the captured image. Hyperspectral imaging therefore offers extremely detailed data about the images it analyzes and is able to detect minute changes in one location, which is valuable for many industries, particularly science, biology, surveillance, astronomy, and agriculture.

in-space manufacturing: the production of materials outside of Earth's atmosphere. While most in-space manufacturing today is limited to the additive manufacturing of tools and other needed objects on the International Space Station, NASA is working to create a sustainable in-space manufacturing capability for long-term missions, which would help provide maintenance, recycling, repair, and fabrication for spacecraft, control systems, and even in-space habitats. With proper robotics, manufacturing and assembly in space could serve as a better alternative to building on Earth and carrying finished structures to space, especially because building in the microgravity environment is much easier than on Earth—and doing so in space allows means structures can be built vastly larger than if made on Earth.

incubators: collaborative programs for nascent startups that focus primarily on developing new ideas that can be evolved into a minimum viable product and functional business. They tend to have flexible timelines and loose constraints, providing the startup or individual with ample room to experiment and grow. This is where a seedling idea is set with ideal conditions; from there, the incubator helps spur growth.

They can be run by separate organizations, government groups, investment groups, or corporations.

Indian Space Research Organization or **ISRO:** the Government of India's space agency, created in 1969. ISRO has gained notable traction in recent decades, in particular with its Polar Satellite Launch Vehicle (PSLV) serving as a low-cost launch option for satellites around the world.

infotainment: a form of "soft news," or a combination of information and entertainment, typically with information embedded in entertaining media.

infrastructure: the basic and fundamental structures, physical and organizational, that allow a system, business, or industry to operate.

Integrated Space Plan or **ISP:** a visual representation of the space ecosystem and the first to illustrate how the various elements of space infrastructure fit together, published by space conglomerate Rockwell International in 1989. The ISP mapped the Western world's space programs, activities, and development opportunities over the next century; it is designed by chronological milestones and necessary developments, with overarching goals designated throughout the future timeline.

Intelsat: a communications satellite service provider founded in 1964 that was responsible for launching the world's first commercial satellite; originally created as an intergovernmental consortium called International Telecommunications Satellite Organization (ITSO, or INTELSAT) headquartered in and predominantly run by the United States, INTELSAT was one of the largest commercial satellite providers and the first globalized network of broadband services. In 2001, not long after the international communications satellite industry was opened to the commercial sector, Intelsat went private in Luxembourg.

The International Charter: Space and Major Disasters: an international effort focused on providing free satellite data and services to relief organizations in the event of a major disaster. It was started by the European Space Agency (ESA) and France's government space agency, the National Centre for Space Studies (CNES), and became an official operation in 2001. The charter is non-binding and currently has seventeen signatories, including the United States National Oceanic and Atmospheric Administration (NOAA) and the government space agencies of Russia, Japan, Germany, India, China, and South Korea; as of 2019, it has had nearly 600 activations to aid disasters around the world ranging from earthquakes to tsunamis to the 2014 Ebola outbreak.

International Space Station or **ISS:** a modular space station that has been in service since it was launched into low Earth orbit in 2001. A multi-national and inter-governmental collaborative project between five space agencies—NASA (United States), JAXA (Japan), ESA (Europe), ROSCOSMOS (Russia), and CSA (Canada)—the ISS houses permanent crews for missions up to six months long; crews are between two six members, though the station has the capacity for a seven-person crew. The ISS serves primarily as a research laboratory for various forms of scientific testing using the unique microgravity environment for breakthrough discoveries not possible on Earth. The work done on the ISS is all for the benefit of humanity, from advances in biology, technology, medicine, pharmaceuticals, astronomy, physics, and more. The space station is also used for observation, exploration, education, and testing of new manufacturing techniques in space; in addition, the ISS works with the commercial sector in a variety of ways, and as the station nears retirement (the last operations are contracted to end in 2030), it is possible that the ISS will convert into a commercial station. The ISS is considered the most expensive single item ever made, costing upwards of $150 billion (inflation unadjusted) by 2010.

International Traffic in Arms Regulations or **ITAR:** a US regulatory regime created in 1976 during the Cold War to restrict the transfer of any US defense or military technology—physical items or technical data—to other countries or non-US persons. ITAR was implemented as a national security measure to control, in particular, arms exports; key materials regulated under ITAR include firearms and weapons, military vehicles, ammunition, defense software, and launch vehicles. Beginning in 1999, satellites became a prime material restricted by ITAR, which has led to increased difficulty for the commercial satellite industry. In addition, ITAR has faced scrutiny for restricting top international students from working on scientific projects in and for the United States.

IP or **intellectual property licensing:** a contract or agreement between an IP owner and a third-party lessee that allows the lessee to purchase rights to the IP (often within some kind of limitation, whether for a certain amount of time or for a specific use). Via licensing, the owner continues to retain their rights to the IP, and the lessee gains access to valuable information without paying to own the IP (or spend the time and money to develop their own IP). Most IP licensing comes from universities or research institutions, commercial businesses, or individual inventors.

IPO or **initial public offering:** the process in which a private company becomes a public company and is the first time shares of the company are available as stock to be publicly traded. An IPO is an important event for a company that allows new investments to come in via purchased stock, and allows the founders, investors, and other pre-IPO shareholders to generate financial liquidity.

JAXA: the Japan Aerospace Exploration Agency is Japan's national government space agency. In 2003, three space-focused organizations merged to create JAXA—the Institute of Space and Astronautical Science (ISAS), the National Aerospace Laboratory of Japan (NAL), and the National Space Development Agency (NASDA)—making the agency responsible for research, technology development, satellite launch, and other space missions (such as asteroid and Moon explorations).

K band: The segment of the radio spectrum with a frequency range of 18 to 27 GHz (gigahertz) and a wavelength range of 1.67 to 1.11 cm. The K band is divided into three sub-bands. The higher frequencies in the K band are used for radar and experimental communications (first used by NASA's Kepler spacecraft); the lowest frequencies are commonly used for satellite communications, satellite television, and radar (especially speed detectors used by

police). A small portion of the K band is available for amateur radio and amateur satellite operators to use.

Kaggle competition: Kaggle, a subsidiary of Google created in 2010, is an online data science community that began with a machine learning competition and now has over one million users. Any member can start ("host") a new competition, which is posted for other community members to participate in. NewSpace company Planet notably hosted a Kaggle competition in 2017 to create accurate satellite dataset labeling of the Amazon basin.

Kardashev Scale: In 1964, Soviet astronomer Nikolai Kardashev created a theoretical scale that he suggested could be used to measure a civilization's progress based on its technological advancement and ability to harness energy. The Type 1 (planetary) civilization can harness all available energy that its home planet receives from its parent star. The Type 2 (stellar) civilization can harness all of the energy of its home planet's parent star; a Dyson sphere is a model of such energy harnessing. The Type 3 (galactic) civilization is able to harness all of the energy within its home galaxy. Our human civilization harnesses five magnitudes less power than Earth receives from the Sun, rendering humanity a Type 0 civilization.

Kármán line: the threshold that separates Earth's atmosphere with low Earth orbit (i.e., where "outer space" begins), which occurs at an altitude of 100 kilometers (62 miles) above mean sea level, according to the Fédération Aéronautique Internationale (FAI). The line is named after Hungarian American astronomer Theodore von Kármán (1881–1963), who first calculated the point at which Earth's atmosphere becomes too thin to support aeronautical flight (which is actually 51.9 miles above sea level). Along with its physical applications, the Kármán line is used for legal and regulatory purposes to delineate between aircraft and spacecraft. In 2005, NASA and the US Air Force changed their definition of the edge of space to 50 miles above sea level, or 12 miles below the Kármán line.

Kepler-452b: a potential planet in the Cygnus constellation that was detected by the Kepler space telescope in 2015. Kepler-452b is notable because, despite its 1,400 light-year distance from our solar system, it is located at approximately the same distance from its parent star as Earth is from the Sun, and is therefore considered in a "habitable zone," resulting in its nickname, "Earth 2.0."

Kibō: the nickname for the Japanese Experiment Module (JEM) on the International Space Station. It is the largest module on the ISS, JAXA's first contribution to the space station, and has been in operation since its assembly completed in 2009. Kibō is home to many scientific experiments, ranging from medicine, biology, Earth observation, astronomy, and biotechnology; it enables testing of manufacturing, communications, and engineering in space; and it allows the inclusion of commercial and educational opportunities.

KSC or **John F. Kennedy Space Center:** one of ten NASA field centers and the primary site for NASA's human spaceflight launches. Located in Merritt Island, on the eastern coast of Florida, KSC is situated near the Cape Canaveral US Air Force Station; the two sites collaborate in various capacities and comprise what is known as Florida's

"Space Coast." KSC was created in 1962 during JFK's presidency and was originally named the NASA Launch Operations Center; President Lyndon B. Johnson gave the facility its current name on November 29, 1963, one week after JFK's assassination. Launches from KSC include the historical Apollo and Space Shuttle programs, and current International Space Station payloads and Commercial Crew Program.

L band: the segment of the radio spectrum with a frequency range of 1 to 2 GHz (gigahertz) and a wavelength range of 30 to 15 cm. The L band is used extensively: by the military for telemetry; for various mobile and telecommunication services; for GPS and other satellite navigation services, because L band waves can penetrate vegetation, clouds, and other weather; and for aircraft surveillance. The L band also contains what is known as the "hydrogen line," a frequency that allows imaging of hydrogen in space and is therefore valuable for astronomy.

Lagrange point: locations in space often described as "parking spots" as they exist in a gravitational equilibrium between the Sun and Earth, which allows objects to remain almost completely still. In Lagrange points, spacecraft require minimal fuel to maintain their position; data communications speeds remain high because the spacecraft never moves too far away from Earth; and the physical locations are shielded from the Sun, so spacecraft don't experience light and heat interference, nor do they need help staying cool. These unique points are therefore ideal locations for space stations, asteroid-hunting, spacecraft, and astronomy alike. The planned James Webb Space

Telescope will station in the Lagrange point known as L2.

LATCOSMOS: a four-year, education-based space development plan for the Latin America and the Caribbean regions that began in 2017 in an effort to encourage these regions to become involved in space activities.

Launch Services Agreement or **LSA:** a contract between a Purchaser (e.g., the US Air Force) and a Launch Agency (e.g., SpaceX) to provide specific launch services. Government LSAs have been crucial in NewSpace for providing various commercial companies with significant funding to develop new launch capabilities.[†]

launch vehicle or **carrier rocket:** a rocket with the capability to carry a payload from Earth to space. A payload could be human crew, satellites, scientific materials, cargo, robotic systems—basically, anything that can be carried. NASA classifies launch vehicles based on payload weight capacity as either small-lift, medium-life, heavy-lift, or super-heavy-lift.

LEO: low Earth orbit is the geographic area of space between the altitudes of 180 km and 2,000 km above mean sea level on Earth. LEO is where most of humanity's space activities have taken place and is currently considered the most economically viable area of space: LEO accounts for many communications, remote sensing, and Earth-imaging satellites; it has housed all space stations to date and is where the ISS resides; and all crewed flights to space have occurred in LEO (apart from the Apollo program from 1968–1972).

licensing: the legal permission granted from one party to another to do, use, or own something. While licensing can refer to anything, such as the use of intellectual property or the right to fly a plane, current space sector regulations require cumbersome and redundant licenses from various government agencies. Each of the following require its own license: launch; re-entry; Earth observation and remote sensing; satellite communications; payloads; safety; spectrum; operating launch; human spaceflight.

Long March: the primary family of rockets operated by the China National Space Administration (CNSA). Long March rockets are an expendable launch system and have had over 300 launches to date. Long March 1, the first model of the rocket family, launched China's first satellite in 1970, making China the fifth nation to achieve successful launch.

Lunar Library: a thirty-million-page archive of human history created by the Arch Mission Foundation and carried as a payload on SpaceIL's Beresheet lunar lander in 2019. The Beresheet crash-landed on the Moon, so the Lunar Library may have shattered—however, its data can still be read and extracted even if it is in pieces. The Lunar Library is the third installation of the Arch Library; its data will survive for billions of years.

lunarians: advocates for lunar activity. In science fiction, a lunar inhabitant.

[†] Not to be confused with the Luxembourg Space Agency.

Luxembourg Space Agency or **LSA:** the official national space agency of Luxembourg. Created in 2018 by then-deputy prime minister and minister of the economy Étienne Schneider, LSA[†] was formed to expand Luxembourg's commercial space endeavors and the role of Luxembourg in the global space economy. LSA is notably different from most other national space agencies in its focus on the commercial sector, space resources, domestic education about space, establishing effective international space regulations, and providing funding and support for space startups. LSA is led by Marc Serres, former head of space affairs at the Luxembourg Ministry of the Economy.

M&A: mergers and acquisitions are the consolidation of companies or company assets through a financial agreement, whether by one company buying and absorbing another; one company buying a majority stake in another company and thereby becoming the latter's parent company; two companies joining together to create one new entity; one company purchasing the assets of another company (typically during the latter's bankruptcy); or a company's executives purchasing a controlling stake in their company's assets and operations, making the company private.

machine learning or **ML**: a subset or application of artificial intelligence where computer systems are programmed to "learn" improved behaviors by adjusting their functions based on patterns recognition. Over time, as the system continues to classify patterns, its algorithms will improve automatically (e.g., email filtering, image recognition, music software that creates new playlists based on the music you've listened to).

M2M or **machine to machine:** the direct communication between devices using embedded hardware that allows two machines to interact with each other (e.g., an ATM receiving authorization from a bank to dispense funds, or a home alarm system that notifies a security company if the correct code is not input).

makerspace: a shared, collaborative, community workspace that typically focuses on a common interest (e.g., space, computers, robotics), and in which the members share resources, ideas, materials, skills, and often work together. As a movement, makerspaces encourage hands-on creativity, education, and access for community members.

member states: a country or state that is a member of an international organization, federation, or confederation. Member states share in the privileges (e.g., funding, voting, access to facilities and resources) and obligations (e.g., contributing finances and resources, participation, adhering to laws and treaties) set by the organization. The United Nations, for instance, has 193 member states and 2 observer states; the observer states can participate in the UN with limitations.

MEO or **medium Earth orbit:** the orbit that occurs at an altitude between 2,000 km (1,243 mi) and 35,786 km (22,236 mi) above mean sea level on Earth. MEO hosts communications satellite constellations as well as the Global Navigation Satellite Systems (GNSS), which provides global

---

[†] Not to be confused with Launch Services Agreement.

positioning and navigation capabilities such as GPS. MEO occurs between low Earth orbit and geosynchronous orbit.

microsatellite or **microsat:** a small satellite with a mass between 10 and 100 kilograms.

microgravity: the near-absence (i.e., extremely low amount) of gravity, as experienced in the space environment. Microgravity renders objects and people "weightless," meaning objects that are extremely heavy on Earth can be moved with ease. The microgravity environment of space is used for research and experiments, and is particularly valuable for medicine, biology, biotechnology, and physics because scientists can more accurately understand the true behavior of molecular structures. Microgravity experiments have yielded incredible advances in medicine, technology, and science throughout the International Space Station's lifespan.

minimum viable product or **MVP:** an early version of a product that contains enough features to satisfy early adopters (i.e., early customers who use a new product or technology before the mass market) and/or attract investment. The MVP is also a way to gather feedback from early adopters in order to continue developing or making changes to the product and its features before releasing the finished product.

Mir: a space station that operated in low Earth orbit from 1986 until 2001. Mir was operated by the Soviet Union until 1986 and then by Russia until its deorbit. It was used as a microgravity research laboratory and to test space technologies. Mir housed crews between three and six astronauts for missions lasting up to six months (shorter missions for larger crews) between 1986 and 1999, and after the end of the Cold War, Mir was accessible to visits by other countries. In 1999, when Russia could no longer afford to fund the space station, commercial space company MirCorp leased Mir, using it as a commercial platform from 2000 to 2001. MirCorp notably arranged for Dennis Tito's visit to Mir, making him the first "space tourist." Despite interest to make Mir into a permanent commercial space station, pressure for Russia to commit to the ISS led to Mir being deorbited in 2001.

module: an independent or detachable unit that is part of a whole, typically a physical structure.

monolith: from the Greek *monolithos* ("single stone"), a massive, singular structure (such as the mysterious Monoliths of Arthur C. Clarke's *Space Odyssey* book series and Stanley Kubrick's seminal sci-fi film adaptation, *2001: A Space Odyssey*). Societally and culturally, "monolithic" indicates a large, centralized and homogenous power—typically one that is rigid and unchanging. In business, "monolithic" can be understood similarly, pointing to an industry that revolves around a singular concept or activity. As such, neither the space sector nor NASA can be considered monoliths, as the industry is both broad and interdisciplinary.

Moore's Law: a golden rule, rather than a natural or physical law, based on Intel co-founder Gordon E. Moore's observation that the number of transistors on a microchip doubled each year while the price dropped by half. Moore's Law is the foundation of exponential technological growth, specifically that the speed and capabilities of a computer will double every two years while the cost reduces by half.

multispectral imaging: images produced by sensors that can measure specific wavelength bands within the electromagnetic spectrum. While regular cameras are only able to capture three wavelength bands (red, green, and blue), multispectral images can capture between three and fifteen bands, both within the visible light range and invisible light spectrums; the latter includes ultraviolet, infrared, and x-ray. Because of this ability to capture a significant amount more data than a typical camera, multispectral imaging was first developed for military uses; it is now commonly used for tracking, mapping, weather forecasting, and detecting weapons like ballistic missiles or landmines in the imaged area.

nanotechnology or **nanotech:** engineering of products or systems on the nanometer scale (one nanometer equals one billionth of a meter). Nanotech encompasses various other fields that are based on seeing and controlling matter on a molecular or atomic level.

National Plan for the Promotion of Space Investment: United Arab Emirates' (UAE) space investment plan, announced in early 2019, which will aim to advance the UAE's space capabilities with foreign and domestic investments.

National Reconnaissance Office or **NRO:** one of the "big five" US intelligence agencies, the NRO is part of the US Intelligence Community and an agency within the Department of Defense that is responsible for the federal government's reconnaissance satellites, from design to launch, and provides satellite intelligence

to various US government agencies. The NRO workforce is a mixture of personnel from the US armed services, the CIA, and private contractors (the latter makes up the majority of the NRO's workers).

NEO or **near-Earth object:** asteroids, comets, and meteoroids that orbit the Sun and whose orbits either come close to or intersect Earth's orbit. Most NEOs are asteroids, and nearly 23,000 are currently tracked by NASA (as of June 1, 2020). NEOs are closely tracked and monitored in order to minimize the possibility of one impacting Earth; they are also considered key targets for space resource mining.

NewSpace or **new space:** the movement and philosophy that emphasizes developing improved, more frequent, and lower-cost access to space, mainly via private sector innovations and efforts. Compared to traditional space programs, NewSpace focuses on space's many applications and opportunities as a means to improve life on Earth (rather than as a tool to establish power or simply generate revenue). The NewSpace movement has existed since as early as the 1980s, but didn't gain widespread momentum until the early 2000s when breakthroughs in technology coupled with strong private sector plans began to lower the barriers to space. Now, entrepreneurial and commercial activity in and around space is the driving force of the whole space sector, from developing launch vehicles and satellites to innovations in Smart Data, robotics, and microgravity.

NextSTEP-2: Next Space Technologies for Exploration Partnerships (NextSTEP) is a NASA partnership model between the private and public sectors, focused on commercial development opportunities that help NASA achieve its myriad goals in space. NextSTEP solicited proposals from commercial space companies, and the twelve selected companies were awarded NASA task orders. The first phase of NextSTEP-2 focused on developing deep space habitat prototypes and awarded task orders to six commercial companies; one of those companies, Axiom Space, was selected in January 2020 to develop a commercial module that will be attached to the ISS.

NIAC: NASA Innovative Advanced Concepts is a program that provides funding to innovative aerospace projects that NASA believes could lead to breakthroughs in aerospace. NIAC selects new recipients every year and is open to the commercial industry, academia, and government.

NOAA or **National Oceanic and Atmospheric Administration:** a United States scientific agency, housed within the Department of Commerce, that monitors the climate, environment, weather, and oceans. The NOAA was created in 1970 as a merger of three existing agencies—the US Coast and Geodetic Survey, the Weather Bureau, and the US Commission of Fish and Fisheries—and is responsible for weather forecasting, predicting climate and weather changes and patterns, preserving and protecting the oceans and coasts, and warning of dangerous weather. As part of the NOAA's duties to improve its capabilities, the agency partners with private sector companies, offers tech transfers and licensing, and provides funding via its Small Business Innovation Research (SBIR) program. The NOAA successfully partnered with NewSpace companies Spire Global and GeoOptics to purchase improved, low-cost

data for GPS radio occultation, and will continue to collaborate with commercial companies for weather modeling and forecasting capabilities.

Node 2 or **Harmony:** a module on the International Space Station known as the "utility hub" as it provides electrical power, electronic data, and connects the laboratory modules of the United States (Destiny node), Japan (Kibō node), and ESA (Columbia node). Harmony was added to the ISS in 2007, is part of the United States Orbital Segment of the space station, and is managed by NASA.

occultation: when an object disappears from view as a result of another object passing in front of it. During a lunar occultation, the Moon passes in front of a star, temporarily hiding the star from view.

open source: products that include permission to be freely used. The idea of open source began in the software realm as a movement to increase open collaboration as a means of improving software development.

optical remote sensing: remote sensing capabilities that image visible, near infrared, and short-wave infrared wavelengths. Spectral, multispectral, and hyperspectral imaging are all forms of optical remote sensing. This form of remote sensing is particularly valuable in the agriculture industry for its ability to monitor crop and vegetation conditions. As optical remote sensing depends on solar radiation reflected in the captured wavelengths, it is not effective in cloudy areas (radar sensors, on the other hand, capture the microwave portion of the electromagnetic spectrum, which is not affected by cloud coverage).

orbit: the regular, repeating path of one celestial body around another celestial body. All orbits are elliptical and are caused by the gravitational pull between the two celestial bodies.

Orbital Library or **LEO Library:** Arch Mission Foundation's second Billion Year Archive initiative. In 2018, SpaceChain launched a CubeSat into low Earth orbit that contains an encrypted, English copy of Wikipedia created by Arch Mission, which is designed to survive for billions of years.

orbital spacecraft: a vehicle or object designed to operate in an Earth orbit—either low Earth orbit, medium Earth orbit, or geosynchronous orbit. Orbital spacecraft vehicles typically remain in low Earth orbit (LEO), but satellites can station in LEO, medium Earth orbit, or geosynchronous orbit. Orbital spacecraft are valuable for communications, Earth observation, space exploration, scientific research, and transportation of humans and cargo.

OSTP: the White House Office of Science and Technology Policy is a government branch within the Executive Office of the President, established in 1976. OSTP is responsible for advising the Executive Office on science and technology's domestic and international impacts on the economy, national security, health, and the environment, among other topics. OSTP also advises the President on the aforementioned topics in respect to government policy, plans, programs, and budgets.

Overview Effect: a term coined in 1987 by Frank White to describe the phenomenon experienced by humans who see Earth from space, in which the viewer is overcome by feelings of universal connectedness and empathy. This shift in awareness leads many astronauts to feel that humanity coming together as a collective to protect and preserve our fragile planet is of the utmost importance.

payload: the carrying capacity of a launch vehicle (or aircraft), often measured by the weight the vehicle can transport into space. Payloads are typically cargo, human crew, satellites, or scientific equipment.

picosatellite or **picosat:** one of the smallest categories of artificial satellites. Picosats have a mass between 0.1 kg and 1 kg.

pivot: when a company (often a startup) makes a significant change to their business strategy or product in response to market needs, changes in industry, customer feedback, or new opportunities.

Polar Satellite Launch Vehicle or **PSLV:** India's expendable, medium-lift launch vehicle, designed and operated by the Indian Space Research Organization (ISRO). Development of the PSLV began in 1978, though the rocket didn't begin flying until 1993. Along with India's payloads, the PSLV has become a viable and inexpensive rideshare option for other space agencies and commercial companies in recent years, having launched over 300 satellites from more than thirty countries. As a low-cost launch option, the PSLV provided commercial companies with crucial and unprecedented access to space.

precision agriculture: a farming strategy that uses technology like satellites, sensors, the Internet of Things, and Big Data to improve efficiency in crop management. Precision agriculture closely monitors various aspects of the crop, such as soil moisture, temperature, and growth patterns, to make informed decisions that pinpoint exactly what the crops need to thrive—including when and how much to water, fertilize, and implement pest management; when and where to plant seeds; and when to harvest the crops. Precision agriculture leverages the technological advances at our disposal to save resources while improving crop health and maximizing crop growth.

quadrillion: one thousand raised to the power of five (10^{15}), or one thousand trillion: 1,000,000,000,000,000.

quantum computing: while conventional computers operate in a binary (i.e., a two-state system, normally 1s and 0s), a quantum computer operates in a three-state system that allows it to solve multi-deterministic problems much faster than a conventional computer.

radar satellites: artificial satellites with radar systems, typically Earth observation radar systems. Space-based radar can be used to image, map, track, and measure various phenomena on Earth or in space.

radio occultation: the change in radio signal that occurs when it crosses Earth's atmosphere, which causes the radio waves to refract; the refraction depends on the atmosphere's temperature, pressure, and water vapor content—meaning the refraction can be used to forecast weather and, over time, monitor climate change.

radio spectrum: the segment of the electromagnetic spectrum from 30 HZ to 300 GHz that is used predominantly for telecommunications. To prevent interference between different transmissions sent by various users, and because the

spectrum is a fixed resource, radio spectrum is heavily regulated. The International Telecommunication Union (ITU) determines how to allocate the spectrum, which private operators can buy or license.

rare Earth element or **REE:** seventeen chemical elements found in Earth's crust that are used for many modern technologies. Neodymium and praseodymium are two REEs necessary for the magnets used in energy-efficient innovations like wind turbines. While REEs are relatively abundant, they are rarely found in concentrated amounts and are difficult to mine.

remote sensing: use of satellite or aircraft to gather information (from a distance) about a target area of Earth's surface. Remote sensing relies on imaging capabilities that can capture portions of the entire electromagnetic spectrum. Remote sensing data is helpful for weather and environmental monitoring, agriculture, tracking, and mapping, among many other applications.

replicator: a fictional machine from television sci-fi series *Star Trek* that can create (and recycle) food and objects on demand. Replicators have inspired various technological advances that seek to create a real-life food printer.

reusability: the ability of a spacecraft, launch system, or certain components of a launch system to be used more than once. Reusability in the space sector is rare, as development of reusable systems is both complex and expensive, but increasing because of its ability to lower launch costs and preserve resources. Most launch systems, by contrast, have been expendable—meaning they can only fly once and either burn up during deorbit or are deorbited in such a way that the remaining material can be discarded.

reusable launch vehicle or **RLV:** spacecraft that can be used more than once; meaning a RLV can launch, reach orbit, deorbit, and re-enter Earth's atmosphere where it can complete a controlled landing and be recovered. Successful reusable launch vehicles include the NASA Space Shuttle, SpaceX's Dragon spacecraft, and Boeing's CST-100 Starliner crew capsule spacecraft.

rideshare: use of extra space on a rocket to carry third-party payloads. Various companies act as rideshare intermediaries, coordinating that extra cargo space as a low-cost, faster alternative for companies to get their payloads into space. Rideshare companies include Nanoracks, Rocket Lab, and Spaceflight Industries.

robotics: technology that combines computer science and engineering with an aim of creating "intelligent" machines for specific purposes. Robotics are valuable for the space industry as they can withstand the harsh space environment and perform tasks like maintenance and repairs of existing orbital spacecraft, in-space construction, surface exploration (e.g., the Mars rover), and more. Robotics are key technologies to enable safe, effective, and efficient in-space work, research, and living.

ROIII or **Return on Investment, Innovation, and Inspiration:** the three-fold measure of benefits derived from investing in the space sector: cost-savings and exponential financial returns, technological and scientific advances and breakthroughs, and motivating citizens to help improve life on Earth.

Roscosmos: the Roscosmos State Corporation for Space Activities is Russia's national space agency, formed in 1992 after the collapse of the Soviet Union, at which point Russia inherited the Soviet space program. Roscosmos collaborates with other international space programs, particularly with its partnership on the International Space Station.

S band: the segment of the radio spectrum with a frequency range of 2 to 4 GHz (gigahertz) and a wavelength range of 15 to 7.5 cm. The S band is particularly valuable for airport surveillance radar used for air traffic control, weather radar, and certain communications satellites (such as those that NASA uses to communicate with the Space Shuttle and the ISS). It is also used for satellite radio and television, WiFi, and wireless devices such as Bluetooth and garage door openers.

satellite: a celestial object in orbit, whether natural (e.g., the Moon, a planet) or human-made (e.g., Sputnik 1 or the Hubble Space Telescope). Human-made satellites are those that are intentionally placed in a specific orbit (e.g., low Earth orbit, geosynchronous orbit) for a specific purpose, such as communications, global positioning and navigation, or Earth observation.

Series A, B, C funding: the first rounds of private investment. Series A occurs after seed funding, once the business has established a performance indicator (customer base, consistent revenue) and is considered a viable investment. Typical Series A rounds pull in between $2 million and $15 million in funding, which goes into optimizing the business. Series B averages between $30 million and $60 million, which is used to fully develop the business and begin growing the enterprise. Series C rounds occur when a business has proven significant success and is ready to scale and expand (e.g., enter new markets, create new products, acquire another company); typical Series C rounds result in hundreds of millions of dollars in investments, and typically set up the company for an initial public offering.

service module or **Zvezda:** an ISS module that most notably consists of the life support systems that allow the ISS crew to survive in space. Zvezda is in the Russian Orbital Segment of the ISS (built and operated by Roscosmos) and is the third module added to the ISS (docked in 2000). Zvezda's layout design is based on Mir's core module.

Shackleton crater: an area in the Moon's south pole that is predicted to be rich with ice (and possibly mineral compounds), making it a desirable location for lunar exploration and mining. Shackleton is uniquely positioned in constant sunlight, making it ideal to generate power with solar panels and for robots to operate properly.

small satellite or **smallsat:** a satellite with a low mass and size, typically under 500 kilograms. Subclasses of smallsats include minisatellites, microsatellites, nanosatellites, and picosatellites (from smallest to largest). Smallsats are far less expensive to manufacture compared to traditional satellites and can be grouped together to form a constellation that provides capabilities similar to a large satellite. While the world's first satellite, Sputnik 1, was a smallsat, the market has recently seen rapid growth, especially with new technological capabilities that can be added to smallsats (e.g., sensors). Smallsat innovations have made many NewSpace startups, like Planet and Spire Global, industry leaders.

smart contracts: self-executing contracts enabled by a decentralized blockchain network, which allows agreements to be made between two parties without external enforcements such as legal systems or financial authorities, and enforces the terms of the contracts with more security than a traditional contract such that funds are only ever dispersed as prescribed.

Smart Data: data that uses algorithms to organize itself, filtering out the "noise" in order to provide actionable information and optimize future analyses (i.e., by presenting the data with valuable insights).

solar arrays: multiple solar panels collecting energy as a single system.

solar flare: sudden explosion of energy on the Sun's surface due to the interaction of magnetic field lines near sunspots.

solar sails: large, reflective sheets used for spacecraft propulsion. Photons from the sun bounce off of the sheet and transfer their momentum, causing a small push in the opposite direction.

Soviet space program: the Space program of the Union of Soviet Socialist Republics was the national space program of the Soviet Union from the 1930s until the USSR's collapse in 1991. Known for its achievements and secrecy, the Soviet space program was the main competition of the United States during the Space Race and successfully beat the US to many firsts, including launching the first artificial satellite into space (Sputnik 1, 1957) and putting the first human into space (Yuri Gagarin, 1961), and the first space station

(Salyut 1, 1971). After the US put humans on the Moon in 1969, the race died down; the two space powers entered into a cooperative agreement in 1975 in which a crewed US Apollo capsule docked with a crewed Soviet Soyuz capsule in space. After the USSR disbanded in 1991, the Soviet space program transitioned into the new Russian Federation's Roscosmos space program.

space debris or **orbital debris:** spacecraft or artificial parts that are no longer controlled from Earth but remain in orbit. Space debris poses a threat to spacecraft in service, as collisions can damage or destroy functioning systems. The higher the orbit, the longer the debris will last; while debris in LEO will deteriorate in a matter of years, debris in geostationary orbit will survive for millions of years. There are currently 23,000 pieces of large orbital debris (larger than 10 cm), 500,000 pieces of debris between 1 cm and 10 cm, and an estimated 100 million + pieces of debris smaller than 1 cm; as pieces of debris collide with one another, they break into smaller pieces of debris. Space debris is considered a serious threat on the horizon, especially with the increase of satellite constellations being launched.

space debris mitigation: techniques to limit and prevent the creation of orbital debris, including maneuvering techniques, designing satellites to endure being impacted by small debris, better end-of-life satellite disposals (into "graveyard orbit," 300 km above geostationary orbit), and depleting energy reserves when a satellite is decommissioned to prevent in-orbit explosions. NASA, ESA, and nine other space agencies around the world formed the Inter-agency Space Debris Coordination Committee

(IADC) to create global standards that will help curtail future debris.

space exploration: the use of various technologies and science to explore off-Earth, whether remotely by telescopes and cameras, or physically by robotic probes or astronauts. The physical exploration of space began during the Space Race in the late 1950s, though astronomical observations date back to the earliest human civilizations.

US Space Force or **USSF:** the US military's sixth branch, established in 2019 and part of the US Air Force. The USSF was created to operate in a military defense capacity.

Space Resources Initiative: a Luxembourg Space Agency initiative launched in 2016 to finance commercial companies focused on space resource mining. LSA initially invested in two resource mining companies, Deep Space Industries and Planetary Resources, but both were later acquired; however, LSA has not been deterred by the high-risk venture and is continuing to fund private companies, which has resulted in over fifty companies to open offices in Luxembourg.

space resource mining: the practice of extracting valuable elements from celestial bodies that are classified as near-Earth objects (NEOs), such as asteroids; there are an expected 100,000 NEOs and they can contain resources including iron, platinum, water, and rare earth elements.

Space Shuttle program: NASA human spaceflight program that followed the Apollo program. Started by President Nixon in 1972, the Space Shuttle program was the first reusable rocket and originally meant to fly fifty times per year in order to serve various national interests. Throughout its lifetime until 2011, the program was both slow and expensive, flying only 135 times, and faced criticism for its minimal scientific and exploration achievements. The Space Shuttle ultimately represented a large step backward from the Apollo program, and the 1986 Challenger shuttle explosion and 2003 Columbia disaster led to even more roadblocks for NASA.

space tourism: human space travel for recreational purposes. Because of the extremely high costs of going to space, only a handful of space tourism experiences have occurred, but Virgin Galactic and other commercial companies have been focused on establishing a full-blown space tourism industry.

space weather: various conditions within the solar system (including the areas outside of Earth's atmosphere, such as the magnetosphere), such as solar wind and geomagnetic storms, which can adversely affect spacecraft electronics and orbits, signals between spacecraft and ground systems, human safety in space, and even human safety in commercial aviation—mainly as a result of increased radiation and high energy charged particles caused by space weather and the phenomena that ensue.

spacecraft: vehicles or machines that are launched into outer space and designed specifically to operate in the space environment. Artificial satellites, space stations, spaceplanes, space capsules, rovers, and space probes are all forms of spacecraft. Spacecraft are often further classified as being crewed or uncrewed.

SpaceIL: an Israeli nonprofit space organization originally created to participate in the

Google Lunar XPRIZE (GLXP). Since GLXP, SpaceIL has been the first private company to attempt a lunar landing, with its Beresheet spacecraft undergoing a crash-landing on the Moon in 2019. In addition to its lunar aspirations, SpaceIL is dedicated to bringing more of Israel's population into the space and STEM industries.

spaceports: also known as a "cosmodrome," spaceports are sites for spacecraft launch and, occasionally, landings. Kennedy Space Center is an example of a spaceport.

SpaceShipOne: the spacecraft created for the 2006 XPRIZE competition by legendary pilot and aircraft designer Burt Rutan (and financially backed by Paul Allen). SpaceShipOne won the XPRIZE and became a signal that commercial efforts could truly be viable. Between the two flights required in the competition, Sir Richard Branson purchased a license to SpaceShipOne's technology and announced the creation of Virgin Galactic.

SpaceShipTwo: Virgin Galactic's first spacecraft, developed by Burt Rutan in partnership with Sir Richard Branson and based off of Rutan's SpaceShipOne spacecraft. SpaceShipTwo was created specifically for space tourism.

Spinoff: NASA's free publication, created in 1976 and published annually, that showcases the products and services that began with or leveraged NASA technology via the Tech Transfer Program. To date, there have been over 2,000 spinoffs that span industries including agriculture, medicine, public safety, and computer technology.

Sputnik 1: the first artificial satellite in history to be placed in orbit. The Soviet Union created Sputnik 1 and launched it on October 4, 1957, effectively spurring the start of the Space Race within the Cold War, as well as the "Sputnik crisis"—a period of public fear in the Western countries about the technological capabilities of the USSR.

Starlink: SpaceX's satellite constellation that is planned to provide global internet access to underserved areas of the world via thousands of small satellites stationed in low Earth orbit. SpaceX has been approved for 12,000 Starlink satellites, and has filed for another 30,000. The astronomical community has criticized the plan, saying that the volume and placement of the Starlink constellation will create light pollution and interfere with scientific observations; additional concerns focus on the long-term space debris that Starlink will cause and propagate.

STEM and **STEAM:** STEM is an academic curriculum focused on educating in the disciplines of science, technology, engineering, and math. While STEM studies focus on scientific concepts, "Arts" (which includes humanities, language, visual arts, media, music, and other art forms) has been added in recent years in an effort to integrate traditional STEM topics with the problem-solving techniques used in the creative process. STEAM studies are often taught in an interdisciplinary approach to teach students critical thinking and the ability to solve complex problems that can be applied in a variety of fields, lead to future innovations, and best sustain and grow the economy.

stratosphere: the second major layer of Earth's atmosphere and where the ozone layer resides. Because of the stratosphere's low temperatures, low air density, and general lack of weather, most commercial airplanes' cruise altitudes occur in the stratosphere. High-altitude pseudo-satellites are positioned in the stratosphere for similar reasons, where they can quickly travel for weather monitoring, communications, imaging, and tracking purposes, among other uses.

suborbital spaceflight: Flights that occur below the Kármán line, still within Earth's atmosphere. An object or spacecraft in suborbital flight is still impacted by enough of the planet's gravity that it will be pulled back down rather than engaging in orbit; many companies use suborbital flights for launch tests. Suborbital space is considered a growing and mostly untapped market; it is already used for scientific experiments, and the emerging commercial companies focused on space tourism will provide trips to space via suborbital flights.

suborbital vehicle: spacecraft designed specifically for suborbital flights. While most spacecraft's velocities determine whether they reach suborbital or orbital space, commercial companies have been developing low-cost—and in some cases, reusable—vehicles with capabilities that aren't meant to function as orbital vehicles. Suborbital vehicles will instead function for testing, scientific, and space tourism.

supersonic flight: airflight traveling at a velocity faster than the speed of sound, mostly used in military capacities.

surface rover: a robotic vehicle designed to explore surfaces of celestial bodies and collect images, samples of the terrain, and other data, depending on the mission objectives. Rovers can be remotely controlled or autonomous; the Mars Curiosity rover, for example, was too far for remote control, so it navigated mostly autonomously after receiving general directions from human-controlled communication systems. Surface rovers have been critical in space exploration and in understanding conditions of other planets and planetary bodies.

sustainable business model: business structures and values that include social benefits via, or in addition to, key services or products. Sustainable business models typically solve broader industry problems and generate significant social value that leads to growth that is not only economic in nature.

Syncom 3: the third satellite of NASA's Syncom ("synchronous communication satellite") program and the first geostationary communication satellite, launched on August 19, 1964.

synthetic-aperture radar or **SAR:** a type of data collection that is used mainly for remote sensing and Earth imaging by being mounted on a moving platform (such as a satellite or aircraft). SAR implements signal processing to create high-resolution 2D or 3D image renderings and is particularly valuable as it can actively image in a continuous manner, regardless of clouds (or other weather) or amount of light (i.e., it can image at night). SAR is used predominantly to monitor large areas over a short period of time; common uses include determining boundaries of an oil spill, locating mineral reserves, and locating ships.

task order: a type of government contract for services that is used when the definite quantity of needed services is not yet known. Instead, the task order is set against a general contract that gives an overview of the required services, and is later issued to provide the specific requirements (when determined and as needed), thereby allowing a great deal of flexibility for the government buyer. NASA uses task orders often, employing them when new needs or objectives arise (e.g., NASA might issue a task order to develop a new lunar lander; companies that have existing Commercial Lunar Payload Services contracts with NASA would be eligible to submit a proposal to bid on the task order).

Technology Transfer Program: NASA program that allows licensing of patented NASA technologies. Since its creation in 1964, the Tech Transfer Program has resulted in approximately 2,000 products or services across various industries, from medicine to transportation, and has yielded broad social and economic returns while promoting innovation.

Telstar 1: NASA communications satellite launched on July 10, 1962 that transmitted the first live transatlantic television broadcast (between the United States and Europe). It was only active for seven months before it stopped communicating (many believe as a result of the Starfish Prime nuclear testing) but remains in low Earth orbit to this day.

Terra Bella: a commercial remote sensing company founded in 2009 and known as SkyBox Imaging until Google purchased it in 2014. As one of the earliest acquisitions of significant value in NewSpace history, Skybox's sale marked an exit for investors that helped establish credibility for the commercial space industry. In 2017, Planet (also a remote sensing and Earth imaging NewSpace company) purchased Terra Bella from Google.

terraforming: the theoretical process of altering the conditions (e.g., atmosphere, temperature, ecology) of another celestial body in an effort to mimic Earth's environment so that it would be habitable by humans.

tricorder: a device featured in the sci-fi universe of *Star Trek* with three primary functions—sensing, computing, and recording—that is used for various types of data collection and analysis (for instance, by scanning a foreign lifeform and then providing details about it). The medical tricorder works similarly by scanning a patient and providing a diagnosis to the doctor. This fictional device has inspired many attempts to create a real-world version.

uncrewed aerial vehicle or **UAV:** an aircraft that flies without a pilot and is instead operated via ground control. UAVs are often used for military purposes, but in recent years have been employed for agricultural, scientific, and environmental applications. Drones and high-altitude pseudo-satellites are two types of UAVs.

US Space Surveillance Network: agency based at New Mexico State University that tracks space debris and predicts any possible collisions with spacecraft or the ISS.

venture capital: a form of private equity funding for startup and early-stage companies deemed to have established growth or growth potential.

vertical takeoff, vertical landing or **VTVL:** one form of takeoff and landing used for launch vehicles. Unlike vertical takeoff and landing (VTOL) vehicles such as helicopters, VTVL vehicles use retropropulsion to land; the technology required for VL is more complex, and the landing process itself is more involved than horizontal landing, which is used by most spacecraft. VTVL gained popularity when commercial space companies in the early 2000s began developing VTVL technologies and rockets; VTVL has been successfully achieved with SpaceX's Falcon 9 rocket.

verticals: a market whose goods or services cater to a specific industry or niche, compared to a horizontal market, which meets the needs of a broad range of markets and customers. Verticals are often newer fields that have high-potential companies and are likely to attract investors. While NewSpace generally overlaps with many other industries and can therefore work with a wide array of customers, industry verticals include spacecraft, launch vehicles, and asteroid mining.

visible light spectrum: the portion of the electromagnetic spectrum that the human eye is able to see (typically, wavelengths between 380 and 740 nanometers). Certain remote sensing instruments measure the visible light spectrum, but many others are able to measure portions of the electromagnetic spectrum that the human eye cannot process.

Voyager: the first aircraft to fly around the world without stopping or refueling. Known formally as the Rutan Model 76 Voyager, the plane was designed by famed aerospace engineer Burt Rutan, and piloted by Burt's brother Dick Rutan along with Jeana Yeager. The nine-day flight began on December 14, 1986 and completed on December 23, setting an endurance record.

WINFOCUS: the World Interactive Network Focused on Critical Ultrasound is a scientific network committed to using ultrasound as a point-of-care device in order to provide medical care to underserved regions of the world. WINFOCUS adopted practices developed for astronauts on the ISS to train over twenty thousand physicians and healthcare providers to perform rapid, complex procedures via remote guidance.

X band: the segment of the electromagnetic spectrum with a frequency range of 8 to 12 GHz (gigahertz) and a wavelength range of 3.75 to 2.5 cm. The X band is used primarily for radar, satellite communications, and wireless computer networks. The X band has civilian, military, and governmental uses that span weather monitoring, vehicle speed detection, maritime vessel and air traffic control, and defense tracking. Parts of the X band are reserved specifically for deep space communications (used most by the NASA Deep Space Network).

XPRIZE: a competition developed by the XPRIZE Foundation in 1996 in an effort to advance private spaceflight. The competition, which eventually took place in 2001, offered a $10 million prize for two successful uncrewed flights to the Kármán Line within a two-week span. Aerospace engineer Burt Rutan ultimately designed SpaceShipOne and won the competition, ushering in a new wave of hope and inspiration for the commercial space sector.

Yutu-2: a robotic lunar rover developed by the China's space agency, CNSA, that was deployed on the Moon's far side on January 3, 2019, via the Chang'e 4 mission to the Moon. Yutu-2 has primarily been exploring the Moon's geography and geology, and is still operational.

Zero gravity or **zero-g:** the term used to describe a sense of weightlessness, which occurs when the gravitational force around an object is neutralized. However, there is never truly "zero gravity" (as proven by Einstein's theory of general relativity, or by the existence of black holes in space) but rather very little gravity (i.e., "microgravity").

REFERENCES

Preface

1   Tran, Phi. "Cell Phone Inventor Martin Cooper Was Influenced by Star Trek." *Adweek,* April 3, 2013. https://www.adweek.com/digital/cell-phone-maker-martin-cooper-was-influenced-by-star-trek.

PART I

Chapter One

1   Adams, Josiah. *Memoir of the Life of John Quincy Adams.* Boston: Crosby, Nichols, Lee & Co., 1860.

2   Jeff Greason (Cofounder and CTO, Electric Sky; Cofounder, XCOR Aerospace), in discussion with the author, March 4, 2017.

Chapter Two

1   NASA. "Behind the Space Shuttle Mission Numbering System." NASA Feature. Last updated December 5, 2015. http://www.nasa.gov/feature/behind-the-space-shuttle-mission-numbering-system.

2   Callahan, Jason. "How Richard Nixon Changed NASA." *Planetary Society,* October 4, 2014. http://www.planetary.org/blogs/guest-blogs/jason-callahan/20141003-how-richard-nixon-changed-nasa.html.

3   Sharp, Tim. "Space Shuttle: The First Reusable Spacecraft." *Space,* December 11, 2017. https://www.space.com/16726-space-shuttle.html.

4   "Space Shuttle Program." *National Geographic,* accessed September 27, 2019. https://www.nationalgeographic.com/science/space/space-exploration/space-shuttle-program.

5   Logsdon, John. *After Apollo? Richard Nixon and the American Space Program.* New York: Palgrave Macmillan, 2015.

6   Wall, Mike. "How the Space Shuttle Was Born." *Space,* June 28, 2011. https://www.space.com/12085-nasa-space-shuttle-history-born.html.

7   Amadeo, Kimberly. "How $1 Spent on NASA Adds $10 to the Economy." *Balance,* June 25, 2019. https://www.thebalance.com/nasa-budget-current-funding-and-history-3306321.

8   Amadeo, Kimberly. "How $1 Spent on NASA Adds $10 to the Economy." *Balance,* June 25, 2019. https://www.thebalance.com/nasa-budget-current-funding-and-history-3306321.

9   Fowler, Wallace. "Anniversary Shows Us That NASA and Space Exploration Are Worth Their Costs." Texas Perspectives, *UT News,* July 21, 2014. https://news.utexas.edu/2014/07/21/anniversary-shows-us-that-nasa-and-space-exploration-are-worth-their-costs.

10 Michael Carey (Cofounder and Chief Strategy Officer, ATLAS Space Operations), in discussion with the author, March 1, 2017.

PART II

Chapter Three

1   Dean, James. "OneWeb Satellites Bringing 250 Jobs to Space Coast." *Florida Today,* May 17, 2016. https://www.floridatoday.com/story/tech/science/space/2016/04/19/oneweb-build-satellites-space-coast/83194754.

Chapter Four

1   John Spencer (Space Architect; Founder and President, Space Tourism Society; Chief Designer, Mars World Enterprises), in discussion with the author, February 1, 2017.

2   Wall, Mike. "First Space Tourist: How a U.S. Millionaire Bought a Ticket to Orbit." *Space,* April 27, 2011. https://www.space.com/11492-space-tourism-pioneer-dennis-tito.html.

3   Jeff Greason (Cofounder and CTO, Electric Sky; Cofounder, XCOR Aerospace), in discussion with the author, March 4, 2017.

4   Anderson, Rebecca, and Michael Peacock. "Ansari X-Prize: A Brief History and Background." *NASA History Program Office.* February 5, 2010. https://history.nasa.gov/x-prize.htm.

5   John Spencer (Space Architect; Founder and President, Space Tourism Society; Chief Designer, Mars World Enterprises), in discussion with the author, February 1, 2017.

Chapter Five

1   Christopher Stott (Cofounder, Chair, and CEO, ManSat), in discussion with the author, May 31, 2017.

2   Pelley, Scott. "U.S., China, Russia, Elon Musk: Entrepreneur's 'Insane' Vision Becomes Reality." *CBS News,* May 22, 2012. https://www.cbsnews.com/news/us-china-russia-elon-musk-entrepreneurs-insane-vision-becomes-reality.

3   Sachdev, Avijeet. "Elon Musk: A Self-Made Entrepreneur." *Huffington Post,* December 3, 2012. https://www.huffpost.com/entry/elon-musk-a-selfmade-entr_b_2214268.

4   Primack, Dan. "Founders Fund Partner Leaves to Launch SpaceX-Focused Fund." *Axios,* December 15, 2017. https://www.axios.com/founders-fund-partner-leaves-to-launch-spacex-focused-fund-1513304489-21aad0b1-e467-4403-94f5-df36d5b95988.html.

5   Deagon, Brian. "Venture Capitalist Steve Jurvetson Eyes Space Boom." *Investor's Business Daily*, March 19, 2015. https://www.investors.com/news/technology/steve-jurvetson-draper-fisher-jurvetson-venture-capital.

6   Klotz, Irene. "SpaceX Flight Opens Door for U.S. Military Payloads." *Reuters,* June 5, 2012. https://www.reuters.com/article/usa-spaceship-military-idINDEE8540FM20120605.

7   Coldewey, Devin. "Trifecta! SpaceX Launches First Mission on Falcon Heavy and Lands All Three Boosters." *TechCrunch,* April 11, 2019. http://social.techcrunch.com/2019/04/11/trifecta-spacex-launches-first-mission-on-falcon-heavy-and-lands-all-three-boosters.

8   Musk, Elon (@elonmusk). "Race to orbit by both teams, although a success by both in close proximity would be amazing & each would count as a win." Twitter, August 5, 2019. https://twitter.com/elonmusk/status/1158631714706427904.

9   Lurio, Charles A. "Rocket Lab Reusable, Starship's Path, Regulation Errors." *Lurio Report* 14, no. 7 (September 2019).

10 Crunchbase. "SpaceX." Accessed January 20, 2020. https://www.crunchbase.com/organization/space-exploration-technologies.

11 Gigafund. "Who We Are." Accessed September 27, 2019. http://www.gigafund.com.

12 Sheetz, Michael. "SpaceX Raising over $300 Million as New Ontario Teachers' Tech Fund Makes Its First Investment." *CNBC,* June 27, 2019. https://www.cnbc.com/2019/06/27/spacex-raising-300-million-more-in-third-funding-round-this-year.html.

13 Mosher, Dave. "SpaceX May Be a $120 Billion Company if its Starlink Global Internet Service Takes Off, Morgan Stanley Research Predicts." *Business Insider*, September 17, 2019. https://www.businessinsider.com/spacex-future-multibillion-dollar-valuation-starlink-internet-morgan-stanley-2019-9.

14 Foust, Jeff. "SpaceX Revamps Smallsat Rideshare Program." *SpaceNews,* August 29, 2019. https://spacenews.com/spacex-revamps-smallsat-rideshare-program.

15 NASA Technology Transfer Office. "Flock of Nanosatellites Provides a Daily Picture of Earth." In *Spinoff*. Washington, DC: NASA, 2016. https://spinoff.nasa.gov/Spinoff2016/pdf/Spinoff2016.pdf.

16 Fernholz, Tim. "A Startup's Constellation of Tiny Satellites Is Now Photographing a Third of Earth's Landmass Every Day." *Quartz,* October 24, 2016. https://qz.com/816126/a-startups-constellation-of-tiny-satellites-is-now-photographing-a-third-of-earths-landmass-every-day.

17 Safyan, Mike. "Planet's First Launch of 2020: 26 SuperDoves on a Vega." Planet. February 13, 2020. https://www.planet.com/pulse/planets-first-launch-of-2020-26-superdoves-on-a-vega.

18   Baylor, Michael. "Planet Labs Targets a Search Engine of the World."
     NASASpaceflight.com, January 29, 2018. https://www.nasaspaceflight.
     com/2018/01/planet-labs-targets-search-engine-world.

19   Crunchbase. "Spire." Accessed September 27, 2019. https://www.crunchbase.
     com/organization/spire.

20   Lee, Alfred. "Briefing: Planet Labs to Close New Funding Round." *Information,*
     April 9, 2018. https://www.theinformation.com/briefings/97550b.

21   Schenker, Jennifer L. "Startup of the Week: Planet Labs." *Innovator,*
     December 10, 2017. https://innovator.news/startup-of-the-week-planet-labs-
     5c4391e6f9e5.

22   Crunchbase. "Spire." Accessed September 27, 2019. https://www.crunchbase.
     com/organization/spire.

23   Messier, Doug. "Four Spire Weather Satellites Launched into Orbit." *Parabolic
     Arc,* September 29, 2015. http://www.parabolicarc.com/2015/09/29/spire-
     weather-satellites-launched-orbit.

24   Sheetz, Michael. "Start-up Spire Global Lands Deal with ESA's Galileo Satellites
     for Predictive Weather Data." *CNBC,* December 11, 2018. https://www.cnbc.
     com/2018/12/11/spire-global-gets-2point7-billion-weather-data-partnership-
     from-galileo.html.

25   Airbus. "Airbus and Orbital Insight Partner on The OneAtlas Platform to Build
     World-Class Geospatial Analytics." Press Release. September 12, 2018. https://
     www.airbus.com/newsroom/press-releases/en/2018/09/airbus-and-orbital-
     insight-partner-on-the-oneatlas-platform-to-b.html.

26   "Orbital Insight and Energy Aspects Partner to Shape the Future of Energy
     Industry Research." Markets Insider, *Business Insider,* July 25, 2018. https://
     markets.businessinsider.com/news/stocks/orbital-insight-and-energy-aspects-
     partner-to-shape-the-future-of-energy-industry-researchglobal-partnership-
     combines-geospatial-analytics-with-in-depth-analyst-expertise-to-provide-
     customers-with-1027397788.

27   Crunchbase. "Orbital Insight." Accessed September 27, 2019. https://www.
     crunchbase.com/organization/orbital-insight-inc.

28   Vance, Ashlee. "Orbital Insight Opens Its Satellite Network to the Masses."
     Businessweek, *Bloomberg,* May 15, 2019. https://www.bloomberg.com/news/
     articles/2019-05-15/orbital-insight-uses-satellite-imagery-to-interrogate-the-
     world.

29   "Orbital Insight." Most Innovative Companies, *Fast Company,* accessed
     September 27, 2019. https://www.fastcompany.com/company/orbital-insight.

30   Nanoracks. "About Nanoracks." Accessed August 4, 2020. https://nanoracks.
     com/about-us.

31   Manber, Jeffrey. "Flying Through Our First 7 Years." Nanoracks. April 5, 2017.
     http://Nanoracks.com/flying-through-our-first-7-years.

32   Dan Katz (CEO, Orbital Sidekick), in discussion with the author, January 1,
     2019.

33   Blundell, Sally. "The Extraordinary Story of How New Zealand Entered the
     Space Race." The Listener, Noted, December 8, 2018. https://www.noted.co.nz/
     money/money-business/rocket-lab-how-new-zealand-entered-space-race.

34   Rocket Lab. "Next Generation Electron Booster on the Pad for Rocket Lab's
     Tenth Mission." News Release. November 5, 2019. https://www.rocketlabusa.
     com/news/updates/next-generation-electron-booster-on-the-pad-for-rocket-
     labs-10th-mission.

35   Crunchbase. "Rocket Lab." Accessed September 27, 2019. https://www.
     crunchbase.com/organization/rocket-lab.

36   Royal Aeronautical Society. "2018 Medals & Awards." News Release. November
     27, 2018. https://www.aerosociety.com/news/2018-medals-awards.

37   Crunchbase. "Spaceflight Industries." Accessed September 27, 2019. https://
     www.crunchbase.com/organization/spaceflight.

38   Spaceflight Industries. "Spaceflight Awarded First GSA Schedule Contract for
     Satellite Launch Services." News Release. February 10, 2016. https://spaceflight.
     com/spaceflight-awarded-first-gsa-schedule-contract-for-satellite-launch-
     services.

39   Lurio, Charles A. "Rocket Lab Reusable, Starship's Path, Regulation Errors."
     Lurio Report 14, no. 7 (September 2019).

Chapter Six

1   Jeff Greason (Cofounder and CTO, Electric Sky; Cofounder, XCOR
    Aerospace), in discussion with the author, March 4, 2017.

2   Messier, Doug. "U.S. Air Force Awards Launcher Development Contracts
    to ULA, Blue Origin & Northrop Grumman." Parabolic Arc, October 10,
    2018. http://www.parabolicarc.com/2018/10/10/air-force-awards-launcher-
    development-contracts-ula-blue-origin-northrop-grumman.

3   Grush, Loren. "The Defense Department Picks Three Companies to Develop
    Rockets for National Security Launches." Verge, October 10, 2018. https://www.
    theverge.com/2018/10/10/17961832/defense-department-launch-service-
    agreement-ula-blue-origin-northrop-grumman.

4   Foust, Jeff. "ULA Selects Blue Origin to Provide Vulcan Main Engine."
    SpaceNews, September 27, 2018. https://spacenews.com/ula-selects-blue-
    origin-to-provide-vulcan-main-engine.

5   Messier, Doug. "U.S. Air Force Awards SpaceX & ULA $727 Million in
    Launch Contracts." Parabolic Arc, February 20, 2019. http://www.parabolicarc.
    com/2019/02/20/air-force-awards-spacex-ula-727-million-launch-contracts.

6   NASA. "NASA, SpaceX Launch First Flight Test of Space System Planned for
    Crew." Press Release. March 2, 2019. http://www.nasa.gov/press-release/nasa-
    spacex-launch-first-flight-test-of-space-system-designed-for-crew.

7   NASA. "NASA, SpaceX Launch First Flight Test of Space System Planned for
    Crew." Press Release. March 2, 2019. http://www.nasa.gov/press-release/nasa-
    spacex-launch-first-flight-test-of-space-system-designed-for-crew.

8   Ian Fichtenbaum (Senior Vice President and Space & Satellite Specialist, American Industrial Acquisition Corporation; Director, Bradford Space group), in discussion with the author, April 28, 2017.

9   Michael Carey (Cofounder and Chief Strategy Officer, ATLAS Space Operations), in discussion with the author, March 1, 2017.

10 Berger, Eric. "In-Depth Study: Commercial Cargo Program a Bargain for NASA." *Ars Technica,* November 8, 2017. https://arstechnica.com/science/2017/11/in-depth-study-commercial-cargo-program-a-bargain-for-nasa.

11 Berger, Eric. "In-Depth Study: Commercial Cargo Program a Bargain for NASA." *Ars Technica,* November 8, 2017. https://arstechnica.com/science/2017/11/in-depth-study-commercial-cargo-program-a-bargain-for-nasa.

12 Berger, Eric. "In-Depth Study: Commercial Cargo Program a Bargain for NASA." *Ars Technica,* November 8, 2017. https://arstechnica.com/science/2017/11/in-depth-study-commercial-cargo-program-a-bargain-for-nasa.

13 NASA Commercial Crew & Cargo Program Office. *Commercial Orbital Transportation Services: A New Era in Spaceflight.* NASA SP-2014-617, 2014. https://www.nasa.gov/sites/default/files/files/SP-2014-617.pdf.

14 Bruce Pittman (Senior Vice President and Senior Operating Officer, National Space Society) in discussion with the author, October 26, 2016.

15 NASA. "NIAC Overview." August 28, 2015. http://www.nasa.gov/content/niac-overview.

16 NASA Technology Transfer Office. "About Spinoff." Accessed September 27, 2019. https://spinoff.nasa.gov/about.html.

17 SpaceX. "PICA Heat Shield." April 5, 2013. https://www.spacex.com/news/2013/04/04/pica-heat-shield.

18 Anthony Freeman (Innovation Foundry, NASA Jet Propulsion Laboratory), in discussion with the author, May 5, 2017.

PART III

Chapter Seven

1   Dennis Wingo (Founder and Chief Executive Officer, Skycorp Inc.), in discussion with the author, June 6, 2016.

2   Venezia, Michael. "What Is the Difference Between GNSS and GPS?" *Symmetry Electronics,* December 16, 2015. https://www.semiconductorstore.com/blog/2015/What-is-the-Difference-Between-GNSS-and-GPS/1550.

3   Collis, Christy. "The Geostationary Orbit: A Critical Legal Geography of Space's Most Valuable Real Estate." *The Sociological Review* 57, no. 1 (May 2009): 47–65. doi:10.1111/j.1467-954X.2009.01816.x.

4   David, Leonard. "Blue Origin's Sweet Spot: An Untapped Suborbital Market for Private Spaceflight." *Space*, August 12, 2016. https://www.space.com/33705-blue-origin-suborbital-private-spaceflight-market.html.

5   "The Integrated Space Plan." *Space Safety Magazine*, October 7, 2012. http://www.spacesafetymagazine.com/spaceflight/integrated-space-plan.

6   "Space Economy: An Overview." *Space Safety Magazine*, accessed October 2, 2019. http://www.spacesafetymagazine.com/space-on-earth/space-economy.

Chapter Eight

1   Michael Potter (Founder, Geeks Without Frontiers; Director, Paradigm Ventures), in discussion with the author, June 13, 2017.

2   David Cowan (Partner, Bessemer Venture Partners; Board Member, Rocket Lab), in discussion with the author, January 14, 2019.

3   Institute of Electrical and Electronics Engineers. "How Small Satellites Are Providing Low-Cost Access to Space." Xplore. November 13, 2018. https://site.ieee.org/sb-uol/how- small-satellites-are-providing-low-cost-access-to-space.

4   GlobeNewswire. "Global Prospects for the Small Satellite Market, 2018-2022." News Release. March 27, 2019. http://www.globenewswire.com/news-release/2019/03/27/1774017/0/en/Global-Prospects-for-the-Small-Satellite-Market-2018-2022.html.

5   SpaceWorks Enterprises. "2019 Nano/Microsatellite Market Forecast, 9th Edition." Accessed December 1, 2019. https://www.spaceworks.aero/wp-content/uploads/Nano-Microsatellite-Market-Forecast-9th-Edition-2019.pdf.

6   EuroConsult. "$22 Billion Market Value for Small Satellites over Next Ten Years." Press Release. July 7, 2016. http://www.euroconsult-ec.com/7_July_2016.

7   Bryce Space and Technology. "Smallsats by the Numbers 2020." Industry Analysis. Accessed February 4, 2020. https://brycetech.com/reports.

8   Bryce Space and Technology. "Smallsats by the Numbers 2020." Industry Analysis. Accessed February 4, 2020. https://brycetech.com/reports.

9   Dave Barnhart (Research Professor, Department of Astronautical Engineering at the University of Southern California), in discussion with the author, May 4, 2017.

10   Bryce Space and Technology. "Smallsats by the Numbers 2020." Industry Analysis. Accessed February 4, 2020. https://brycetech.com/reports.

11   EuroConsult. "$22 Billion Market Value for Small Satellites over Next Ten Years." Press Release. July 7, 2016. http://www.euroconsult-ec.com/7_July_2016.

12   GlobeNewswire. "Global Prospects for the Small Satellite Market, 2018-2022." News Release. March 27, 2019. http://www.globenewswire.com/news-release/2019/03/27/1774017/0/en/Global-Prospects-for-the-Small-Satellite-Market-2018-2022.html.

13   "Small-Satellite Launch Service Revenues to Pass $69B by 2030." *Space Daily,* January 9, 2019. http://www.spacedaily.com/reports/Small_satellite_launch_service_revenues_to_pass_69B_by_2030_999.html.

14   Dillow, Clay. "Why Small Satellites Are So Big Right Now." *Fortune,* August 4, 2015. https://fortune.com/2015/08/04/small-satellites-newspace.

15   Foust, Jeff. "NASA and NOAA Emphasize Value of Commercial Earth Science Data." *SpaceNews,* March 5, 2019. https://spacenews.com/nasa-and-noaa-emphasize-value-of-commercial-earth-science-data.

16   SpaceFab.US. "Space Telescopes." Accessed March 10, 2019. http://www.spacefab.us/space-telescopes.html.

17   SpaceFab.US. "SpaceFab.US Awards Space Telescope Time for Research." April 1, 2019. http://www.spacefab.us/updatesnews/spacefabus-awards-space-telescope-time-for-research.

18   Lars Krogh Alminde (Cofounder and Chief Commercial Officer, GomSpace), in discussion with the author, February 28, 2017.

19   Dave Barnhart (Research Professor, Department of Astronautical Engineering at the University of Southern California), in discussion with the author, May 4, 2017.

20   Taylor, Shane. "3D Printing & Space (Part 3): NASA." *3D Printing Industry,* February 20, 2014. https://3dprintingindustry.com/news/3d-printing-space-part-3-nasa-23887.

21   PR Newswire. "Global Additive Manufacturing Markets for Space Industry Applications 2017-2027 - The Next Frontier for 3D Printing." Press Release. August 17, 2017. https://www.prnewswire.com/news-releases/global-additive-manufacturing-markets-for-space-industry-applications-2017-2027---the-next-frontier-for-3d-printing-300505437.html.

22   Rocket Crafters. "Revolutionary Star-3D Hybrid Rocket Engines: Powering the Future of Space Access." Accessed October 4, 2019. http://www.rocketcrafters.com.

23   Messier, Doug. "Relativity Space Raises $140 Million In Series C Round." *Parabolic Arc,* October 1, 2019. http://www.parabolicarc.com/2019/10/01/relativity-space-raises-140-million-in-series-c-round.

24   Sheetz, Michael. "A Tiny Start-up Based in Brooklyn Has a 3D-Printed Rocket Engine It Says Is the Largest in the World." *CNBC,* February 20, 2019. https://www.cnbc.com/2019/02/20/brooklyn-rocket-start-up-launcher-gets-largest-single-piece-3d-printed-engine.html.

25   Sheetz, Michael. "A Tiny Start-up Based in Brooklyn Has a 3D-Printed Rocket Engine It Says Is the Largest in the World." *CNBC,* February 20, 2019. https://www.cnbc.com/2019/02/20/brooklyn-rocket-start-up-launcher-gets-largest-single-piece-3d-printed-engine.html.

26   Cowan, David. "Space Tech Investing, Part 1." *The Full Ratchet: Venture Capital Demystified.* Podcast audio, January 19, 2017. http://fullratchet.net/124-space-tech-investing-part-1-david-cowan.

27   Scott, Alwyn. "Exclusive: Boeing's Space Taxis to Use More than 600 3D-Printed Parts." *Reuters,* February 3, 2017. https://www.reuters.com/article/us-boeing-space-exclusive-idUSKBN15I1HW.

28   Boeing. "HorizonX: Who We Are." Accessed October 9, 2019. http://www.boeing.com/company/key-orgs/horizon-x.

29   Boyle, Alan. "Boeing HorizonX Co-Leads Funding Round for Morf3D Additive Manufacturing Startup." *GeekWire,* April 24, 2018. https://www.geekwire.com/2018/boeing-horizonx-morf3d.

30   Santana, Marco. "3-D Printing for Satellites? Harris Has a Plan." *Orlando Sentinel,* August 11, 2017. https://www.orlandosentinel.com/business/os-bz-3d-printing-satellites-20170811-story.html.

31   Schwab, Katharine. "MIT Invented The Material We'll Need To Build In Space." *Fast Company,* January 6, 2017. https://www.fastcompany.com/3066988/mit-invented-the-material-well-need-to-build-in-space.

32   NASA. "Latest Updates from NASA on 3D-Printed Habitat Competition." 3D-Printed Habitat Challenge Feature. Last updated March 27, 2019. http://www.nasa.gov/directorates/spacetech/centennial_challenges/3DPHab/latest-updates-from-nasa-on-3d-printed-habitat-competition.

33   Tan, Yvette. "This House Was 3D-Printed in Just 24 Hours." *Mashable,* March 3, 2017. https://mashable.com/2017/03/03/3d-house-24-hours.

34   Marks, Paul. "Interview: Elon Musk on What's Next for SpaceX." *NewScientist,* May 25, 2012. *Internet Archive.* https://web.archive.org/web/20120526103005/https://www.newscientist.com/blogs/onepercent/2012/05/spacex-the-apple-of-spacefligh.html?DCMP=OTC-rss&nsref=online-news.

35   John Paffett (Founder and Managing Director of KISPE Ltd.; Managing Director of Applied Space Solutions Ltd.; Member of the Board of Swedish Space Corporation), in discussion with the author, December 10, 2017.

36   Morgan Stanley. "Space: Investing in the Final Frontier." Morgan Stanley Research. July 2, 2019. https://www.morganstanley.com/ideas/investing-in-space.

37   Morgan Stanley. "Space: Investing in the Final Frontier." Morgan Stanley Research. July 2, 2019. https://www.morganstanley.com/ideas/investing-in-space.

38   O'Callaghan, Jonathan. "Blue Origin Launches New Shepard Rocket For 11th Time As It Prepares For Human Flights This Year." *Forbes,* May 2, 2019. https://www.forbes.com/sites/jonathanocallaghan/2019/05/02/blue-origin-launches-new-shepard-rocket-for-11th-time-as-it-prepares-for-human-flights-this-year.

39   Bezos, Jeff. "Innovation Spotlights." Fireside Chat, re:MARS from Amazon, Las Vegas, June 6, 2019.

40   George T. Whitesides (CEO, Virgin Galactic), in discussion with the author, January 28, 2019.

41   Jeff Garzik (Cofounder and CEO, Bloq, Inc.), in discussion with the author, November 15, 2018.

Chapter Nine

1   Stewart Bain (Cofounder and CEO, NorthStar Earth & Space), in discussion with the author, November 16, 2017.

2   Hollingham, Richard. "What Would Happen If All Satellites Stopped Working?" Future, *BBC,* June 10, 2013. http://www.bbc.com/future/story/20130609-the-day-without-satellites.

3   Clifford W. Beek (CEO, Cloud Constellation Corporation – SpaceBelt™; Cofounder, Star Asia Technologies PTE, Ltd; Board Member, CMC – Asia (Renewable Energy); Board Member, Advanced Training & Learning Technology), in discussion with the author, January 3, 2019.

4   SpaceBelt. "SpaceBelt Data Security as a Service." Accessed October 2, 2019. http://spacebelt.com.

5   Clifford W. Beek (CEO, Cloud Constellation Corporation – SpaceBelt™; Cofounder, Star Asia Technologies PTE, Ltd; Board Member, CMC – Asia (Renewable Energy); Board Member, Advanced Training & Learning Technology), in discussion with the author, January 3, 2019.

6   Hossain, Faisal. "Data for All: Using Satellite Observations for Social Good." *Eos,* October 14, 2015. https://eos.org/opinions/data-for-all-using-satellite-observations-for-social-good.

7   "Human Migration." *Springer Nature,* March 1, 2017. http://www.nature.com/news/human-migration-1.21547.

8   Centre for Remote Imaging, Sensing and Processing (CRISP). "Principles of Remote Sensing." CRISP Research. Accessed March 10, 2019. https://crisp.nus.edu.sg/~research/tutorial/optical.htm.

9   Wichner, David. "World View Balloon Flight from Tucson Successful after Five Days." *Arizona Daily Star,* October 6, 2017. https://tucson.com/business/world-view-balloon-flight-from-tucson-successful-after-five-days/article_e8a14c57-5815-508f-8e72-9300d99533fd.html.

10 Cofield, Calla. "High-Altitude Balloon Company Wants to Open a New Market at the Edge of Space." *Space,* February 24, 2017. https://www.space.com/35828-high-altitude-balloon-space-port-grand-opening.html.

11 Tom Olson (Director of Business Development, Avealto Ltd.), correspondence with the author, January 27, 2019.

12 Internet World Stats. "World Internet Users Statistics and 2019 World Population Stats." Accessed March 10, 2019. https://www.internetworldstats.com/stats.htm.

13 Grush, Loren. "OneWeb Set to Launch First Satellites in Quest to Provide Global Internet Coverage from Space." *Verge,* February 27, 2019. https://www.theverge.com/2019/2/27/18242120/oneweb-650-satellite-constellation-arianespace-soyuz-launch.

14   Grush, Loren. "FCC Approves SpaceX's Plans to Fly Internet-Beaming
     Satellites in a Lower Orbit." *Verge,* April 27, 2019. https://www.theverge.
     com/2019/4/27/18519778/spacex-starlink-fcc-approval-satellite-internet-
     constellation-lower-orbit.
     Brown, Mike. "SpaceX: Why Starlink Depends on Starship to Fuel the Future
     of Humanity." *Inverse,* March 2, 2020. https://www.inverse.com/innovation/
     spacex-elon-musk-details-how-starlink-starship-are-inextricably-linked.

15   Porter, Jon. "Amazon Will Launch Thousands of Satellites to Provide
     Internet around the World." *Verge,* April 4, 2019. https://www.theverge.
     com/2019/4/4/18295310/amazon-project-kuiper-satellite-internet-low-earth-
     orbit-facebook-spacex-starlink.

16   Scott, Kat. "Forest Recognition: Planet Launches Kaggle Competition." Planet
     Labs. April 20, 2017. https://www.planet.com/pulse/forest-recognition-planet-
     launches-kaggle-competition.

17   Zolli, Andrew. "Planet Becomes First Private-Sector Data Provider to Directly
     Support the International Charter on Space and Major Disasters." Planet Labs.
     August 13, 2018. https://www.planet.com/pulse/planet-international-charter-
     space-and-major-disasters.

18   Zolli, Andrew. "Planet Becomes First Private-Sector Data Provider to Directly
     Support the International Charter on Space and Major Disasters." Planet Labs.
     August 13, 2018. https://www.planet.com/pulse/planet-international-charter-
     space-and-major-disasters.

19   Scott, Kat. "Forest Recognition: Planet Launches Kaggle Competition." Planet
     Labs. April 20, 2017. https://www.planet.com/pulse/forest-recognition-planet-
     launches-kaggle-competition.

20   Yong, Ed. "The Space Station Is Becoming a Spy Satellite For Wildlife." *Atlantic,*
     July 6, 2016. https://www.theatlantic.com/science/archive/2016/07/the-
     international-space-station-becoming-a-spy-satellite-for-tiny-animals/490112.

21   Gareth Keane (Partner, Promus Ventures), in discussion with the author,
     November 1, 2016.

22   Foust, Jeff. "President Signs Commercial Satellite Weather Bill." *SpaceNews,*
     April 21, 2017. https://spacenews.com/president-signs-commercial-satellite-
     weather-bill.

23   Van Wagenen, Juliet. "GeoOptics Talks Benefits of Commercial Weather
     Contract with NOAA." *Via Satellite,* October 7, 2016. https://www.
     satellitetoday.com/innovation/2016/10/07/geooptics-talks-benefits-
     commercial-weather-contract-noaa.

24   National Oceanic and Atmospheric Administration (NOAA), email to the
     author, April 24, 2019.

25   National Oceanic and Atmospheric Administration (NOAA), email to the
     author, April 24, 2019.

26   Sheetz, Michael. "Satellite Builder and Data Business Spire Raises $40 Million
     as IPO Plans Come into View." *CNBC,* September 25, 2019. https://www.cnbc.
     com/2019/09/25/satellite-data-company-spire-raises-40-million-with-ipo-
     plans-in-view.html.

27   Liebhold, Peter. "The Crop of the 21st Century." National Museum of American History (blog). July 13, 2018. https://americanhistory.si.edu/blog/precision-farming.

28   Goedde, Lutz, Maya Horii, and Sunil Sanghvi. "Pursuing the Global Opportunity in Food and Agribusiness." *McKinsey & Company,* July 2015. https://www.mckinsey.com/industries/chemicals/our-insights/pursuing-the-global-opportunity-in-food-and-agribusiness.

29   Grand View Research. "Precision Farming/Agriculture Market Size, Share & Trends Analysis Report By Offering (Hardware, Software, Services), By Application (Yield Monitoring, Irrigation Management) And Segment Forecasts, 2019 - 2025." Industry Analysis. May 2019. https://www. grandviewresearch. com/industry-analysis/precision-farming-market.

30   Richard Godwin (President, Space Technology Holdings LLC), in discussion with the author, June 8, 2017.

31   Soper, Taylor. "Bayer Partners with Planetary Resources to Use Space Data to Boost Agriculture on Earth." *GeekWire,* May 31, 2016. https://www.geekwire. com/2016/bayer-inks-partnership-planetary-resources-use-satellite-images-agricultural-products.

32   Messier, Doug. "Planetary Resources, Bayer Sign MOU on Space Data." *Parabolic Arc,* May 31, 2016. http://www.parabolicarc.com/2016/05/31/planetary-resources-bayer-sign-mou-space-data.

33   Henry, Caleb. "Planet Labs Acquires BlackBridge." *Via Satellite*, July 15, 2015. https://www.satellitetoday.com/innovation/2015/07/15/planet-labs-acquires-blackbridge.

34   "Climate Corp To Use Satellite Imagery From RapidEye." *AgriMarketing,* May 14, 2015. https://www.agrimarketing.com/ss.php?id=96090.

35   Parkhurst, Emalie. "Monsanto's 'Data + Analytics' Frontier." The Digital Matrix, *Medium,* February 26, 2018. https://medium.com/emalies-test-publication/monsantos-data-analytics-frontier-6cd47eed7869.

36   "Satellites vs. Drones: The Technology in Your Vegetables." Planet Stories, *Medium,* April 18, 2018. https://medium.com/planet-stories/satellites-vs-drones-the-technology-in-your-vegetables-5794eea4b738.

37   Corning. "Orbital Sidekick and Corning Release High-Fidelity Hyperspectral Images from Space." News Release. April 26, 2019. https://www.corning.com/worldwide/en/about-us/news-events/news-releases/2019/04/Orbital-sidekick-and-corning-release-high-fidelity-hyperspectral-images-from-space.html.

38   Fábio Teixeira (Cofounder, Hypercubes), in discussion with the author, January 15, 2019.

39   ORBCOMM. "Industrial IoT and M2M Tracking, Monitoring and Control Solutions." Accessed March 10, 2019. https://www.orbcomm.com.

40   McClelland, Calum. "What Is IoT? - A Simple Explanation of the Internet of Things." *IoT For All,* May 13, 2019. https://www.iotforall.com/what-is-iot-simple-explanation.

41   Woodie, Alex. "5 Ways Big Geospatial Data Is Driving Analytics In the Real World." *Datanami,* May 21, 2015. https://www.datanami.com/2015/05/21/5-ways-big-geospatial-data-is-driving-analytics-in-the-real-world.

42   Stevenson, Alexandra. "The Next Generation of Hedge Fund Stars: Data-Crunching Computers." DealBook, *New York Times,* November 14, 2016. https://www.nytimes.com/2016/11/15/business/dealbook/the-next-generation-of-hedge-fund-stars-data-crunching-computers.html.

43   Pearson, Matthew. "Future Farming: Climate Change, Satellites and Smart Irrigation." Fleet Space Technologies. September 1, 2018. https://www.fleet.space/news/future-farming-climate-change-satellites-and-smart-irrigation.

44   Pearson, Matthew. "Future Farming: Climate Change, Satellites and Smart Irrigation." Fleet Space Technologies. September 1, 2018. https://www.fleet.space/news/future-farming-climate-change-satellites-and-smart-irrigation.

45   Flavia Tata Nardini (Cofounder and CEO, Fleet Space Technologies), in conversation with the author, April 24, 2017.

46   Rafal Modrzewski (CEO, ICEYE), in discussion with the author, March 6, 2019.

47   International Data Corporation. "IDC Forecasts Revenues for Big Data and Business Analytics Solutions Will Reach $189.1 Billion This Year with Double-Digit Annual Growth Through 2022." Industry Analysis. April 4, 2019. https://www.idc.com/getdoc.jsp?containerId=prUS44998419.

48   Maddox, Teena. "How IoT Will Drive the Fourth Industrial Revolution." *ZDNet,* March 6, 2019. https://www.zdnet.com/article/how-iot-will-drive-the-fourth-industrial-revolution.

Chapter Ten

1   Harari, Yuval. *Homo Deus: A Brief History of Tomorrow.* New York: HarperCollins, 2017.

2   Harari, Yuval. *Homo Deus: A Brief History of Tomorrow.* New York: HarperCollins, 2017.

3   Wang, Brian. "The Solar System Is Big Enough to Hold the Space Plans of Elon Musk and Jeff Bezos Which Combined Look like Babylon 5." *NextBigFuture,* October 30, 2016. https://www.nextbigfuture.com/2016/10/the-solar-system-is-big-enough-to-hold.html.

4   The World Counts. "Depletion of Natural Resources Statistics." Accessed November 18, 2019 and January 13, 2020. http://www.theworldcounts.com/counters/environmental_effect_of_mining/depletion_of_natural_resources_statistics.

5   Frank, Adam. "Are Humans Evolved To Explore And Expand Into Space?" Cosmos & Culture, *National Public Radio,* August 23, 2016. https://www.npr.org/sections/13.7/2016/08/23/491020152/are-humans-evolved-to-explore-and-expand-into-space.

6   Stern, Marlow. "Elon Musk of Tesla Motors Discusses Revenge of the Electric Car." *Daily Beast*, last updated July 13, 2017. https://www.thedailybeast.com/elon-musk-of-tesla-motors-discusses-revenge-of-the-electric-car.

7   Hedgecock, Sarah. "How One Former Astronaut Is Prepping For A Trip Outside The Solar System." *Forbes*, May 13, 2016. https://www.forbes.com/sites/sarahhedgecock/2016/05/13/mae-jemison-and-the-100-year-starship.

8   NASA Technology Transfer Office. *Spinoff*. Washington, DC: NASA, 2015. https://spinoff.nasa.gov/Spinoff2015/pdf/Spinoff2015.pdf.

9   Svitil, Kathy. "Space-Based Solar Power Project Funded." CalTech. April 28, 2015. https://www.caltech.edu/about/news/space-based-solar-power-project-funded-46644.

10   M. D. Kelzenberg et al., "Ultralight Energy Converter Tile for the Space Solar Power Initiative." Paper presented at the *IEEE 7th World Conference on Photovoltaic Energy Conversion (WCPEC) (A Joint Conference of 45th IEEE PVSC, 28th PVSEC & 34th EU PVSEC)*, Waikoloa Village, HI, June 10–15, 2018. https://doi.org/10.1109/PVSC.2018.8547403.

11   Shapiro, Fred R. "Notes and Queries." *The Yale Book of Quotations*. New Haven: Yale University Press, 2006.

12   Jones, Andrew. "Chang'e-4 Updates: Yutu-2 Roves into Overtime, Returns More Images." Planetary Society (blog). April 22, 2019. http://www.planetary.org/blogs/guest-blogs/2019/change-4-updates-day-4.html.

13   Narayanan, Aparna. "Isreal's SpaceIL Fails To Become First Company To Successfully Land On Moon." *Business News Daily*, April 11, 2019. https://www.investors.com/news/moon-landing-spaceil-first-private-company-spacex-launch.

14   Yonatan Winetraub (Cofounder, SpaceIL), in discussion with the author, November 9, 2016.

15   Bezos, Jeff. "Innovation Spotlights." Fireside Chat, re:MARS from Amazon, Las Vegas, June 6, 2019.

16   Clifford, Catherine. "Jeff Bezos Dreams of a World with a Trillion People Living in Space." Make It, *CNBC*, May 1, 2018. https://www.cnbc.com/2018/05/01/jeff-bezos-dreams-of-a-world-with-a-trillion-people-living-in-space.html.

17   Becker, Rachel. "Amazon Boss Jeff Bezos Wants to Start Shipping Packages to the Moon." *Verge*, March 2, 2017. https://www.theverge.com/2017/3/2/14797704/jeff-bezos-blue-origin-amazon-lunar-shipping-cargo-delivery-moon.

18   U.S. Congress. House. Committee on Science, Space, and Technology. *Private Sector Lunar Expansion: Hearing before the Subcommittee on Space.* 115th Cong., 1st sess., September 7, 2017. https://www.govinfo.gov/content/pkg/CHRG-115hhrg27174/pdf/CHRG-115hhrg27174.pdf.

19   Grush, Loren. "Jeff Bezos Unveils Mock-up of Blue Origin's Lunar Lander Blue Moon." *Verge*, May 9, 2019. https://www.theverge.com/2019/5/9/18550258/blue-origin-moon-lunar-lander-jeff-bezos-space.

20 Thomas, Cathy Booth. "The Space Cowboys." *Time* 169, no. 10 (2007).

21 Takeshi Hakamada (Cofounder and CEO, ispace), in discussion with the author, November 23, 2016.

22 Takeshi Hakamada (Cofounder and CEO, ispace), in discussion with the author, November 23, 2016.

23 Messier, Doug. "Sumitomo Becomes Corporate Partner of Ispace's Lunar Program." *Parabolic Arc,* August 27, 2019. http://parabolicarc.com/2019/08/27/sumitomo-becomes-corporate-partner-of-ispaces-lunar-program.

24 Takeshi Hakamada (Cofounder and CEO, ispace), in discussion with the author, November 23, 2016.

25 Jurvetson, Steve. "Moon Base Alpha—Strategies for Low Cost Lunar Settlement Workshop." Flickr. August 23, 2014. https://www.flickr.com/photos/jurvetson/30929394984.

26 Harper, Lynn D., Clive R. Neal, Jane Poynter, James D. Schalkwyk, and Dennis Ray Wingo. "Life Support for a Low-Cost Lunar Settlement: No Showstoppers." *New Space* 4, no. 1 (March 2016): 40–49. https://doi.org/10.1089/space.2015.0029.

27 Harper, Lynn D., Clive R. Neal, Jane Poynter, James D. Schalkwyk, and Dennis Ray Wingo. "Life Support for a Low-Cost Lunar Settlement: No Showstoppers." *New Space* 4, no. 1 (March 2016): 40–49. https://doi.org/10.1089/space.2015.0029.

28 Jurvetson, Steve. "Moon Base Alpha—Strategies for Low Cost Lunar Settlement Workshop." Flickr. August 23, 2014. https://www.flickr.com/photos/jurvetson/30929394984.

29 Vance, Ashlee. "The Silicon Valley Heavyweights Who Want to Settle the Moon." *Bloomberg,* September 5, 2019. https://www.bloomberg.com/news/articles/2019-09-05/the-silicon-valley-heavyweights-who-want-to-settle-the-moon.

30 Vance, Ashlee. "The Silicon Valley Heavyweights Who Want to Settle the Moon." *Bloomberg,* September 5, 2019. https://www.bloomberg.com/news/articles/2019-09-05/the-silicon-valley-heavyweights-who-want-to-settle-the-moon.

31 Wall, Mike. "NASA Awards $45.5 Million for Private Moon Lander Work on Project Artemis." *Space,* May 17, 2019. https://www.space.com/nasa-private-moon-landers-funding-artemis.html.

32 Smith, Rich. "NASA Disses the Usual Suspects in Latest Moon Contract Awards." *Motley Fool,* June 10, 2019. https://www.fool.com/pwa/investing/2019/06/10/nasa-disses-the-usual-suspects-in-latest-moon-cont.aspx.

33 Astrobotic. "Astrobotic Selects United Launch Alliance Vulcan Centaur Rocket to Launch Its First Mission to the Moon." Press Release. August 19, 2019. https://www.astrobotic.com/2019/8/19/astrobotic-selects-united-launch-alliance-vulcan-centaur-rocket-to-launch-its-first-mission-to-the-moon.

34   Astrobotic. "Astrobotic Selects United Launch Alliance Vulcan Centaur Rocket to Launch Its First Mission to the Moon." August 19, 2019. https://www.astrobotic.com/2019/8/19/astrobotic-selects-united-launch-alliance-vulcan-centaur-rocket-to-launch-its-first-mission-to-the-moon.

35   NASA. "NASA Announces Next Phase of Commercial Lunar Payload Services." Press Release. July 30, 2019. http://www.nasa.gov/press-release/nasa-announces-call-for-next-phase-of-commercial-lunar-payload-services.

36   NASA. "NASA Announces Industry Partnerships to Advance Moon, Mars Technology." Press Release. July 30, 2019. http://www.nasa.gov/press-release/nasa-announces-us-industry-partnerships-to-advance-moon-mars-technology.

37   NASA. "NASA Announces Industry Partnerships to Advance Moon, Mars Technology." Press Release. July 30, 2019. http://www.nasa.gov/press-release/nasa-announces-us-industry-partnerships-to-advance-moon-mars-technology.

38   Smith, Rich. "NASA's Multibillion-Dollar Bet on the Moon: Good News for Space Companies, and for Taxpayers Too." *Motley Fool,* June 22, 2019. https://www.fool.com/pwa/investing/2019/06/22/nasas-multibillion-dollar-bet-on-the-moon-good-new.aspx.

39   Bridenstine, Jim. "This Is Our Sputnik Moment." *OKG News*, November 7, 2016. https://okgrassroots.com/?p=642815.

40   Foust, Jeff. "NASA and JAXA Reaffirm Intent to Cooperate in Lunar Exploration." *SpaceNews*, September 25, 2019. https://spacenews.com/nasa-and-jaxa-reaffirm-intent-to-cooperate-in-lunar-exploration.

41   Japan Aerospace Exploration Agency. "ANA HOLDINGS and JAXA Partner to Create a New Space Industry Centered Around Real-World Avatars." Press Release. September 6, 2018. https://global.jaxa.jp/press/2018/09/20180906_avatarx.html.

42   Wolf, Michael. "Meet Space Food X, Japan's New Initiative to Feed People in Space." *Spoon*, March 28, 2019. https://thespoon.tech/meet-space-food-x-japans-new-initiative-to-feed-people-in-space.

43   Japan Aerospace Exploration Agency. "ANA HOLDINGS and JAXA Partner to Create a New Space Industry Centered Around Real-World Avatars." Press Release. September 6, 2018. https://global.jaxa.jp/press/2018/09/20180906_avatarx.html.

44   Kalil, Tom. "Bootstrapping a Solar System Civilization." The White House. October 14, 2014. Archived Obama White House Website. https://obamawhitehouse.archives.gov/blog/2014/10/14/bootstrapping-solar-system-civilization.

45   Metzger, Philip T., Anthony Muscatello, Robert P. Mueller, and James Mantovani. "Affordable, Rapid Bootstrapping of the Space Industry and Solar System Civilization." *Journal of Aerospace Engineering* 26 (2012): 18-29. 10.1061/(ASCE)AS.1943-5525.0000236.

46 Kalil, Tom. "Bootstrapping a Solar System Civilization." The White
    House. October 14, 2014. Archived Obama White House Website. https://
    obamawhitehouse.archives.gov/blog/2014/10/14/bootstrapping-solar-system-
    civilization.

47 Metzger, Philip T., Anthony Muscatello, Robert P. Mueller, and James
    Mantovani. "Affordable, Rapid Bootstrapping of the Space Industry and
    Solar System Civilization." Journal of Aerospace Engineering 26 (2012): 18-29.
    10.1061/(ASCE)AS.1943-5525.0000236.

48 Elvis, Martin, and Tony Milligan. "How Much of the Solar System Should We
    Leave as Wilderness?" Acta Astronautica 162 (September 2019): 574–580.
    arXiv:1905.13681.

49 Dvorsky, George. "Humans Will Never Colonize Mars." Space, Gizmodo, July
    30, 2019. https://gizmodo.com/humans-will-never-colonize-mars-1836316222.

50 World Nuclear Association. "What Is Background Radiation?" Accessed
    October 3, 2019. http://www.world-nuclear.org/uploadedFiles/org/Features/
    Radiation/4_Background_Radiation%281%29.pdf.

51 United States Nuclear Regulatory Commission. "NRC: High Radiation Doses."
    Updated October 2, 2017. https://www.nrc.gov/about-nrc/radiation/health-
    effects/high-rad-doses.html.

52 Dvorsky, George. "Humans Will Never Colonize Mars." Space, Gizmodo, July
    30, 2019. https://gizmodo.com/humans-will-never-colonize-mars-1836316222.

53 Cuthbertson, Anthony. "The First Ever Asteroid Mining Mission Is Set
    to Launch by 2020." Newsweek, August 10, 2016. https://www.newsweek.
    com/asteroid-mining-mission-launch-space-unlimited-economic-
    expansion-488949.

54 Shaer, Matthew. "The Asteroid Miner's Guide to the Galaxy." Foreign Policy,
    April 28, 2016. https://foreignpolicy.com/2016/04/28/the-asteroid-miners-
    guide-to-the-galaxy-space-race-mining-asteroids-planetary-research-deep-
    space-industries.

55 Williams, Georgia. "Rare Earths Outlook 2019: EV Production to Drive
    Demand." Investing News Network, December 19, 2018. https://investingnews.
    com/daily/resource-investing/critical-metals-investing/rare-earth-investing/
    rare-earth-outlook.

56 Rare Earth Technology Alliance. "What Are Rare Earths?" Accessed October 3,
    2019. http://www.rareearthtechalliance.com/What-are-Rare-Earths.

57 Massachusetts Institute of Technology. "Rare Earth Elements Supply
    and Demand." Mission 2016: The Future of Strategic Natural Resources
    (blog). Accessed October 3, 2019. http://web.mit.edu/12.000/www/m2016/
    finalwebsite/problems/ree.html.

58 Massachusetts Institute of Technology. "Rare Earth Elements Supply
    and Demand." Mission 2016: The Future of Strategic Natural Resources
    (blog). Accessed October 3, 2019. http://web.mit.edu/12.000/www/m2016/
    finalwebsite/problems/ree.html.

59   Chandler, David L. "Clean Energy Could Lead to Scarce Materials." *MIT News,* April 9, 2012. http://news.mit.edu/2012/rare-earth-alternative-energy-0409.

60   Chandler, David L. "Clean Energy Could Lead to Scarce Materials." *MIT News,* April 9, 2012. http://news.mit.edu/2012/rare-earth-alternative-energy-0409.

61   Chandler, David L. "Clean Energy Could Lead to Scarce Materials." *MIT News,* April 9, 2012. http://news.mit.edu/2012/rare-earth-alternative-energy-0409.

62   Colorado School of Mines. "Graduate Programs." Accessed October 4, 2019. https://space.mines.edu/graduate-programs.

63   Whaley, Monte. "School of Mines Hopes to Launch First-Ever Space Mining Program." *Denver Post,* August 23, 2017. https://www.denverpost. com/2017/08/23/school-of-mines-could-launch-space-mining-program.

64   "Luxembourg Sets aside 200 Million Euros to Fund Space Mining Ventures." *Reuters,* June 3, 2016. https://www.reuters.com/article/us-luxembourg-space-mining-idUSKCN0YP22H.

65   Ghalitschi, Kamran. "Why the Fund Industry Chooses Luxembourg Non-Bank Lending In the European Union." *HedgeNordic,* October 11, 2018. https:// hedgenordic.com/2018/10/why-the-fund-industry-chooses-luxembourg.

     The Heritage Foundation. "Luxembourg Economy: Population, GDP, Inflation, Business, Trade, FDI, Corruption." Accessed April 10, 2019. https://www. heritage.org/index/country/luxembourg.

66   Luxembourg. The Official Portal of the Grand Duchy of Luxembourg. "New Space Law to Provide Framework for Space Resource Utilization." Press Release. June 3, 2016. https://space-agency.public.lu/dam-assets/press-release/ 2016/2016_06_03PressRelease_MeetingAdvisoryBoard.pdf.

67   Zaleski, Andrew. "Luxembourg Leads the Trillion-Dollar Race to Become the Silicon Valley of Asteroid Mining." *CNBC,* April 16, 2018. https://www.cnbc. com/2018/04/16/luxembourg-vies-to-become-the-silicon-valley-of-asteroid-mining.html.

68   Daley, Jason. "Will Luxembourg Lead the Race for Space Mining?" Smart News, *Smithsonian,* October 9, 2016. https://www.smithsonianmag.com/ smart-news/will-luxembourg-lead-race-space-mining-180959031.

     Luxembourg. The Official Portal of the Grand Duchy of Luxembourg. "Luxembourg to Launch Framework to Support the Future Use of Space Resources." Press Release. February 03, 2016. https://space-agency.public.lu/ dam-assets/press-release/2016/2016_02_03PressReleaseAnnouncementSpaceR esourceslu.pdf.

69   Messier, Doug. "Luxembourg Lost $13.7 Million on Planetary Resources Investment." *Parabolic Arc,* November 19, 2018. http://www.parabolicarc. com/2018/11/19/luxembourg-lost-137-million-planetary-resources-investment.

70   Messier, Doug. "Firmamentum Wins Contract to Manufacture Comsat Component in Space." *Parabolic Arc,* October 10, 2016. http://www. parabolicarc.com/2016/10/10/firmamentum-wins-contract-manufacture-comsat-component-space.

71 Tethers Unlimited, Inc. "SpiderFab™: Orbital Manufacturing and Construction Technologies." Retrieved from archive February 3, 2020. Internet Archive. https://web.archive.org/web/20191014024524/http://www.tethers.com/SpiderFab.html.

72 Tethers Unlimited, Inc. "The KRAKEN® Arm: Compact, High-Dexterity Robotic Arm for Nanosatellites." Retrieved from archive February 3, 2020. Internet Archive. https://web.archive.org/web/20190707061914/http://www.tethers.com/KRAKEN.html.

73 Boyle, Alan. "Tethers Unlimited works on technologies for 'LEO Knight' Satellite Servicing Robot." *GeekWire*, May 22, 2019. https://www.geekwire.com/2019/tethers-unlimited-works-technologies-leo-knight-satellite-servicing-robot.

74 Tethers Unlimited, Inc. "Refabricator: A Recycling and Manufacturing System for the International Space Station." Retrieved from archive February 3, 2020. Internet Archive. https://web.archive.org/web/20190729003132/http://www.tethers.com/Refabricator.html.

75 NASA. "NASA's Dragonfly Project Demonstrates Robotic Satellite Assembly." September 13, 2017. http://www.nasa.gov/mission_pages/tdm/irma/nasas-dragonfly-project-demonstrates-robotic-satellite-assembly-critical-to-future-space.html.

NASA. "The Dark Side of the Crater: Learning How to Explore the Moon's Poles." Mission Feature. July 25, 2017. http://www.nasa.gov/ames/feature/the-dark-side-of-the-crater-how-light-looks-different-on-the-moon-and-what-nasa-is-doing.

76 NASA.. "NASA's First Astrobee Robot 'Bumble' Starts Flying in Space." Mission Feature. Last updated June 20, 2019. http://www.nasa.gov/image-feature/ames/look-no-hands-nasa-s-first-astrobee-robot-bumble-starts-flying-in-space.

77 NASA. "Remote Manipulator System (Canadarm2)." NASA Feature. Last updated October 23, 2018. http://www.nasa.gov/mission_pages/station/structure/elements/remote-manipulator-system-canadarm2.

78 Messier, Doug. "Made In Space to Demonstrate Manufacture of Exotic Optical Fiber in Space." *Parabolic Arc,* July 19, 2016. http://www.parabolicarc.com/2016/07/19/space-demonstrate-manufacture-exotic-optical-fiber-space.

79 Host, Pat. "Made In Space Taps Northrop Grumman as Subcontractor." *Via Satellite,* April 26, 2016. https://www.satellitetoday.com/innovation/2016/04/26/made-in-space-taps-northrop-grumman-as-subcontractor.

80 SpaceFab.US. "World's First App Controlled Space Telescope." Accessed October 04, 2019. http://www.spacefab.us.

81 SpaceFab.US. "World's First App Controlled Space Telescope." Accessed October 04, 2019. http://www.spacefab.us.

82 Garfield, Leanna. "An PhD Student Invented a Robot That Can Grow Fruits and Vegetables on Mars." *Business Insider,* April 19, 2016. https://www.businessinsider.com/mit-student-invented-robot-for-food-in-space-2016-4.

83   Garfield, Leanna. "An PhD Student Invented a Robot That Can Grow Fruits and Vegetables on Mars." *Business Insider,* April 19, 2016. https://www.businessinsider.com/mit-student-invented-robot-for-food-in-space-2016-4.

84   Andrew Barton (Aerospace Technology Consultant; Venture Partner, Syndicate 708), in discussion with the author, November 12, 2016.

85   Jeff Greason (Cofounder and CTO, Electric Sky; Cofounder, XCOR Aerospace), in discussion with the author, March 4, 2017.

86   Bezos, Jeff. "Innovation Spotlights." Fireside Chat, re:MARS from Amazon, Las Vegas, June 6, 2019.

87   Bezos, Jeff. "Innovation Spotlights." Fireside Chat, re:MARS from Amazon, Las Vegas, June 6, 2019.

88   Bezos, Jeff. "Jeff Bezos Discusses Space Flight and His Vision for Blue Origin." Produced by *GeekWire.* Pathfinder Awards, Seattle Museum of Flight, 2016. YouTube video, 01:11. October 23, 2016. https://www.youtube.com/watch?v=VNwE3sRWxHw.

89   Foust, Jeff. "Industry Sees New Opportunities for Space Manufacturing." *SpaceNews,* December 06, 2017. https://spacenews.com/industry-sees-new-opportunities-for-space-manufacturing.

90   Glover, Rich. "Microgravity Production = Advanced Manufacturing Innovation = Neutral Force Processing (NFP)." LinkedIn. June 28, 2019. https://www.linkedin.com/pulse/microgravity-production-advanced-manufacturing-neutral-rich-glover.

91   Glover, Rich. "Space Commercialization – Part 1; Are You a Supporter or a Doer?!" LinkedIn. May 9, 2016. https://www.linkedin.com/pulse/space-commercialization-part-1-you-supporter-doer-rich-glover.

92   Mahoney, Erin. "Synthetic Biology." NASA Feature. Last updated August 3, 2017. http://www.nasa.gov/content/synthetic-biology.

93   Menezes, Amor A., Michael G. Montague, John Cumbers, John A. Hogan, and Adam P. Arkin. "Grand Challenges in Space Synthetic Biology." *Journal of The Royal Society Interface* 12, no. 113 (December 2015): 1–7. https://doi.org/10.1098/rsif.2015.0803.

94   Cumbers, John. "Can We Redesign The Modern City With Synthetic Biology? Could We Grow Our Houses Instead Of Building Them?" *Forbes,* September 26, 2019. https://www.forbes.com/sites/johncumbers/2019/09/26/can-we-redesign-the-modern-city-with-synthetic-biology-could-we-grow-our-houses-instead-of-building-them.

95   Cumbers, John, and Niko McCarty. "Meet the 8 Tech Titans Investing in Synthetic Biology." *SynBioBeta,* September 15, 2019. https://synbiobeta.com/meet-the-8-tech-titans-investing-in-synthetic-biology.

96   Cumbers, John. "Can We Redesign The Modern City With Synthetic Biology? Could We Grow Our Houses Instead Of Building Them?" *Forbes,* September 26, 2019. https://www.forbes.com/sites/johncumbers/2019/09/26/can-we-redesign-the-modern-city-with-synthetic-biology-could-we-grow-our-houses-instead-of-building-them.

97   Cumbers, John. "Can We Redesign the Modern City with Synthetic Biology? Could We Grow Our Houses Instead of Building Them?" *Forbes*, September 26, 2019. https://www.forbes.com/sites/johncumbers/2019/09/26/can-we-redesign-the-modern-city-with-synthetic-biology-could-we-grow-our-houses-instead-of-building-them.

98   Mahoney, Erin. "Synthetic Biology." NASA Feature. Last updated August 3, 2017. http://www.nasa.gov/content/synthetic-biology.

99   Menezes, Amor A, Michael G Montague, John Cumbers, John A Hogan, and Adam P Arkin. "Grand Challenges in Space Synthetic Biology." *Journal of The Royal Society Interface* 12, no. 113 (December 2015): 1–7. https://doi.org/10.1098/rsif.2015.0803.

100 Foy, Kylie. "Scientists Look to Synthetic Biology and 3-D Printing for Life Support in Space." *Phys.Org*, July 29, 2019. https://phys.org/news/2019-07-scientists-synthetic-biology-d-life.html.

Chapter Eleven

1   International Space Station Program Science Forum. *International Space Station Benefits for Humanity.* 2nd ed. Washington, DC: NASA, 2015. https://www.nasa.gov/sites/default/files/atoms/files/jsc_benefits_for_humanity_tagged_6-30-15.pdf.

2   Patel, Neel. "A Medical Revolution Underway in Orbit." *Inverse*, July 13, 2016. https://www.inverse.com/article/18198-future-space-medicine-nasa-telemedicine-iss-eric-topol.

3   "Counting the Many Ways the Space Station Benefits Humankind." *International Space Station Feature.* Last updated June 13, 2019. http://www.nasa.gov/mission_pages/station/research/news/b4h-3rd-ed-book.

4   International Space Station Program Science Forum. *International Space Station Benefits for Humanity.* 2nd ed. Washington, DC: NASA, 2015. https://www.nasa.gov/sites/default/files/atoms/files/jsc_benefits_for_humanity_tagged_6-30-15.pdf.

5   Space Tango. "Our Story." Accessed January 20, 2020. https://spacetango.com/about.

6   NASA. "15 Ways the International Space Station Is Benefiting Earth." NASA Space Station Research. August 6, 2017. http://www.nasa.gov/mission_pages/station/research/news/15_ways_iss_benefits_earth.

7   Carlson, Emily, and Mika Ono. "Exploring the Elusive World of Life's Most Vital Proteins." *Live Science,* April 17, 2013. https://www.livescience.com/28734-vital-proteins-explained-nigms.html.

8   NASA. "Bringing Space Station Ultrasound to the Ends of the Earth." International Space Station Feature. Last updated April 4, 2019. http://www.nasa.gov/mission_pages/station/research/news/b4h-3rd/hh-bringing-space-station-ultrasound.

9   Foust, Jeff. "Industry Sees New Opportunities for Space Manufacturing."
     SpaceNews, December 6, 2017. https://spacenews.com/industry-sees-new-
     opportunities-for-space-manufacturing.

10   Space Tango. "Our Story." Accessed January 20, 2020. https://spacetango.com/
     about.

11   Space Tango. "Tango Lab." Accessed May 10, 2019. https://spacetango.com/
     tangolab.

12   Space Tango. "What's Flying? A Look at Space Tango NG-10 Payloads."
     November 19, 2018. https://spacetango.com/whats-flying-a-look-at-space-
     tango-ng-10-payloads.

13   Space Tango. "Space Tango Provides Updates from OA-9 Mission." June 13,
     2018. https://spacetango.com/space-tango-provides-updates-from-oa-9-
     mission.

14   Space Tango. "Space Tango Unveils ST-42 for Scalable Manufacturing in Space
     for Earth-Based Applications." November 15, 2018. https://spacetango.com/
     st-42/.

15   James A. M. Muncy (President and Founder, PoliSpace), in discussion with the
     author, March 25, 2017.

16   "SpacePharma." Most Innovative Companies, *Fast Company,* accessed May 10,
     2019. https://www.fastcompany.com/company/spacepharma.

17   SpacePharma. "Simply Microgravity." Accessed May 10, 2019. https://www.
     space4p.com.

18   Yossi Yamin (Cofounder and CEO, SpacePharma), in conversation with the
     author, January 17, 2017.

19   Christopher Stott (Cofounder, Chair, and CEO, ManSat), in discussion with
     the author, May 31, 2017.

20   Christopher Stott (Cofounder, Chair, and CEO, ManSat), in discussion with
     the author, May 31, 2017.

21   Sloat, Sarah. "The ISS Will Retire in 2028." *Inverse,* May 19, 2016. https://www.
     inverse.com/article/15852-nasa-chief-announces-a-2028-expiration-date-for-
     the-iss-it-is-inevitable.

22   Minkel, JR. "Is the International Space Station Worth $100 Billion?" *Space,*
     November 1, 2010. https://www.space.com/9435-international-space-station-
     worth-100-billion.html.

23   NASA. "Economic Development of Space." International Space Station Feature.
     Last updated August 3, 2017. http://www.nasa.gov/mission_pages/station/
     research/benefits/economic_development.

24   NASA. "Economic Development of Space." International Space Station Feature.
     Last updated August 3, 2017. http://www.nasa.gov/mission_pages/station/
     research/benefits/economic_development.

25   NASA Commercial Crew & Cargo Program Office. "CCDev." Accessed
     February 5, 2020. https://www.nasa.gov/offices/c3po/partners/ccdev_info.
     html.

26 Smith, Rich. "The Truth About NASA's Plan to 'Privatize the Space Station."
    Motley Fool, June 30, 2019. https://www.fool.com/investing/2019/06/30/the-
    truth-about-nasas-plan-to-privatize-the-space.aspx.

    NASA. "NASA Opens International Space Station to New Commercial
    Opportunities." Press Release. Last updated July 17, 2019. http://www.nasa.
    gov/press-release/nasa-opens-international-space-station-to-new-commercial-
    opportunities-private.

27 NASA. "NextSTEP I: Commercial Destination Development in Low Earth
    Orbit Using the International Space Station." NEXTStep Feature. Last updated
    August 27, 2019. http://www.nasa.gov/nextstep/issport.

28 Grush, Loren. "An Inflatable Space Habitat Is Getting Attached to the ISS
    This Weekend." *Verge,* last updated April 15, 2016. https://www.theverge.
    com/2016/4/12/11416290/nasa-inflatable-space-habitat-international-space-
    station-beam.

29 Foust, Jeff. "NASA Planning to Keep BEAM Module on ISS for the Long Haul."
    Space News, August 12, 2019. https://spacenews.com/nasa-planning-to-keep-
    beam-module-on-iss-for-the-long-haul.

30 Simberg, Rand. "Bigelow Aerospace Shows Off Bigger, Badder Space Real
    Estate." *Popular Mechanics,* October 28, 2010. https://www.popularmechanics.
    com/science/space/news/bigelow-aerospace-ba2100-hotel.

31 NASA. "Space Station's Expandable Habitat." International Space Station
    Feature. Last updated August 6, 2017. http://www.nasa.gov/image-feature/
    space-stations-expandable-habitat.

32 Muoio, Danielle. "Space Stations for Tourists Could Be Here as Soon as 2020."
    Business Insider, April 14, 2016. https://www.businessinsider.com/bigelow-
    aerospace-station-could-support-space-tourism-2016-4.

33 Wall, Mike. "Bigelow Aerospace Launches New Company to Operate Private
    Space Stations." *Space,* February 20, 2018. https://www.space.com/39752-
    bigelow-space-operations-private-space-stations.html.

34 Davis, Jason. "A Company You've Never Heard of Plans to Build the World's
    First Private Space Station." *Planetary Society,* January 3, 2017. http://www.
    planetary.org/blogs/jason-davis/2016/20170103-axiom-profile.html.

35 Foust, Jeff. "A Stepping-Stone to Commercial Space Stations." *Space Review,*
    July 15, 2019. http://www.thespacereview.com/article/3033/1.

36 Foust, Jeff. "Axiom to Fly Crew Dragon Mission to the Space Station." *Space
    News,* March 5, 2020. https://spacenews.com/axiom-to-fly-crew-dragon-
    mission-to-the-space-station.

37 Wall, Mike. "1st Private Space Station Will Become an Off-Earth
    Manufacturing Hub." *Space,* June 05, 2017. https://www.space.com/37079-
    axiom-commercial-space-station-manufacturing.html.

38 "The Axiom Space Tests Key Space Station Acrylic Sample on ISS in Alpha
    Space's MISSE Facility." *Yahoo Finance,* May 13, 2019. https://finance.yahoo.
    com/news/axiom-space-tests-key-space-160000689.html.

Chapter Twelve

1   Shahin Farshchi (Partner, Lux Capital), in discussion with the author, May 12, 2017.

2   Jacobson, Robert C. "Space: Humanity's Gateway to Infinite Wealth, Sustainability for All." *Medium,* October 16, 2018. https://medium.com/@ spaceguitar/space-humanitys-gateway-to-infinite-wealth-sustainability-for-all-72d5196883c4.

3   Bilton, Nick. "A Conversation With Steve Jurvetson, Space Investor and Rocket Maker." Bits, *New York Times,* March 17, 2014. https://bits.blogs.nytimes. com/2014/03/17/qa-with-steve-jurvetson-space-investor-and-rocket-maker.

4   Buzek, Jerzy. "Investment in Space Sector Is 'Not an Extravagance but a Necessity.'" *Parliament Magazine,* February 2, 2015. https://www. theparliamentmagazine.eu/articles/opinion/investment-space-sector-not-extravagance-necessity.

5   Yonatan Winetraub (Cofounder, SpaceIL), in discussion with the author, November 9, 2016.

6   Amaresh Kollipara (Chief Revenue Officer, OffWorld; Founder, Earth2Orbit), in discussion with the author, July 20, 2019.

7   Friedman, Josh. "Entrepreneur Tries His Midas Touch in Space." *Los Angeles Times,* April 22, 2003. https://www.latimes.com/archives/la-xpm-2003-apr-22-fi-spacex22-story.html.

8   "The 5 Stages of Technology Adoption." *On Digital Marketing,* accessed May 1, 2019. https://ondigitalmarketing.com/learn/odm/foundations/5-customer-segments-technology-adoption.

     Everett, Roger. *Diffusion of Innovations.* 5th ed. New York: Free Press, 2003.

9   Andrew Barton (Aerospace Technology Consultant; Venture Partner, Syndicate 708), in discussion with the author, November 12, 2016.

10   Rob Coneybeer (Managing Director of Shasta Ventures), in discussion with the author, October 3, 2019.

11   Frank Salzgeber (Head of the Technology Transfer and Business Incubation Office, European Space Agency), in discussion with the author, September 10, 2018.

PART IV

Chapter Thirteen

1   Jeff Greason (Cofounder and CTO, Electric Sky; Cofounder, XCOR Aerospace), in discussion with the author, March 4, 2017.

2   Steve Goldberg (Operating Partner, Venrock), in discussion with the author, November 1, 2016.

3   Mark Boggett (CEO & Managing Partner, Seraphim Capital), in discussion with the author, June 13, 2017.

Chapter Fourteen

1   Higginbotham, Brian. "The Space Economy: An Industry Takes Off." U.S.
     Chamber of Commerce. October 11, 2018. https://www.uschamber.com/
     series/above-the-fold/the-space-economy-industry-takes.

2   Bryce Space and Technology. "Start-Up Space: Update on Investment in
     Commercial Space Ventures. 2020." Industry Analysis. Accessed March 9, 2020.
     https://brycetech.com/download.php?f=Bryce_Start_Up_Space_2020.pdf.

3   Space Angels. "Space Investment Quarterly: Q1 2018." General Industry
     Trends. April 10, 2018. Retrieved from archive August 3, 2020. Internet
     Archive. https://web.archive.org/web/20180426112624/https://www.
     spaceangels.com/post/space-investment-quarterly-q1-2018.

4   Manessis, George. "Boeing Leads Gains in Stocks Linked to Space
     Exploration." *CNBC,* August 17, 2017. https://www.cnbc.com/2017/08/17/
     kenshos-space-index-soars-past-the-sp.html.

5   Pressman, Aaron. "Space Startups Grabbed the Imagination-and Dollars–Of
     Tech Investors." *Fortune,* January 10, 2019. https://fortune.com/2019/01/10/
     space-startups-spacex-bezos-vc.

6   Space Angels. "Space Investment Quarterly: Q1 2018." General Industry
     Trends. April 10, 2018. Retrieved from archive August 3, 2020. Internet
     Archive. https://web.archive.org/web/20180426112624/https://www.
     spaceangels.com/post/space-investment-quarterly-q1-2018.

7   Sheetz, Michael. "Morgan Stanley Says 2019 Could 'Be the Year for Space,' Led
     by the Likes of SpaceX and Blue Origin." *CNBC,* November 28, 2018. https://
     www.cnbc.com/2018/11/28/morgan-stanley-says-2019-could-be-the-year-for-
     space.html.

8   Space Angels. "Space Investment Quarterly: Q1 2019." General Industry
     Trends. April 9, 2019. Retrieved from archive August 3, 2020. Internet Archive.
     https://web.archive.org/web/20190612014607/https://www.spaceangels.com/
     post/space-investment-quarterly-q1-2019.

9   Bryce Space and Technology. "Start-Up Space: Update on Investment in
     Commercial Space Ventures. 2020." Industry Analysis. Accessed March 9, 2020.
     https://brycetech.com/download.php?f=Bryce_Start_Up_Space_2020.pdf.

10   Foust, Jeff. "'Golden Period' for Space Startup Investment Continues."
     SpaceNews, September 12, 2018. https://spacenews.com/golden-period-for-
     space-startup-investment-continues.

11   Pressman, Aaron. "Space Startups Grabbed the Imagination-and Dollars–Of
     Tech Investors." *Fortune,* January 10, 2019. https://fortune.com/2019/01/10/
     space-startups-spacex-bezos-vc.

12   Bryce Space and Technology. "Start-Up Space: Update on Investment in
     Commercial Space Ventures. 2020." Industry Analysis. Accessed March 9, 2020.
     https://brycetech.com/download.php?f=Bryce_Start_Up_Space_2020.pdf.

13   Bryce Space and Technology. "Start-Up Space: Update on Investment in
     Commercial Space Ventures. 2020." Industry Analysis. Accessed March 9, 2020.
     https://brycetech.com/download.php?f=Bryce_Start_Up_Space_2020.pdf.

14 Mithril. "Built to Last." Accessed September 27, 2019. https://www.mithril.com.

15 Sorensen, Jodi. "New Financing, New Acquisition." *Spaceflight*, June 21, 2016. https://spaceflight.com/new-financing-new-acquisition.

16 Loizos, Connie. "Peter Thiel's Other Fund, Mithril Capital Management, Raises $600 Million." *TechCrunch*, April 1, 2016. http://social.techcrunch.com/2016/04/01/peter-thiels-other-fund-mithril-capital-management-raises-600-million.

17 Pham, Sherisse. "SoftBank Already Has a $100 Billion Tech Fund. Now It's Launching Another." *CNN*, May 9, 2019. https://www.cnn.com/2019/05/09/tech/softbank-vision-fund-2/index.html.

18 Crunchbase. "OneWeb." Accessed September 27, 2019. https://www.crunchbase.com/organization/oneweb.

19 SoftBank Group. "Vision." Corporate Philosophy, Vision and Values. Accessed September 27, 2019. https://group.softbank/en/corp/about/philosophy/vision.

20 Sheetz, Michael. "Space Startup Adds $1.25 Billion from SoftBank and Others to Mass Produce Internet Satellites." *CNBC*, March 18, 2019. https://www.cnbc.com/2019/03/18/oneweb-adds-1point25-billion-from-softbank-and-others-for-satellites.html.

21 Anthony Freeman (Innovation Foundry, NASA Jet Propulsion Laboratory), in discussion with the author, May 5, 2017.

22 Sheetz, Michael. "Super Fast Travel Using Outer Space Could Be $20 Billion Market, Disrupting Airlines, UBS Predicts." *CNBC*, March 18, 2019. https://www.cnbc.com/2019/03/18/ubs-space-travel-and-space-tourism-a-23-billion-business-in-a-decade.html.

23 Foust, Jeff. "A Trillion-Dollar Space Industry Will Require New Markets." *SpaceNews*, July 6, 2018. https://spacenews.com/a-trillion-dollar-space-industry-will-require-new-markets.

24 Wang, Brian. "SpaceX BFR will make multi-trillion dollar space industry by 2030." *Next Big Future*, February 11, 2018. https://www.nextbigfuture.com/2018/02/spacex-bfr-will-make-multi-trillion-dollar-space-industry-by-2030.html.

25 Sheetz, Michael. "Super Fast Travel Using Outer Space Could Be $20 Billion Market, Disrupting Airlines, UBS Predicts." *CNBC*, March 18, 2019. https://www.cnbc.com/2019/03/18/ubs-space-travel-and-space-tourism-a-23-billion-business-in-a-decade.html.

26 Monsanto. "Monsanto to Acquire the Climate Corporation, Combination to Provide Farmers with Broad Suite of Tools Offering Greater On-Farm Insights." News Release. October 2, 2013. https://monsanto.com/news-releases/monsanto-to-acquire-the-climate-corporation-combination-to-provide-farmers-with-broad-suite-of-tools-offering-greater-on-farm-insights.

27 Foust, Jeff. "Google's Skybox Imaging Has New Name, Business Model." *SpaceNews*, March 9, 2016. https://spacenews.com/googles-skybox-imaging-has-new-name-business-model.

Foust, Jeff. "Planet to Acquire Terra Bella from Google." *SpaceNews,* February 3, 2017. https://spacenews.com/planet-to-acquire-terra-bella-from-google.

28   Foust, Jeff. "Northrop Grumman to Acquire Orbital ATK." *SpaceNews,* September 18, 2017. http://spacenews.com/northrop-grumman-to-acquire-orbital-atk.

29   Schingler, Robbie. "Planet to Acquire Boundless to Further Support U.S. Government Business." Planet Labs. December 18, 2018. https://www.planet.com/pulse/planet-to-acquire-boundless.

30   "UrtheCast Closes Geosys Acquisition, Secures US$12 Million Term Loan and Provides Corporate Update." *SpaceRef,* January 15, 2019. http://www.spaceref.com/news/viewpr.html?pid=53574.

31   Northrop Grumman. "Northrop Grumman to Acquire Orbital ATK for $9.2 Billion." News Release. September 18, 2017. https://news.northropgrumman.com/news/releases/northrop-grumman-to-acquire-orbital-atk-for-9-2-billion.

32   Henderson, Richard. "Virgin Galactic Hits $2.3bn Valuation in Public Launch." *Financial Times,* October 28, 2019. https://www.ft.com/content/8e86eb5a-f992-11e9-a354-36acbbb0d9b6.

33   Browne, Ryan. "Richard Branson's Virgin Galactic Is Set to Be the First Space-Tourism Company to Go Public." *CNBC,* July 9, 2019. https://www.cnbc.com/2019/07/09/richard-branson-space-unit-virgin-galactic-plans-to-go-public-wsj.html.

34   Browne, Ryan. "Richard Branson's Virgin Galactic Is Set to Be the First Space-Tourism Company to Go Public." *CNBC,* July 9, 2019. https://www.cnbc.com/2019/07/09/richard-branson-space-unit-virgin-galactic-plans-to-go-public-wsj.html.

35   Henderson, Richard. "Virgin Galactic Hits $2.3bn Valuation in Public Launch." *Financial Times,* October 28, 2019. https://www.ft.com/content/8e86eb5a-f992-11e9-a354-36acbbb0d9b6.

36   Foust, Jeff. "Virgin Galactic Expects Rapid Conclusion of SpaceShipTwo Test Flights after Downtime." *SpaceNews,* April 19, 2019. https://spacenews.com/virgin-galactic-expects-rapid-conclusion-of-spaceshiptwo-test-flights-after-downtime.

37   Grush, Loren. "The Italian Air Force Plans to Fly Researchers on One of Virgin Galactic's Flights to Space." *Verge,* October 2, 2019. https://www.theverge.com/2019/10/2/20893210/virgin-galactic-italian-air-force-research-human-spaceflight-vss-unity.

38   Moynihan, Ruqayyah, and Thomas Giraudet. "Richard Branson Wants Virgin Galactic to Send People to Space Every 32 Hours by 2023." France, *Business Insider,* September 10, 2019. https://www.businessinsider.com/branson-virgin-galactic-people-space-every-32-hours-2019-9.

39   Sheetz, Michael. "Satellite Builder and Data Business Spire Raises $40 Million as IPO Plans Come into View." *CNBC,* September 25, 2019. https://www.cnbc.com/2019/09/25/satellite-data-company-spire-raises-40-million-with-ipo-plans-in-view.html.

40   George T. Whitesides (CEO, Virgin Galactic), in discussion with the author, January 28, 2019.

41   Meagan Crawford (Managing Partner, SpaceFund; Cofounder, Eden Growth Systems; Cofounder, Delta-V), in discussion with the author, January 23, 2019.

42   Meagan Crawford (Managing Partner, SpaceFund; Cofounder, Eden Growth Systems; Cofounder, Delta-V), in discussion with the author, January 23, 2019.

Chapter Fifteen

1   Van Espahbodi (Cofounder and Managing Partner, Starburst Aerospace), in discussion with the author, June 28, 2017.

2   Simon Worden (Chair, Breakthrough Prize Foundation for Breakthrough Initiatives), in discussion with the author, August 8, 2017.

3   Joerg Kreisel (CEO, JKIC), email to the author, October 9, 2019.

PART V

Chapter Sixteen

1   Bob Werb (Cofounder, Space Frontier Foundation), correspondence with the author, December 23, 2019.

2   Mack, Eric. "Thirty-Million-Page Backup of Humanity Headed to Moon Aboard Israeli Lander." *CNET*, February 24, 2019. https://www.cnet.com/news/backup-of-humanity-on-its-way-to-the-moon-aboard-israeli-lander.

3   Musk, Elon (@elonmusk). "As individuals, we will all die in blink of an eye on a galactic timescale. What can live on for long time is civilization…" Twitter, June 24, 2018. https://twitter.com/elonmusk/status/1011139030476451840.

4   SpaceChain. "The Arch Mission Foundation and SpaceChain Create Orbital LibraryTM, First Archive in Space." Mission Feature. February 1, 2019. https://spacechain.com/the-arch-mission-foundation-and-spacechain-create-orbital-library.

5   Boyle, Alan. "How Satellites and Blockchain Go Together." *GeekWire*, February 1, 2019. https://www.geekwire.com/2019/satellites-blockchain-go-together.

6   Arch Mission Foundation. "The Lunar Library: Genesis (SpaceIL, 2019)—The First Library on Another Celestial Body." Mission Feature. Accessed October 9, 2019. https://www.archmission.org/spaceil.

7   Mack, Eric. "Thirty-Million-Page Backup of Humanity Headed to Moon Aboard Israeli Lander." *CNET*, February 24, 2019. https://www.cnet.com/news/backup-of-humanity-on-its-way-to-the-moon-aboard-israeli-lander.

8   Arch Mission Foundation. "Conrad Challenge (Blue Origin, 2019)—Arch Mission Meet Blue Origin." Mission Feature. Accessed October 9, 2019. https://www.archmission.org/conrad-challenge.

9   Howell, Elizabeth. "Lagrange Points: Parking Places in Space." *Space*, August 22, 2017. https://www.space.com/30302-lagrange-points.html.

10   Arch Mission Foundation. "Our Missions." Accessed October 9, 2019. https://www.archmission.org/missions.

11   Ryssdal, Kai, and Bridget Bodnar. "What It Means to Be a Futurist." *Marketplace*, December 5, 2016. https://www.marketplace.org/2016/12/05/what-it-means-be-futurist.

12   Don Brancato (Chief Strategy Architect, Boeing), in discussion with the author, May 4, 2017.

13   Don Brancato (Chief Strategy Architect, Boeing), in discussion with the author, May 4, 2017.

14   Kay, Alan. "How to Invent the Future I." Lecture. Stanford, Center for Professional Development, May 9, 2017. YouTube video, 58:01. May 25, 2017. https://www.youtube.com/watch?v=id1WShzzMCQ.

15   Jewell, Catherine. "Giving Innovation Wings: How Boeing Uses Its IP." *World Intellectual Property Organization Magazine,* February 2014. https://www.wipo.int/wipo_magazine/en/2014/01/article_0004.html.

16   Jewell, Catherine. "Giving Innovation Wings: How Boeing Uses Its IP." *World Intellectual Property Organization Magazine,* February 2014. https://www.wipo.int/wipo_magazine/en/2014/01/article_0004.html.

17   Jewell, Catherine. "Giving Innovation Wings: How Boeing Uses Its IP." *World Intellectual Property Organization Magazine,* February 2014. https://www.wipo.int/wipo_magazine/en/2014/01/article_0004.html.

18   Greenberg, Joel. "Positron Dynamics Paves the Road to the Final Frontier." Deep Technology—Dissected, *Medium*, January 9, 2017. https://medium.com/dissected-by-propel-x/positron-dynamics-paves-the-road-to-the-final-frontier-d00e60133b67.

19   Will Porteous (General Partner and COO, RRE Ventures), in discussion with the author, May 9, 2017.

Chapter Seventeen

1   Dave Barnhart (Research Professor, Department of Astronautical Engineering at the University of Southern California), in discussion with the author, May 4, 2017.

2   SpaceIL (@TeamSpaceIL). "The dream goes on! Morris Kahn just announced the launching of Beresheet 2.0 #Beresheet2.0 #IsraeltotheMoon." Twitter, April 13, 2019. https://twitter.com/TeamSpaceIL/status/1117108316554125312?s=20.

3   Garun, Natt. "Israeli Team Will No Longer Send a Second Spacecraft to the Moon." *Verge*, June 15, 2019. https://www.theverge.com/2019/6/25/18758794/spaceil-beresheet-2-moon-spacecraft-new-objective-challenge.

4   SpaceIL (@TeamSpaceIL). "'This is part of my message to the younger generation: Even if you do not succeed, you get up again and try.' - Morris Kahn." Twitter, April 15, 2019. https://twitter.com/TeamSpaceIL/status/1117691935085486080?s=20.

5   Dezsö Molnár (Staff Inventor, WET Design), in discussion with the author, January 12, 2019.

6   Yonatan Winetraub (Cofounder, SpaceIL), in discussion with the author, November 9, 2016.

7   Cohen Gilliland, Haley. "The World's Smallest Big Rocket Company." *MIT Technology Review*, June 26, 2019. https://www.technologyreview. com/s/613757/dave-masten-rocket-company-reinvent-nasa.

8   Cohen Gilliland, Haley. "The World's Smallest Big Rocket Company." *MIT Technology Review*, June 26, 2019. https://www.technologyreview. com/s/613757/dave-masten-rocket-company-reinvent-nasa.

9   Kuhns, Matthew. "Masten Space Systems and P3 Technologies Team to Offer Line of Electric Pumps." Masten Space Systems. July 15, 2019. https://www. masten.aero/blog.

10 Sean Mahoney (CEO, Masten Space Systems), in conversation with the author, July 31, 2019.

11 Cohen Gilliland, Haley. "The World's Smallest Big Rocket Company." *MIT Technology Review*, June 26, 2019. https://www.technologyreview. com/s/613757/dave-masten-rocket-company-reinvent-nasa.

12 Griffin, Tren. "A Dozen Things I Learned Being Involved in One of the Most Ambitious Startups Ever Conceived (Teledesic)." *25iq*, July 23, 2016. https://25iq.com/2016/07/23/a-dozen-things-i-learned-being-involved-in-one-of-the-most-ambitious-startups-ever-conceived-teledesic.

13 Foust, Jeff. "Exos Seeks To Revive Armadillo Rocket Technology." *SpaceNews*, May 11, 2015. https://spacenews.com/exos-seeks-to-revive-armadillo-rocket-technology.

14 Foust, Jeff. "Exos Seeks To Revive Armadillo Rocket Technology." *SpaceNews*, May 11, 2015. https://spacenews.com/exos-seeks-to-revive-armadillo-rocket-technology.

15 Beal Aerospace. "Home." Accessed September 10, 2019. https://www.beal-aerospace.com.

16 Breakstone, Alan. "Will Spacex Succeed…Where Beal Failed?" *Space Future*, March 26, 2003. http://www.spacefuture.com/journal/journal. cgi?art=2003.03.26.will_spacex_succeed;l=channel.

17 Reingold, Jennifer. "Hondas in Space." *Fast Company*, February 1, 2005. https://www.fastcompany.com/52065/hondas-space.

18 Millard, Doug. "Iridium: Story of a Communications Solution No One Listened To." *New Scientist*, August 3, 2016. https://www.newscientist.com/ article/mg23130850-700-iridium-story-of-a-communications-solution-no-one-listened-to.

19 Bezos, Jeff. "Innovation Spotlights." Fireside Chat, re:MARS from Amazon, Las Vegas, June 6, 2019.

20 Isidore, Chris. "RadioShack Will Take Its Pitch to Space." Money, *CNN*, May 2, 2001. https://money.cnn.com/2001/05/02/companies/space_advertising/ index.htm.

21 Messier, Doug. "Henry Vanderbilt on XCOR's Bankruptcy." *Parabolic Arc,* November 10, 2017. http://www.parabolicarc.com/2017/11/10/henry-vanderbilt-xcors-bankruptcy.

22 Jeff Greason (Cofounder and CTO, Electric Sky; Cofounder, XCOR Aerospace), in discussion with the author, April 21, 2020.

23 Foust, Jeff. "XCOR Aerospace Files for Bankruptcy." *SpaceNews,* November 10, 2017. https://spacenews.com/xcor-aerospace-files-for-bankruptcy.

24 Messier, Doug. "Henry Vanderbilt on XCOR's Bankruptcy." *Parabolic Arc,* November 10, 2017. http://www.parabolicarc.com/2017/11/10/henry-vanderbilt-xcors-bankruptcy.

25 Messier, Doug. "Luxembourg Lost $13.7 Million on Planetary Resources Investment." *Parabolic Arc,* November 19, 2018. http://www.parabolicarc.com/2018/11/19/luxembourg-lost-137-million-planetary-resources-investment.

26 Foust, Jeff. "Planetary Resources Revising Plans after Funding Setback." *SpaceNews,* March 12, 2018. https://spacenews.com/planetary-resources-revising-plans-after-funding-setback.

27 Foust, Jeff. "Asteroid Mining Company Planetary Resources Acquired by Blockchain Firm." *Space,* November 2, 2018. https://www.space.com/42324-asteroid-mining-company-planetary-resources-acquired.html.

28 Guillermo Söhnlein (Cofounder and CEO, Blue Marble Exploration), in discussion with the author, December 6, 2018.

29 Simon Worden (Chair, Breakthrough Prize Foundation for Breakthrough Initiatives), in discussion with the author, August 8, 2017.

Chapter Eighteen

1 Brandon Farwell (Partner, XFund), in discussion with the author, February 11, 2019.

2 Kartik Kumar (Cofounder, satsearch), in discussion with the author, October 6, 2019.

3 Lisa Rich (Cofounder, Hemisphere Ventures and Xplore), call with the author, December 12, 2019.

4 Chris Biddy (Cofounder and CEO, Astro Digital), in discussion with the author, February 27, 2019.

5 Jason Dunn (Cofounder and Director, Made In Space), in discussion with the author, November 3, 2016.

6 Federico Sciammarella (President and CTO, MxD), in discussion with the author, November 2, 2016.

7 Jason Dunn (Cofounder and Director, Made In Space), in discussion with the author, November 3, 2016.

8   Musk, Elon. "A Conversation With Elon Musk About Starship." Produced by *Everyday Astronauts*. SpaceX Starship Update, Cameron County, Texas, 2019. YouTube video, 17:05. October 1, 2019. https://www.youtube.com/ watch?v=cIQ36Kt7UVg&feature=youtu.be&t=230.

9   Frank Salzgeber (Head of the Technology Transfer and Business Incubation Office, European Space Agency), in discussion with the author, September 10, 2018.

10   Kartik Kumar (Cofounder, satsearch), in discussion with the author, October 6, 2019.

11   Daniel Faber (CEO, Orbit Fab), in discussion with the author, January 3, 2019.

12   Ulanoff, Lance. "Elon Musk: Secrets of a Highly Effective Entrepreneur." *Mashable*, April 13, 2012. https://mashable.com/2012/04/13/elon-musk-secrets-of-effectiveness/#dHzYc5SgAaqH.

13   Monica Jan (Cofounder and former Managing Partner of LightSpeed Innovations), in discussion with the author, June 11, 2017.

14   Starburst Aerospace. "Some Facts About Starburst." Accessed October 9, 2019. http://starburst.aero.

15   Van Espahbodi (Cofounder and Managing Partner, Starburst Aerospace), in discussion with the author, June 28, 2017.

16   Monica Jan (Cofounder and former Managing Partner of LightSpeed Innovations), in discussion with the author, June 11, 2017.

17   Ellen Chang (Cofounder and Board Member, Syndicate 708), in discussion with the author, June 9, 2017.

18   Shaun Arora (Managing Director, MiLA Capital), in discussion with the author, March 12, 2019.

19   Shaun Arora (Managing Director, MiLA Capital), in discussion with the author, March 12, 2019.

20   Moonshot Space Company. "The MoonShot Model." Accessed October 10, 2019. https://www.moonshotspace.co/model.

21   Moonshot Space Company. "Reuniting Humanity and Space." Accessed October 10, 2019. https://www.moonshotspace.co/about.

Chapter Nineteen

1   Ian Fichtenbaum (Senior Vice President and Space & Satellite Specialist, American Industrial Acquisition Corporation; Director, Bradford Space group), in discussion with the author, April 28, 2017.

2   Gupta, Nayanee, Bhavya Lal, and Emily J. Sylak-Glassman. *Global Trends in Civil and Commercial Space*. Washington, DC: Institute for Defense Analyses: Science & Technology Policy Institute, 2015. https://www.ida.org/~/media/ Corporate/Files/Publications/STPIPubs/2015/d5682final.ashx.

3   Rick Tumlinson (Founding Partner, SpaceFund; Cofounder, Deep Space Industries, Space Frontier Foundation, Orbital Outfitters, New Worlds Institute), in discussion with the author, December 20, 2018.

PART VI

Chapter Twenty

1   Murtaugh, Dan. "Space May Be Next Frontier for Earth's Crude Oil Giants, Analyst Says." *Bloomberg,* April 23, 2017. https://www.bloomberg.com/news/articles/2017-04-23/space-the-final-frontier-seen-for-earth-s-crude-oil-giants.

2   Foust, Jeff. "UAE to Establish Space Investment Plan." *SpaceNews,* January 22, 2019. https://spacenews.com/uae-to-establish-space-investment-plan.

3   Australia. Department of Industry, Innovation and Science. "Australian Space Agency." June 18, 2018. https://www.industry.gov.au/strategies-for-the-future/australian-space-agency.

4   Australia. Department of Industry, Innovation and Science. "Australian Space Agency." June 18, 2018. https://www.industry.gov.au/strategies-for-the-future/australian-space-agency.

5   LATCOSMOS. "Why Are We Doing This?" Accessed October 7, 2019. https://www.latcosmos.org/why.

6   Business Wire. "Teleglobal Brings Broadband Access and Mobile Connectivity Services to Rural Communities in Indonesia via SES Networks." Press release. April 24, 2019. https://www.businesswire.com/news/home/20190423006035/en/Teleglobal-Brings-Broadband-Access-Mobile-Connectivity-Services.

7   Radu, Sintia. "The Global Race to Space." *US News,* August 27, 2018. https://www.usnews.com/news/best-countries/articles/2018-08-27/60-years-after-nasa-a-global-space-race.

8   Kyu Hwang (Space Industry Consultant, DecisionBox), in discussion with the author, July 25, 2019.

9   ispace. "Japan Airlines Becomes Corporate Partner of ispace's HAKUTO-R Program." News. February 22, 2019. https://ispace-inc.com/news/?p=1042.

10   Messier, Doug. "Infostellar Closes $7.3 Million Series A Round for Satellite Antenna Sharing Platform." *Parabolic Arc,* September 13, 2017. http://www.parabolicarc.com/2017/09/13/infostellar-closes-73-million-series-satellite-antenna-sharing-platform.

11   Yamaguchi, Mari. "Japanese Space Startup Aims to Compete with US Rivals." *Phys.org,* May 15, 2019. https://phys.org/news/2019-05-japan-space-startup-aims-rivals.html.

12   Sheetz, Michael. "Japanese Government Launches $940 Million Fund for Space Start-ups." *CNBC,* March 20, 2018. https://www.cnbc.com/2018/03/20/japan-offers-940-million-to-boost-nations-space-startups.html.

13   Wang, Kent. "China's Space Program Soars." *Asia Times,* March 25, 2019. https://www.asiatimes.com/2019/03/opinion/chinas-space-program-soars.

14   Wang, Kent. "China's Space Program Soars." *Asia Times,* March 25, 2019. https://www.asiatimes.com/2019/03/opinion/chinas-space-program-soars.

15   Foust, Jeff. "New Opportunities Emerging for U.S.-China Space Cooperation."
     SpaceNews, April 8, 2019. https://spacenews.com/new-opportunities-
     emerging-for-u-s-china-space-cooperation.

16   Moss, Trefor. "In China's New Space Odyssey, 80 Startups Race to Get Into
     Orbit." *Wall Street Journal,* Updated November 11, 2019. https://www.wsj.com/
     articles/chinese-startups-push-into-space-business-1541851211.

17   Moss, Trefor. "In China's New Space Odyssey, 80 Startups Race to Get Into
     Orbit." *Wall Street Journal,* Updated November 11, 2019. https://www.wsj.com/
     articles/chinese-startups-push-into-space-business-1541851211.

18   "5 Developments in NewSpace for 2018." NewSpace, *Nanalyze,* December 23,
     2017. https://www.nanalyze.com/2017/12/5-developments-newspace-2018.

19   India. Department of Space. Indian Space Research Organisation. "ISRO
     Crosses 50 International Customer Satellite Launch Mark." News Release.
     Accessed July 10, 2019. https://www.isro.gov.in/isro-crosses-50-international-
     customer-satellite-launch-mark.

20   Mathewson, Samantha. "India Launches Record-Breaking 104 Satellites on
     Single Rocket." *Space,* February 15, 2017. https://www.space.com/35709-india-
     rocket-launches-record-104-satellites.html.

21   Bartels, Meghan. "India Will Launch Its Own Astronauts to Space by 2022,
     Government Says." *Space,* August 29, 2018. https://www.space.com/41657-
     india-will-launch-astronauts-in-2022.html.

22   Singh, Surendra. "New Space Company to Facilitate Isro Tech Transfer to
     Industry." *Times of India,* last updated February 21, 2019. https://timesofindia.
     indiatimes.com/india/new-space-company-to-facilitate-isro-tech-transfer-to-
     industry/articleshow/68087995.cms.

23   Luca del Monte (Senior Manager, European Space Agency), in discussion with
     the author, August 6, 2019.

24   Frank Salzgeber (Head of the Technology Transfer and Business Incubation
     Office, European Space Agency), in discussion with the author, September 10,
     2018.

25   Marc Serres (CEO, Luxembourg Space Agency), in discussion with the author,
     February 22, 2019.

26   Grand Duchy of Luxembourg. Luxembourg Space Agency. "Milestones." Accessed
     January 28, 2020. https://space-agency.public.lu/en/agency/timeline.html.

27   "Étienne Schneider, Architect of Luxembourg's Space Sector, To Step Down
     In February 2020." *SpaceWatch.Global.* Accessed January 28, 2020. https://
     spacewatch.global/2020/01/etienne-schneider-architect-of-luxembourgs-
     space-sector-to-step-down-in-february-2020.

28   Grand Duchy of Luxembourg. Luxembourg Space Agency. "Milestones."
     Accessed January 28, 2020. https://space-agency.public.lu/en/agency/
     timeline.html.

Chapter Twenty-One

1   James Dunstan (Founder, Mobius Legal Group, PLLC), in discussion with the author, May 1, 2017.

2   U.S. Library of Congress. Congressional Research Service. *Commercial Space: Federal Regulation, Oversight, and Utilization*, by Daniel Morgan. R45416, version 2, updated. 2018. https://fas.org/sgp/crs/space/R45416.pdf.

3   Siraj, Amir. "Why Congress Must Act Quickly to Reform U.S. Space Law." *Harvard Political Review*, September 28, 2017. http://harvardpolitics.com/united-states/the-dangers-of-stagnancy-and-the-need-for-norms-in-u-s-space-law.

4   Davenport, Christian. "Companies Flood Earth's Orbit With Satellites, But No One's Directing Traffic." *Washington Post,* July 26, 2016. https://www.washingtonpost.com/business/economy/companies-flood-earths-orbit-with-satellites/2016/07/22/9db2e522-49ee-11e6-90a8-fb84201e0645_story.html.

5   Jeremy Conrad (Cofounder and CEO, Quartz; Founding Member, Lemnos Labs), in discussion with the author, October 6, 2017.

6   Rex Ridenoure (Cofounder and CEO, Ecliptic Enterprises Corporation), in discussion with the author, September 21, 2017.

7   U.S. Congress. House. Committee on Science, Space, and Technology. *Private Sector Lunar Expansion: Hearing before the Subcommittee on Space.* 115th Cong., 1st sess., September 7, 2017. https://www.govinfo.gov/content/pkg/CHRG-115hhrg27174/pdf/CHRG-115hhrg27174.pdf.

8   James Dunstan (Founder, Mobius Legal Group, PLLC), in discussion with the author, May 1, 2017.

9   David Livingston (Founder, The Space Show®), in discussion with the author, June 27, 2017.

10 Bowles, Norman. "Part 1: The Office of Commercial Space Transportation–Pre FAA." *Commercial Space Transportation* (blog), accessed February 19, 2020. http://www.commercialspacetransportation.com/ocst-1.

11 Bowles, Norman. "Part 1: The Office of Commercial Space Transportation–Pre FAA." *Commercial Space Transportation* (blog), accessed February 19, 2020. http://www.commercialspacetransportation.com/ocst-1.

12 Bowles, Norman. "Part 2: The Office of Commercial Space Transportation–Pre FAA." *Commercial Space Transportation* (blog), accessed February 19, 2020. http://www.commercialspacetransportation.com/ocst-2.

13 Bowles, Norman. "Part 2: The Office of Commercial Space Transportation–Pre FAA." *Commercial Space Transportation* (blog), accessed February 19, 2020. http://www.commercialspacetransportation.com/ocst-2.

14 Bowles, Norman. "Early History of Commercial Space Transportation." *Commercial Space Transportation* (blog), accessed February 19, 2020. http://www.commercialspacetransportation.com.

15 Bowles, Norman. "Early History of Commercial Space Transportation." *Commercial Space Transportation* (blog), accessed February 19, 2020. http://www.commercialspacetransportation.com.

16 Foust, Jeff. "Congress Launches Commercial Space Legislation." *Space Review,* May 26, 2019. http://www.thespacereview.com/article/2759/1.

17 U.S. Department of Transportation. Federal Aviation Administration. Final Rule. "Human Space Flight Requirements for Crew and Space Flight Participants; Final Rule, 14 CFR Parts 401, 415, 431, 435, 440 and 460." *Federal Register* 71, no. 241 (December 15, 2006): 75616. https://www.govinfo.gov/content/pkg/FR-2006-12-15/pdf/E6-21193.pdf.

18 U.S. Department of Transportation. Federal Aviation Administration. Office of Commercial Space Transportation. *New Regulations Govern Private Human Space Flight Requirements for Crew and Space Flight Participants.* Last updated December 30, 2016. https://www.faa.gov/about/office_org/headquarters_offices/ast/human_space_flight_reqs.

19 Foust, Jeff. "House Passes Commercial Space Bill." *SpaceNews,* November 17, 2015. https://spacenews.com/house-passes-commercial-space-bill.

20 Lurio, Charles A. "Rocket Lab Reusable, Starship's Path, Regulation Errors." *Lurio Report* 14, no. 7, September 4, 2019.

21 U.S. Congress. House. Committee on Science, Space, and Technology. *The Commercial Space Landscape: Innovation, Market, and Policy: Hearing before the Committee on Science, Space, and Technology, Subcommittee on Space and Aeronautics.* 116th Cong., 1st sess., July 25, 2019. https://science.house.gov/imo/media/doc/Stallmer%20Testimony2.pdf.

22 Lurio, Charles A. "Rocket Lab Reusable, Starship's Path, Regulation Errors." *Lurio Report* 14, no. 7, September 4, 2019.

23 Abrahamian, Atossa. "How a Tax Haven Is Leading the Race to Privatise Space." *Guardian,* September 15, 2017. http://www.theguardian.com/news/2017/sep/15/luxembourg-tax-haven-privatise-space.

24 Christopher Stott (Cofounder, Chair, and CEO, ManSat), in discussion with the author, May 31, 2017.

25 U.S. Federal Communications Commission. *FCC Fact Sheet: Streamlining Licensing Procedures for Small Satellites.* Report and Order, DA/FCC #: FCC-19-81, Docket/RM: 18-86. Washington, DC, August 2, 2019. https://docs.fcc.gov/public/attachments/DOC-358437A1.pdf.

26 Jones, Harry W. *The Recent Large Reduction in Space Launch Cost.* Moffett Field, CA: NASA Ames Research Center, 2018. https://ttu-ir.tdl.org/bitstream/handle/2346/74082/ICES_2018_81.pdf?sequence=1&isAllowed=y.

27 Hammes, T.X. "Cheap Technology Will Challenge U.S. Tactical Dominance." *Joint Force Quarterly* 81 (April 2016): 76–85. https://ndupress.ndu.edu/Portals/68/Documents/jfq/jfq-81/jfq-81_76-85_Hammes.pdf.

28 "Oil Price Fall Starts to Weigh on Banks." *Financial Times,* November 26, 2014. https://www.ft.com/content/c9f4e9e8-757c-11e4-b1bf-00144feabdc0.

29 Wingo, Dennis. *Creating a Bold and Courageous 21st Century American Space Policy.* International Institute of Space Commerce, 2017. https://iisc.im/portfolio-items/creating-a-courageous-21st-century-space-policy/.

30 Dennis Wingo (Founder and CEO, Skycorp Inc.), in discussion with the author, June 6, 2016.

31 Foust, Jeff. "International and Commercial Interest in the Moon." *Space Review,* April 24, 2019. http://www.thespacereview.com/article/3223/1.

32 Van Espahbodi (Cofounder and Managing Partner, Starburst Aerospace), in discussion with the author, June 28, 2017.

Chapter Twenty-Two

1 Redd, Nola Taylor. "Space Junk: Tracking & Removing Orbital Debris." *Space,* March 8, 2013. https://www.space.com/16518-space-junk.html.

2 Whitehead, Joanna. "Fascinating Footage Shows One of Aviation's Busiest Days." *Independent,* July 3, 2018. https://www.independent.co.uk/travel/news-and-advice/flights-sky-map-worldwide-air-traffic-aviation-busiest-day-june-a8428451.html.

3 NASA Johnson Space Center. "Frequently Asked Questions." Astromaterials Research & Exploration Science: Orbital Debris Program Office. Accessed September 10, 2019. https://orbitaldebris.jsc.nasa.gov/faq/#.

4 NASA. "Frequently Asked Questions: Orbital Debris." Last updated September 2, 2011. https://www.nasa.gov/news/debris_faq.html.

5 Kordella, Scott. "Op-Ed | Protecting Low Earth Orbit from Becoming the New Wild West." *SpaceNews,* March 16, 2019. https://spacenews.com/op-ed-protecting-low-earth-orbit-from-becoming-the-new-wild-west.

6 Bilby, Ethan. "Extreme Space Weather Can Wreak Havoc on Earth—These Tools Help Warn of the Dangers Ahead." *Phys.Org,* January 23, 2019. https://phys.org/news/2019-01-extreme-space-weather-wreak-havoc.html.

7 Messier, Doug. "Space Weather Blackout Could Cost U.S. $40 Billion Per Day." *Parabolic Arc,* January 19, 2017. http://www.parabolicarc.com/2017/01/19/space-weather-blackout-cost-40-billion-day.

8 NASA. "July 12, 1962: The Day Information Went Global." NASA History Feature. Last updated January 30, 2018. http://www.nasa.gov/topics/technology/features/telstar.html.

9 Pickrell, Ryan. "Trump Signs Executive Order to Protect the US from a 'Debilitating' EMP Attack." *Business Insider,* March 26, 2019. https://www.businessinsider.com/trump-signs-executive-order-electromagnetic-pulse-attack-2019-3.

10 Smith, Marcia. "DeFazio Succeeds in Killing Space Frontier Act." *SpacePolicyOnline.Com,* December 22, 2018. https://spacepolicyonline.com/news/defazio-succeeds-in-killing-space-frontier-act.

11 Foust, Jeff. "One Small Step for U.S.-China Space Cooperation." *SpaceNews,* July 10, 2017. https://spacenews.com/one-small-step-for-u-s-china-space-cooperation.

12 Foust, Jeff. "One Small Step for U.S.-China Space Cooperation." *SpaceNews*, July 10, 2017. https://spacenews.com/one-small-step-for-u-s-china-space-cooperation.

13 Nanoracks. "Kuang-Chi and Nanoracks Announce Agreement on Near Space 'Traveler' Program." News. March 22, 2018. http://Nanoracks.com/near-space-traveler-program.

14 Zhuo, Chen. "Japan Accelerates Space Militarization Process." *China Military*, February 25, 2019. http://english.chinamil.com.cn/view/2019-02/25/content_9433921.htm.

    Erwin, Sandra. "Defense Intelligence Report: China in Steady Pursuit of Space Capabilities to Outmatch U.S." *SpaceNews*, January 16, 2019. https://spacenews.com/defense-intelligence-report-china-on-steady-pursuit-of-space-capabilities-to-outmatch-u-s.

15 West, Jessica. "It's Time to Speak out about India's Reckless Anti-Satellite Test." *Space Review*, April 15, 2019. http://www.thespacereview.com/article/3695/1.

16 Werner, Debra. "Boycott Indian Launchers? Industry Reacts to India's Anti-Satellite Weapon Test." *SpaceNews*, March 27, 2019. https://spacenews.com/reactions-to-indian-asat.

17 Rajagopalan, Rajeswari. "A First: India to Launch First Simulated Space Warfare Exercise." *Diplomat*, June 12, 2019. https://thediplomat.com/2019/06/a-first-india-to-launch-first-simulated-space-warfare-exercise.

18 Michael Clive (High Pressure Systems Engineer; Former Engineer for XCOR Aerospace and SpaceX), in discussion with the author, March 28, 2017.

19 U.S. Air Force. "U.S. Space Force Fact Sheet." United States Space Force. December 20, 2019. Retrieved January 20, 2020. https://www.spaceforce.mil/About-Us/Fact-Sheet.

20 Marc Serres (CEO, Luxembourg Space Agency), in discussion with the author, February 22, 2019.

21 James Dunstan (Founder, Mobius Legal Group, PLLC), in discussion with the author, May 1, 2017.

Chapter Twenty-Three

1   Armin Ellis (Founder, the Exploration Institute; Formerly: Mission Systems Concepts, NASA Jet Propulsion Laboratory), in discussion with the author, August 21, 2019.

2   *Encyclopædia Britannica Online*, s.v. "California Gold Rush." Accessed January 10, 2019. https://www.britannica.com/topic/California-Gold-Rush.

    Clark, Karen. "How Many Gold Rushes Were There in the 19th Century?" *Sciencing*, April 24, 2017. https://sciencing.com/many-gold-rushes-were-there-19th-century-19423.html.

3   "China Beat Columbus to It, Perhaps." *Economist*, January 12, 2006. https://www.economist.com/books-and-arts/2006/01/12/china-beat-columbus-to-it-perhaps.

PART VII

Chapter Twenty-Four

1   Anthony, Sebastian. "The Apollo 11 Moon Landing, 45 Years on: Looking Back at Mankind's Giant Leap." *ExtremeTech,* July 21, 2014. http://www.extremetech. com/extreme/186600-apollo-11-moon-landing-45-years-looking-back-at-mankinds-giant-leap.

2   Dickerson, Kelly. "Here's What David Bowie's Song 'Space Oddity' Is Really About." *Business Insider,* January 11, 2016. https://www.businessinsider.com/ david-bowie-song-space-oddity-meaning-2016-1.

3   Dickerson, Kelly. "Here's What David Bowie's Song 'Space Oddity' Is Really About." *Business Insider,* January 11, 2016. https://www.businessinsider.com/ david-bowie-song-space-oddity-meaning-2016-1.

4   Roddenberry, Gene. "A Quote by Gene Roddenberry." Goodreads. Accessed October 4, 2019. https://www.goodreads.com/quotes/623122-star-trek-was-an-attempt-to-say-that-humanity-will.

5   Marcellino, William. "How 'Star Trek' Inspired a Boy to Become a Scientist." Rand Corporation. August 26, 2016. https://www.rand.org/blog/2016/08/star-trek-at-50-how-the-tv-series-inspired-a-boy-to.html.

6   Grannum, Gillian. "*Star Trek* Was RAND Corporation Predictive Programming." *Shift Frequency,* January 22, 2013. https://www.shiftfrequency. com/jurriaan-maessen-captain-kirks-predecessor-star-trek-was-rand-corporation-predictive-programming.

7   Liebling, Rick. "The Economics of Science Fiction." Adjacent Possible, *Medium,* August 2, 2018. https://medium.com/adjacent-possible/the-economics-of-science-fiction-c8a3b7fd21a5.

8   March, Stephanie. "NASA's Astronaut Program Receives Record Number of Applications Ahead of Mars Mission." *ABC News,* May 23, 2016. https:// www.abc.net.au/news/2016-05-23/mars-mission-spurs-renewed-interest-in-becoming-nasa-astronaut/7437300.

9   Eschrich, Joey. "Futurist Brian David Johnson Leaves Intel, Joins ASU." *ASU Now,* January 4, 2016. https://asunow.asu.edu/20151231-futurist-brian-david-johnson-leaves-intel-joins-asu.

10   Cilderman, Matt. "Science Fiction Investing, Part 1." *Seeking Alpha,* September 14, 2012. https://seekingalpha.com/article/867431-science-fiction-investing-part-1.

11   Arbesman, Sam. "Building the Future: Merging Science Fact & Science Fiction." Lux, *Medium,* June 14, 2016. https://medium.com/lux-capital/ building-the-future-merging-science-fact-science-fiction-6e230c70c866.

Chapter Twenty-Five

1   Ray Podder (Founder, GROW), in discussion with the author, January 13, 2017.

2 Daniel Abraham (Author, *The Expanse*), in discussion with the author, March 1, 2019.

3 Michael Clive (High Pressure Systems Engineer; Former Engineer for XCOR Aerospace and SpaceX), in discussion with the author, March 28, 2017.

4 Christopher Stott (Cofounder, Chair, and CEO, ManSat), in discussion with the author, May 31, 2017.

5 Larry Niven (Science Fiction Author), in discussion with the author, April 12, 2019.

6 Nahum Romero (Space Artist), in discussion with the author, November 1, 2016.

7 Penn Arthur (Cofounder and CEO, Inhance Digital), in discussion with the author, July 8, 2017.

8 Jeremy Conrad (Cofounder and CEO, Quartz; Founding Member, Lemnos), in discussion with the author, October 6, 2017.

9 Shahin Farshchi (Partner, Lux Capital), in discussion with the author, May 12, 2017.

10 Richard Godwin (President, Space Technology Holdings LLC), in discussion with the author, June 8, 2017.

11 Peter Platzer (Cofounder and CEO, Spire Global), in discussion with the author, November 23, 2016.

12 Mandy Sweeney (VP of Operations, Museum of Science Fiction), in discussion with the author, March 10, 2017.

13 John Spencer (Space Architect; Founder and President, Space Tourism Society; Chief Designer, Mars World Enterprises), in discussion with the author, February 1, 2017.

14 Lynette Kucsma (Cofounder and Chief Marketing Officer, Natural Machines), in discussion with the author, March 9, 2017.

Chapter Twenty-Six

1 Fischer, Dennis. "A Brief History of Science Fiction Films." In *Science Fiction Film Directors, 1895-1998*. Vol. 1. Jefferson, NC: McFarland & Company, 2000.

2 Clark, Travis, and John Lynch. "The 10 Highest-Grossing Movies of All Time, Including 'Avengers: Endgame.'" *Business Insider*, July 22, 2019. https://www.businessinsider.com/highest-grossing-movies-all-time-worldwide-box-office-2018-4.

3 Bishop, Bryan. "Star Wars Just Made 2015 the Biggest Year in US Box Office History." *Verge*, December 29, 2015, https://www.theverge.com/2015/12/29/10686180/star-wars-the-force-awakens-2015-box-office-record.

4 The Wealth Record. "*Star Wars* Net Worth." January 16, 2019. https://www.thewealthrecord.com/celebs-bio-wiki-salary-earnings-2019-2020-2021-2022-2023-2024-2025/other/star-wars-net-worth.

5 Box Office Mojo. "'Martian', 'Gravity' and 'Interstellar': Comparing the Recent Successes of Three Top Tier Sci-Fi Films." Accessed May 10, 2019. https://www.boxofficemojo.com/showdowns/chart/?id=martiangravity.htm.

6   Caixin Global. "The Hurdles 'The Wandering Earth' Overcame to Become a Smash Hit." *China Film Insider,* March 22, 2019. http://chinafilminsider.com/the-hurdles-the-wandering-earth-overcame-to-become-a-smash-hit.

7   Rahman, Abid. "Filmart: Renny Harlin on His Festival Opener 'Bodies at Rest,' Plans for a 'Long Kiss Goodnight' Sequel." *Hollywood Reporter,* March 18, 2019. https://www.hollywoodreporter.com/news/renny-harlin-talks-long-kiss-goodnight-sequel-hopes-1195329.

8   Mendelson, Scott. "Box Office: 'How To Train Your Dragon 3' Tops $170M, 'Wandering Earth' Tops $560M." *Forbes,* February 17, 2019. https://www.forbes.com/sites/scottmendelson/2019/02/17/box-office-wandering-earth-how-to-train-your-dragon-lego-taraji-henson-liam-neeson-kevin-hart.

Chapter Twenty-Seven

1   Young, Angelo. "Libertarians in Space: Is 'Alien: Covenant' a Parable about the Privatization of Space?" *Salon,* May 16, 2017. https://www.salon.com/2017/05/15/libertarians-in-space-is-alien-covenant-a-parable-about-the-privatization-of-space.

2   Liebling, Rick. "The Economics of Science Fiction." Adjacent Possible, *Medium,* August 2, 2018. https://medium.com/adjacent-possible/the-economics-of-science-fiction-c8a3b7fd21a5.

3   Liebling, Rick. "The Economics of Science Fiction." Adjacent Possible, *Medium,* August 2, 2018. https://medium.com/adjacent-possible/the-economics-of-science-fiction-c8a3b7fd21a5.

4   Liebling, Rick. "The Economics of Science Fiction." Adjacent Possible, *Medium,* August 2, 2018. https://medium.com/adjacent-possible/the-economics-of-science-fiction-c8a3b7fd21a5.

5   Leonhardt, Megan. "What If the Moon Had Its Own Currency? The Author of 'The Martian' Has an Idea." *Money,* November 16, 2017. http://money.com/money/5025583/andy-weir-martian-artemis-interview-money.

6   Liebling, Rick. "The Economics of Science Fiction." Adjacent Possible, *Medium,* August 2, 2018. https://medium.com/adjacent-possible/the-economics-of-science-fiction-c8a3b7fd21a5.

Chapter Twenty-Eight

1   Vance, Ashlee. "Elon Musk, the 21st Century Industrialist." *Bloomberg Businessweek,* September 14, 2012. https://www.bloomberg.com/news/articles/2012-09-13/elon-musk-the-21st-century-industrialist.

2   Kardashev, Nikolai S. "Transmission of Information by Extraterrestrial Civilizations." *Soviet Astronomy* 8, no. 2 (Sept.–Oct. 1964): 217–221. http://adsabs.harvard.edu/full/1964SvA.....8..217K.

3   McFadden, Christopher. "Sizing Up a Civilization With the Kardashev Scale." Interesting Engineering. February 28, 2019. https://interestingengineering.com/sizing-up-a-civilization-with-the-kardashev-scale.

4   Cesar Sciammarella (former Apollo project engineer), in discussion with the author, September 23, 2019.

EX ASTRIS, AD ASTRA

1   O'Neill, Gerard K. *The High Frontier: Human Colonies in Space*. New York: William Morrow & Co., 1976.

Enabling a Trillion-Dollar Space Industry

1   Farrah, Jeff. "US Rule Changes Could Mean More Startups Would Need Government Approval to Hire Immigrants." *TechCrunch*, March 11, 2019. http://social.techcrunch.com/2019/03/11/u-s-rule-changes-could-mean-more-startups-would-need-government-approval-to-hire-immigrants.

2   John Paffett (Founder and Managing Director of KISPE Ltd,; Managing Director of Applied Space Solutions Ltd.; Member of the Board of Swedish Space Corporation), in discussion with the author, December 10, 2017.

3   David Cowan (Partner, Bessemer Venture Partners; Board Member, Rocket Lab), in discussion with the author, January 14, 2019.

4   Whitehead, Joanna. "Fascinating Footage Shows One of Aviation's Busiest Days." *Independent*, July 3, 2018. https://www.independent.co.uk/travel/news-and-advice/flights-sky-map-worldwide-air-traffic-aviation-busiest-day-june-a8428451.html.

5   Grush, Loren. "As Commercial Spaceflight Takes off, the Aviation Industry Gets Protective of Airspace." *Verge*, May 16, 2019. https://www.theverge.com/2019/5/16/18535813/commercial-spaceflight-federation-aviation-falcon-heavy-airspace-faa-traffic.

6   Grush, Loren. "As Commercial Spaceflight Takes off, the Aviation Industry Gets Protective of Airspace." *Verge*, May 16, 2019. https://www.theverge.com/2019/5/16/18535813/commercial-spaceflight-federation-aviation-falcon-heavy-airspace-faa-traffic.

7   U.S. Congress. House. Committee on Commerce, Science, and Transportation. *New Entrants in the National Airspace: Policy, Technology, and Security Issues for Congress: Hearing before the Committee on Commerce, Science, and Transportation*. 116th Cong., 1st sess., May 8, 2019. https://www.commerce.senate.gov/services/files/e45ac125-b1dd-4d98-9055-678788cf5f7e.

8   Dennis Wingo (Founder and CEO, Skycorp Inc.), in discussion with the author, June 6, 2016.

9   Center for Responsive Politics. "Lobbying Spending Database Defense Aerospace, 2019." Defense Aerospace. Accessed March 9, 2020. https://www.opensecrets.org/federal-lobbying/industries/summary?cycle=2019&id=D01.

10 Burns, Caleb B., Sarah B. Hansen, and Robert L. Walker. "2018 NDAA Imposes Sweeping New Revolving Door Restrictions on Lobbying Activities by Former Senior DOD Officials." Wiley Rein LLP. January 12, 2018. https://www.wileyrein.com/newsroom-articles-2018-NDAA-Imposes-Sweeping-New-Revolving-Door-Restrictions-on-Lobbying-Activities-by-Former-Senior-DOD-Officials.html.

11 Jane Kinney (Assistant Director, Commercial Spaceflight Federation), in discussion with the author, March 2019.

12 Christopher Stott (Cofounder, Chair, and CEO, ManSat), in discussion with the author, May 31, 2017.

13 Sadlier, Greg, Maike Halterbeck, and Will Pearce. *Google Lunar XPRIZE Market Study 2014: A Report to the XPRIZE Foundation.* London: London Economics, 2014. https://londoneconomics.co.uk/wp-content/uploads/2015/08/LondonEconomics-GLXPMarketStudy2014-MediaSummary-PUBLISHED030815.pdf.

14 NASA. "NASA Makes Dozens of Patents Available in Public Domain." Press Release. Last updated August 6, 2017. http://www.nasa.gov/press-release/ nasa-makes-dozens-of-patents-available-in-public-domain-to-benefit-us- industry.

15 Bays, Jonathan, Tony Goland, and Joe Newsum. "Using Prizes to Spur Innovation." *McKinsey & Company*, July 2009. https://www.mckinsey.com/business-functions/strategy-and-corporate-finance/our-insights/using-prizes-to-spur-innovation.

16 Ubois, Jeff, and Thomas Kalil. "The Promise of Incentive Prizes." *Stanford Social Innovation Review*, Winter 2019. https://ssir.org/articles/entry/the_promise_of_incentive_prizes.

17 Kenneth Davidian (Director of Research, AST; Program Manager, FAA Center of Excellence for Commercial Space Transportation), in discussion with the author, March 2019.

18 Rathi, Anil. "To Encourage Innovation, Make It a Competition." *Harvard Business Review,* November 19, 2014. https://hbr.org/2014/11/to-encourage-innovation-make-it-a-competition.

19 Yasemin Denari (Former Marketing Manager, Google), in conversation with the author, October 10, 2019.

20 NASA Jet Propulsion Laboratory. "NASA's JPL Seeking Applicants for First Space Accelerator." News Release. March 19, 2019. https://www.jpl.nasa.gov/news/news. php?feature=7353.

21 NASA Jet Propulsion Laboratory. "JPL Entrepreneurs." Office of Technology Transfer at JPL. Accessed October 9, 2019. https://ott.jpl.nasa.gov.

22 Farrington, Robert. "Student Loan Forgiveness For Engineering Majors." *College Investor*, February 2, 2018. https://thecollegeinvestor.com/21311/student-loan-forgiveness-engineering-majors.

23 *Fairness in Forgiveness Act* of 2017. HR 2992. 115th Cong., 1st sess., *Congressional Record* 164.

24   Maycotte, H. O. "How Makerspaces Are Inspiring Innovation At Startups." *Forbes*, February 2, 2016. https://www.forbes.com/sites/homaycotte/2016/02/02/how-makerspaces-are-inspiring-innovation-at-startups.

25   Kalish, John. "High-Tech Maker Spaces: Helping Little Startups Make It Big." All Tech Considered, *National Public Radio*, April 30, 2014. https://www.npr.org/sections/alltechconsidered/2014/04/30/306235442/high-tech-maker-spaces-helping-little-startups-make-it-big.

26   Cole, Ian. "TechShop Is Dead, The Maker Movement Is Strong." *Medium*, November 27, 2017. https://medium.com/@ian.cole/techshop-is-dead-the-maker-movement-is-strong-8f30bb7c718c.

27   Lynch, Matthew. "Why Makerspaces Are the Key to Innovation." *Tech Edvocate*, January 19, 2017. https://www.thetechedvocate.org/why-makerspaces-are-the-key-to-innovation.

28   Pearlman, Robert, ed. "NASA's Fiscal Year (FY) 2019 Budget." *CollectSPACE*, February 2, 2018. http://www.collectspace.com/ubb/Forum3/HTML/005257.html.

     NASA. *FY 2019 Budget Estimates*. February 12, 2018. https://www.nasa.gov/sites/default/files/atoms/files/nasa_fy_2019_budget_overview.pdf

29   Ardalan, Davar. "Introducing the 2019 Presidential Innovation Fellows." *U.S. General Administration Services* (blog), February 13, 2019. https://www.gsa.gov/blog/2019/02/13/introducing-the-2019-presidential-innovation-fellows.

30   Park, Todd. "Wanted: A Few Good Women and Men to Serve as Presidential Innovation Fellows." The White House. May 23, 2012. Archived Obama White House Website. https://obamawhitehouse.archives.gov/blog/2012/05/23/wanted-few-good-women-and-men-serve-presidential-innovation-fellows.

31   Colleen Howard (STEM professional development educator), in discussion with the author, March 2019.

32   Elizabeth Kennick (Executive Director, Teachers in Space Inc.), in discussion with the author, July 31, 2019.

33   Foust, Jeff. "A Trillion-Dollar Space Industry Will Require New Markets." *SpaceNews*, July 6, 2018. https://spacenews.com/a-trillion-dollar-space-industry-will-require-new-markets.

34   Bezos, Jeff. "Innovation Spotlights." Fireside Chat, re:MARS from Amazon, Las Vegas, June 6, 2019.

35   Listner, Michael. "Asteroid Mining: To Infinity and Beyond, But What Are the Legal Implications?" *Space Safety Magazine,* April 26, 2012. http://www.spacesafetymagazine.com/space-exploration/asteroid-mining/commercial-space-leap-earth-orbit-legal-implications.

36   William Miller (Principal, SpaceCap Investments), in discussion with the author, January 17, 2019.

37   Secretary of the Air Force Public Affairs. "'Space Pitch Day' Yields Innovative Technologies and New Partners for the Air Force." U.S. Air Force News Release November 8, 2019. https://www.af.mil/News/Article-Display/Article/2012708/space-pitch-day-yields-innovative-technologies-and-new-partners-for-the-air-for.

38   NASA. "NASA Selects Over 100 Small Business Projects for Space Innovation." Press Release. Last updated August 6, 2017. http://www.nasa.gov/press-release/nasa-selects-over-100-small-business-projects-to-advance-space-innovation.

39   Tassey, Gregory. "A Technology-Based Growth Policy." *Issues in Science and Technology*, March 6, 2017. https://issues.org/a-technology-based-growth-policy.

40   U.S. Office of Management and Budget. *Budget of the United States Government, Fiscal Year 2019*. Washington, DC: U.S. Government Publishing Office, 2018. https://www.whitehouse.gov/wp-content/uploads/2018/02/budget-fy2019.pdf.

41   Kollipara, Amaresh. "Opening Keynote by Amaresh Kollipara - Disrupt Space Summit 2017." Produced by Disrupt Space. Disrupt Space Summit, 2017. YouTube video, 33:16. April 14, 2017. https://www.youtube.com/watch?v=1GCvmgsvrZ8.

42   Karina Drees (CEO, Mojave Air and Space Port), in discussion with the author, December 12, 2016.

43   Wingo, Dennis. "Zero G, Zero Tax: Enabling Private Space Enterprise Through Tax Incentives." *Ad Astra* 19, no. 1 (Spring 2007). https://space.nss.org/zero-g-zero-tax.

44   William Miller (Principal, SpaceCap Investments), in discussion with the author, January 17, 2019.

45   Van Espahbodi (Cofounder and Managing Partner, Starburst Aerospace), in discussion with the author, June 28, 2017.

46   Thorpe, David. "Investment Schemes Offer Tax Relief to Encourage Investment in Small or Medium-Sized Companies." *What Investment*, October 5, 2018. https://www.whatinvestment.co.uk/eis-and-seis-tax-breaks-explained-2381293.

47   Kartik Kumar (Cofounder, satsearch), in discussion with the author, October 10, 2019.

48   Higginbotham, Brian. "The Space Economy: An Industry Takes Off." U.S. Chamber of Commerce. October 11, 2018. https://www.uschamber.com/series/above-the-fold/the-space-economy-industry-takes.

Breaking Into NewSpace

1   Comstock, Doug, David Lockney, and Coleman Glass. "A Structure for Capturing Quantitative Benefits From the Transfer of Space and Aeronautics Technology." Paper No. IAC-11.E5.2.2, 62nd International Astronautical Congress, Cape Town, South Africa, October 3–7, 2010.

2   Anthony Freeman (Innovation Foundry, NASA Jet Propulsion Laboratory), in discussion with the author, May 5, 2017.

3   Sam Reiber (General Counsel, Cognis Group; Director, IP Technology Exchange, Inc.), in discussion with the author, October 31, 2016.

4   Eric Golden (Managing Director, Armory Securities), in conversation with the author, June 17, 2017.

INDEX

ABOUT THE AUTHOR

Robert C. Jacobson is a multi-faceted entrepreneur, industry leader, and mentor with over ten years of experience advising private investors in the potential of the space sector. His professional career has been characterized by an innate talent for early recognition of transformative industry developments, such as emerging sectors, new business trends and cycles, and enabling technologies.

Robert was one of the earliest members and a principal with Space Angels (formerly Space Angels Network), the first space-focused angel group in the world and the leading source of capital for aerospace startups. At Space Angels, his extensive network in the space industry was instrumental in developing strategic partnerships with other space organizations and recruiting early members for the group. He later cofounded The Aerospace & Defense Forum, a global aerospace and defense leadership community that currently consists of over 2,000 industry senior executives and professionals. In 2017, Robert became one of the first team members of Arch Mission Foundation and was subsequently part of the three successful space missions: the Solar Library payload in Elon Musk's Tesla Roadster, now orbiting the Sun (via SpaceX's Falcon Heavy, 2018); the LEO Library, with the first English copy of *Wikipedia* in low Earth orbit (via a SpaceChain CubeSat, 2018); and the Lunar Library, a thirty-million-page archive on the Moon (via SpaceIL's Beresheet Moon lander, 2019). Today, Robert serves as the founder and chief executive officer of Space Advisors™, a financial and strategic consulting firm that mentors startups and advises private investors in the potential of the space program for the benefit of humanity.